TYCOON

The Life of James Goldsmith

D1326908

TYCOON

The Life of James Goldsmith

GEOFFREY WANSELL

GRAFTON BOOKS

A Division of the Collins Publishing Group

LONDON GLASGOW
TORONTO SYDNEY AUCKLAND

Grafton Books
A Division of the Collins Publishing Group
8 Grafton Street, London W1X 3LA

Published by Grafton Books 1987

British Library Cataloguing in Publication Data

Wansell, Geoffrey
Tycoon: the life of James Goldsmith.
1. Businessmen – Great Britain –
Biography
I. Title
338'.04'0924   HC252.5.G6

ISBN 0-246-12921-2

Set in Linotron Imprint by
Rowland Phototypesetting Ltd
Bury St Edmunds, Suffolk
Printed in Great Britain by
Mackays of Chatham Ltd, Chatham, Kent

For Jan

Contents

Part 4 Melodrama

Part 5 Raider on Wall Street

List of Illustrations

Preface

Tycoons are the gladiators of the modern financial world. Their battles, and their achievements, are now reported with the breathless enthusiasm that was once reserved for sportsmen and movie stars. Yet unlike either they usually have no desire for fame or publicity. To succeed they need the private confidences of other powerful men and women. Theirs is a secret world that they wish to sustain.

So it is hardly a surprise that Jimmy Goldsmith, one of the most remarkable international tycoons to have emerged in the past quarter of a century, can seem elusive. To many in Paris, London or New York he resembles nothing more than a great beast of the financial jungle who deliberately avoids coming to the water-hole until dusk. In the past thirty years he has become what the *Wall Street Journal* describes as "one of the world's richest and most influential men", but he has rarely chosen to reveal anything about himself.

Though I worked for him for nearly two years as a columnist on his British newsmagazine *Now!* I knew him little better than anyone else. He would appear from time to time, a tanned, tall man with a boyish smile, who seemed almost embarrassed to be rich and powerful. For ever courteous and charming, he never once matched the stereotype of the belligerent, self-seeking tycoon that the British headlines and gossip columns so relentlessly described.

Yet Jimmy Goldsmith could never – by any stretch of the imagination – be called conventional. There is none of the restraint of a financier about him. He lives out the fantasies of others with a flamboyance that is unmistakable. His takeovers have been some of the largest and most controversial in the history of the European and United States economies. His political opinions have attracted the strongest criticism in France and Great Britain. His unorthodox private life has been the subject of persistent speculation throughout the world. It is a lack of inhibition that still attracts the strongest reactions. To his enemies he is always a monster, to his friends always an angel.

But for those who are neither friends nor enemies he is a curiously enigmatic figure, a man surrounded by myths rather than realities. The more I saw of him the more determined I became to try to unravel the two, and to describe as accurately as any outsider can the passions of a man once called "the re-incarnation of Charles Foster Kane". In the attempt I have spent much of the past five years examining the world of someone who precisely fits Webster's definition of a tycoon as a "businessman of exceptional power, wealth and influence".

Rather than rely on myth and rumour, however, I asked Sir James Goldsmith himself to explain in detail the reasons behind his actions and his decisions. Though he was reluctant initially, and did not particularly want any book to be written about him, he finally agreed to talk because he wanted this biography to "be accurate rather than otherwise". As the book progressed we met for many hours in London, Paris and New York.

At no stage did he attempt to influence my opinions or change my conclusions, any more than he ever refused to answer my questions, but his generosity in talking to me provided an exceptional opportunity to compare the truth of the myths that surround him with the realities, and at the same time to observe at close quarters the entrepreneur who has been called "the most powerful predator on Wall Street". What emerged was a far more complicated picture than any of the previous descriptions of him – or indeed of any other successful tycoon – had prepared me for.

But I did not rely on Jimmy Goldsmith alone to complete the portrait. I also spoke to more than 300 people in France, Britain and the United States who knew him and had worked with him during his career. I cannot name each and every one of them, but I would like to thank particularly a group who have observed him over a number of years. In France these include Gilberte Beaux, Humbert Frèrejean, Claude-Henry Leconte, Maurice Lignon, Digby Neave, David de Rothschild, Ambroise Roux, Tom

Sebestyen, Olivier Todd, and Sam White. In Britain they include Jeffrey Archer, Anthony Blond, Nigel Dempster, Roman Eisenstein, Jack Greenhalgh, Lady Falkender, Tony Fathers, Joe Haines, Charles Hambro, Ronnie Payne, Ken Riley, Lord Rothschild, Jacob Rothschild, the late Anthony Shrimsley, Jim Slater, Hugh Stephenson, Lord Thomas, Rollo Watts, Sir Gordon White, and Selim Zilkha. In the United States there are also Chris Anderson, Arnaud de Borchgrave, Joe Flom, Milton Glaser, Roy Godson, Floyd Hall, John Park, Robert S. Pirie, and John Tigrett.

I must also thank the members of the Goldsmith family, particularly the late Madame Marcelle Goldsmith, Teddy Goldsmith and Lady Annabel Goldsmith; as well as Sir James's personal staff, including Charles Filmer, Catherine Toplis, Jean Moffat and Edith Mikolajczak.

But there is another group to whom I am especially grateful, those who agreed to speak to me on the strict understanding that their names would never be disclosed. To them I offer my profound, but private, thanks.

I must finally thank my editors in London, Paris and New York – especially Richard Johnson in London – for their support; my agent Andrew Hewson, whose enthusiasm for this book rivalled my own; and my friends Marcel Berlins, Giles Clark, Stephen du Sautoy, Rivers Scott and Tom Shields, who have all lent me help and advice over the past five years. But, most of all, I must thank my wife Jan for her unwavering encouragement throughout all that time. No one else should be held responsible for my conclusions, however; those are mine alone.

Geoffrey Wansell
December 1986

Prologue

Jimmy Goldsmith was a mess. When he woke shortly before dawn on the morning of 10 July 1957 he did not look like a tycoon destined to become one of the world's richest men: quite the opposite. As the rays of the sun started to filter through the slatted window shutters of his apartment near the Eiffel Tower in Paris, they revealed a tall, unshaven, bald young man, who looked more like a prisoner on Devil's Island than an ambitious entrepreneur. His chestnut hair had fallen out, his china-blue eyes were closing with styes, and his neck was red with boils. He was just twenty-four but he looked fifty. And he looked like a man whom the fates had chosen to destroy.

The reason was straightforward enough: that day he was to be declared bankrupt.

Jimmy Goldsmith could hardly believe it. Just three years before he had been one of the most famously handsome young men of his age, the flamboyant playboy who had eloped with the beautiful heiress to a $75-million fortune and married her in Scotland. And in the past three years his company, Laboratoires Cassene, had become one of the success stories of France: "a phenomenon in pharmaceuticals", according to one newspaper. From one employee he had expanded to more than 400, selling everything from adrenalin cream to vapour rub, cold remedies to nasal sprays, hormone pills to cortisone derivatives, and every chemist and doctor in France had seemed enthusiastic. The turnover had grown to nearly one and a half million pounds a year. He had negotiated the French rights to sell Alka-Seltzer and the famous cold cure Lantigen B, and the previous October he had even bought a half-finished factory from a scrap-dealer to build a manufacturing plant and research laboratories. But he had expanded too far, too fast.

The previous winter things had not been too bad. Colds and 'flu meant that business was good for a company selling antibiotics, but with the first buds of spring it had become only too clear that Laboratoires Cassene might not survive. As the days passed his hair began to fall out. Then in May it looked as though help had arrived. He negotiated a 50:50 partnership with two Italians in exchange for their financial backing. But three weeks later they came back demanding 80 per cent of his company in exchange for their money. Jimmy Goldsmith refused to negotiate.

"I can imagine circumstances," he told them, "when a man who was much in love with a beautiful mistress would rather see her dead than in the arms of someone else."

The Italians could hardly believe their ears. Here was a twenty-four-year-old with no money, refusing an offer of help because he would rather see his business fail than lose control of it. Surely, no sane man could refuse their offer. What they did not know was that Jimmy Goldsmith had always been perfectly prepared to be thought insane, eccentric or extravagant; providing he could control his own destiny.

As June drew to a close Jimmy Goldsmith tried desperately to raise the money he needed from the banks, and to persuade his creditors to "wait a little longer". But by the evening of 9 July 1957 he knew that when his bills were presented to the bank the next day there would not be enough money to pay them.

"In the circumstances I slept very well," he remembers now. "It was over. I was finished." When he woke next morning he did not bother to get up, or to shave. It was not that he was particularly depressed; there was simply nothing to be done, and no point in going to the office. Eventually, to cheer himself up, he decided to go out to lunch.

"At a corner kiosk I bought the *Paris-Presse*, to see if my bankruptcy had made the newspapers," he remembers. "But when I opened it the first thing I saw were big headlines saying 'BANK STRIKE'. I couldn't believe it."

For the first time in twenty years the staff of every French bank had decided to go on strike. Not a single one had opened that morning, and – more important still – not a single bill had been presented for payment. Jimmy Goldsmith was not bankrupt; at least not for the moment.

"It galvanized me. I realized I had extra time." Suddenly he was his old self again. When he got to the restaurant he rushed downstairs to the telephone and rang a friend at Agence-France Presse to find out how long the strike would last – at least a week he was told.

Jimmy Goldsmith bounded back upstairs two at a time, but not before he had made one more call, to his company's biggest competitor in the pharmaceutical industry in France, Laboratoires Roussell. He had decided then and there to take advantage of his extraordinary good luck and pay off his debts – by selling his business. All he wanted to keep were the royalties to Lantigen B, because that would pay for the rent and upkeep of his apartment and his family.

"During the next eighteen days or so I managed to sell almost everything else to Roussell," he explains. "They gave me £120,000, and I went away on holiday to Spain for two months to recuperate."

Thirty years later the man who was to become a billionaire in his own right and "the most powerful predator in the stock market jungle" was to tell his friends: "It was a spectacular example of luck. The gods stopped scowling that day. I still took reckless risks after that – I can't say it taught me not to. But I never considered any success certain again.

"I am always absolutely aware of the perils out there. What the experience taught me was fear. The next time there was even a flicker of success I capitalized on it at once, because I was determined not to see it vanish again."

From that day forth the financier who was to be called "a modern Mongol chieftain, a Sultan of these times" by more than one newspaper, would always tread his own path and never again allow himself to be caught without a means to escape – and enough money to pay the bills. In matters of business Sir James Michael Goldsmith was never to forget the lessons of 1957.

From that day forth he continued to rely on his own intuition – and his own luck. And by doing so he became one of the most extraordinary, flamboyant and unconventional tycoons in history, as well as one of the richest men the world has ever known.

PART 1

Dynasty

1

The Goldschmidts of Frankfurt

Jimmy Goldsmith was not the first member of his family to feel different – or persecuted by fate. To some extent every Goldsmith for 500 years had felt separate, an outsider in a harsh world. After all, the Goldschmidt dynasty had begun with Moses von Schaffhausen, a middle-aged goldsmith in Nuremburg, Germany, forced to wear a red peaked cap and a yellow ring fastened to his coat to identify him as a Jew. That was not the limit of his persecution. On the third Sunday in Lent in 1499 his house, and all the other houses belonging to Jews in the city, were confiscated by the mayor on behalf of the Holy Roman Emperor. Jews were not to be trusted, or allowed a home in Nuremburg. Undeterred Moses von Schaffhausen set off with his family down the valley of the river Main towards Frankfurt, the greatest commercial centre in Germany, in search of a new, safer home.

The journey took several years, and it was not until 1519 that Moses von Schaffhausen finally settled in Frankfurt. Almost all the Jewish families from Nuremburg had settled in the ghetto there, alongside others from Ulm and Augsburg in the south, and Cologne in the north. The Rothschilds also arrived at about this time, attracted by the comparative freedom enjoyed by Jews in Frankfurt. Commerce, not religion, was the prime consideration of the city council and as a result Jews were welcome – at least, they were welcome to do business. In 1521 Moses von Schaffhausen followed accepted practice and adopted the name of his craft. After moving into a house on the west side of the Judengasse, known as The Golden Swan, he became Moses Goldschmidt. The house remained in the Goldschmidt family until its demolition in 1883.

For the Goldschmidts, the move from Nuremburg was a success. They might still be prohibited by city law from walking "two together in the vicinity of the Town Hall" and prevented from offending "Christian ears with strange or sudden sounds", but otherwise they were free to do business providing they continued to live within the ghetto. When Moses Goldschmidt died in 1531 there were still only thirty-two houses with fewer than 300 inhabitants there, but by 1610 there were 3,000 Jews squeezed into barely 200 houses.

Moses Goldschmidt's sons prospered. Joseph became the first Jew to extend his interests beyond money-lending and pawnbroking into the world of government finance, and was mentioned by name in the records of sixteenth-century Europe for his services in raising loans for the city of Frankfurt and the Archbishop of Cologne, among others. His success was short-lived, however. He was brought to trial on charges of forgery, mainly because of the failure of two noble families to pay their debts. Though Joseph steadfastly denied the charges, he was persecuted until his death in 1572.

Over the next 200 years, Joseph's descendants established one of the most significant banking dynasties in Germany, often in collaboration with their cousins, the Bischoffsheims. Being prohibited from marrying outside the ghetto most of the great Jewish families intermarried. It was a habit that was to persist for generations. But their horizons extended far beyond the ghetto: Frankfurt's Jewish families went wherever there seemed an opportunity to do business. After Cromwell had allowed the Jews back into England in the mid-seventeenth century, the Goldschmidts had established themselves as money lenders in London, and the Napoleonic Wars provided new opportunities in Europe. By 1800 the Bischoffsheims were banking in France, and by 1821 they had moved into Amsterdam. Nine years later they were established in Belgium.

Never quite as flamboyant as the Rothschilds, the Bischoffsheims and the Goldschmidts nevertheless carried out financial transactions for almost every European government in the first half of the nineteenth century. After 1815 the Rothschilds increased their influence in London, but the freedom offered by the City attracted one of the Goldschmidts' most adventurous cousins, Louis Bischoffsheim. In 1840 he opened a bank off Throgmorton Street, and by 1846 he had gone into partnership with his cousin Solomon Goldschmidt. With the arrival of Louis Napoleon in France in December 1851 the climate for an entrepreneurial banking family with links throughout Europe blossomed. The Industrial Revolution had spread tarmacadamed roads across the continent, and now the expansion of the railways demanded vast sums of money, as well as men to find it and lend it. The Goldschmidts and the Bischoffsheims did precisely that: with effortless, and relentless, efficiency. The spread of railways across Europe was their particular concern, and they attended to it with diligent determination. By 1860 they had financed, and taken a share in, railway lines throughout France, and were on the brink of doing the same in Germany, Luxembourg, Italy and Belgium.

Like the Rothschilds, the Goldschmidts and the Bischoffsheims were not deterred by national boundaries. The Rothschilds had built up their own intelligence network, to which every Jewish family, to some extent, was privy, and they used it to ensure that they were better informed than any of their competitors. As the philosopher and poet Heinrich Heine was to say: "Money is the God of our time, and Rothschild is his prophet."

Most of the governments of Europe came to depend on the Rothschilds, and their lesser-known cousins the Goldschmidts, for money in an emergency. The Rothschilds lent money for the relief of the Irish famine of 1847, to the British government for the Crimean War and to help them buy a half share in the Suez Canal in 1876. (As Disraeli told Queen Victoria: "Four million sterling! And almost immediately. There was only one firm that could do it – Rothschilds.") Throughout Europe the Jewish banking dynasties which had originated in Frankfurt played an ever-increasing part in commercial life and gradually became accepted among the aristocracies of their new countries.

But when Bismarck's Prussian troops marched into Frankfurt in the summer of 1866 to end its ancient independence and annex it to the new Germany, some members of the Goldschmidt family left—but not all. The well-established banking firm founded by Benedict Hayum Goldschmidt fifty years earlier, was too prosperous, and too important, to close down overnight. Besides, the

Frankfurt market was in the middle of an unexpected boom: it had provided almost all the funds for the victorious Unionist armies in the American Civil War, principally because the city had developed a reputation for placing both North and South American bonds. So, as Bismarck guided Germany's expansion, he did so with the financial assistance of the Goldschmidt family.

But Benedict Hayum Goldschmidt (who had refused a baronetcy from Bismarck) had decided, at the age of seventy-one, to retire to Paris and leave two of his fourteen children, Maximilian and Adolph, in charge of the family bank. Under their guidance the Goldschmidts became one of the pioneers of joint stock banking in Europe, as the old private banks were gradually replaced by larger institutions. Until in 1893 they too decided to leave Frankfurt and to close the family bank. Maximilian and Adolph Goldschmidt, now aged fifty and fifty-five, had never been able to agree on the bank's policy, and they both had other interests.

In 1878, Maximilian had married Minka, youngest daughter of Baron Willy Rothschild, the head of the Rothschild family in Frankfurt, and not long afterwards had founded a private bank in Frankfurt under the name Goldschmidt-Rothschild. After Baron Willy's death in 1901, Maximilian was granted the right to adopt the title of Baron von Goldschmidt-Rothschild and inherited a great estate of houses in Frankfurt, where he continued to live until 1940, when he died at the age of ninety-seven. Even in his nineties Maximilian kept a car and would drive out into the Frankfurt woods with one of his two mistresses. In 1939, when visited by two members of the Gestapo, he instructed his butler to say, "Tell them I did not send for them". So powerful was he that the two men left, never to return.

Adolph, too, had made a good match. In 1866 he had married Alice Emma Moses from London, daughter of the industrialist Wilhelm Merton who founded the Frankfurt firm Metallgesellschaft. An intensely religious Jew, Merton had changed his family name to Moses. Adolph Goldschmidt and Alice Moses had four children: Carl, born a year after their marriage, in 1867; Edward in 1868; Nellie in 1871; and Frank in 1878. Upright and respectable, Adolph and Alice were popular figures in Frankfurt city life, but in 1893, after the decision was taken to close the family bank, they moved to Paris. The move was not a success, and in 1895 they decided to settle in Alice's native country, England. After all they had many connections there, and Alice's sister Amelia was married to Sir George Jessel, the Solicitor General and Master of the Rolls.

A smallish man with a white goatee beard, Adolph Goldschmidt's first step was to take a house at 14 South Street, just off Park Lane, then one of the most fashionable addresses for Jews in London. He was comfortably a millionaire, and could well afford it. His cousin Henry Bischoffsheim lived round the corner in South Audley Street, and another cousin, Moritz Adolphus von Goldschmidt, lived in Mount Street, barely 200 yards away. Branches of the family had become an integral part of the establishment in late Victorian England. The restrained and careful Alice Goldschmidt set about creating a home fit for a millionaire, supervising both the appointment of staff and the furnishing with her natural diffidence but firm discipline.

Like his cousins, Adolph Goldschmidt was only too anxious to be part of the English way of life. So anxious, in fact, that he bought a 2,500-acre country estate not far from Newmarket, in Suffolk, and just west of the solid market town of Bury St Edmunds. The entire estate took its name from the small village at its heart, Cavenham, and the manor house was called Cavenham Hall. Adolph, Alice and two of their sons, Edward and Frank, settled in London and Suffolk. The eldest son, Carl, who had not wanted to leave Germany, never cared for England, and began gambling in the casinos of Europe; while the only daughter, Nellie, married in 1894, shortly before the family arrived in London. Her husband was Ernst von Marx, the son of an old business acquaintance of her father's. A lawyer, who had converted to Christianity from Judaism, von Marx later became a senior civil servant in Germany.

The rest of the Goldschmidt family were quite content in London and Suffolk, despite the hostility shown to Jews by the English. They accumulated an impressive collection of *objets d'art*, including Louis XV and XVI furniture, clocks and vases, German silver and oriental porcelain and china, and started to hold house parties. Adolph even took up polo, so keen was he to appear English. Frankfurter Deutsch, the dialect of the ghetto, was spoken only when there were no guests. At one party in Cavenham Hall he even instructed one of his grandsons, Nellie's son, to stay in his room in case the boy's German accent disturbed the English guests.

Adolph was rich enough to live on his fortune and did not set up as a banker in London. But he took advantage of his family connections to become a sleeping partner in Helbert Wagg & Co, a merchant bank which was to become part of Schroder Wagg, one of the most respected firms in the City of London. He invested his considerable fortune in what he felt were the safest bonds, those issued by the Tsar of Russia and the Kaiser in Germany, as well as trying Mexican silver shares and South African gold shares. He also joined a syndicate known as the Central Mining Investment Corporation which controlled mines in South Africa and had interests in the De Beer diamond and oil business. His cousin Henry Bischoffsheim was another member of the syndicate. But for the most part he and Alice settled down to the life of an English country squire: hunting, shooting and fishing, mixed with a little fox hunting and weekend house parties.

Edward and Frank Goldschmidt were equally determined to adopt the manners of their new country. Indeed, they were so anxious to do so that, barely a year after their arrival from Paris, they decided to adopt the name Goldsmith, though they failed to persuade their parents to do the same. Edward, known as Teddy, was regarded as the better looking and the better shot of the brothers, but it was Frank who made the more significant mark on English society.

Born on 22 November 1878, and aged sixteen when the family moved to England, Frank Goldsmith was first educated at home by a private tutor and then sent to a crammer's in Cheltenham to study for his university matriculation. By May 1897 he had progressed well enough to be awarded a place at Magdalen College, Oxford, to study law. It was a considerable achievement for the son of a recent Jewish immigrant. Until 1871 neither Oxford nor Cambridge had accepted Jewish undergraduates who had usually attended London University – founded partly on the initiative of another member of the Goldsmid family, Isaac. But now that Oxford was open to Jews, no ambitious young man, especially one anxious to seem as English as possible, could refuse the chance to go there.

Slightly smaller but no less handsome than his elder brother,

Frank Goldsmith was a success at Oxford. Rich enough to enjoy it, and intelligent enough to profit from the experience, he graduated in 1900 with a good second in jurisprudence, and the determination not only to study to become a barrister but, more important, to set out on a political career as well. One of his cousins, Herbert Jessel, was already making a name for himself as a member of the London County Council (LCC), and Frank decided to follow a similar path. While qualifying as a barrister and being called to the bar of the Inner Temple in 1903, he decided to stand as an independent "municipal reform" candidate for the Westminster City Council. He fought and won easily the council's Conduit ward, which included his father's house in South Street. It was November 1903, and he was not quite twenty-five.

In the autumn of 1904 Frank Goldsmith went on to stand as one of two "municipal reform" candidates for the St Pancras South ward in the LCC elections. His Progressive Party opponent was considerably better known than he was: the critic and playwright George Bernard Shaw. But Frank was not in the least dismayed. He knew the elections were of considerable importance to London's Jewish community, because, for the first time, the LCC was to take charge of the city's elementary education. This became a crucial issue in the election, and it became one of Frank Goldsmith's principal interests in politics. But it was his good looks and charm as much as his campaigning which convinced the electors of St Pancras South. When he won the seat comfortably, Shaw remarked tartly that "beauty had beaten brains", and even *The Times* reported: "'The best looking man gets my vote' was a remark frequently made by the electors."

To celebrate his success, and to indicate to the world his determination to support his new King and Country, Frank Goldsmith decided to volunteer to join the local army regiment near the family home, the Duke of York's Loyal Suffolk Hussars. He was welcomed with a commission, and spent his weekends when not on manoeuvres entertaining his fellow volunteer officers at Cavenham Hall. Dashing, charming and undeniably handsome, he looked every inch the British officer, even if he had spent the first sixteen years of his life in Germany; just as he looked every inch the young politician with a future as he spent his weeks energetically pursuing a career on the London County Council, and particularly its interests in education.

In 1907 Frank Goldsmith resigned his seat on the Westminster City Council to concentrate on his political activities in the LCC, and later that year he retained his seat in St Pancras South. His enthusiasm was rewarded with the post of whip for the Municipal Reform Party, which supported the national Conservative Party. This did not escape the notice of the Conservative and Unionist Party, nor did it escape his Frankfurt cousins. Through his work for the LCC Frank increasingly came into contact with his cousin Herbert Jessel, who was not only chairman of the London Municipal Society, but also the Unionist Member of Parliament for St Pancras, a seat he had inherited from his father-in-law, Sir Julian Goldsmid. It seemed only a matter of time before Frank Goldsmith followed his cousin into the House of Commons. It was. By the age of thirty-one, he was a British Member of Parliament.

In January 1910, Asquith, the Liberal Prime Minister, was forced to call a general election over the House of Lords' refusal to approve David Lloyd George's radical "people's budget". The Unionist party offered Frank Goldsmith the chance to fight a parliamentary seat in the constituency of North-West Suffolk, based at Stowmarket, not far from Cavenham Hall. It was certainly not a safe seat: the Liberals had held it since their landslide victory at the last general election in 1906, although the Unionists had won it in 1900 and 1895.

In his published election address Frank Goldsmith declared himself "opposed to the payment of Members of Parliament", and "opposed to single chamber government". His opinions were firmly those of any member of the English middle classes. After a brisk but bitter fight against the Liberals, he won the seat by 5,311 votes to 4,666, a majority of 645. It was a remarkable success, as the country as a whole had turned against the Unionists. In barely six years he had laid the foundations of what looked like a long and successful political career, and one which might even take him into a future Conservative and Unionist Cabinet.

In the first months of 1910 Frank Goldsmith set about familiarizing himself with the habits of Parliament, aided by Herbert Jessel and his experience of the ways of the London County Council. It was, however, a considerable achievement for a young Jew to be elected to the House of Commons. The entry of Jews into Parliament was a comparatively recent phenomenon, following a struggle led, predictably, by a Rothschild. Lionel Rothschild had become the first Jewish MP in 1858. Other Jews had followed him, all members of the Liberal Party which, under Lord John Russell, had supported the cause of Jewish emancipation. By the turn of the century support for both the Liberal and the Unionist parties was almost equally divided among Jewish candidates. Indeed, in January 1910, the thirty-two Jewish candidates were split evenly between the two parties. When Frank Goldsmith entered the House of Commons in 1910, he joined a notable group of Jewish MPs, including Lionel de Rothschild, Sir Harry Samuel, Sir Philip Magnus and Alfred Strauss. Whatever the party, there was pressure on every one of them to represent the interests of the Jewish community, as well as those of their own constituents.

Although Asquith's Liberal government had been returned to power, it was clear that they were losing popular support. After the sudden death of King Edward VII in May, the new king, George V, attempted to settle the bickering between the Liberal and Conservative parties over the reform of the House of Lords to allow a radical liberal legislature by suggesting a Constitutional Conference. Eight politicians, four from each of the two senior parties, met in June at 10 Downing Street behind closed doors, but failed to reach agreement. Asquith called another general election, and in December Frank Goldsmith appealed to the electors of Suffolk for the second time in eleven months. He won again, although with the narrower majority of 191 votes.

Frank's first year in the House had been one of acute political excitement, nourished not only by two general elections, but also by a long series of full-dress debates in the House of Commons on the future of the House of Lords, in which every leading political figure of the day took part. It was an astonishingly exciting time for a young man to enter Parliament, and he was never to forget it. Like every other ambitious young MP he dreamed of influencing the affairs of his country, and he had every reason to expect he would. After all, in just six years he had been elected to Westminster City Council, the LCC and the House of Commons; he had been elected a Freemason, made a member of the influential Tattersall's committee controlling horse racing at Newmarket, and become a Justice of the Peace in Suffolk, as well as a county alderman. He had achieved all this with ease and grace, but within a few years it was all to be snatched away.

In the years before the First World War, Frank Goldsmith was a young Tory on the rise. He did not speak often in the chamber, but when he did it was usually on education and helping the poor and the mentally and physically handicapped. He joined backbench committees, and began to establish a reputation for being a likeable, articulate and promising politician. He was at his happiest in the smoking room, away from women whom he considered to be best suited to domestic life and the family, or to play and pleasure; they were not to be taken entirely seriously. It was a view he shared with many of his friends, and one which he passed on to his sons.

Frank Goldsmith's circle included the young Winston Churchill, only four years his senior and recently appointed First Lord of the Admiralty; Sir Edward Carson, the leader of the Irish Unionists; and another rising young politician, F. E. Smith. They played cards together regularly in the St James's Club, off Pall Mall. But just as he seemed to have settled comfortably into his new life, Frank Goldsmith, Conservative and Unionist MP for Stowmarket, Captain in the Loyal Suffolk Hussars, was caught up in the anti-German feeling that was sweeping across Europe. In 1914, fanned by Lord Northcliffe's *Daily Mail*, the resentment became hysteria, and to be German in England was to wear a stigma the Jews of Frankfurt would have recognized. Frank Goldsmith suddenly found himself an outcast in his new country. The outbreak of war at the beginning of August 1914 was to transform his life. In a matter of weeks his political future was destroyed in a frenzy of "spy-mania". He was not alone. In the first ten months of the war two great statesmen, Lord Haldane and Prince Louis of Battenberg, who had rendered England the incalculable service of preventing the demobilization of the fleet, were also forced from office. Nor were politicians the only people to suffer. Harmless old people who had forgotten to take out naturalization papers found themselves suddenly threatened with internment in a country which they had been proud to call their own; and bakers' shops with German-sounding names were looted. In the face of all this, Frank Goldsmith could not save himself.

Ironically, it was another member of the Goldschmidt family who sealed Frank Goldsmith's fate. Ernst von Marx, his sister Nellie's husband, by then a respected civil servant in the Kaiser's Germany, sent him a telegram in the first weeks of war. It asked "How can you consider fighting for anyone other than your fatherland?" and was sent, not through diplomatic channels, but by ordinary mail. The local postmaster could hardly avoid seeing it. To those who knew Frank Goldsmith only as the dashing Oxford man from Cavenham Hall it came as a profound shock, just as it did to Frank Goldsmith himself who never forgave his brother-in-law. He had never considered fighting for any country other than England: why else would he have spent ten years as a volunteer officer in his local regiment?

Demands that he should be stripped of his commission in the Suffolk Hussars were followed by riots in his Stowmarket constituency. Bewildered, he found himself paying the hospital bills of the local men who had defended him in the villages near Cavenham.

Frank Goldsmith soon realized that he could not remain in England. Even in the London clubs, where he had spent so much of his time in the past ten years, men whom he had come to regard as his friends turned against him, although Winston Churchill and another old friend, Lord Bessborough, remained loyal and helped him to keep his commission. Bitterly upset and determined to prove his innocence, he asked for the first posting abroad that the War Office could arrange for him.

Through no fault of his own, and like so many Goldschmidts in the past, Frank Goldsmith suddenly found himself an outsider. It was to change his life, and his son Jimmy would never forget it.

2

Monsieur le Major

As he polished his Sam Browne belt, and folded his cotton khaki shirts into the trunk while he prepared to leave for Southampton and the troopship in the first days of 1915, Captain Frank Goldsmith of the Loyal Suffolk Hussars suspected that he would never live in England permanently again. The humiliation of being called "pro-German" was too great. He could not understand what he had done wrong. Why had so many Englishmen turned against him – an English army officer about to fight in a war against Germany? But in the spring of 1915 when the first important battle of the war opened in the Dardanelles, he found himself fighting not Germans but Turks.

On 25 April 1915 British and Australian troops landed on the sands of Gallipoli to find themselves confronted by well prepared and well entrenched Turkish troops. By the end of 1915 it was clear that the British and Australian troops had not the slightest hope of victory, and in the middle of December their evacuation began. The campaign had been an unmitigated failure, costing thousands of lives. Captain Frank Goldsmith had served at Gallipoli through-out the campaign, bravely and without hesitation, but it did nothing to increase his respect for the British establishment – a coalition led by Lloyd George had replaced the Liberal government – who were supposed to be directing the fate of the British Army.

Together with a quarter of a million other troops, Frank Goldsmith was kept in the Middle East, in Egypt, to guard the Suez Canal from potential attack by the Turks. Newly promoted to the rank of Major, he served under General Allenby, and helped to provide the British with some of their only victories during the darkest days of the war. By December 1917 Allenby's army had taken Jerusalem and given Lloyd George a "Christmas present" for the British people.

After the victory in Jerusalem, Major Frank Goldsmith MP returned to England and told his old colleagues in the Unionist party that he no longer wished to remain the Member of Parliament for Stowmarket. He had spent his time on leave from the desert in Paris where, in 1917, he had fallen in love with a French girl called Jacqueline Franc. He had decided to join her in France and now he set about organizing his departure from England for good. Some of his old friends tried to dissuade him, but his mind was made up. In any case, those connections he still had with England were beginning to break down.

If the anti-German feeling of the war years had hurt Frank, it had mortally wounded Adolph Goldschmidt who had long believed the British to be the most civilized people in the world. Throughout the war Adolph and Alice had stayed mainly in London, rarely going out; memories of Cavenham Hall had become too painful. On 6 April 1918 Adolph died at his London home at the age of eighty. The death certificate read simply "Pneumonia", but it could equally well have read "Despair". Now only Frank's mother and elder brother remained in England.

By the time the Armistice was declared in November 1918 Frank Goldsmith had finalized his plans to leave England. In December he saw his parliamentary constituency taken over by his old friend and Suffolk Hussars colleague Walter Guinness, from whom he had inherited the seat eight years before. The Liberal Party did not even consider putting up an opposition candidate.

Paris was now to be Frank Goldsmith's home, just as it had been the home of his grandfather Benedict Hayum when he left Frankfurt in 1866. The Goldschmidt family had enjoyed considerable commercial success there, and there was no reason why they should not do so again.

Frank Goldsmith had received a small inheritance from his grandfather, but his father's death provided him with enough money to launch himself in business. Part of his father's money had disappeared with the Tsar and the Kaiser; his painstakingly collected bonds largely worthless. But, according to *The Times*, Adolph

Goldschmidt's estate was worth £364,000. The old man had left £1,000 to his confidential clerk and £500 to his butler, but the rest was to be divided among his family. Alice Goldschmidt had inherited a sizeable sum from her own parents and did not need the support of her sons. So Frank Goldsmith hardly needed to find a job, but it was not in his nature to sit about doing nothing and, at forty, his appetite for adventure was as keen as ever.

At first he bought shares in a rapidly expanding chain of cinemas which seemed to him to have a considerable future in Europe, but he quickly decided to sell them again when an opportunity to invest in the hotel industry came up. With Henri Ruhl and the Comte de la Rouchefoucauld, he set out to rejuvenate a hotel company which came to be known as the Hôtels Réunis. By chance he had stumbled on a career that suited him admirably. His charm was as considerable as it had always been, and so was his sense of style. After the disappointments of England, he rather relished a peripatetic life which would allow him to live comfortably without maintaining a string of personal servants. His effortless enthusiasm and drive were rare enough to endear him to thousands; his relationship with the Rothschilds and his own family in France was more than useful; but it was his delight in the luxurious, and his determination to see that his guests were always well catered for, which enabled him, within a decade, to establish himself as one of the most powerful and popular hoteliers in Europe.

In January 1922 Frank Goldsmith paid a last formal visit to his former home. His mother Alice had died at the age of seventy-eight in London, and his father's estate was to be broken up and sold. Only his elder brother Teddy was still living in England permanently (in London), and even though Alice Goldschmidt had left more than £135,000 in her will none of her children wanted to sustain the 2,500 acres in Suffolk or the house off Park Lane. They decided that it would be better to sell everything.

On Wednesday 24 May 1922, the estate of A. B. H. Goldschmidt at Cavenham Park in Suffolk and 14 South Street, Park Lane, came under the auctioneer's hammer, at Messrs Christie, Manson and Woods in St James's Square, London. It attracted a great deal of interest, particularly among collectors. The sale of "French Decorative Furniture, Objects of Art, Porcelain and Tapestry" lasted two full days, and raised a little over £13,000. On Friday 26 May, the sale of Adolph Goldschmidt's pictures followed and raised almost as much. The gallery Colnaghi's paid nearly £2,000 for a painting by Danbigny.

The Goldschmidts' last connections with England were broken and there was nothing to draw Frank Goldsmith back again regularly. Adolph Goldschmidt's children and grandchildren were never to feel anything but outsiders there, so strong was the memory of their humiliation.

By 1928 the company that Frank Goldsmith had founded, Hôtels Réunis, controlled forty-eight of the finest hotels in France, including the Hôtel Scribe and the Hôtel Astoria in Paris, and the impeccable Carlton in Cannes. He also managed all the principal hotels in Monte Carlo, including the Hôtel de Paris and the Hermitage. Still an amateur businessman, however, he did not always own the hotels he managed, but he nevertheless established himself as one of Europe's perfect hosts. He moved around France from suite to suite taking Jacqueline Franc with him. The winter was spent in Monte Carlo, the summer at Trouville on the Channel coast. In the spring they visited London and Paris. Still with the style of an Edwardian English gentleman, "Monsieur le Major", as he became known, was one of the people who gave the 1920s their particular flavour in Europe. In his hotel dining rooms young women swooned at the feet of men twice their age, and in his suites the Aga Khan and J. P. Morgan entertained on their summer trips around Europe.

Monsieur le Major travelled around Europe with no small pomp and no little circumstance. A string of porters always carried his suitcases from the hotel to his waiting Rolls-Royce, and from the car to the waiting train's first-class compartment. He did not like long car journeys, so his chauffeur drove on ahead to meet him at the station on his arrival. He took a small private pleasure in bringing the foyer of the hotel he was leaving to a halt as his entourage swept through.

Frank took Jacqueline Franc with him whenever he could, for one reason above any other: they were keen to have children. "It is part of the Goldsmith tradition," Frank would explain to her. "My grandfather was one of fourteen children, remember." But despite visits to specialists, she was unable to conceive. Finally, it was discovered that there might be a blockage in one of her Fallopian tubes, and without hesitation she decided to have the operation that her specialist recommended. She was told that it would be quite straightforward.

If there was a whisper of concern in Frank Goldsmith's mind he did not show it to the beautiful young French girl as she packed to go to the clinic in the outskirts of Paris. She had the finest medical advice that France could provide, and the best surgeon. He had seen to that. And it was a straightforward operation. Everyone told him so. There was nothing whatever to worry about. And Jacqueline seemed so happy.

Tragically, however, the operation went wrong. Jacqueline Franc never recovered from the anaesthetic, and she died before Frank could reach the clinic. None of the doctors could explain what had happened. It seemed as if, yet again, the world had saved its cruellest blow for the Goldsmith family. Just as he had watched his political career destroyed through no fault of his own, Frank Goldsmith now lost the one woman he had ever loved; and all because he had wanted to perpetuate the Goldsmith name.

For nearly six months Monsieur le Major retired behind the doors of his suite in the Hôtel Scribe in Paris, and for the rest of his life, a picture of Jacqueline would never be far away.

It was on a trip to Cannes in the autumn of 1927, that Monsieur le Major was finally to meet the woman who would continue the Goldsmith name. At the time, though, he was travelling with someone else – one of five famously beautiful sisters from a Catholic family called Mouiller. They came from Vichy in the Auvergne where their father, who also ran a hotel, had been a member of the elected local government before the First World War. A socialist, he became a municipal councillor in Vichy, but financial difficulties had eventually forced the family to move. The hotel was sold and they settled on the Côte d'Azur. Since the end of the war the two elder sisters had married, and it was in the company of one of the married sisters that Frank Goldsmith was travelling from Paris. He intended to entertain her at his hotels, and while he was in Cannes he would also supervise the alterations needed to prepare the Carlton Hotel for the coming winter season.

When Frank Goldsmith and his companion stepped down from the Blue Train, they were met by the retinue of porters that traditionally greeted his arrival in a city that boasted one of his hotels, and they were also met by the lady's younger sister, Marcelle. A striking, uninhibited blonde, aged twenty-three, Marcelle Mouiller was slightly surprised not to find her elder sister accompanied by her husband, but nevertheless she was quite happy to escort her and Major Goldsmith to Monte Carlo for lunch on the following afternoon. In the next few days Marcelle and her sister went everywhere with Frank, and it rapidly became quite clear that she had taken a fancy to him. When the week's visit to Cannes came to an end Marcelle accompanied them to the station, "so that I can see the inside of the famous Blue Train," she told her sister. When they reached the train Marcelle seemed fascinated by the magnificent oak panelling of the train's sitting rooms, and the hand-stitched white linen of the sheets and head rests. And, almost before anyone had noticed it, the express slipped quietly out of the station. Although she was wearing only a light blue summer dress over her swimming costume, Marcelle was not in the least perturbed, and she was determined not to be put off at the first stop. After all, for a young girl who had never been to Paris here was the perfect opportunity. Even at the age of twenty-three the young woman, who was later described proudly by her son Jimmy as "an Auvergne peasant", was not daunted by the prospect of an adventure, or a husband – even if he was forty-eight.

In Paris Marcelle Mouiller stayed with her sister, content to be entertained on most evenings by the charming Major, who seemed to know everyone. There were visits to Ciros and the Ritz, dinner at his hotels. Any other young girl who had hardly travelled more than 100 kilometres from her home town might have been overwhelmed. But Marcelle Mouiller was not. She had inherited a fierceness of spirit, and a pride, that captivated almost everyone she met. By the time Frank Goldsmith celebrated his forty-ninth birthday at the end of November, they were lovers. By March 1928 she was pregnant and early in November their son Edward (like his uncle known as Teddy) was born in a Paris clinic.

Frank Goldsmith decided that his new family needed a more permanent home than his hotel suites; those he would keep for business. By the time that Marcelle had left the clinic with their new son, Monsieur le Major had taken the lease on a comfortable apartment, at 43 rue Emile-Meunier, near the Bois de Boulogne. It was large enough for the staff that he believed his new family now demanded. A nurse and cook were hired at once, as was a maid, and later a governess. The apartment might not actually have been on the Avenue Foch, but it was in the suitably fashionable 16th *arrondissement*.

As he watched his young son grow Frank Goldsmith realized that something in his life had changed. The private uncertainty that he had sometimes felt in the past had all but disappeared. He was established. His success in France had even been recognized in England: in 1926 he had become a director of the independent Savoy group of hotels, which included Claridges and The Berkeley. Perhaps the time had come to marry. So on 29 June 1929, while on a business trip to London, he and Marcelle were married at the Register Office in Hanover Square, not far from his father's old home in Mayfair. Little had really changed; Monsieur le Major still intended to tour his hotels as he had always done, only now he would take with him a rather larger entourage than before, because his wife and son, not to mention their maid and nanny, would be travelling with him.

Into this magnificently cossetted, and not exactly conventional, life a second son was born on 26 February 1933. He was christened James Michael. Now there were two sons to sustain the Goldsmith name. What Frank and Marcelle did not know was how seriously their new son would take his birthright. He knew exactly what was expected of every male member of the family: success, and reputation. "Can there be anything more important than the family name?" he says now. "It is absolutely vital. Its continuance is a fundamental biological instinct."

3

The Sporting Life

It was a gilded childhood. The soft breath of affluence that blew across Jimmy Goldsmith's early years convinced him that life should never be lived in any other way. Dinner was always a matter of white tie and tails; parties were always extravagant and peopled by the celebrated; the girls were always pretty, but usually bored. It was the time of *Private Lives*, when Noël Coward and Gertrude Lawrence played out their stuttering romance on the balcony of a hotel on the Riviera that was almost certainly managed by his father, Monsieur le Major. The world of the soup kitchen and the dole queue never penetrated the cocoon of wealth that was wrapped around him.

When not at home in Paris, Jimmy Goldsmith spent the first years of his life in some of the grandest hotel suites in Europe. He was welcome in every city from Monte Carlo to Biarritz, from London to Locarno, a boy for whom the terrace of the Carlton at Cannes, or the first-floor suite at Claridges in London, was as much a playground as the Bois de Boulogne.

The small boy who had inherited his mother's fierce blue eyes, and his father's wide, boyish face accepted the luxury that surrounded him without hesitation. Everything was provided for him, so why should that not always be the case? Jimmy Goldsmith revelled in his affluence, and saw no need whatever to be ashamed of it. Indeed, no matter what might happen in the future he vowed he would always try to make sure that the same luxury always surrounded him. Even when he had no money, twenty years later, he still employed a valet and a cook. Jimmy Goldsmith never learned the meaning of temperance or restraint. There had been no one to teach him those supposed virtues, any more than there had been anyone to teach him that life was not always fun.

Jimmy Goldsmith spent every spring in Paris with his parents, with a trip to London for a few weeks so that his father could discuss the future of the Savoy group of hotels. Then it was back to Paris before visiting Trouville, and on to the Côte d'Azur. Everywhere the porters brought the hotel lobbies to a halt as the Goldsmith retinue arrived. Express trains were held up for them to reach the station, yachts kept waiting at the dock, cars always at their disposal. Millions might have given anything to sample, even for a day, such a gilded existence, but to those born into it, there seemed nothing exceptional, nothing untoward, in the pursuit of pleasure as well as profit.

It did not take Jimmy Goldsmith long to develop his own version of his father's style, adding his own individual variation. Luxury was all very well, but it needed a little excitement. He took to gambling. After all, that too was part of the family tradition. He had heard his father talk about his own brother Charles (Carl), who had become so addicted to playing roulette in the casino in Ostend, and had lost so often, that he had become convinced that his bad luck was due to the subtle and mysterious powers of another player, the King of the Belgians – a claim for which there was not the slightest justification. (Charles ended his days in a house in the grounds of a Swiss sanatorium, when the excitement of roulette – not to mention the inheritance from his father and mother – had been lost.) So, by the age of six Jimmy Goldsmith had developed a passion for gambling, and particularly for the new gambling machines, predecessors of the one-armed bandit, which had just begun to appear in some of his father's hotels in the South of France as an adjunct to the casino.

One morning in the early summer of 1939 he watched, hypno-tized, as an American woman struggled to make one of the machines in the drawing room adjacent to the foyer of the Hôtel de Paris in Monte Carlo disgorge its fortune in exchange for her steady supply of one-franc pieces. When she finally gave up the struggle and retired to the terrace, she gave him her last franc. There was no stopping him. He rushed across the drawing room, grabbed a chair and pushed it up to the machine. Standing on the seat he could just reach the handle and, more important, he could push one of his own precious supply of coins into the machine. Without a pause he pulled the handle, and seconds later found himself surrounded by a huge pile of money. Jimmy Goldsmith had won the jackpot.

Without a moment's hesitation he set off in search of a waiter to help him collect his winnings; a Goldsmith did not stoop to filling his own pockets. In fact it took not one waiter but two to sweep up the one-franc pieces and assemble them on "a fine silver platter" which Jimmy Goldsmith remembers to this day. He was intent on displaying his luck to his parents, and in particular to his mother. In fact, an anxious duty manager had already thought it wise to tell the Goldsmiths about their son's exploits.

Marcelle Goldsmith and her husband were having lunch in the hotel's dining room when they saw their six-year-old son striding confidently towards them in front of a waiter carrying a huge pile of coins on a silver tray. Frank, however, told him that he was not to have the money until he was older.

"Why not?" Jimmy demanded. "I won it!"

"A boy of your age should not be gambling," Frank replied.

But Jimmy Goldsmith had no intention of giving back his winnings. He grabbed the tray from the astonished waiter and took off across the foyer. In the hotel's manually operated lift, he pushed the sliding gates shut with his foot and proceeded to take himself up as quickly as he could away from the wrath of his parents. As he rose through the Hôtel de Paris's magnificent marble and carpeted stairs, he heard his parents running up after him. He was making for his family's suite where he intended hiding his winnings. But by the time the Hôtel de Paris's lift shuddered to a halt Major Goldsmith and his wife had almost caught up with their son. Immediately Jimmy Goldsmith shut the lift doors again, and set off back down towards the foyer. He had calculated that by the time he got back downstairs his parents would be so out of breath they might give him enough time to hide some of his winnings at least, and beat a hasty retreat. Even at the age of six Jimmy Goldsmith did not intend to have his independence threatened, or be separated from what was rightfully his.

That was to be one of the last times that Jimmy Goldsmith stayed at the Hôtel de Paris as a boy. The years when girls were sent to finishing schools on the Côte d'Azur were coming to an end. The autumn afternoons when his father would welcome the English Prince of Wales to one of his hotels, while his mother looked after another of the guests, Mrs Wallis Simpson, had passed. By this time Edward had given up the throne to marry Mrs Simpson, and in Munich the British Prime Minister Neville Chamberlain was meeting Adolf Hitler.

To his guests Monsieur le Major seemed cheerful enough, but he was worried about the future. He had already despatched his eldest son Teddy to school in England with his nanny: first to Surbiton and then to a preparatory school in Seaford on the Sussex coast. But no matter how concerned he may have been in private, he intended to make sure that the prospect of a German invasion remained remote to his guests. He took the same view in public as *The Tatler* correspondent who reported on 6 September 1939 that "although the crisis in Europe robbed Deauville of many of its most regular supporters before Grand Prix days, there was still a good attendance for a very exciting day's racing".

In the sunny autumn of 1939 he tried to console his wife with the thought that there was always something they could do. After all, he was one of the most prominent hoteliers in France. Marcelle Goldsmith was not convinced. She had refused to let Teddy travel back to school in England at the beginning of the new term, and the prospect of an Italian invasion was preoccupying her. Reluctantly, Frank Goldsmith agreed to let his wife and sons leave the comfort of the Carlton to take refuge, first on the Channel coast at Trouville, and then with one of Marcelle Goldsmith's old friends in a village high in the Pyrenees. For his part he was determined to stay in Cannes, at least for the time being. The fact that he was a member of one of the most famous Jewish families in Europe hardly occurred to him. "My father was never really conscious of anti-semitism," his son Jimmy was to explain years later.

By the beginning of December 1939, however, Frank Goldsmith was only too well aware that no Jewish family was safe from the Gestapo; even the Rothschilds were preparing to leave France. If he wanted to save himself and his family he had to act quickly. The Rothschilds thought that the best hope of escape lay in going to England, and the most likely place to find a boat was the port of

Bayonne on France's south-west coast. From there it was a short trip across the Bay of Biscay to safety. Shortly before Christmas Major Goldsmith told his wife to leave the Haut Pyrenees and set out for the French coast. He would join the family in Bayonne.

Monsieur le Major did not intend to panic, however. He instructed his chauffeur Nelo to prepare the Rolls-Royce, pack all they would need for the two-day journey, and be ready to leave the following morning. He offered a lift to a Jewish friend, Sydney Beer, who had also realized that the time had come to leave France.

Neither man thought that the trip would present many difficulties as they set off from the courtyard of the Carlton Hotel with rugs wrapped over their knees. They were wrong. Although there were few obvious signs of danger as they motored through the wintry countryside towards the Pyrenees, by the time they reached the old town of Carcassone things were quite different. The town was surrounded by soldiers who had blocked every road to the coast; there was no way that a Rolls-Royce could penetrate the cordon. It began to look as though they would never reach Bayonne. Not sure what else to do, Major Frank Goldsmith decided to have lunch.

Once again the notion that life was to be enjoyed rather than endured came to his rescue. At a neighbouring table were two French soldiers and an officer, also intent on getting to the coast. With their help, and after a distinctly disturbing episode in which the soldiers drew their guns and prepared to shoot their way out, Major Frank Goldsmith managed to avoid the road blocks and escape from Carcassone. A day later he joined his family in Bayonne. But when he got there he realized that the Goldsmiths were not the only family to have worked out that the port offered the best hope for escape from France. A boat was not going to be easy to find.

The town was crammed with people, each and every one of them apparently intent on watching the quayside for the sight of a ship. There was little or no food, and it was only because his wife had reached there two days earlier, and secured one of the few hotel rooms, that they had anywhere to sleep. Ignoring the rumours that there would be no boats and that the Germans were about to bomb the town, Marcelle Goldsmith sat steadfastly on the quayside. After three days of waiting, she was rewarded. A Dutch freighter slipped into the mouth of the Adour river, and as many passengers as it could take embarked for the voyage across the Bay of Biscay to England. "The captain took 5,000 on a ship designed for no more than 400," Teddy Goldsmith remembers. "When he berthed, he announced he would take British-born citizens first, which of course none of us were, but my father told him that he'd been a British MP, and the captain let us on board."

They were not the only Jewish family to escape on that ship: among the other passengers was Evelyn de Rothschild and his two sisters, and their governess. It was, in fact, the last ship to escape from Bayonne before the German Army arrived. But even on board ship the danger had not quite passed. In the Bay of Biscay a U-boat fired a torpedo at the freighter, but fortunately it slipped harmlessly past, and the submarine disappeared. "There was a terrible panic on the ship when that happened," Teddy Goldsmith recalls. "Everyone was screaming, because there weren't nearly enough lifeboats for 5,000 people, and we all thought we were going to drown." But after four days at sea the freighter sailed quietly into Southampton.

As the family settled into a suite at Claridges again, one they had stayed in before, everything in London seemed much as it had always done on their visits. There were more precautions taken at night, with the blackout, but by the time the first months of 1940 had passed the escape from Bayonne seemed to Teddy and Jimmy almost like an adventure in a magazine. If there had been any danger, they had certainly forgotten it. Frank, however, was planning his family's future. He thought it would be best if they took refuge in the West Indies. They had friends in the hotel industry there, and he doubted that the war in Europe would ever reach the Caribbean. In the first months of 1940 he organized their passage by ship, and sorted out his financial affairs. His flat in Paris had been seized by the Germans, and he had not been able to bring much money from Cannes. But he was still a director of the Savoy, and he always kept some money in England.

For his own part, Frank had decided to try to re-enlist in the British Army. But his request to be taken back into his regiment was turned down, even though he appealed to his old friends Lord Bessborough and Winston Churchill, the new Prime Minister. He was sixty-one years old, they pointed out to him, with four years' war service already; the British government was not about to recruit veterans approaching their old-age pensions, at least not yet. Reluctantly Monsieur le Major decided he might as well go with his wife and sons. So, in the early summer of 1940, the family set sail from Liverpool for the rather less austere surroundings of the Bahama Islands. Monsieur le Major had been invited to manage the Royal Victoria Hotel in Nassau and it seemed an entirely appropriate place in which to bring up a young family.

The next four years were peaceful enough. Frank was occupied with running the hotel where they lived at first, and the boys were looked after by a black maid called Jane. The only slight difference, as his sons reminded one another, was that "It was the first time that he had actually worked for someone else, rather than for his own company." But the boys could hardly have asked for more comfortable surroundings in which to survive a war. It meant they could resume their old habits from France.

"We used to collect sea shells," Teddy Goldsmith remembers, "and use them to gamble, because some of them were quite valuable." The appetite for games of chance had not deserted either of Frank Goldsmith's sons. "My preoccupation at the time was games of dice, like craps," Jimmy Goldsmith recalls now, though he was barely seven years old at the time. While they played on the beaches or indulged their other passion, for poker, their mother helped run a canteen for trainee air force pilots, which had been organized by the wife of the British colony's new Governor. Once more the family took part in the familiar round of parties, dinners and conversation, punctuated by gentle afternoons of rest out of the sun.

The two boys were supposed to be attending the islands' Belmont School, but they had little success. Teddy Goldsmith had "some dedication", according to one school report, but his younger brother was principally described as "lazy" or "uninterested". School was not one of the seven-year-old Jimmy Goldsmith's passions. For a good part of the time he contrived to be as far away from it as possible. When Frank asked him why he was not interested in learning to read, Jimmy told him gravely that when he grew up he was going to be a millionaire, and would have somebody to read to him. There was no need for him to learn in the first place.

There was no way to make Jimmy Goldsmith do anything he did

not care to. Bribery, threats, punishment, force – nothing worked. He simply gritted his teeth, looked whoever was telling him off straight in the eye, and did precisely what he wanted. His parents were prepared to accept his eccentricity for a time, including his new hobby of chicken farming for a profit, but after two years in the Bahamas they knew they had to do something about it. On the advice of friends they decided to despatch both boys to St Andrews College, in Ontario, Canada, where they had heard that the discipline was strict and the regime controlled.

Jimmy Goldsmith loathed every moment he spent at St Andrews College. "There was no heating in the school. We used to dress to go to bed it was so cold," he remembers now. "I used to put on two pullovers over my pyjama, and five pairs of socks, as well as stuff newspapers under the mattress just to keep warm." Teddy recalled: "In the winter we had to boil the ink, it was so cold." Jimmy Goldsmith was determined to escape. But to do that he knew he needed money. He decided to do the only thing that presented itself to a boy of nine in Canada in the winter: trap animals. He started setting traps at night, and coming back during the day to find what he had caught.

"I used to trap skunk, rabbit, and, occasionally, wild mink – which was, of course, a bonanza." He would then sell his furs in Toronto. By the time he was ten he had raised "a bit of money", and he had plans for it. That Christmas he decided to run away from school. "We couldn't go home during the holidays, because it was complicated flying from Toronto to the Bahamas while the war was still on, so I decided to go to New York. I'd been there with my father and I reckoned it was going to be more fun than staying and freezing in Toronto."

Without telling his elder brother, he simply took himself by train across the Canadian border, arrived at Grand Central Station, took a taxi to the Waldorf-Astoria on Park Avenue, installed himself in a room, and set out to enjoy himself. It took his parents and the school several days to locate him.

"When they arrived, they were rather upset, but I thought it was great fun." The memory still amuses him. Throughout his life he has never quite been able to escape an image of himself as the perpetually naughty schoolboy: the one always getting into scraps and scrapes, but, just as surely, getting out of them. It has become part of his character.

Returned to St Andrews, Jimmy Goldsmith did nothing to change his ways, especially when it came to anything even remotely athletic. He refused point blank to co-operate with any effort to turn him into a boy that a public school might call a "sportsman". And he took particular pleasure in demonstrating his dislike of the school's annual cross-country race. Every boy was expected to do his best and reach the finish in the school's quadrangle to be cheered by the staff and parents. Not James Michael Goldsmith. In the school sanatorium suffering from measles, his brother Teddy remembers only too clearly: "As I lay in bed I heard all the names called as they finished the race: but I didn't hear Jimmy's." Finally, almost a quarter of an hour after the last boy had come panting into the quadrangle, Teddy Goldsmith heard, "Come on, Goldsmith, you bugger, get a move on." He climbed on to his bed to look out of the window and see what was going on. There was the tall figure of his eleven-year-old brother studiously strolling rather than running into the quadrangle. "He was carrying a bag of toffees in one hand, and the Toronto *Sporting Chronicle* in the other," Teddy remembers, "and he completed the race by walking across the finishing line, to a deafening silence."

Teddy Goldsmith is convinced that "Jimmy considered it beneath his dignity to run. He walked the whole way deliberately. He didn't mind people kicking him. If they knocked him down, he'd just get up again. It was very typical of him." Whatever else Jimmy Goldsmith may have minded, he did not mind being noticed. Being an outcast did not worry him in the least. If he did not care to run, or do anything else, there would be no false effort, no half-hearted attempt. He would rather finish ostentatiously last than somewhere in the middle at something he did not want to do. It was an approach that he has never abandoned, no matter how unpopular or eccentric it made him appear.

However, like Adolph Goldschmidt before him, Frank Goldsmith wanted his sons, above all else, to have the manners and education of English gentlemen: that meant Magdalen College, Oxford, his old college, for Teddy; and Eton for Jimmy. If the Goldsmiths were to make their mark again, they would need to prove their education and intelligence, and understand the workings of the English aristocracy. Eton and Oxford provided that. If people called him a snob, he did not care. To become a part of English life had originally been Frank Goldsmith's dream. He was not to know that his son Jimmy was convinced that the only way to make a mark in the world was to do precisely the opposite: stand out from the crowd at all times. That meant no one could forget the Goldsmith name.

In February 1945, shortly before his younger son's twelfth birthday, Major Goldsmith despatched both boys to England to further their education as "gentlemen". Initially Teddy and Jimmy were to go to Millfield in Somerset, run by the formidable R. J. O. ("Boss") Meyer; Teddy to cram for Oxford entrance, Jimmy to prepare for the common entrance examination at thirteen and Eton.

The boys had at least one advantage when they arrived at Millfield: they could speak fluent French. Their mother had addressed them in little else throughout their childhood, partly because she had hardly known any English when she had married and partly because she was determined that her sons should speak the two languages that reflected the dual nationality that their father had arranged for them. Major Frank Goldsmith, on the other hand, had addressed his sons in English throughout their childhood. He had not taken such trouble to conceal the accent of the Frankfurt ghetto just to hear another accent, that of the French countryside, spoil his sons' chances of being English gentlemen.

Jimmy Goldsmith still did not much care for school. Indeed Millfield could hardly have been called an appropriate choice for a boy who disliked all aspects of athleticism as thoroughly as he did. Millfield's principal interest was sporting achievement, even though Robert Bolt, the playwright, was a master at the school. But Millfield had one great advantage for Jimmy Goldsmith: it accepted the unconventional. Founded by Meyer only a decade before, it reflected its headmaster's unusual view of the world. An international golfer who was also a former cricket captain of Somerset, Meyer was an enthusiastic gambler, whether on horses, gold shares or the outcome of one of his pupils' races. The young gambler and the inveterate one were almost made for each other. They understood the same language. Jimmy still took some delight in outwitting the school authorities. Bets on horse races – strictly against the formal rules –

were despatched by postal order or delivered by other boys. Even so Meyer got Jimmy Goldsmith into Eton. "It's doubtful if anyone else could have done," Teddy Goldsmith says now.

PART 2

Playboy

4

The Nonconformist

By the time he arrived at Eton in the autumn of 1946 Jimmy Goldsmith was a confident boy of almost six feet, with a clear idea of what he wanted from the world. It was simple enough: to enjoy himself. His plans did not include doing much in the way of academic work. He would wear the black frock coat, stiff collar and top hat that tradition demanded, but he did not intend to conform in any other way.

"At Eton I was part of a group which consisted of misfits, eccentrics or rebels," he recalls now. "As far as I could see, the virtues that the school prized were conforming and being good at games. I was good at neither. I was a bit foreign, and certainly not good at games. Scholarship – although at that time I was no great scholar – would not have compensated."

Receiving a generous allowance of £1 a week from his father, he proceeded to take an interest in other things. He ignored most classes, paying as little attention as he could get away with, and steadfastly refused to take part in all sports. Waterloo may have been won on the playing fields of Eton, but it was not a battle that Jimmy Goldsmith was interested in. The only Sporting Life that engaged his attention was the newspaper that chronicled the day's horse racing; his one intellectual challenge, the complicated variations of bets he could have. He took considerable care to study form and kept an accurate record of every horse that made him a profit. If he could not get to the races himself he would try to persuade other boys to put bets on for him, or he would telephone his bookmakers. Who knows, one day it might present a means of escape.

"The only thing I was any good at at Eton was mathematics," he remembers, "and I wasn't much good at that." But when his housemaster asked him what he was going to specialize in, he replied briskly, "Mathematics." Jimmy Goldsmith can recall the look of horror on the man's face to this day. "He looked at me very coldly, and said, 'I don't want any mechanics in my house.' And that was the end of that."

That remark coloured forever Jimmy Goldsmith's attitude to English public schools. "Mathematics was the most scurrilous, undignified thing that they could imagine. It was dirty. All they wanted anyone to do was Greats."

Jimmy Goldsmith did not mind in the least if the school thought him eccentric. In fact he took considerable pride in it. To demonstrate his disdain for convention he began to throw extravagant dinner parties in the hotels of nearby Windsor, and taking his fellow pupils to the races there whenever he could. His allowance was hardly enough to sustain quite such a flamboyant lifestyle, but he usually managed to win enough, or borrow enough from his father when things got difficult. Yet, in spite of his determination to do so, Jimmy Goldsmith did not cut a particularly distinctive figure at Eton in his years there. Certainly he was nothing like as famous as "Tiny" Armstrong Jones, who coxed the Eton boat. Indeed, Charles Hambro, who was later to become his close friend and business partner, recalls now: "I don't think I knew of Jimmy's existence at Eton, and he did not know of mine: even if we were contemporaries." Jimmy remained something of a loner. He seemed both too sure of himself and too shy at the same time. He looked as though he never felt entirely comfortable.

His brother Teddy, by contrast, was particularly happy. A year after Jimmy left Millfield for Eton, he went up to Magdalen College, Oxford, where his father had been an undergraduate fifty years before. To Jimmy the life of an undergraduate seemed much more appealing than the life of an Eton schoolboy, but there was not much chance that he would follow Teddy. He remained determined not to take any interest whatsoever in examinations. His parents, who were by this time gratefully back in France after their years in the Caribbean (Monsieur le Major was once again in charge of the affairs of the Hôtels Réunis), might have nursed their private ambitions for him, but there was nothing he could do about that.

One dull, weekday afternoon in the autumn of 1949, Jimmy Goldsmith invested the considerable sum of £10 on three horses running at a race meeting at Lewes, Sussex, and he linked the bets into an accumulator. If one won, the winnings would be invested on the next, and if that also won, an even larger bet would go on to the third. To his enormous surprise and delight, the three horses won, bringing him a little over £8,000 in cash. It was a king's ransom for a boy only a few months beyond his sixteenth birthday, and to this day he can still remember the names of the three horses: Bartisan, Your Fancy and Merry Dance. From that day onwards he would defend his gambler's instinct to anyone: "A gambler knows when to play his luck, and when not to, when to keep on and when to give up, and that is a good thing for a businessman." It had provided him with a way of escape.

He proceeded to take most of the members of his house out to dinner to celebrate. At dinner he announced, "A man of my means should not remain a schoolboy, even at Eton." He had decided to leave school there and then. Neither the school nor his parents were to be offered any alternative. The following morning he set off for Oxford to visit his brother. That evening he was invited to play chemin de fer at 167 Walton Street. It was there that his education proper began.

The British publisher Anthony Blond, then also an undergraduate at Magdalen, recalls: "There was no lodging house in Oxford more bizarre than 167 Walton Street, which was run by a Swiss lady called Maxie. On the top floor lived two men dressed entirely in black – as was their apartment which boasted a coffin in the corner containing a skeleton. Below that lived a Jewish antique dealer and nightclub owner; and a constant visitor was another Oxford undergraduate, John Aspinall."

Educated at Rugby, Aspinall was one of the most flamboyant undergraduates of his day. Muscular, genial and uninhibited, he habitually organized gambling parties, wherever and whenever he could, and invited as many of his friends as he thought would be "amusing". One of the regular players at Aspinall's table was Teddy Goldsmith, and it was only to be expected that he would bring his younger brother Jimmy. When Anthony Blond first caught sight of

Jimmy Goldsmith he was playing chemin de fer with Aspinall and
his brother Teddy at Walton Street. Before the end of his first
evening Jimmy Goldsmith had lost almost half of his £8,000.

"What Jimmy hadn't realized about the games at Walton Street,"
explains Digby Neave, a contemporary at Eton who had arrived at
Oxford the year before as an undergraduate, "was that he was the
only one in the game playing with real money. All the rest of us
used IOUs. Most of the time we were just passing pieces of paper
about. But if someone turned up with real money it was a sensation."
But Jimmy Goldsmith did not mind losing in the least. After the
rigid life of Eton, Walton Street was a revelation. And it introduced
him to the other passion that was to rule his life: beautiful
women.

One of the inhabitants of the ground floor of 167 Walton Street
was a woman who was to remain in his mind for years to come.
The mistress of one of the regular players at John Aspinall's table,
she wore a garment that hypnotized Jimmy Goldsmith. "It
was an elaborate silk dressing gown, tied at the waist, which
had small holes cut out in it so that her nipples could show through.
I'd never seen anything like it." As his brother Teddy remembers,
"The first thing Jimmy did when he got to Oxford was to go
out and get himself a girlfriend. He pinched her from a famous
seducer."

Life was suddenly transformed for Jimmy Goldsmith. Now he
could leave school, and live as and where he chose. When he
telephoned his parents in France, Major Goldsmith and his wife,
aware that their younger son had not passed a single academic
examination in his school career, accepted the inevitable: they could
not make him stay at school but they did persuade him to follow
his father's example and go to a crammer's to prepare for Oxford.
Jimmy did not take too much persuading.

Eton, too, accepted the inevitable. The school realized that it
could not contain a restless young man of sixteen, who looked
twenty-one, and who suddenly found himself substantially richer
than most of the masters who taught him. Reluctantly the headmaster agreed that he should be allowed to leave, and – as tradition
dictated – he took part in the school's "going down" ceremony at
which he was presented with a book, suitably engraved in Latin by

the headmaster which is still in Jimmy Goldsmith's house in Paris.
"It proves to everyone that I haven't been sacked," he tells anyone
who asks.

In November he set out for the rather less traditional surroundings
of a cramming college not far from Tunbridge Wells in Kent. For
the journey he bought himself a car: a 1928 Singer. He couldn't
drive, and he had hardly sat behind the wheel of a car, let alone
taken a driving test, but that did not deter him in the slightest. A
young man setting out in the world, with his financial backing,
should have a car. After all his father had had a Rolls-Royce, so
why shouldn't he have a car of his own? Over the next few months,
he would teach himself to drive.

Not everything went according to plan, however. After he had
been at the crammer's only a few weeks, Jimmy Goldsmith got
involved in a fight with one of the college's academic staff. The
man was knocked down and injured. In the circumstances Jimmy
Goldsmith thought it prudent to withdraw, and he did so without
even pausing to collect his car.

Back in Oxford again he fell back into the round of card games
and visits to the races as energetically as ever. He devoted himself
to "making whoopee", as his father called it, by filling his time with
poker, parties and pretty girls. The fact that he did not possess a
single academic qualification, beyond the school certificate – or
show the slightest sign of getting one – did not concern him in the
slightest.

Anthony Blond vividly remembers Jimmy Goldsmith's months
in Oxford. "There was an electric quality about Jimmy, aged sixteen.
I dare say there was at age six. His preoccupations seemed to be
sex, gambling and the outrageous. By which I mean he enjoyed
sensationalism in any form, and from any source." Teddy Goldsmith
also remembers: "For a year and a half we gambled all day, that's
all we did. It took up all our time."

When the poker game started every morning at 167 Walton Street,
there was no more enthusiastic player than Jimmy Goldsmith. After
a brief interlude for lunch, and perhaps a trip to the local race
meeting, he and his friends would return to Oxford for supper and
another expedition, this time to the local greyhound racing, before
going back to Walton Street for the ritual late night game of chemin

de fer. All that mattered was having as good a time as possible; the future would look after itself.

The idyll could not last for ever. No matter how little they may have devoted themselves to their studies, final examinations were rapidly approaching for Teddy Goldsmith and John Aspinall. There was the question of work, and a career to consider. After Teddy's finals in the summer of 1950 both brothers left Oxford. In the absence of anything better to do they had decided to go back to France and discuss their future with their father. When they arrived they discovered that he had decided that they had both better "try" the hotel business. He would speak to his friends.

By the time the Parisians returned to their city after the August holiday in 1950, Frank Goldsmith had found a place for Teddy at a hotel school in Lausanne, Switzerland. But he had also decided that it might be wiser to keep a closer eye on his younger son. With that in mind he organized a job for him in the kitchens of one of Paris's "à discretion" restaurants, the Luce in Montmartre, where young couples could eat and drink as much as they liked for 500 francs. He was to "learn a little of what goes on", and to see if he liked it. Jimmy was not over-pleased.

A life of collecting plates, washing dishes and generally clearing up after the chef, did not appeal to him. Besides now it was more difficult to find time for pretty girls as he was living directly under his mother's nose, in a room in the servants' quarters of the Scribe hotel. What he wanted was a post in a hotel in a different place altogether, where he could have his own flat and do exactly as he liked. After weeks of subtle pressure, he persuaded his father that he would learn more in a hotel where the Goldsmith name was not quite so well known. By the end of October Monsieur le Major had arranged for his son to become second in command of the hors d'oeuvres department of Madrid's Palace hotel. With a sigh of relief, Jimmy Goldsmith left Paris.

Once again, the Major's plans for his son did not work out as he intended. Jimmy Goldsmith certainly travelled to Madrid, and he set himself up in a splendid apartment in the Ruis Alacone, a short walk along the Plaza de las Cortes from the Palace hotel; but he showed no inclination whatsoever to learn the hotel trade. In fact, he took considerable pains not to set foot in the kitchens of the hotel, devoting his time instead to discovering the delights of Madrid's nightlife. He had even found a new means of gambling: on the outcome of the fronton matches that he went to see in the late afternoon. That was a small diversion before the parties every evening. Before long his old friends began to visit him. "Jimmy seemed to know everybody in Madrid by the time I got there" Digby Neave remembers. He watched fascinated as his friend "gambled on the ugly women winning at fronton—because the odds were more favourable—and when that didn't work, changed over to betting on the pretty women winning." Neither worked. Jimmy got further and further into debt. He even persuaded his friend to cash in the return part of his airline ticket so they could go on enjoying themselves, and he still studiously avoided the Palace hotel.

"When his father rang to ask why he hadn't been to the hotel Jimmy would make excuses. Once he told him that he had broken his arm," Neave remembers. "So that morning we went out to the local chemist and bought some plaster to do Jimmy's arm up, in case any of the Major's friends were asked to check. I told him I thought I could manage it." Duly plastered by his friend, Jimmy Goldsmith proceeded to throw another party. It was the act of an unrepentant schoolboy, still thumbing his nose at authority: refusing to conform. He was determined to enjoy himself for as long as he could get away with it. After five months, even Monsieur le Major's patience wore thin. He rang up and instructed Jimmy to go to the Palace hotel.

The next day Jimmy Goldsmith presented himself at the hors d'oeuvres department. But, predictably, he did not take his new responsibilities all that seriously. That evening he went back to his apartment carrying a huge bag of caviar. "There was a reception for General Franco," he told Neave, "and I didn't think the General would begrudge us some of his caviar. We can have a party." The next day was his last at the hotel. Major Goldsmith summoned him to London. Accompanied by Digby Neave, Jimmy left Madrid on aeroplane tickets sent to them by the Major. On the plane the two young men wondered how angry Monsieur le Major would be about Jimmy's debts which had reached almost £2,000.

In fact, Major Goldsmith was unable to control his affection for his younger son. "When Jimmy arrived at his suite in the Berkeley hotel, Frank poured out glasses of champagne for everyone," Neave recalls. But Major Goldsmith also knew that something had to be done to calm his son down. In desperation he had asked one of the family's solicitors to see if he could find somewhere for his son to go, where there would not be too many temptations. After three weeks the solicitor had returned triumphant. "There are places available in the Melbourne fire brigade at the moment, Major Goldsmith, which I am assured would be an entirely appropriate place for your son. They have also indicated that they would be prepared to accept him on the basis of his attendance at Eton."

Marcelle Goldsmith had thrown up her hands in horror. "You cannot possibly send him to Australia!" Teddy remembers: "She broke down sobbing. She was sure that Jimmy was going to fall off a ladder and kill himself." Major Goldsmith reassured his wife at once. He too could not imagine his son as a fireman, particularly as an Australian fireman.

After considerable thought, Major Goldsmith decided that he would pay his son's debts only on the condition that he did his National Service at once. His solicitor was instructed to make sure he ended up as far as possible from London, and Digby Neave had to march the somewhat disconsolate Jimmy Goldsmith to Victoria to sign up. He would eventually have been called up for National Service in any case as he had dual British–French nationality.

In a matter of days Jimmy Goldsmith found himself transported to an army training camp near Oswestry on the Welsh border for basic training. "I hated it almost as much as St Andrews in Toronto," he says. But to the surprise of some of his friends, he was not destroyed by the rigours of army life. Posted to the 55th Regiment of the Royal Artillery, he was selected to train as an officer ("Anyone from a good school was in those days"), and was sent to the training school at Mons. To the delight of his father, he emerged as a second lieutenant, and was posted back to Wales where he was put in charge of the more difficult young men the regiment had to cope with. The poacher had turned gamekeeper, "and very effectively too", in the words of one fellow officer.

Not that he had lost the appetite for "whoopee". Bored, and intensely cold, Jimmy Goldsmith telephoned his old friend Digby Neave and suggested they took a trip to Spain, to get some sunshine.

The two young men duly set off, first for Barcelona and then for Sitges; and Jimmy Goldsmith set about enjoying himself again. He found a beautiful girl from Liverpool and proceeded to pursue her all round the Costa Brava, while Digby Neave looked on in astonishment. "He had always had this knack of finding pretty girls, but we'd only been there for two days when he found the most beautiful girl you can imagine." Back in Wales, Jimmy Goldsmith kept up with the girl from Liverpool. Life could not be allowed to be all work and no play.

The Royal Artillery did not cure him of his interest in sex, gambling and the outrageous, any more than it sapped his confidence. But the army did convince him of the virtue of occasionally curbing the exuberant flamboyance that had been so much part of his character since his childhood, and sometimes replacing it with restraint. "The army did more to make a reasonable man out of me than anything else," he insists.

He despised the reticence of the English and their appetite for hypocrisy and secrecy, and he was to exploit his dislike of the English class system with unexpected success. He proved that it was possible to storm the high points of English and European society, by marching firmly against the tide and disregarding almost every tenet of accepted thought and wisdom. And he started doing that the moment he left the British Army in April 1953. "In Europe the eldest sons knew exactly what they were going to do. They were going to run the family estates. The younger sons knew as well – they were to go into the army, or the Church, or a profession." Jimmy Goldsmith had no intention of doing any of those things. He had decided he was going to "revive the family fortunes" by starting out to rebuild the Goldsmith name in business.

There was no Cavenham Hall now, no substantial inheritance to help him begin. His father did not even own the hotels that he managed so splendidly. He was a shareholder and a director, certainly, but his suites were provided by Hôtels Réunis; Frank Goldsmith could never have afforded to pay for them himself. But Jimmy Goldsmith was determined nevertheless to prove that no one had to conform to succeed. He relished being out of step, no matter how extraordinary that may have made him appear. After his experiences at Eton he knew very well that "For anyone from that culture, going into industry was an incredibly eccentric thing to do". The idea appealed to him tremendously.

When his two years of National Service came to an end in April 1953, Jimmy Goldsmith set out to establish himself in business. He had no wish to stay in London, simply hanging around with his old Oxford friends. Besides, they were already establishing their careers. Digby Neave had gone into insurance with Lloyds; and John Aspinall had launched himself as a professional gambler. He was determined to go back to France, where he felt more at home. An opportunity might present itself there. In Paris, his father welcomed him back and provided the same small servant's room on the seventh floor of the Hôtel Scribe that he had lived in two years earlier. But this time his son did not try to find an excuse to leave Paris again. He wanted to start making his own living. The only difficult question was – what exactly he should do.

The answer came almost at once. Teddy explains: "Jimmy and I had both French and British passports and we could decide whether to do our National Service in one country or the other. I had deferred my British National Service while I was at Oxford, and had ended up back in Paris after the hotel school trying to start a small business. I had forgotten to do anything about my French National Service. In the spring of 1953 I was arrested and thrown in jail as a deserter." It turned out to be a mistake. His call-up papers had been sent to the wrong address. But rather than submit to the rigours of the Army of the French Foreign Legion, Teddy Goldsmith rapidly decided to serve in the British Army. Not knowing what else to do, he left two small companies in the hands of his younger brother. It was the start of Jimmy Goldsmith's business career.

Not that the companies were exactly promising. Started with friends from the Traveller's Club in Paris, Teddy worked in one small company called Dagonal ("named after the fish God of the Philistines") and in another, Lucifer, manufacturer of "safe" electrical plugs. But he had so underestimated his costs that each plug he sold actually lost money. Undeterred he had also stumbled into another in the pharmaceutical business rather in the same way that his father had stumbled into hotels in 1918. On a recent aeroplane flight from London to Paris a friend from the Traveller's Club had met Dr William Moss, the inventor of Lloyd's Adrenalin Cream, which Moss claimed alleviated the worst effects of rheumatism. Before the flight was over he had been persuaded to allow Teddy Goldsmith to become the cream's licence holder and distributor in France.

To prove the sensational qualities of his new adrenalin cream, which he named Adremad, Teddy decided to launch it by experimenting on the most famously sore joints in France. These belonged to Worden the Second, a racehorse, whose owners had hoped might have a chance to win Europe's richest horse race, the Prix de l'Arc de Triomphe, in October 1952. But rheumatism seemed to have put paid to his chances. Teddy Goldsmith arranged for the adrenalin cream to be rubbed into the animal's sore knees. Miraculously it came third in the race, and Adremad became the talk of France.

By the time that Jimmy Goldsmith took over his brother's company, however, the excitement had worn off. Dagonal was effectively bust. "The cream didn't do any harm, but there was not much proof that it did anyone very much good either," Jimmy remembers. "The electrical plugs were hopeless. We had the help of a young PR man, Claude-Henry Leconte, and there was no money." But he was not in the least dismayed. "It had a licence, and a letterhead, and something to get to grips with." It was what he had been looking for, no matter how unpromising it seemed.

After renting an office from Hôtel Réunis in the rue de la Paix, just across the boulevard des Capucines from the Hôtel Scribe, Jimmy Goldsmith set out to become a businessman. But, within the next twelve months, it was not his commercial acumen that was to make him one of the most famous young men in Europe; it was his reputation as a rich young playboy, who had fallen suddenly, and spectacularly, in love.

5

Gypsy

In the first months of 1953 Christina and Maria Isabella Patino were the talk of Paris. After an American education they arrived just as the city was rediscovering its confidence and style, and they had taken it by storm. Their father, Señor Don Antenor Patino, had been Bolivian ambassador to London during the war years. In 1947 he had inherited $150 million from his father. With interests in mining, his fortune was matched by only a handful of families, the Gettys, the Hunts and, perhaps, the Rothschilds.

Few people knew, however, that Don Antenor Patino's father, Simon, was an illiterate Bolivian Indian who had worked as a greengrocer's assistant before exploring the Andes and discovering one of the richest veins of tin in South America in 1899. For the next forty-five years Simon Patino and his family had not only dominated their country and its population of five million, but also founded a worldwide empire. In 1951 his son had seen a revolution on the horizon, and moved what remained of their assets in Bolivia abroad. By the time the left-wing nationalists came to power in 1952, Don Antenor was living in Europe, where he planned to re-establish the Patino dynasty by ensuring that his two strikingly beautiful daughters made suitable marriages. With that very much in his mind, he had settled in Paris in a magnificent apartment on the avenue Foch. The girls' mother, from whom he was separated, was the Duchess of Durcal, a relation of King Alfonso of Spain.

To Señor Patino's delight, a number of potentially acceptable suitors had presented themselves in a matter of months, and his elder daughter Christina soon announced her intention of marrying the Prince Marc de Beauveau-Craon, whose family lived in a château near Nancy. Isabel, however, was less easily settled. Ravishingly beautiful, and with a dramatic temper, she had always been the more independent of the two girls – she was called "Gypsy" by her friends – but Señor Patino had not counted on her being quite so emphatic in her dislike for the string of eligible and titled young men that he had contrived to steer towards her. For her part Isabel Patino was not too keen on her father's ambitions for her; she wished to make her own choice of a husband, in her own time. One man to whom she had confided her fears was Teddy Goldsmith, whom she met regularly at parties in Paris while he was struggling to make a success of his new firm Dagonal.

"She always seemed to want to be different, and not just sit about looking pretty," he remembers. "But there were hundreds of young men pursuing her." Not surprisingly Teddy told Isabel Patino about his brother Jimmy who was just about to come out of the British army. But before he could introduce them he was arrested and speedily despatched to do his own National Service in England. It was not until the eve of Isabel Patino's eighteenth birthday in June 1953 that he finally introduced her to the man with whom she was destined to spend the rest of her tragically short life.

As the memory of war gradually faded, Europe had begun to relax, and as it did so a sense of optimism flooded back into its cities. In London the change was signalled by the Festival of Britain on the south bank of the Thames, but the new confidence was demonstrated to the world by the Coronation of the new young English Queen in June 1953.

On the night of the Coronation every hotel dining room in London was packed with people celebrating the beginning of what *The Times* called "a second Elizabethan age". And Señor Don Antenor Patino was giving a dinner party for his daughter Isabel at his favourite London hotel, Claridges; it was the eve of her eighteenth birthday, 4 June. When he asked who she would particularly like to invite, she had suggested Teddy Goldsmith, and his new wife Gill.

When the dinner was over, Teddy Goldsmith suggested to Isabel that she might like to go on with them to Al Burnett's Stork Club in Swallow Street where Jimmy's Eton contemporary Mark Birley was throwing a party. Jimmy would be there on one of his regular visits to London.

Jimmy Goldsmith had met beautiful girls before. Indeed, he had met rich, beautiful, young girls before. But when they were introduced by his brother at the Stork Club, he noticed there was more to Isabel Patino than most of the other rich girls he had met. She had a temper and a temperament to match his own. She did nothing by halves: when she laughed she threw her head back and laughed out loud; when she was annoyed she looked as though she could cut his throat. She was every bit as fiery, and every bit as uninhibited as he was: and – even more bewitching – she saw no reason why any man should be allowed to dominate her. She made it very clear to her new admirer that she was not in the least intimidated by him. For his part Jimmy Goldsmith could hardly believe it: at the age of twenty he was completely captivated.

That evening Jimmy Goldsmith and Isabel Patino fell in love, and they did so with a ferocity that the world would come to hear of. Over the next few weeks their attraction grew into such an all-consuming passion that they could hardly bear to be separated. Back in Paris, they met whenever they could. By the beginning of September it was abundantly clear that – whatever Señor Patino might have wished – his daughter was not interested in more eligible suitors, not even the King of the Belgians, who had expressed his enthusiasm to meet her.

Señor Patino did not know it, but his daughter had grown exceptionally close to the flamboyant young man that his friends told him had a reputation for being a gambler and a playboy. Isabel Patino and Jimmy Goldsmith were lovers. In November 1953 they decided to marry. Jimmy Goldsmith was delighted. He was hopelessly in love with her, though he knew that he would be accused of fortune-hunting, for Antenor Patino had made it clear that he intended to leave everything to his daughters.

"We'll get married at once," he told her, beaming. "I'll speak to your father at once. He will understand, I'm sure."

Isabel Patino did not reply. She hardly dared. She knew how little her father would understand, and she was afraid of what he might do. So she just squeezed her young lover's hand, and kissed him.

In Antenor Patino's magnificent office, Jimmy Goldsmith came straight to the point.

"I intend to marry your daughter Isabel," he explained. "We are very much in love, and we would like to get married as quickly as possible."

In seconds the fifty-six-year-old Bolivian was beside himself with rage. He had not brought his daughter to Paris to marry a flamboyant young man with no name, no money and a reputation for being a gambler. The Patinos were a great Bolivian family; Catholic, respected, and rich. His advisers told him constantly that he was one of the six richest men in the world. He had no intention whatsoever of allowing his daughter to marry the twenty-year-old son of a Jewish hotelier. He had seen adventurers before.

"I am afraid that is quite impossible," he told Jimmy Goldsmith, as politely as he could. "She is far too young." But Jimmy did not look in the least perturbed.

Antenor Patino's rage almost overcame him.

"Young man, we come from an old Catholic family."

"Perfect. We come from an old Jewish family."

"But it is not our habit to marry Jews," Antenor Patino went on, in exasperation.

"It is not our habit to marry Red Indians," Jimmy Goldsmith replied tartly.

Within a few minutes Jimmy Goldsmith found himself on the pavement outside the office, having lost all hope of receiving Antenor Patino's blessing. Worse, Don Antenor had told him that he had no intention of allowing Maria Isabella to marry him "at any price".

For the first time in his life he hardly knew what to do. In desperation he set off to tell Isabel what her father had said. But she was nowhere to be found. After searching frantically, he discovered that Antenor Patino had suddenly despatched her on a trip to North Africa with a chaperone. She had already left for Casablanca.

In a panic Jimmy Goldsmith assumed the worst: Isabel was to be consigned to a nunnery, something unthinkable. The insult to the Goldsmith family name was bad enough – were the Goldsmiths not respectable enough for any family in the world, let alone a Bolivian one? – but now the woman he intended to marry might be harmed. Jimmy Goldsmith reacted violently, as he was to do whenever the family name was threatened in the future. In the words of one friend he went "slightly mad"; the exaggerated and the dramatic qualities that had always been a part of his character surfaced at once. In a matter of hours he had decided to follow her to Casablanca, bring her back with him to France, and then take her anywhere that they could marry without parental consent as the legal age of consent was eighteen. There was no one else to protect her, and he was determined that they should become Mr and Mrs James Michael Goldsmith.

Hardly had Isabel Patino set off for Casablanca than Jimmy Goldsmith was chartering a plane and asking two friends in Paris – Digby Neave, whom he had encouraged to launch a French insurance broking company, and John Train, a lawyer – to accompany him.

"There's not a moment to lose," he told Neave, who was in the middle of a business meeting. "We have to go at once. We may never see Isabel again."

When the three men took off from Le Bourget airport just outside Paris in an eight-seater De Havilland Dove on that November afternoon, it seemed like an adventure worthy of Hollywood in the 1930s. There was the beautiful heroine, heiress to one of the largest fortunes the world had ever known; her angry father; and the misunderstood playboy who loved her and intended to rescue her, whatever the cost. If he had not been in quite such a state, Jimmy Goldsmith might have enjoyed every minute, but as it was he sat "in a terrible state" for the entire journey, chewing his handkerchief.

"The crew weren't allowed to rest on the flight," Digby Neave remembers. "They just had to keep on and on. We landed in Madrid, to refuel, but there was no time to stretch our legs. We just had to keep going. By the time we reached Casablanca, the crew were exhausted." Neave and John Train suggested they should all rest but Goldsmith would hear none of it. "He started telephoning everyone in sight, anybody who might know something, while John and I were only allowed a trip to the Casbah. He told us not to go too far in case we had to leave again suddenly." They did.

They had been in Casablanca for only two hours when Jimmy discovered that Antenor Patino had out-manoeuvred him. Just after he had taken off from Le Bourget, Isabel Patino had landed there.

Antenor Patino had got wind of his young adversary's plan and had ordered her home. He intended to supervise her future personally. More excited than ever, Jimmy Goldsmith decided to go ahead with the second part of his own plan at once. He would arrange for Isabel Patino to elope with him.

Shouting instructions from a public telephone box, Jimmy Goldsmith started to organize his next step. First he had to make sure that Isabel could leave France, and for that she had to have her passport. He told his secretary in Paris to go round and tell the maid at Antenor Patino's home that she had been instructed by Señor Patino to collect his daughter's passport at once so that it could be given a new visa. "In fact she told the housekeeper that she was from a driving instructor, and that Isabel had decided to take driving lessons, so they needed her passport to stamp it," Jimmy Goldsmith recalls now. "My secretary then arranged for Isabel to be collected from her father's home and taken to Le Bourget to be put on board a plane for England."

Then he telephoned a firm of London solicitors, Withers and Partners, to ask if they could suggest a solution to his problem. One of the firm's partners, Ian Scott Smith, agreed to look into it, and to meet him at London's Heathrow Airport when he arrived.

If Don Antenor Patino had actually been consulted about this elaborate plan to abduct his daughter he might well have told Jimmy Goldsmith not to be so childish. Certainly some of Jimmy Goldsmith's friends believe that he had accepted that the marriage was inevitable. But, as Digby Neave explains, "By this time Jimmy was in rather a state, and would have found it difficult to believe anything that Patino said to him." No reconciliation was ever mooted. He just plunged ahead with his plans, while the two-man crew of his De Havilland Dove slept. That was just as well. He had already decided to tell them, as soon as they woke up, that they had to take off for London at once. On the way they could stop off at Jersey, to refuel, and he would telephone Paris to see if everything had gone according to plan. It had.

Jimmy Goldsmith was met at London airport by his solicitor, wearing a black bowler hat and a rather cheerful expression.

"I believe we may have found a way for you to marry, Mr Goldsmith," Ian Scott Smith told him. "My Scottish partners have

decided that they believe you will be able to marry in Scotland
without consent. No one has done so for more than twenty years,
but we believe the law is still valid."

A delighted Jimmy Goldsmith climbed into his solicitor's large
black Daimler and was taken to be reunited with his fiancée. Almost
at once they were despatched to Scotland for what was to become
the most publicized elopement of the post-war years. Not since
Jessica Mitford had decided to escape her family's clutches in the
1930s had a couple's romantic flight so delighted the headline
writers. In the next few days sightings of the couple were reported
everywhere. But, astonishingly, they were never found. On the
journey north from London they had done the perfectly obvious
thing: they had stopped off to see Teddy Goldsmith at his officers'
training camp, Eaton Hall, near Chester, but by the time the posse
of pursuing journalists thought of checking with his brother, Jimmy
and Isabel were on the move again.

By the time they reached Edinburgh, on 13 December, their
elopement had captured the popular imagination: the *Daily Mirror*
was calling them "The Runaway Heiress and the Playboy" on its
front page. "When I ran off with Isabel I never, never expected it
to be a press story. It never occurred to me for one second," Jimmy
Goldsmith says now. In the South of France Frank Goldsmith and
his wife had listened to news of it with just as much interest and
amusement as everyone else. Whenever they were asked by a visiting
reporter whether their son had been in touch with them, Monsieur
le Major would say firmly: "The boys in my family are not in the
habit of asking permission when they want to get married. My son
Teddy, who is twenty-five, informed me that he was getting married
only a few minutes before his wedding." Privately Frank Goldsmith
found his son's escapade quite hilarious.

In Paris Don Antenor Patino still did not approve of this "foolish
infatuation", as he called it, and he approved of it even less, now
that it made him appear a fool. He could not forgive himself for
allowing his daughter to escape from Paris. Now he was more
determined than ever to find her, and bring her back to Paris before
she could marry anyone. He had already hired private detectives to
help him do it. The newspapers could trumpet the "true love" of
the "romantic young couple" as much as they liked, his daughter

was still under-age, and still his responsibility. Don Antenor Patino decided to set off for Edinburgh to supervise the search for his daughter.

In the week before Christmas Antenor Patino set himself up in residence in a suite in the Caledonian hotel at the west end of Princes Street and began discussions with his lawyers and private detectives. They all assured him that it would be only a matter of time before the couple were tracked down. Then, to Señor Patino's great surprise, his wife, the Duchess of Durcal, arrived. They had not lived together for almost a decade, and for most of that time the Duchess had been suing him, acrimoniously, for divorce. Their persistent arguments had become part of his life, so their sudden "reconciliation" came as a shock. Besieged by the world's press on the one hand, and his wife on the other, a dismayed Don Antenor Patino took to arriving and leaving his hotel suite by the rear luggage lift in order to avoid anyone he did not wish to talk to.

By the time her mother arrived to help in the search, Isabel was living quietly in the home of one of Jimmy Goldsmith's Scottish solicitors and Jimmy was staying nearby. The Daimler had been swapped for a less conspicuous Standard Vanguard, and they were planning to take a trip round Scotland to avoid Antenor Patino's detectives for the three weeks that they had to wait under Scottish law before they could marry. The solicitors had arranged for friends all over Scotland to accommodate the young couple. For their part Jimmy Goldsmith and Isabel Patino had not the slightest intention of changing their minds about getting married. "Why should we – we are very much in love," they told anyone who asked.

In spite of the detectives and the threats of the "legal consequences", Jimmy Goldsmith and Isabel Patino duly posted the formal notice of their intention to marry on 29 December 1953 at the Chief Registrar's Office in Edinburgh. The law did not require them to state precisely which Registrar in the south of Scotland they would be asking to conduct the ceremony, so they did not.

Don Antenor Patino responded at once. As soon as the Hogmanay celebrations were over, he sought an "interim interdict" from the Scottish High Court to prevent the issue of a marriage certificate to his daughter. The application was granted. But once again Antenor Patino had underestimated his adversary. Jimmy Goldsmith im-

mediately lodged notice of appeal against the court's decisions, and
he and Isabel remained in hiding.

Had Señor Patino but known it, his daughter by this time was
actually less than four miles away in the Prestonfield House Hotel
in the south-western suburbs of Edinburgh. She and Jimmy Goldsmith had toasted their first Scottish Hogmanay together there, with
a piper and whisky, and were planning their honeymoon. In a
granite house once used by Bonnie Prince Charlie to hide from his
pursuers, they spent their days playing cards and reading as they
waited for the last week to elapse before they could get married.
Isabel was still wearing the black suit she had left Paris in more
than two weeks before: there had been no chance to buy a trousseau.

The newspapers were still full of their story. To the reporters
chasing them it was a real-life version of John Buchan's novel *The
Thirty-nine Steps*. More than one innocent young Scottish couple
were roused from their beds after midnight on the urging of inquisi-
tive reporters. In London news editors demanded fresh details of
"the likely whereabouts of the runaway heiress and her playboy".
The *Daily Mirror* took more interest than most, but they had an
advantage because one of their reporters had arranged an exclusive
story through the solicitors. Jimmy Goldsmith and Isabel Patino
were symbols of a new Britain. Free-spirited, independent and
intent on taking their own advice, and no one else's, they epitomized
the new generation.

To those who paid little attention to the story, beyond the
headlines, it may have seemed that Jimmy Goldsmith was little
more than a playboy intent on grabbing the chance of an easy life
by marrying a rich, and beautiful, young woman. The innuendo
that he was merely an adventurer was to hurt him deeply for years
to come: just as Don Antenor Patino's private detectives were to
breed a suspicion of anyone who tried to pry into his affairs.

A High Court judge in Edinburgh accepted his appeal against
Don Antenor Patino's "interim interdict", and he and Isabel were
free to marry on 7 January 1954. Triumphant, they planned their
wedding, and Isabel telephoned her mother. "For God's sake let's
stop all this," she told the Duchess of Durcal. "There's no point
any more. You've lost, and in any case I think I might be pregnant."
There was a stunned silence on the end of the telephone.

Though they had studiously stayed in separate houses, and in separate rooms in hotels, Isabel Patino had discovered that she was going to have her young lover's child. Though neither she nor Jimmy Goldsmith had known it when they set off to elope, the knowledge only further intensified their determination that nothing was going to stand in their way. "To me marriage is having a child, not signing a piece of paper," her delighted young lover had told her. And she had smiled.

Defeated by the mountains of publicity, her daughter's pregnancy, and their future son-in-law's refusal to be put off by intimidation, threats or legal action, Antenor Patino and his wife accepted the inevitable. The Duchess of Durcal told her daughter, "We will not do anything more to stop you, if this is what you want." Her daughter burst into tears on the other end of the phone. The battle was over.

Shortly before four o'clock on 7 January 1954, as the grey Edinburgh dusk began to creep across the city, Jimmy Goldsmith and Isabel Patino slipped quietly out of the gravel drive of Prestonfield House and turned south for Kelso. To escape the attention of newspapermen and private detectives, they rode in the back of a butcher's van.

Just over an hour later the meat van delivered them to the Registrar's Office in Kelso, some forty miles outside Edinburgh across the Lammermuir Hills. A comfortable, honest town, with granite houses and cobbled streets, it nestled on the edge of the river Tweed. Sir Walter Scott had once called it "the most romantic place in Scotland", and there could hardly have been a more appropriate place for this particular wedding. At 5.30 that afternoon, with the bride wearing the simple black two-piece in which she had first escaped from Paris, and the bridegroom wearing a dark suit, under the fur-collared coat that was to appear on countless front pages, Jimmy Goldsmith married Isabel Patino in the tiny Registrar's office, where the linoleum creaked on the floor, and the stately tick of the clock on the wall was the only accompaniment to their vows. Not a single flashbulb greeted them as they walked out into the soft heathery night. The tall confident young man and his beautiful pregnant young wife slipped away to celebrate in private.

It was not until the following day that Mr and Mrs James

Goldsmith emerged from hiding. With a style that came to typify him, Jimmy Goldsmith had decided to give a lunch party for his solicitors, and all the others who had helped him marry, at the George Hotel in Edinburgh. On the way to his wedding reception he bought his new young wife several pairs of nylon stockings. It was the first opportunity for several weeks that he had had the chance to do anything as commonplace as shopping. As Mrs Isabel Goldsmith sat down to lunch she showed every sign of being utterly happy, while her husband looked triumphant, slightly mischievous, and just as much in love. In the *Daily Mirror* the columnist Cassandra commented: "Not since the Stone of Scone was swiped from underneath the Coronation Chair in Westminster Abbey had the public been treated to such a feast of sentimental fun."

No one knew then just how short-lived that fun would turn out to be.

6

Little Isabel

As they walked across the runway at Heathrow airport, on their return to London in January 1954, the new Mr and Mrs James Goldsmith still looked every bit the recklessly romantic young couple that had stolen the newspaper headlines. They blinked as the flashbulbs went off around them, and tried to look as though they were not just a touch embarrassed at the sensation they had caused. They held hands, laughed at their own private jokes, and argued constantly about anything and nothing; oblivious to everything around them, except the birth of their first child. Their future seemed golden.

Whatever the cynics may have suspected about the playboy's intentions towards the heiress, Jimmy Goldsmith continued to tell anyone who would listen that he wanted no part of the Patino fortune. It was a matter of honour to prove to the Patinos that no Goldsmith was ever to be dismissed lightly.

Antenor Patino showed no sign of relenting. In spite of the reconciliation between Isabel and his wife, he was now trying to get his daughter's marriage annulled in the Scottish courts. Anthony Blond remembers: "Jimmy and Isabel were staying at the Ritz in London, and I went to see them. Jimmy was jubilant that his campaign had succeeded, with the help of the *Daily Mirror*, and their marriage had come off; but now Papa Patino had gone back to Scotland to persuade a Scottish judge to declare the marriage null and void." Antenor Patino was prepared to do anything in his power to rid himself of his rebellious son-in-law. But the Scottish judges were not impressed by him, and his mission failed. When he arrived back in London by train Antenor Patino was again besieged by reporters. "She can now look after herself, and her husband," he said grimly at the station. "They can expect no financial assistance from me." Isabel Patino was to be disinherited.

The defeat of the Patino family was complete. "Jimmy was the David who had smitten a Goliath," as Anthony Blond puts it, "and the battle had made him an international hero." The only problem was that he was a hero with £2,000 in debts from his elopement, and a foundling business in France. The new Mr and Mrs Goldsmith did not even have anywhere to live.

Once again Frank Goldsmith came to the rescue. When the young couple arrived in Paris in January 1954, he provided them with a suite at the Hôtel Scribe which was theirs for as long as they wanted it. Isabel was deeply touched. She had hardly had a chance to meet her new parents-in-law during her extraordinary courtship, but now she took great comfort from the fact that, no matter how frosty the relations with her own father and mother may have become, her new family showed every sign of taking her to their hearts. She planned for the birth, saw her friends in Paris and looked for an apartment; while Jimmy went back to resurrecting what was left of Teddy's Dagonal and selling Lloyd's Adrenalin Cream. In April they told those of their friends who did not know that she was expecting a baby, and that they intended to leave Paris in late May to spend a few weeks in Cannes before the birth due towards the end of June. On the morning of Wednesday 12 May 1954, however, everything changed.

"When you're twenty a year is a very long time," Jimmy Goldsmith says now. "We met in June, and by the time we married in January a lifetime seemed to have passed." The moment that the lifetime came to an end is etched in his memory.

When he woke up on that May morning in 1954 the sun was streaming through the curtains of their fifth-floor suite, but the noise of the cafés opening their doors and setting out their tables on the boulevard des Capucines below did not disturb him. Nor did they wake his beautiful young wife. She lay asleep beside him, her black hair and magnificent Latin face framed by the white linen pillow. She seemed as serene as a goddess as her breathing gently lifted the lace counterpane that covered her.

"The night before, Isabel and I had dined alone," Jimmy Goldsmith recalls. "It had been an unusually hot evening for May and we had dinner on the terrace of a restaurant in the old village of Montmartre, looking down over Paris." As they talked about the future it seemed as though nothing could ever threaten their life together. The world had watched them overcome every obstacle to get married, until even the notoriously cynical English columnist Cassandra had called their elopement "as romantic as a motorized version of Lorna Doone". Nothing could go wrong now. "They were transparently happy," Madame Marcelle Goldsmith remembered later. "No one who saw them could possibly doubt it."

So Jimmy Goldsmith did not bother to wake his young wife before he set off to his office that morning. The pregnancy had not been difficult, but she still needed rest. Nevertheless there was a faint whisper of concern in his mind: Isabel had hardly stirred as he left. When he got to his office he telephoned his mother to ask if she would go and make sure that Isabel was all right.

Shortly before 10 o'clock Madame Goldsmith quietly let herself into the fifth-floor suite that lay directly above her own. Isabel was still asleep. "I went across and took her hand," Madame Goldsmith recalled later, "and it was quite limp."

Within an hour Isabel had been transported across Paris to the Hartmann Clinic on the banks of the Seine at Neuilly, and Jimmy had begun to telephone doctors around the world, to bully and cajole them to come to Paris and treat his wife. When he was not on the telephone he paced up and down the clinic's corridors seizing anyone who passed to ask for news about her. Then he began telephoning again. There was nothing else he could do.

In fact there was nothing that anyone could do. Three of France's most respected brain surgeons had realized within minutes of her arrival at the Hartmann Clinic that eighteen-year-old Isabel had suffered a massive cerebral haemorrhage. Their only hope of saving her life was to trepan her skull to relieve the pressure of the blood clot. Without that, even with the help of their new life-support machines, she was unlikely ever to regain consciousness. That evening the surgeons operated. In the early hours of the next morning they announced that the operation had not been a failure, but that it would be some time before they knew exactly what its effect would be. By that evening, Thursday 13 May, the doctors were warning Jimmy Goldsmith that they might not be able to save his wife's life. However, there was still the child to consider.

On Friday morning it was decided that the baby's life had to be saved at once. Shortly after eleven o'clock a five-and-a-half-pound baby daughter was delivered to Mr and Mrs James Goldsmith by caesarian section. But her mother did not know it. She was still unconscious.

Within twelve hours Isabel Goldsmith was dead. A further attempt to relieve the pressure on her brain by trepanning failed, and a little after eleven in the evening a priest delivered the last rites. For an instant she had almost seemed to wake: the priest thought she might have whispered something, perhaps *"L'enfant, l'enfant"*. But there was no hope. Shortly before midnight Jimmy Goldsmith and the doctors took the agonizing decision to switch off the life-support machines and allow his wife to die peacefully.

In the early hours of Saturday morning, 15 May 1954, Jimmy Goldsmith walked out of the Hartmann Clinic into the darkness, ignoring everyone. Perhaps he blamed himself for his young wife's death, for the doctors had told him that the haemorrhage had developed as a result of her pregnancy, or perhaps he felt that once again the fates had turned against the Goldsmiths. No one could tell, and he told no one himself. A legend would grow up that she had died in childbirth, but he would not bother to deny it. From that day onwards the man who was to become one of the most famous tycoons in the world lived every day as though it were his last. There was nothing to lose. He had already lost everything.

All Paris, and most of Europe, seemed to go into mourning with Jimmy Goldsmith. For just as the marriage had captured the popular imagination, so Isabel's death seemed an unfair and bitter end to the fairytale. At the funeral there were 600 people inside L'Eglise St Honoré-d'Eylau, and a vast crowd waited outside. *Le Figaro* noted the next day that there were "some 3,000 people, the majority of them women and young girls, pressed on to the pavements of the Place Victor Hugo outside, making it necessary to call the police". The mourners took more than an hour to file past the catafalque bearing Isabel's embalmed body, while the church echoed to the sound of Beethoven's funeral march. *Le Figaro* reported that the congregation "included five duchesses, a princess, two marquesses, two counts and the ambassadors of most of the South American states." There were also many members of the Rothschild family, as well as the Goldsmiths and the Goldschmidts. The old ties had not been severed.

While the congregation filed slowly out of the church Jimmy Goldsmith stood alone. As he was to say later, "It was a greater shock than anyone can ever imagine. We'd known each other less than a year." Looking back now he can still recall the fiery-eyed girl with a temper of quicksilver as vividly as if she had never left him. But he was not to fill his home with her picture as his father had done with portraits of Jacqueline Franc. He had a more concrete memorial. Less than two kilometres away his baby daughter still lay in an incubator. He had decided to christen her Isabel Marcella Olga, in memory of her mother. She was all that Jimmy Goldsmith had left of his wife – or Don Antenor Patino had left of his daughter.

After the funeral Major Goldsmith advised his son to get away from Paris for a while. It was advice which, eventually, Jimmy Goldsmith was to accept. But he did not go away until he had ensured the future care and safety of his daughter. He discussed it first with his own mother, and then with the Duchess of Durcal, who had returned to Paris for her daughter's funeral. After some thought he agreed that the Duchess should have little Isabel in her care for a few weeks as soon as the baby was well enough to leave the hospital. But he insisted that he should provide a nanny for her, so that when he came back to Paris it would be a simple matter for her to move into the home he was already planning to provide for her. "Jimmy wanted to make a gesture of goodwill towards the Patinos," his brother Teddy explains. "He thought it was for the best, and it would leave him time to find an apartment."

He left Paris in June for West Africa and returned at the end of July. In Ghana he had visited an old friend, Geoffrey Bing QC, a former British Member of Parliament, and he had started a small branch of his pharmaceutical company in neighbouring Liberia. On his return he agreed to extend the time his daughter could stay with her grandmother. ("Jimmy was still anxious to keep the peace," Digby Neave explains.) Besides, the extension gave him a little more time to find somewhere suitable to live. With his mother's help he set about looking for an apartment, while taking every

chance he could to go and see his young daughter. The arrangement
seemed to work admirably. He was delighted with little Isabel's
progress. The English nanny he had found, Deborah Cockbill, had
proved a great success, and the Duchess of Durcal seemed genuinely
pleased to see him.

By the beginning of September he had found an apartment on
the fifth floor of 23 rue Marbeau, overlooking the Bois de Boulogne,
barely half a kilometre from the flat in which he had spent part of
his own childhood. Large and comfortable, it had three bedrooms
and its own terrace. With some pride he told the Duchess of Durcal
that he would like to arrange for Isabel to move into his new
apartment on 14 September, just three days after her christening at
the Church of Nôtre Dame in Chantilly. "Without hesitation the
Duchess agreed," he recalls.

But when he arrived in Versailles to collect his daughter as
planned, he found the door to the Duchess's hotel suite locked. He
knocked, but there was no reply. He knocked again. Still no sound
from inside. At first he thought something must be wrong, but then
he realized that the Patino family had never intended to hand their
granddaughter back to him. In a rage he knocked the door down
with his shoulder, and burst into the suite. It was empty. There
was no sign of his daughter, her nanny or the Duchess. But there
was every sign that they had left in a hurry.

Still in a rage, he rushed back to his parents' suite in the Hôtel
Scribe to see his mother. "He just paced up and down shouting,"
she remembered later. "He could not understand how anyone could
have done such a thing. But he was determined that they were not
going to get away with it. They had kidnapped his daughter."
Controlling his anger, he consulted his lawyers. That afternoon,
four months to the day after his wife's death, he issued a writ in the
civil court of Paris alleging that "unknown persons" had kidnapped
little Isabel.

Once again Jimmy Goldsmith was about to live out his private
life in the public eye. By the time that *Le Figaro* reported the affair
the following morning he was at the centre of a case that was to
provoke as much excitement in France as the kidnapping of Charles
Lindbergh's baby son had done in the United States twenty-two
years earlier. But by then it was also quite clear that Isabel Goldsmith

had not been kidnapped by "unknown persons". On Thursday 16 September, the Duchess of Durcal issued separate proceedings in the civil court of Paris for custody of her granddaughter. She claimed that Jimmy Goldsmith was "not a fit person" to look after his child. The feud with the Patino family continued.

Sharp at three o'clock in the afternoon of Friday 17 September Judge Ausset, one of the most eminent members of the French judiciary, took his seat in a panelled courtroom in the great Palais de Justice on the Ile de la Cité, in the heart of Paris. Before him, representing the Duchess of Durcal, stood the most renowned advocate in France, Maître René Floriot. Outside the court Floriot had told *Le Figaro*, "I will certainly not miss making the point that since the beginning of July Madame Patino has had care of the baby with the total accord of the father. One is thus surprised that he now suddenly wishes to take back little Isabel." Floriot added carefully that his client was not only claiming that Jimmy Goldsmith could not give his daughter the care she required, but also that he travelled a lot.

"Monsieur Goldsmith is convinced that we want to take away his child," Floriot told the court gravely in his opening address, "and, indeed, he believes that we have already taken her to Spain. What a mistake. It was only when Madame Patino saw her son-in-law in a state of excitement, of which he later provided such abundant proof by forcing the door of her suite at the Hôtel Trianon, that she decided to put the little girl in security, fearing that her father would take her away at the risk of her already fragile life."

Called to give evidence, an undeniably agitated Jimmy Goldsmith told Judge Ausset: "My child was taken to an unknown place without my permission. They have literally kidnapped her, which makes me very angry."

His own advocate, the restrained Maître Allehaut, then explained to Judge Ausset: "My client alone has the right to determine who should care for his child: and the excited state he is in, for which he is being reproached, in fact demonstrates his affection for his daughter."

Anxious to determine precisely who was presently looking after the child, Judge Ausset asked Maître Floriot if he would "perhaps be kind enough to tell me her whereabouts".

"I will, of course, your honour, but not in front of Monsieur Goldsmith."

Still standing in the witness box, Jimmy Goldsmith was white with rage. He suggested icily: "At least my own mother has led a blameless bourgeois existence for thirty years, which could hardly be said for Madame Patino, who is, after all, currently suing her husband for divorce."

For his part Judge Ausset asked only for a little less invective and for rather more facts. Having ascertained that Jimmy Goldsmith had rented an apartment in which Isabel was to have her own large sunny room, and a nanny – as well as the attentions of her paternal grandmother who was to live at the apartment "to ensure that she receives every proper attention" – Ausset decided that he had better see the place for himself. He told the court that he intended to take such an unusual step in view of the seriousness of the case. The hearing stood adjourned until Saturday morning.

Outside the courtroom Jimmy Goldsmith was even less restrained than he had been inside it. He was considering "suing the Patino family for defamation of character", he told the crowd of waiting reporters. "They said it was not good enough for my baby – three bedrooms, a veranda, a cook and a valet." But few of the watching reporters believed he could be a match for Maître Floriot, whatever he might say.

By ten o'clock on Saturday morning, 18 September, alerted by the newspapers, a considerable crowd had gathered outside the Palais de Justice. By the time that Judge Ausset and the court officials arrived thirty minutes later, the police were having some difficulty in keeping the crowd in order. Undeterred, Ausset led an extraordinary procession along the banks of the Seine, across into the 16th *arrondissement*, and to the entrance of a handsome building at number 23, rue Marbeau. The crowd blocked the small street entirely. Ausset and his officials climbed to the fifth floor. When they finally walked across the landing and opened the double doors, Judge Ausset was clearly impressed. After half an hour of careful inspection, he announced that he would deliver his judgement at two o'clock that afternoon in the Palais de Justice. With that he marched back down the stairs, and out into the crowded street.

By the time Jimmy Goldsmith and his mother returned to the

court, shortly before two o'clock, the crowd that had followed them all morning had grown even larger. It was now not only stopping the traffic, but also engulfing the nearby flower market. The road was almost impassable. No one could recall a case like it since the war.

Promptly at two Judge Ausset walked back into his courtroom and settled himself impassively to deliver his judgement. Jimmy Goldsmith and his mother sat on one side of the courtroom, while the Duchess of Durcal sat opposite them. The only participant not present was Isabel Goldsmith. Her father still had no idea of her whereabouts.

Ausset told the packed court that the apartment he had seen that morning in the rue Marbeau was "comfortable, even luxurious", that it had the benefit of being airy and even had a terrace. Inclining his head slightly towards her, he went on to say that Madame Goldsmith had promised to "occupy herself maternally" with the child in question, and that she represented "substantial moral qualities to the court". Looking across at the Duchess of Durcal, Judge Ausset continued sternly that the young man "whose daughter is the subject of these custody proceedings" was "clearly in a most enviable financial situation" and that "any excitement that he might have shown at the Hôtel Trianon was clearly the result of his distress and anxiety to know the whereabouts of his daughter".

After twenty minutes Ausset announced his formal decision: Isabel Goldsmith was to be returned to her father by four o'clock the following afternoon. Jimmy Goldsmith hugged his mother with delight. Once again the Patino family had been vanquished, "Floriot or no Floriot", and the law had proved a defence against the suspicions of others. It was a lesson that Jimmy Goldsmith would never forget. He watched the Duchess of Durcal leave the courtroom in silence, after he had heard Floriot tell Judge Ausset that his clients "would consider an appeal against this judgement". The judge listened unmoved, and then repeated his instructions that little Isabel should be returned to her father "without fail by four tomorrow afternoon".

At 3.45 in the afternoon of Sunday 19 September 1954 a black Citroën drew up outside number 23 rue Marbeau and Miss Deborah Cockbill climbed out carrying the most famous four-month-old in

France. Without a word Jimmy Goldsmith opened the door to his apartment building and showed them in. Little Isabel was at home with her father.

7

Facing Bankruptcy

Yet again Jimmy Goldsmith had lived out his life in headlines. For the second time in less than a year he had found himself presented in the newspapers, and in the courts, as a petulant, irresponsible, argumentative young man who was a great deal too rich, and far too idle for someone of just twenty-one years of age. He was too flamboyant, too outrageous and far too keen on sensation to be taken quite seriously, his detractors said. It was less than just, but it was partly true.

In a Europe just emerging from austerity, he became the first of the post-war breed of bright young things: proof that life had changed after the drab years. In the solid comfort of their now rebuilt homes, the less adventurous could live out their lives by watching his exploits. They might not always approve, but that did nothing to dim his fascination for them. Years of hotel suites and the finest parties, of the smartest resorts and the flashiest friends had not equipped Jimmy Goldsmith to consider that there might be any other way of life.

But since little Isabel had come home to his new apartment, something had changed. Now Jimmy Goldsmith knew that he *had* to work. After their defeat the Patinos would be watching for the slightest sign that he could not support his daughter, and he had no intention of allowing them to seize her back. His own parents had told him that they would help in any way they could – his mother had stayed at rue Marbeau with him as she had promised in court, but that could not go on for ever. Besides, he had decided that making a fortune was now a matter of some urgency. He would prove once and for all that the Goldsmiths were a great family, whom no one could afford to overlook.

With the furious energy that he had previously reserved for enjoying himself, Jimmy Goldsmith set out to create a fortune every bit as large as Don Antenor Patino's. He knew it would not be easy – his father had no money to speak of, his brother Teddy's company was not exactly successful, and he had almost nothing – but that did not deter him.

For the next three years Jimmy Goldsmith poured his energies into his new businesses with a ferocity that astounded his friends. "He suddenly started working eighteen hours a day at his office in the rue de la Paix, not going out much in the evenings, and dedicating himself to building up the companies that I had left him," his brother Teddy recalls. "He hardly saw anyone at all for months," his mother remembered. There was no time now for gambling or nightclubs. There was too much to do and too little time, and in any case there was no one he wanted to go out with now. The memory of Isabel was still fresh in his mind. By the spring of 1955, Jimmy Goldsmith had made a discovery: business could be just as much fun as gambling, especially if you treated it in much the same way. It was a matter of moving your chips around as quickly as possible for the maximum profit, and trusting your luck and judgement. It was a style that he never abandoned.

Not that he had a great deal to work with. Adremad, the adrenalin cream, was all right as far as it went, but it was not exactly overwhelming French chemists. What he needed was more products for his pharmaceutical range and a sales force. Then he saw an opportunity. In the harsh days after the war, the major American and English manufacturers had hardly had time to develop their European marketing, and the products that they had developed for Britain and the United States were not all available in Europe. Jimmy Goldsmith decided to get licences for pharmaceutical products that were not available in France, and launch them there. After all, his brother had not done too badly with Lloyd's Adrenalin Cream. There was no reason why that should not work again, and again.

Two of the first licences that he obtained for distribution in France were the vaccine Lantigen B and the nasal spray Rhinosterin.

He was intent on launching them on to the French market with all possible speed – that required a marketing campaign, and salesmen. To begin with he had had neither. Then, on 21 April 1953, he had hired a young part-time public relations man, Claude-Henry Leconte, to help out. After Isabel's death he had gone on to the offensive. "I had to sell myself, because there was nobody else," Jimmy Goldsmith remembers. "I used to go round and present the products to doctors. I rather enjoyed it all. I'd never done anything like it before." It did not take him long to realize that, with more salesmen, he could expand his business. Determined to succeed as quickly as possible, he approached another small French pharmaceutical company, Distriphar, which had its own sales force, to see if they would be prepared to help him sell the products he had a licence for on a freelance basis. Distriphar already had one or two other pharmaceutical products, including Alka-Seltzer and Vick Inhalant, as well as the licence on some cosmetics, and he was convinced that they could handle his products as well. Run by a chemist with a shop, the Pharmacie Anglaise, close to his father's hotel, Distriphar agreed to try and sell his products. The partnership began so well that, by the beginning of 1955, Jimmy Goldsmith was suggesting that they might go further and found a new company together specifically to distribute their pharmaceutical products. The chemist was only too pleased to become the company's chairman, because only a qualified chemist was allowed to head a company in the pharmaceutical industry in France. He was equally happy to leave its running to the energetic Goldsmith.

By the time Teddy Goldsmith returned to Paris after his National Service, the company he had started with only a secretary had about a hundred employees, as well as a warehouse in the Place Gabriel-Péri. Not that this was exactly grand. There was no telephone, simply a large, almost empty room, in which the staff had to pack the goods that the salesmen had persuaded the chemists to order. Telephone calls had to be made in the bar across the street and if a customer wanted to place an order by phone they too had to telephone the bar, where the patron had agreed to take messages.

One of the salesmen from Distriphar who joined Jimmy Goldsmith's new company, which he had called Laboratoires Cassene, after an aunt, was a young man from the South of France, Maurice

Lignon, who liked his new employer at once. "As soon as he started in the business he launched a competition between the salesmen to see who could sell the most," Lignon remembers. He won the first three competitions outright. "Each time my salary was doubled, and the third time I won a car. From then on we were often together, discussing the future." Lignon, who still works in the pharmaceutical industry in France, remembers that his young employer "was very dynamic and would never sit still; his head was always buzzing with ideas. He wanted to revolutionize the pharmacy business, and he was always thinking up new products."

The only difficulty was that Jimmy Goldsmith still had no money. His new company was active enough, but it lacked hard cash. On Teddy's return, Jimmy gave him 30 per cent of the company and they went into business together. "We used to have to have three shifts a day working to fill the bundles at Gabriel-Péri," Teddy says now, "because we had to send out 200 bundles a day. There was no space, and there was no money." But there was boundless energy, enthusiasm and plenty of ideas.

In particular it had struck Jimmy Goldsmith forcibly that brand-name drugs in France allowed the chemists only a 30 per cent profit margin, whereas if the drugs lacked a brand name – were simply Aspirin rather than, for example, Aspro – they allowed the chemists a profit of more than 40 per cent. With that in mind he started to manufacture these "generic" products, like Vitamin B_{12} and Aspirin, without the benefit of a brand name, as quickly as he could, to offer them to every chemist he thought might be attracted by the bigger profit margin. The idea worked. "In two years Jimmy accomplished what others would have done in ten," Maurice Lignon explains now. Laboratoires Cassene rapidly became a pharmaceutical company to be reckoned with in France.

By the summer of 1956 he had established a business with an annual turnover of more than one and a half million pounds. And he was not going to stop there. That autumn, he bought a half-finished factory, which had been designed to make ski-lifts, from a scrap metal dealer. "It was a great big hangar of a place, and we finished it," he remembers. "It was tremendous. We put in research laboratories, everything, and business went extremely well, we were innovating in research, advertising, development, marketing, and things had started to take off. We were a major commercial success."

Nevertheless, Jimmy Goldsmith still lacked money. Not that he intended to alter his life to suit his income. No Goldsmith was going to live in a garret and starve, especially not one with a small daughter and her nanny to support. "He had a butler, but no money," Lignon says. "Often the butler or I would pay for the taxi when he went home." The two men had moved with the company into slightly grander offices in the rue de la Pépinière, opposite the Gare St Lazare, and were distributing a wider and wider range of products. They even tried to launch one or two new ones, including a shaving foam called Rise in an aerosol can, a distinctly adventurous development for France at that time. But the cans did not work all that well, and the launch was a failure. Jimmy Goldsmith even found himself buying a licence which the company he was paying appeared not to own. "The whole thing lost a fortune," he says now. Once again it underlined his enthusiasm and revealed his inexperience.

The craving for expansion at any price, the rush to launch more and more on to the market, the need to keep moving at all costs, stretched their strained resources to the limit, and beyond. "Cassene was an incredible success in a way," Jimmy Goldsmith explains, "but also an incredible failure. It was a commercial and marketing success, but it was based on no money, complete financial naivety and hope." He had bought the factory on credit, and he was expanding "way ahead of myself". That was all right in winter, "when anybody who sells Vick's Vapour Rub and Lantigen B and antibiotics should do tremendously well", but now he could also see the better weather coming, "and I knew that in the summer I was going to be in very serious trouble".

By the spring of 1957, Jimmy Goldsmith realized that his financial difficulties were acute. He was finding it harder and harder to raise enough money even to pay his workers each week. Teddy Goldsmith gave his brother all the money he could lay his hands on. "Every month Jimmy used to sit down and try to think up schemes to raise money. He was desperate, he didn't know how he was going to pay the bills." In fact Jimmy Goldsmith could hardly have gone on as long as he did without the support of his 400 or more workers:

"They were wonderful," he recalls; "it was quite touching. They were prepared to give up their pay to see us continue."

In the absence of a better idea, Jimmy Goldsmith seized on his generic products as the obvious way to solve his financial difficulties. Only this time he decided to try and make deals with the major pharmaceutical wholesalers up and down the country, so that they could also take advantage of the extra profits that previously only the chemists themselves had been able to enjoy. He had discovered that if he appointed specific, exclusive wholesalers for his generic products in every region, they would be treated as retailers and be able to earn the larger profits. So he insisted that, if they wanted to stock his more profitable products, they would have to place a minimum order of £25,000. In a frenzy of activity, he and Maurice Lignon started telephoning wholesalers around France with the details of their new offer.

Goldsmith did not leave it at simple telephone calls. He decided to hire an aeroplane and travel around to visit the wholesalers who seemed interested in his new scheme. That way he might just be able to lay his hands on enough money to pay his debts and his workers, and to stay out of the bankruptcy court. "We hired this little plane from Le Bourget," Lignon remembers, "and Jimmy and I went from town to town signing contracts with wholesalers."

The two young men from Laboratoires Cassene were not alone, however. They took a secretary with them on the trip – Ginette Lery, who had joined the company in the autumn of 1956. A spare, slight young woman, with longish blonde hair and pale complexion, at first she had been a little overwhelmed by the relentless energy of her young employer, but as the months passed they had become very close. The daughter of a worker on the Paris Metro, she was nothing whatever like Isabel Patino, but she seemed to care intensely for the restless young man so desperate to prove that he could make his way in the financial world. They had become friends, and then lovers. By the spring of 1957 Ginette Lery was as anxious as Jimmy Goldsmith to see the company saved. She had watched in horror as his hair had slowly but steadily begun to fall out. "It must be the worry," she told him firmly. When he began to develop a series of boils, she was quite sure. She had no intention of allowing him to fly around France without her; even if it did turn out to be a mad idea.

"We would just have left one wholesaler," Lignon recalls, "and Jimmy would telephone another a hundred miles away to ask him if he was interested in becoming his exclusive agent. The man would usually tell him 'I'll see you in two or three days'; but Jimmy would shout back: 'I'll see you in two or three hours', and we would rush back to the plane again." When he was not actually visiting new wholesalers, Jimmy Goldsmith would hold meetings with his existing marketing teams. "He would never waste any time." The pyrotechnics may have been unexpected in the French pharmaceutical industry, but they were extremely successful. The wholesalers took his products, and paid for them on the spot.

"Jimmy came back to Paris with about £200,000," Teddy Goldsmith remembers, "and we thought our troubles were over. All we had to do now was pack up all the orders quickly, ship them off to the wholesalers, and put the money in the bank. Everything was all right."

But they had reckoned without the reaction of the other French pharmaceutical companies. Most businessmen were not at all sympathetic to someone who thought he could suddenly overturn the established system of trading. Several of the other major French companies held a meeting in Paris and decided to tell the wholesalers that had agreed to become his exclusive agents that they would give them "only the lowest possible margin in future" if they did not renounce their agreements with him. There was even the hint that a wholesaler who did not return Jimmy Goldsmith's generic goods might find that the rest of France's major pharmaceutical companies would refuse to deal with him.

Teddy Goldsmith remembers it vividly. "The other manufacturers seemed to gang up and write a letter to all our new wholesalers saying: 'If you do this deal with Goldsmith we won't sell you any of our products.'" The threat was enough; the wholesalers had no alternative but to send all their products back, and the bills of exchange that had been so painstakingly collected were cancelled. The young man with a new factory and a research team working on new products suddenly found himself exactly where he had been a few months before: on the verge of bankruptcy. As Jimmy Goldsmith accepts now, "I had expanded too fast with no capital and no knowledge of finance, and I had to pay the consequences." He had products, but no money.

There was only one thing to do: sell part of the company. There had been one or two approaches in the past from some of his major suppliers, including an Italian company, as well as the French giant Laboratoires Roussell. He had to take one up.

"When I saw the summer coming along I started negotiations with the Italians we had been doing business with, and they seemed interested. They came for a great many meetings, but they always ended up asking for more information of some kind. They knew I had terrible problems, and they were just hanging on to get the best deal they possibly could." The negotiations dragged on for weeks until, finally, a deal seemed to have been done. The Italians would provide an injection of capital to help Laboratoires Cassene over its financial difficulties, and in exchange they would become equal partners in the company. At last the worst was over. Even though it meant that Jimmy Goldsmith would no longer be in sole control of his own company, at least there would be some sort of future for the business he had built up over the past two and a half years.

In the last week of June, however, the Italians returned to his office. Jimmy Goldsmith recalls their conversation only too clearly.

"They said: 'We have changed our minds. We want 80 per cent of your business now.' I told them that that wasn't the basis of the deal. 'That is correct,' they said, 'but that is still what we require.' 'Well, there's no deal then,' I said in a fury. 'But you're going to go bust in about three weeks!'

"I can imagine circumstances," Jimmy Goldsmith told them fiercely, "when a man who was much in love with a beautiful mistress, would rather see her dead than in the arms of someone else." And he ushered the dazed Italians towards the door.

"That is exactly what I said, and exactly what I felt," he remembers, "because I really loved that business. I loved it as much as you could possibly love a business. I had created every brick. I'd built it, recruited everybody, designed every pack, every bit of advertising, everything."

A despondent Jimmy Goldsmith looked around to see if he could find anyone else to help. "I tried desperately to borrow money. My life was split between bankers, trying to raise money; and creditors, trying to stave them off. Some of our suppliers were so worried that they started to visit me." In the evenings he would pace round his new apartment in rue de Lübeck where he now lived with Ginette Lery and little Isabel, as well as the nanny.

"On 9 July I realized I had failed. Bills of exchange which I did not have the money to honour were due to be presented at the bank the following day and I expected to be declared a bankrupt at once. That was a great deal more serious in France than many people realized. It meant the end of a man's career. It was impossible to recover from it. At that time the dishonour was enormous."

That night he decided to forget his troubles. "Ginette and I went to the cinema on the Champs Elysées, and then home to bed." Ironically, the film they went to see was Mike Todd's *Around the World in Eighty Days*, starring David Niven, itself an enormous gamble that few movie men had truly believed would ever come off, but which had turned out to be an international hit. It was also a little nostalgic. For Major Goldsmith had played whist in the Reform Club in Pall Mall, just as Phineas Fogg had done in the film, and had wagered on the result, though usually less spectacularly than Fogg. As he walked home along the grand boulevard it seemed to Jimmy Goldsmith that unlike Fogg's, his gamble was destined to fail.

It was the strike by bank staff, the first in France for twenty years, that saved Jimmy Goldsmith from ruin. Even so, the sale to his competitor, Laboratoires Roussell, was not straightforward: negotiations took longer than anyone expected, because Laboratoires Cassene's difficulties had not disappeared overnight. It looked as if the bank strike might end before agreement was reached. Indeed, on the evening before the bank staff were due to return it still looked as though the bankruptcy could happen. Teddy Goldsmith remembers sitting at a pavement table of a restaurant near their offices that evening having dinner with his brother and the chemist from Pharmacie Anglaise who was still connected with the company. "The only sound you could hear was this charming old man weeping. The tears were running down his face, because he would have lost his pharmacy if the company had actually been declared bankrupt.

But halfway through dinner there was a telephone call, and Jimmy came back rubbing his hands, saying 'It's settled, they've bought it.'"

Jimmy Goldsmith had escaped. And remarkably well. Laboratoires Roussell had not only agreed to take over his company, together with its debts, but they had also paid him £120,000 for it, and allowed him to keep the royalties on the sales of Lantigen B in France: more than enough to keep even an ambitious young man of twenty-five reasonably comfortable while he decided what to do next. Maurice Lignon was to be transferred to Laboratoires Roussell, along with the stock.

Tom Sebestyen, who had first met Teddy at Oxford and who had joined Laboratoires Cassene the previous year, says that the events of 1957 had a crucial impact: "They convinced Jimmy that a company did not run on its own. He discovered that things that should have been checked – particularly whether money owing to them had been collected – hadn't been; and that gave him a shock. But it also gave him a preoccupation with cash, which became an absolutely fundamental part of his character. The idea that cash would always take care of itself left him for ever."

Jimmy Goldsmith agrees. Other businessmen might run their concerns with vast debts, but from that day onwards he would always prefer to have substantial amounts of hard cash available to meet any contingency. He was to borrow money many times in the future, but he would never forget that reserves of hard cash made him feel comfortable.

"What the experience taught me was fear," he explains now. "I still took reckless risks afterwards, but I never considered any success certain after that. My antennae became very very sharp, and they still are to this day. Whereas my colleagues are always relaxed, I am always absolutely aware of the perils. 1957 was a very important date in my life because it was miraculous, and it was the only really lucky thing that ever happened to me in business."

As Tom Sebestyen puts it: "Under this terribly tough exterior, there is a very sensitive man, who could not bear the thought of being declared a bankrupt."

After the summer of 1957 Jimmy Goldsmith became a distinctly conservative financier, no matter how much of a gambler he appeared on the surface. Early in August he and Ginette departed gratefully for Spain for a two-month holiday.

PART 3

Entrepreneur

8

The Slimming Business

There is no English word for *entrepreneur*. Like Jimmy Goldsmith it is French, and like him it has developed English and American connections. The Oxford English Dictionary and Webster's both pay tribute to its French origins in the last quarter of the nineteenth century when they define it as "the organizer of an economic venture, especially one who organizes, owns, manages and assumes the risks of a business". There could be no better definition of what Jimmy Goldsmith had in mind. He was prepared to undertake almost any risk to create a business life for himself, and a new Goldsmith dynasty.

When he returned to France in the autumn of 1957 he had £120,000 from his sale of Laboratoires Cassene, and the royalties on the sales of the vaccine Lantigen B. "Those brought me in quite enough money to live on comfortably," he recalls now, "but I didn't just want to sit about doing nothing." That had never been his style. He wanted to go back into business as quickly as possible.

The only business he knew was pharmaceuticals. Without hesitation he started negotiations to buy another small drug company, Laboratoire Laffort, which had a factory in the Loire region of France. Little had changed: he was still prepared to risk everything in business, he went back to working in his old office in the rue de la Paix and Ginette Lery was still his secretary. Lignon had gone, but Claude-Henry Leconte was still there. And he was still trying to sell drugs to chemists and doctors as energetically as he always had. There were licences to be negotiated, products designed, advertising planned, launches organized, and all at the same hectic pace.

One significant change in his style had emerged since the sale of Cassene. He had realized that he might need help from time to time. Although he was devoted to his brother Teddy, he knew that he was probably not the right person to take into business with him as his interests lay in other directions. Teddy and his wife Gill, with their two young daughters Dido and Clio, were living in England. After Cassene the two brothers agreed to split up, and go their own way. So for the moment it looked as though Jimmy Goldsmith would go on alone. Then, quite accidentally, he found a financial supporter and adviser who became first his business partner and then his friend.

In the summer of 1957, while Jimmy Goldsmith had been flying round France in his hired Beechwood aircraft, a new bank had quietly opened its doors on the ground floor of 23, rue de la Paix, underneath his father's offices. The Banque d'Arbitrage et de Crédit was run by one of four Baghdad-born brothers called Zilkha, who had also recently started branches in Geneva, London and New York (one brother was responsible for each branch). Anxious for customers for their new Paris office, the staff had sent a leaflet to every tenant in their office building offering the bank's services. One of the recipients of the leaflet was Jimmy Goldsmith. Not long after his return from Spain he invited the manager of the bank to see him and, to his surprise, asked, "I would rather like to know what you think you could do to help me." Before the meeting was over the manager had suggested to his prospective client that he should meet his principals, and in particular the brother in overall charge of their European branches, thirty-year-old Selim Zilkha, whose offices were in London.

Jimmy Goldsmith went to London to meet him. Their first meeting came as something of a shock, Selim Zilkha recalls. He was not accustomed to such confidence in young men five years or more his junior, even though his staff in Paris had briefed him. He watched, fascinated, as Goldsmith paced up and down his small office, outlining his plans for the future: the companies he wanted to buy, the innovations in marketing drugs that he wanted to make, the products that he wanted to launch. As was to happen time and time again in the future, Jimmy Goldsmith's enthusiasm was infectious. In less than a month, Jimmy Goldsmith and Selim

Zilkha had become business colleagues. Shortly afterwards they became friends. It was a friendship that neither man would ever threaten or give up.

With the support of this shortish young man with dark wavy hair and slight Iraqi accent, Jimmy Goldsmith pressed ahead with his plans to expand his interests in newly developing drugs. His plans were not limited to France: he was considering launching a similar drug company in England, and he had two products in mind for it already. "What people do not understand about Jimmy is that business is both his hobby and his passion," Zilkha says now. "He probably enjoys it more than anything else he does."

"The only difficulty was that I was a capitalist without capital," Jimmy Goldsmith explains. That was not quite true, the royalties on Lantigen B would have comfortably sustained a less ambitious man, but to go further he certainly needed the financial help that Selim Zilkha could bring him, as well as his connections in the City of London, where he had worked for Hambros merchant bank. He had already decided on the kind of rapid expansion plan that he needed: and it was not just to be in France.

The American company Schering had recently patented two new derivatives of the drug cortisone, called prednisone and prednisolone, and Jimmy Goldsmith wanted to develop them for the French and British markets. As ever, he was anxious to push ahead as quickly as he could with manufacturing and marketing them under licence from Schering. But that turned out to be rather more complicated than he had first thought, not least because the American company had already licensed the rights to manufacture the drug to major manufacturers in Europe, including Lepetit in Italy and Laboratoires Roussell in France. Undeterred, Jimmy Goldsmith persuaded Lepetit to sub-license the rights to the British market to him, and agreed that Laboratoires Roussell would manufacture the actual tablets for him in their factory in Britain.

To handle the deal Jimmy Goldsmith set up an English company, under the chairmanship of his friend Captain Julian Snow, Labour Member of Parliament for Lichfield and Tamworth. The company was to be named Ward Casson, partly because Julian Snow's middle name was Ward, and partly because of its echoes of Cassene.

In November 1957 Ward Casson duly opened offices in Victoria

Street in London, and Snow announced to the press that his co-director Jimmy Goldsmith would concentrate on highly special-ized drugs used in the treatment of rheumatism. When Snow was asked about his new partner's reputation for being something of a playboy, he retorted loyally, "He is a very serious young man, all those stories about him being a playboy are just so much nonsense." But the headlines still haunted him.

Jimmy Goldsmith divided his time between London and Paris, staying in the rue de Lübeck for part of the time, and in a suite at the Ritz hotel in London the rest. "It was survival: big activity, big launches, but that's all."

The first months of 1958 were promising. Ward Casson seemed to be going well, and Laffort had started to take over one or two smaller laboratories, including a small one in Paris called Neotherap. Jimmy Goldsmith even decided to buy another factory. No sooner had he done so than he merged both companies into a new organiz-ation, which he called SPHAL, and to celebrate the expansion of his French businesses again, he contacted Maurice Lignon, who had been sold to Laboratoires Roussell along with Cassene. By the end of 1958 the former partners were reunited.

Lignon's brief was to "clean up" what remained of Neotherap, and make the new SPHAL work. "Jimmy hadn't paid anything for the company, but he had taken on its liabilities," Lignon remembers. "So I set about cancelling the old orders and dismissing the medical visitors so that we could make changes and concentrate on just one or two products. One of the first we produced as SPHAL was a gargle in the form of an aerosol spray called 'Collargent'. Within a few months we were selling more than we could produce."

Yet again Jimmy Goldsmith had a commercial success on his hands, but once again he soon realized that he did not have enough money to capitalize on it. This time, however, he had something to sell other than the company itself to get the money he needed: the royalties to Lantigen B. They would give him enough money to expand in France and England. Without hesitation he sold his rights to the royalties on Lantigen B to Laboratoires Roussell. Maurice Lignon remembers, "Lantigen was a success too, and the sales were going up, so the rights would have enabled Jimmy to have lived comfortably for the rest of his life. But that wouldn't have been his style. So he sold them quickly for half what he should have got for them."

What Maurice Lignon did not know was that Jimmy Goldsmith had other plans for the money he had raised, beyond pushing on with the sales of Collargent: he also wanted to expand in England.

Ward Casson's cortisone derivatives were proving successful. The tablets that Laboratoires Roussell were supplying them from their English factory were identical to those sold by other companies, but the crucial difference was that Ward Casson was selling them at a little over £12 for a thousand, barely a fifth of the £60 a thousand being charged by some of the other major drug companies. By the autumn of 1958 Ward Casson had even secured a contract to supply the major London teaching hospitals. The company looked to have a substantial future.

But once again Jimmy Goldsmith came up against the established order in the world of medicine; and once again he became convinced that the major drug companies were conspiring to try and force him out of business. "We had the identical product to everyone else, manufactured by the identical people in England. The only difference was the price." As Julian Snow was to say later: "The attacks against us became almost hysterical."

In December 1958 Professor Max Rosenheim and Dr Eric Ross of the University College Hospital Medical School in London wrote a letter to the medical journal *The Lancet* attacking Ward Casson's cortisone tablets. "The tablets do not break up as quickly as they should," they wrote, and warned their fellow doctors of the dangers of "substandard" cortisone tablets. They had not specifically suggested that Ward Casson's tablets were substandard, but the implication was clear enough. Julian Snow replied angrily in the next edition of *The Lancet*: "Ever since his firm began to force prices down it has been continuously slandered." But it was too late. The innuendo was enough. The damage had been done.

Jimmy Goldsmith offered to produce the independent tests he had had carried out on his cortisone tablets, and to submit them to the Medical Research Council, but to no avail. Questions were asked in the House of Commons about these "cheap imported products", and although the Minister of Health, Derek Walker-Smith, suggested dryly that "the sharp drop in prices was the result of increased competition", the impression was created that Ward Casson was somehow trying to pass off unsatisfactory, imported, cortisone tablets on an unsuspecting British public.

"In fact they were exactly the same tablets that everybody else was selling, and they were manufactured by exactly the same people," Jimmy Goldsmith says now. "If I had been manufacturing them myself then I might have made a mistake, but I wasn't. The cortisone tablets I was selling were made for Ward Casson under sub-licence from an Italian company. And they weren't even imported, Ward Casson was owned from France, but that was the only imported thing about them."

There was little or nothing he could do. To those who remembered him only from the newspaper headlines, Jimmy Goldsmith was once again portrayed as the rather too rich young man who was a little too foreign to be trusted in England; still the playboy rather than the businessman. The memory of it angers him still. "The only 'crime' we committed was that we broke the cartel prices and sold the products to British hospitals at a price which gave us a good profit but was well below the cartel prices. The only unusual thing about our 'cheap imported products' – which they were not – was that they were less expensive."

The suspicions that Jimmy Goldsmith had long nurtured about the British establishment and established companies were confirmed. His determination to make a profit for himself, regardless of the accepted traditions of the established companies who had organized a cartel for their own advantage, meant he felt he could seldom expect to be treated fairly if he chose to ignore their methods.

No matter how much entrepreneurial skill and energy he might demonstrate he seemed for ever destined to battle obstacles placed in his path by those who did not know him, to protect their own interests and the established order. Not for the first time the tiny flame of paranoia that had always lain at the heart of his character was fanned into fire. It made him more determined than ever. There was nothing he relished more than a fight.

It would take him many years to win that fight in England. For the moment, although he finally managed to refute the claim that he was importing substandard delta-cortisone tablets into Britain, the public debate had taken its toll of his business. After another brush with the drug companies over tetracycline it became all too clear that the prospects for Ward Casson, which he had made part of a small public company in Britain called Clinical and General Industries, were not growing any rosier. Not for the first time, or the last, the public image of him in England as a young man in too much of a hurry to be entirely trustworthy had taken a decisive toll. He began to wonder whether he might not be better off remaining in France for a time. There he never encountered the same suspicions, and SPHAL was operating reasonably successfully, even though he had recently paid little attention to it and his small laboratories, because of the fuss in England.

"At one stage Jimmy only came back once a fortnight to see me," Lignon explains, "and even with the profits from the sale of the royalties to Lantigen B there was still a desperate shortage of money." After examining the figures, Jimmy Goldsmith reluctantly concluded he would have to sell some of his French companies to survive, and once again Maurice Lignon was to go with them. Laffort and Neotherap were sold to Laboratoires Sarbach, and in their place he launched a new company called Laboratoire Lanord. For the second time in two years Lignon was sold by his employer along with his companies.

There were other attractions to remaining in France. It was still his home, of course, but, more important, it allowed him a privacy that he had never enjoyed in England. There he was always the eloping playboy, in France that was hardly mentioned. In England he would never feel exactly at home, in France he could conduct himself as he pleased, and lead as unconventional a life as he chose. That was a quality he had always prized, and all the more important now in view of his relationship with Ginette Lery.

In May 1959 – almost exactly five years after the birth of little Isabel – she gave birth to his second child, a son, whom they named Manes. They were not married, something which had never worried the Goldsmith family, but now there was a son to continue the family tradition. If he still had one or two beautiful young companions in England when he went there on business, that too was part of the family tradition. Ginette Lery knew very well that beautiful young women were almost his only hobby. And he was still fascinated by the prospects of a financial success in England.

Perhaps it was the birth of his son, or perhaps it was simply the chance of a good deal that put the notion of clothes for mothers and their children into his mind, no one – not even he – is quite sure. But there is no doubt that before his son was six months old, in the last weeks of 1959, Jimmy Goldsmith had begun negotiations to buy a chain of twenty-eight old-fashioned chemist shops in England, called Lewis and Burrows, from Charles Clore. They needed modernization, but he was convinced that they could form the basis for a new kind of chemists, which he believed should take a more specific interest in mothers and their small children. Such a chain, Pre-Natal, existed in France, and the idea had never been copied in England. He had a scheme worked out, and even though he had no means of financing it, he knew it would work.

He confided in Selim Zilkha who was so convinced by his argument that in the first days of 1960 he gave up banking and went into business as an equal partner with Jimmy Goldsmith. For the next two years they sat at desks opposite each other in London, creating a chain of shops that would come to be known as Mothercare from Charles Clore's twenty-eight discarded chemists.

The City of London then was a dramatically different place from today. It was still a village, a tiny, gossipy square mile where everyone knew each other, or of each other. Bowler hats were still worn, and umbrellas were neatly rolled. The staff at the weekly newspaper the *Investors Chronicle* wrote their copy in longhand. Takeovers were usually matters of agreement, rather than dispute, although Charles Clore had recently begun to upset the applecart by stamping round the City attempting, and often succeeding, by less delicate means. For the most part, however, tradition was everything. It was not so much what you knew as who that counted most. An extravagant, restless twenty-seven-year-old French-born former playboy, even if he was an old Etonian, and his thirty-three-year-old Baghdad-born partner were not exactly commonplace in the City of London. News of their arrival, and their intentions, travelled fast.

So did rumours of their style. Jimmy Goldsmith had not entirely lost his old appetite for "making whoopee". He still liked to gamble, although it was now more often on cards than on horses, more backgammon than greyhound racing. He liked to play cards at the private parties organized by his old friend from Oxford John Aspinall, who was talking about starting his own gaming club in London when the British gaming laws changed. And there were also the attractions of young and pretty girls. Jimmy Goldsmith had never lost his appetite for beautiful girls, and he had no intention of concealing it. The English might find that difficult to understand, even accuse him of being eccentric or a cad, but they did not know the Goldsmith family. It was a disregard for the traditions of the City of London that would come to horrify his enemies.

Not that he had abandoned France: not at all. At almost the same moment he was negotiating with Charles Clore, Jimmy Goldsmith saw Maurice Lignon again. "I had dinner with him one evening," Lignon recalls, "and I told him that I had just heard of a product in the United States for tanning yourself without sun – called Man Tan. We could launch it in France under a new name, say Night Tan." At dinner he looked across at his former employer, and insisted: "We have to do something with it in Europe."

"But I've only got 20,000 francs," Jimmy Goldsmith replied.

"That doesn't matter. Let's do it anyway."

Jimmy Goldsmith went to his new partner in England to discuss the deal. Before long Selim Zilkha had arranged a loan of 20,000 francs to help Lanord exploit the idea in France. In exchange he took 50 per cent of the company.

A delighted Jimmy Goldsmith hired Maurice Lignon for the third time, to launch Man Tan as quickly as possible. To do it, he was given the office in the rue de la Paix. Lewis and Burrows could provide the basic raw materials he needed to produce the new product from England. With Zilkha's support, and the English chain of shops there was a chance of success, even if there was not a great deal of money. "This time I decided to inaugurate a new system in the pharmaceutical field in France," Lignon recalls, "immediate payment." Neither he nor Jimmy Goldsmith intended to see their success disappear for a third time.

Within three months Night Tan was a success, and they were unable to meet demand. But there was a snag. "We launched the product so quickly that we hadn't made searches about the trade mark, and we started packaging the product as Night Tan," Lignon remembers. "But we suddenly had to change it to Right Tan when we found that someone already had the name Night Tan." In fact that did nothing to halt its success. Lanord again became a company with a future, but Selim Zilkha and Jimmy Goldsmith were more concerned with their twenty-eight chemist's shops in England. They may have been equal partners on both sides of the Channel, but there was little doubt about where their principal interest lay in the first months of the 1960s: it was in England.

In October 1960, Jimmy Goldsmith rented a house on a short lease in London, to replace his usual suite in the Ritz hotel. It was now to be his home for part of each year, because Zilkha and he had agreed that he would need to spend at least two weeks of every month in London. Overlooking the west side of Regent's Park, Jimmy Goldsmith's new house was 22 Sussex Place, a fine Georgian building with ornate columns. Spacious, and with a touch of grandeur in its high ceilings and tall casement windows, it was an entirely suitable residence for a young businessman on the rise. And, more important still, it meant that he did not have to be separated completely from his family. After discussing the move with Ginette, who was excited but a little anxious that she would not feel "very comfortable" in England, Jimmy Goldsmith brought her and little Isabel to London with him. Isabel's nanny told a slightly surprised gossip columnist from one English newspaper, "He wants Isabel to be brought up as English, that is why we have come to live here." None the less his nomadic habits had not disappeared. Two months after he moved his family into Sussex Place he was back in Cannes spending the Christmas holiday with Ginette, his father and his mother, at the Carlton Hotel. Mr and Mrs John Aspinall were also guests there at the time.

John Aspinall was still one of his closest friends. Since their time at Oxford a decade earlier the two men had grown closer. They would speak to each other on the telephone almost every day, Aspinall regaling his younger friend with stories of his exploits at the gaming tables. Not long before, Aspinall had opened the Clermont Club in Berkeley Square, Mayfair, taking advantage of the relaxation in the English gambling laws. It became one place Jimmy Goldsmith could usually be found when he was not working. Beneath the Clermont one of his Eton contemporaries, Mark Birley, was also about to open a restaurant and nightclub, and name it after his wife, Annabel, the younger daughter of the Marquis of Londonderry. In the years ahead both places were to play a crucial part in Jimmy Goldsmith's life. At the Clermont he would play backgammon and cards in its magnificent William Kent rooms, designed in 1742, aware that he was among friends, and that his privacy – and his desire to do what he liked – would be respected. Downstairs in Annabel's he would drink as sparingly as he always had, but he would still wolf his food with the appetite of a ravenous schoolboy. Jimmy Goldsmith had emerged as a confident, if boisterous, young businessman with a considerable talent for balance sheets and a taste for parties. Indeed in late May 1961 he gave such a grand one that once again he hit the newspaper headlines.

John Aspinall was in the habit of giving a party every year just before the Derby, and he asked Jimmy Goldsmith if this time he could give it in a marquee in the communal gardens outside his house at Sussex Place, which were for the use of all the residents of the terrace. Without a moment's hesitation, Jimmy Goldsmith agreed and duly warned the residents of his street that Maples, the London furniture shop, would be arriving to erect the tent. What he neglected to tell them was that the "tent" was in the shape of the Taj Mahal, and so large it would take a team of men more than a week to erect it.

"It's so huge it looks like a village," one of the terrace's anguished residents told a visiting reporter as the dome of the marquee rose seventy feet above the gardens. By the time the £12,500 canvas structure was completed some of the local residents were collecting signatures for a petition of protest. But Jimmy Goldsmith remained impassive, smiling cheerfully when they, or the team of reporters who gathered to look at it in amazement, spoke to him. He deliberately did not tell anyone that it was really John Aspinall's tent – the whole affair was far too much fun for that. In fact, the furore over the size of the tent turned out to be rather more fun than the party itself. "It was an absolutely perishing evening," one of the guests recalls, "and I am sure at least half the people there caught pneumonia." But John Aspinall was not downhearted, and Jimmy Goldsmith had enjoyed the whole affair hugely.

Not everything was proving to be quite such fun. Although Right Tan was forging ahead in France the plans to launch a new kind of chemist's shop in England were proving difficult. In their tiny London office, Selim Zilkha and Jimmy Goldsmith tried everything they could think of to breathe life into the Lewis and Burrows chain. They refurbished the shops, improved their design, altered the kind of products they stocked, and varied the kind of assistants that served in them. They looked for fresh ways of attracting people who had never heard of them, and began to refine the notion that they could transform some of them into shops selling "everything for the mother-to-be and her baby, and children under five".

In March 1961 they had bought fifty more shops to add to the twenty-eight of Lewis and Burrows; these were the W. J. Harris chain of pram and nursery furniture shops, destined to become the very first of their shops to open under the name Mothercare. As they prepared to open the first of those the two partners started refining their Pre-Natal idea by opening two completely new Lewis and Burrows chemist shops in affluent London suburbs – Ealing and Kingston – with departments specially designed for mothers and their young children on the first floor. They soon dropped the pharmacy and concentrated on the pre-natal department. The experiments turned out to be expensive. As the new chain expanded so did the losses, until by the end of 1961 they had lost more than £200,000. They had to find more money to keep their idea alive.

In the first weeks of 1962 the inevitable crunch came. It was perfectly obvious that Jimmy Goldsmith could not keep up with his partner in supplying their new business with financial aid. Zilkha, with his background in banking and his family's support from the United States, was prepared to continue to pour money into the new company, but Goldsmith was simply not able to match him pound for pound.

"I had decided long before then that I would never accept a less than equal partnership with anyone," Jimmy Goldsmith explains now. "So in the first weeks of 1962 I came to the conclusion that I had no alternative but to sell out. I could not afford to keep up with Selim." He offered to sell his half share in Lewis and Burrows and the foundling Mothercare chain to his partner. In return he offered to buy back Zilkha's share in his French company Lanord. Reluctantly, he decided to return to what he felt he knew best: France and the pharmaceutical industry. After all Right Tan had proved that he could be successful there, and it would help him pay back Selim Zilkha over the next few years.

Shortly after his twenty-ninth birthday in February 1962, a saddened Jimmy Goldsmith found himself back in Paris, sitting opposite Maurice Lignon again, much as he had done six years before. Little had changed. Lanord had no large staff to speak of, no expensive offices, but it made a healthy profit. There was still the rue de Lübeck apartment, which he had kept on. And Ginette and his two children moved back to Paris with him. But no matter how much at home he may have felt in France, there was still the suspicion in his mind that he had been forced out of England: he was more determined than ever to go back, and he had an idea which might provide him with the opportunity to do so.

"Like everybody else I used to go to America from time to time to find ideas to copy." On one trip to the United States he had observed a slimming product called Metrecal, which he thought he could develop profitably for the market in France. "Metrecal was a big success in the United States. So I decided to go out and copy it, and then adapt it for France by making it taste better. That's all I did." But he had no intention of suffering the difficulties of Right Tan and Night Tan again.

"I wanted to find a name as close as I could to Metrecal, so I started looking up all the old names that had been registered years before." It did not take long before he found a small company in France which had a similar name. Within a month he had taken it over, and by doing so had gained the right to use its name and trademark. Jimmy Goldsmith was now the proprietor of the old-established French pharmaceutical company Laboratoire Milical, which had long had an interest in slimming products. Barely two months later he had launched Milical on to the French market. It tasted better than Metrecal and it was to provide him finally with a firm commercial foundation.

As he had expected Jimmy Goldsmith soon found himself in conflict with a major drug company. Metrecal's American manufacturer, the giant Mead Johnson corporation, took grave exception to their product apparently appearing in France under a name very like theirs. Barely a month after Milical reached the shops the Americans issued a suit against him for using their name. "The strange thing was they weren't suing me for using their idea, which I was," he recalls, "but for using their trademark." He was ready for that.

He even launched a cheeky suit in return: he charged the Americans with using *his* company's name. The Milical name and company, he argued in the court papers, "have been in existence for many years, and certainly far longer than the new American product". A man less prepared to take a calculated commercial risk might not have done so, but Jimmy Goldsmith had always believed that fortune favoured the bravest entrepreneur. This time he was right. He won the case, and confirmed his right to use the name Milical on his slimming product in Europe.

The battle turned out to be well worth it. Milical became the foundation of Jimmy Goldsmith's fortune in France. Within a year he had launched the product all over Europe, and had established branches of the Lanord company in Holland, West Germany, Scandinavia and Italy, as well as in Great Britain. By the time he had done all that he had begun to lose interest in Lanord, and was looking for a new challenge. As Maurice Lignon puts it, "He found the day to day running of things a waste of time. That wasn't his style. He had to be creating something new to play with all the time." "If he hasn't got a battle on his hands, Jimmy's not altogether happy," says his brother Teddy. Certainly he seemed to thrive on the setbacks and conflicts that plagued his earliest years. Jimmy Goldsmith still loved a fight, and for him the commercial battle was almost more important than the victory.

9

A Tale of Two Cities

Even though he had no business interests in London for the moment, Jimmy Goldsmith still liked to go there regularly. In Paris there were Ginette, Manes and little Isabel as well as Laboratoire Lanord, but in London there were John Aspinall and Selim Zilkha, and the possibilities of a little "whoopee" at the Clermont Club and elsewhere with his old friends. So, although he was no longer involved in Mothercare, he told anyone who asked, "I am always on the lookout for something new in England." In fact, as 1962 developed there was another, more private, reason for his trips to London.

Few people knew it at that time, but Jimmy Goldsmith had fallen in love again. Late in 1961 he had been introduced to the singularly beautiful Lady Sally Crichton-Stuart, who was then just twenty-one and had been married to the Marquis of Bute's brother, Lord James Crichton-Stuart, for a little over two years. The daughter of an English army colonel, she was one of the most striking young women in England, and after her marriage had rapidly become one of the country's leading models. A touch over 5ft 8in in height, with sensuous brown eyes, she had been voted debutante of the year in 1958 in the London "season", and in June 1959 had made what seemed to be a spectacularly successful marriage. It had turned out to be a failure.

In the early months of 1962 Jimmy Goldsmith and Sally Crichton-Stuart fell passionately in love. He threw himself into the affair with every bit as much vigour as he pursued his company's fortunes in France. Everywhere they went together he seemed possessed by Sally, even though they were both, theoretically, attached to someone else. By the early summer they were staying together as often as they could, without attracting undue attention, in his suite at the Ritz in Piccadilly. He would spend the weekends in England with Sally, while he looked for the right opportunity to relaunch his business career in London, and the weekdays in France with Ginette and his family. It was not an arrangement that a more conventional person might have entered into, but Jimmy Goldsmith had never given a fig for convention. He saw no reason why he should not have precisely the same life as the hero of Alexander Korda's 1953 film comedy, *The Captain's Paradise*, in which Alec Guinness had played a cheerful ferry captain plying between Gibraltar and Tangier with a wife in each port to suit each side of his personality. On the voyage across the Straits, Guinness would alter the picture standing on his sea locker. There were some in the City of London convinced Jimmy Goldsmith did much the same thing.

His attitude was that of a young man who had always seen himself as someone apart, above convention. There had always been mistresses in the Goldschmidt family, and there would be many more. What was important was whether they were well treated. Women were to be enjoyed certainly, but they were not to be used, or taken advantage of. Jimmy Goldsmith believed in treating women well. He was loyal and generous to both Sally Crichton-Stuart and Ginette Lery, but he did not try to conceal his behaviour from either of them. It would have been hypocritical, and he could not bear hypocrisy. That was one of the sins of the English.

By the summer of 1963, it seemed as if he had finally rediscovered the love he lost with Isabel Patino's death. "Everyone was convinced they were going to get married," one of his friends at the time recalls. "They used to have tremendous rows, but they were very much in love." Now thirty, he had an arrangement that millions of young men longed for, a beautiful companion in London, and a loving companion in France. Yet if he gave the impression of being one of Europe's most carefree bachelors, it was partly an illusion, for in private he was also a most devoted lover. No matter how outrageous he may have appeared, he was a long way from being a promiscuous boor without a conscience. Indeed, that was the cause of his greatest problem. Precisely because he was determined to remain loyal to Ginette, and to their son Manes, Jimmy Goldsmith wanted to legitimize his first-born son. But he also wanted to sustain his relationship with Sally Crichton-Stuart. After a great deal of heart-searching, and endless discussions with both Sally and Ginette, he decided to marry Ginette. After all, he would not be able to marry Sally Crichton-Stuart until her divorce was completed, which could take some time, and his marriage would ensure that his son was legitimate, even if it only lasted for a comparatively short time.

The marriage was not the action of a ruthless, ambitious young man, just intent on temporarily "doing the right thing": rather the reverse. Jimmy Goldsmith remained loyal to the shy, unassuming and gentle young Ginette for far longer than many of his friends predicted in the heat of his affair with Sally Crichton-Stuart. "For me getting married is having children, not a piece of paper," he was to say again and again.

So, in the first weeks of 1963, Jimmy Goldsmith quietly married Ginette Lery in Paris, to the delight of his mother who thoroughly approved of the home-loving French girl and was less certain about her son's passion for the much more glamorous young aristocrat from England. To those who saw it only from the outside it might have seemed an unbalanced relationship, but to him it represented a commitment to the traditions of the family, and the legitimacy of his son Manes. Besides he had told Sally Crichton-Stuart that he would eventually marry her. Indeed he had proved it. After his marriage to Ginette he held a party for Sally at Maxim's in Paris. "Everyone was convinced it was an engagement party," one old friend explains now. "It was naughty, but it was typically Jimmy."

Sally Crichton-Stuart, however, had no intention of letting Jimmy Goldsmith do exactly as he liked. She intended to keep her young admirer up to the mark, and she made no secret of her passion to be courted. After his marriage to Ginette, she flirted with other men and succeeded in making him just a little jealous. For a time he found it amusing, but gradually it began to irritate him, especially as Ginette seemed happier and more content than she had ever been. Then, in August 1963, Ginette discovered she was pregnant again.

Jimmy Goldsmith was not entirely sure what to do. He did not want to lose Sally Crichton-Stuart, but he also felt great affection for his young wife in France. When news of Ginette's pregnancy got back to England his future with Sally Crichton-Stuart was decided for him. She left him. Jimmy Goldsmith was not unduly concerned. They had had rows before. But this time things were different. Now Sally was by no means certain that Jimmy Goldsmith would divorce his new wife and marry her.

When the new Madame Ginette Goldsmith bore him his third child, a daughter Alix, on 3 January 1964, Sally Crichton-Stuart's mind was made up. Even though Jimmy Goldsmith telephoned her regularly for months, there was no reconciliation.

In December 1967 she was divorced, and in October 1969 Sally Crichton-Stuart married for the second time. Her new husband was the spiritual leader of the Ismaili sect of the Shi'ite Muslim community in the world, the Aga Khan, and she became the Begum Aga Khan. For his part Jimmy Goldsmith remained married to Ginette Lery far longer than any of his friends predicted, even though in a matter of months he was to immerse himself in an even more tempestuous and longer-lasting affair with another beautiful young Englishwoman.

Whatever the complications of his personal life, Jimmy Goldsmith never neglected his ambitions to relaunch his business career in England. Right Tan and Milical were now established successes in France, and with Maurice Lignon's help he had expanded them rapidly across Europe. The full range of his slimming and pharmaceutical products were bringing him a profit of some £120,000 a year. But now he wanted to do more. He needed a new objective to get his adrenalin running again. As soon as the commercial future of Right Tan and Milical looked assured, he decided to sell part of his French company. Once he had done that he bought a new company, Laboratoires Gustin, and called his principal company Gustin-Milical, to reflect his success.

"The first time I saw a flicker of success after 1957 I immediately sold a third of my company to capitalize on it," Jimmy Goldsmith says now. "I wanted to consolidate so that if things fell off again, I would not be in danger of going broke."

So, shortly before his daughter Alix was born, he sold a third of Laboratoire Lanord, which was by then well on the way to dominating the slimming foods industry in France, to his cousin Baron

Alexis de Gunzburg, whose grandfather had founded the French Shell Oil company and who came from the Russian strain of the Goldschmidt family – "the Rothschilds of Russia". Once again Jimmy Goldsmith looked to his own dynasty: Alexis's grandmother had married his grandfather's sister, his great-aunt.

Not that he got very much hard cash for his sale. In spite of his aristocratic background Alexis de Gunzburg was not vastly rich, even if his mother was. The price he paid for one-third of his cousin Jimmy's company was mainly in the shares of the French mineral water and soft drink company, Source Perrier, of which he was a director. Perrier had bought the rights to the famous mineral water from its English owner, Lord Harmsworth, in 1951, and had seen the company grow spectacularly in the ensuing fifteen years as they expanded into soft drinks – with the French rights to Pepsi-Cola – as well as into confectionery.

Jimmy Goldsmith's Perrier shares had the twin benefits of giving him both financial security and enough potential borrowing power to launch a return to the City of London, the plan that was still uppermost in his mind. As his affair with Sally Crichton-Stuart stumbled and finally collapsed, he was more intent than ever on returning to London. But he was not planning a massive invasion, rather a financial commando raid. He was convinced that there was nothing to lose and a great deal to gain by mounting an attack on the commanding heights of British business. Besides, the risk was part of the attraction.

The tactics were those that he had gradually refined over the past decade in France – to find weak companies in difficulty, take them over, sell off those assets which did not help their principal objective, develop their management, and use the new company – together with the cash the sale of assets had raised – as the stepping stone for the next attack on a different company. His ground rules were clear: never to accept less than a majority shareholding, and never to let the momentum of acquisition slow down while conditions on the stock market were right. His attack resembled that of a mercenary force rushing to seize an objective before the defenders realize how few their attackers are.

Indeed, as 1963 drew to a close, it was the timing of the assault that was to become Jimmy Goldsmith's prime interest. He was convinced that the financial climate was right to do so, but that it would be right only for a limited period. Other financial analysts might shake their heads in disagreement and advise caution, but he ignored them. But he still could not afford much. It was going to be a matter of buying small companies that were not doing all that well, and were going cheap. That way he might get a bargain, exploit the company's potential – particularly if it happened to own a household name – and build up his assets.

Once again France was to provide the inspiration for his commercial life. The success of his slimming business had given him an idea for his next move in England. He would go into slimming products there too. As the basis for the assault he used the English arm of his old Lanord company, which had become part of Gustin-Milical in France, to buy shares in England. He purchased more than 60,000 shares in the small British public company Procea Products, which was responsible for the slimming breads which had just begun to make their appearance in Britain: Procea and Nutrex. The company made the essential ingredients in a factory on the Slough bypass at Colnbrook. It was not a very promising prospect. Procea was rather run down, and in the four years since it had become a public company its performance had been "uninspiring" according to the *Financial Times*. But when he joined the board of directors, in the middle of January 1964, the newspaper added approvingly, "This 20 per cent holding, which ought to make Mr Goldsmith the principal shareholder, puts him in a strong position to inject some health and energy into the business."

Suddenly Jimmy Goldsmith was back in England, and now he was in a hurry. The frustrations of the past were behind him, and there was nothing to distract him. As Sir Alec Douglas-Home prepared to contest his first general election as Conservative Prime Minister – his party had held power for thirteen years – Jimmy Goldsmith set out to conquer British industry. Procea Products was not the only company he was interested in.

The difficulty was that he did not have enough money to accomplish everything he wanted to, as quickly as he was sure he needed to. To find it he went to see one of England's most famous, but also most elusive financial geniuses, Sir Isaac Wolfson, founder and chairman of Great Universal Stores. Then in his late sixties

Wolfson was still extremely active, and was more than prepared to consider lending an adventurous young businessman a little money when he needed it, provided the young man was prepared to pay him a distinctly advantageous rate of interest in return. Jimmy Goldsmith can still remember vividly going to see Wolfson, to whom he had been introduced by Charles Clore, in his flat in Portland Place not far from Regent's Park.

"Isaac Wolfson was an old-fashioned money lender," Goldsmith recalls, "and he couldn't sleep at night. So after he woke up at four o'clock in the morning he used to like to be busy. But the only way he could get anybody to come and see him at that time in the morning was if they really needed money. Those in the direst trouble used to have to go at five o'clock, but those in the least did not have to be there until nine. I was, of course, always there at five. But when I came out at 5.45 it was usually Roy Thomson coming in behind me." Jimmy Goldsmith did not object in the least to the time, or what he calls the "usurious" rates of interest: "The fact that he took extra interest was absolutely right because he took extra risk. There was nothing wrong with it at all. Isaac Wolfson used to lend me money when nobody else would, and I was extremely grateful to him for doing so."

With the help of Sir Isaac Wolfson's money Jimmy Goldsmith forged ahead in England, keeping up the momentum of acquisitions. In March 1964 he bought shares in the ailing chocolate company Carson's of Bristol, which put Harvey's Bristol Cream sherry and other liqueurs into chocolates, and he became its chairman. By April 1964, when Harold Wilson had become the first socialist Prime Minister in Britain since 1951, Jimmy Goldsmith had also become the majority shareholder in Procea Products, after a brief battle for control with the firm's seventy-two-year-old chairman Dr Douglas Kent-Jones. In October 1964 he started to buy shares in the old established biscuit firm Carrs of Carlisle, as well as in the famous sweet makers J. A. & P. Holland, renowned for glueing up the teeth of generations of English schoolchildren with "Walter's Palm Toffee". After a fight with the catering and grocery company Joe Lyons for Carrs, and a bitter disagreement between the board of directors and the surviving members of the Holland family, Jimmy Goldsmith got control of both companies. But he did not stop there.

As soon as the first wave of the invasion was completed Jimmy Goldsmith decided to put all his new companies into a single holding company in London, and thereby consolidate his British activities. Significantly, he decided to call his new, principal, company Cavenham Foods, in memory of his grandfather's estate in Suffolk. He briefly even considered changing his name by deed poll to Goldschmidt, but, finally, decided against it. He preferred to sound English rather than German.

By the beginning of 1965 the *Sunday Times* was reporting with some interest that the merchant bankers Keyser Ullman "were working on a scheme to consolidate the British interests of Mr 'Jimmy' Goldsmith, the slightly enigmatic figure who has surprised the Stock Market in the past year with a succession of bids and deals". The commando force had stormed the beach.

No sooner had they done so than Jimmy Goldsmith offered to buy out all the shares that he did not own in Carson's chocolates and Holland's toffees, and he also bought Elizabeth Shaw's mint chocolates to add to his assortment of confectionery companies.

In their formal offer to the shareholders of the existing companies in July 1965, Cavenham Foods' directors, and their chairman Jimmy Goldsmith, emphasized "the ample scope for reorganization" in the new group, and explained that their company would have an annual turnover of £27.5 million (with £11 million from manufacturing confectionery, biscuits, groceries and bread ingredients, £7.75 million from wholesaling tobacco, £7.25 million from wholesaling confectionery, and £1.5 million from paper interests). The group had eleven food factories and six paper and allied products factories at present, the directors explained, but they planned to concentrate operations in seven food factories and four paper factories. The only cloud on the horizon was the profit forecast – just £215,000, less than one per cent of turnover.

But the *Sunday Times* for one was impressed. "Cavenham Foods, the new bakery and confectionery group which will result from the merger of the James Goldsmith controlled food companies, looks like becoming one of the most interesting shares on the Stock Exchange," it commented, calling it "the Instant Company", and complimenting its founder on "an exceptionally strong team of comparatively young men".

One of these young men was Jack Greenhalgh, a marketing man from Procter & Gamble, who had worked in frozen foods. He described his new employer then as "just about the most dynamic, most intelligent person I'd ever met and I thought he was going to be a great success. I wanted to be a part of it. I also thought it was going to be a lot of fun." Jimmy Goldsmith and Greenhalgh were photographed together beaming in the newspaper that his friend and fellow borrower Roy Thomson would own within two years.

On 6 August 1965 the mergers that brought Cavenham Foods into existence were complete, and Jimmy Goldsmith set about in earnest the task of sorting out the fifty-one active companies that made up his group. He explained to his staff and shareholders that Cavenham was to be a company manufacturing food and wholesaling confectionery and tobacco "and that any activities which were incompatible with this purpose would be sold or closed". It did not take him long to begin to sell off those parts of the new Cavenham that did not fit into his plans. Within a matter of weeks he had disposed of some of the printing and paper interests. He then reorganized Cavenham into four operating divisions, Bakery, Confectionery, Grocery and Wholesaling, and gave each a general manager and board of directors. To back them up he provided two centralized service divisions, Distribution and Export, and a tiny headquarters staff, which he would run. It was still the philosophy of the commando unit, and he was still leading from the front.

Every weekend he returned to Paris to see Ginette and the children. She was not anxious to return to London, the experience of her earlier expedition in 1960 was still too fresh in her mind, and she preferred the habits and the friendships of the city in which she had grown up. Besides, she also knew that when her husband was not working he was unlikely to be sitting at home contentedly playing with his children; he would usually rather be out.

As restless as ever, Jimmy Goldsmith would pace up and down at home or in his office, grabbing newspapers from the table, or profit and loss reports from his surprised staff and tearing them up after he had read them. In the canteens of his factories in Bristol or Slough he would seize his lunch, sit down beside one of his employees and say suddenly, "I'm Jimmy Goldsmith. What do you do?"

Slightly bewildered, the employee would reply, "Well I'm in the Accounts department," and before he could say another word Goldsmith would ask, "Oh really, and how's the money coming in?" If the answer was "Not frightfully well, you see we've got this slight problem . . ." the division's general manager or sales manager would receive a note that same afternoon saying, "I hear there is a slight problem in collecting our debts." The Cavenham managers came to call it "Jimmy Goldsmith's creative nosiness", and it was a style he was never to abandon.

For all his energetic determination and his nosiness, however, the development of Cavenham did not go precisely according to plan. For a start, modernizing the Carson's factory in Bristol took longer and cost more than the company had predicted, and then profits did not leap up quite as quickly as the *Sunday Times*, and others, had expected. By the middle of 1965 he was warning the shareholders of Carson's chocolates that "the reorganization which will follow will inevitably be a lengthy and expensive operation" and he went on to explain "the material benefits are unlikely to be realized in the immediate future". He even added, "We do not hope for substantial recovery in 1965 and we are looking to 1966 as being the year for a proper return on the capital employed on the Group turnover."

In fact, by the end of 1965 Cavenham Foods was operating at a trading profit in everything except Carson's chocolates. It supplied 3 per cent of the bread eaten in Britain, and 15 per cent of the toffees. It may not have been quite the elegant business that his cousins the Rothschilds might have relished, but a bridgehead in England had been established. Now he intended to capitalize on it.

Life was still not all work, however. Indeed, while he was developing Cavenham Jimmy Goldsmith had found another new interest in England. In the late summer of 1964, he embarked on an affair with another beautiful and aristocratic young Englishwoman, a relationship which lasted far longer than even he might have expected.

Lady Annabel Birley had known Jimmy Goldsmith slightly for a long time. Her husband Mark had been one of his contemporaries at Eton, and John Aspinall's Clermont Club was above her husband's nightclub, Annabel's, named in her honour. In fact, on the night of the club's spectacular opening party in March 1963 Annabel Birley had watched Jimmy Goldsmith's romance with her old friend Sally Crichton-Stuart start up again, temporarily. And three months later she had wiped away a few of her friend's tears as it came to an end again. But, even so, Annabel Birley had not paid all that much attention to Jimmy Goldsmith. "He wasn't really my type," she was to tell her friends later, "I thought he was a bit jet-setty." Besides, she had a great many other things on her mind. For a start there were her three children, Rupert, Robin and Jane, all of whom were under ten; and there was also her relationship with her husband Mark, whom she had married ten years before after "coming out" as débutante in the summer of 1952. His life and hers were no longer quite as close as they had been. She was busy during the day with her children, and he now worked every night, coming home to their house, Pelham Cottage in South Kensington, in the early hours of the morning to sleep for part of the following day. When he had been in advertising, or working in his leather and silk shop off Bond Street their life together had been a good deal easier. Annabel and Mark Birley had paid a price for his success.

Now twenty-nine, tall and ash blonde, with strong features, Annabel Birley was a Londonderry, Lady Annabel Vane-Tempest-Stewart, the second daughter and third child of the 8th Marquis. Her grandmother, Lady Londonderry, had been one of the most famous hostesses in England in the 1920s and 1930s, entertaining the King and Queen as well as the Prime Minister of the day at her house at 101 Park Street near the foot of Park Lane. Her father had inherited the family estates in Cleveland, not far south of Newcastle-upon-Tyne and in Ireland, shortly after the war. A place in the world was hers by the simple fact of birth. But even if that had not been the case Annabel Birley would still have made a mark. She was as fiercely independent as the Londonderrys had always been, capable not only of knowing her own mind, but also translating her thoughts into action.

Annabel Birley may not have had quite the perfect porcelain beauty of Sally Crichton-Stuart, but there was more rebellion, and more passion in her eyes. Certainly the streak of her Irish temper flashed in the candlelight at dinner. She had not slipped into the mindless circuit of modelling, Caribbean holidays and the pursuit of a respectable, and aristocratic, husband that so many of her débutante friends had chosen. After she and Lady Carey Coke, daughter of the Earl of Leicester, had been given the grandest ball of the 1952 débutante season by her grandmother, which attracted a crowd of more than 2,000 to see the new Queen Elizabeth II attend her first private engagement after her father's death, Lady Annabel Stewart had decided to become a journalist. With her father's help she had found herself a job on Lord Rothermere's *Daily Mail*; and was about to take it, until, quite suddenly, she fell in love with Mark Birley.

Since her marriage at the age of nineteen, in March 1954, the attractions of the handsome young advertising man and entrepreneur had begun to fade slightly. She was still a strikingly beautiful young woman, whom many men admired from afar – but the demands of her husband's new nightclub had seen the excitement of her life wane steadily.

So it was not entirely a surprise that, in the summer of 1964, Lady Annabel Birley began to take more and more of an interest in Jimmy Goldsmith. Although she knew only too well that she would not be the first to fall for the flamboyant young man, she was fascinated by him.

Annabel Birley stood up to him, and he adored it. The more she argued, the more he seemed to like it, and the more intrigued she became. The more he tried to dominate her, the more she rebelled, until she thought she saw a vulnerability and a tenderness that many others had missed beneath the brashness and bluster. By the end of August 1964, Jimmy Goldsmith and Annabel Birley had become lovers, and for the next year they conducted their affair in the discreet surroundings of his suite at the Ritz Hotel.

10

Houdini or the Master Builder?

By the autumn of 1965, with a mixture of resourcefulness, financial legerdemain, luck and determination, Jimmy Goldsmith had assembled a group with a turnover of nearly £30 million a year (some £150 million or $210 million a year at today's prices), almost 6,000 employees and assets of more than £7 million. Before anyone in the City of London had noticed it, the commando force he had led ashore just twenty-one months earlier had seized an odd assortment of companies, including one or two of the household names that he had set his heart on, and moulded them into Cavenham Foods. At thirty-two he had finally secured a firm bridgehead in Britain, even if it was made up of "badly managed or loss-making companies", as he described them himself. But he could not stop there. Speed was still the essence of his strategy; each acquisition had to be turned rapidly to his advantage to finance the next attack. He could not afford to stand still. Ambition was one thing, achievement quite another. Now the invasion had to be made to work. Things did not go precisely according to plan.

In November 1965 Jimmy Goldsmith hit his first major obstacle in the unlikely form of a Birmingham-based wholesale tobacco and confectionery group called Singleton and Cole, which boasted an annual turnover of about £22 million. He had decided it was to be the next target for a takeover, and before he began negotiations with the company itself he had taken the precaution of buying a 20 per cent holding from one of the City of London's most conspicuously successful young men, Jim Slater of Slater Walker Securities, a thirty-six-year-old former accountant, who had launched into investment banking with considerable success. Jim Slater was as tall as

Jimmy Goldsmith, but nowhere near as flamboyant or cosmopolitan. Nevertheless, the two men were to become close friends, and shortly after they first met, in the autumn of 1965, Jim Slater sold him his holdings in Singleton and Cole.

On the surface there was nothing wrong with the idea. Initially Jimmy Goldsmith simply wanted to merge his wholesaling division with Singleton's division to create a new, larger, wholesaling division for his Cavenham group of companies. In the last weeks of 1965 he began talks with the chairman of Singleton and Cole, George Waddington, to see if he could bring it about.

The negotiations did not start auspiciously. On his first visit to Birmingham Jimmy Goldsmith hired a car to drive from London – only to have it break down on the M1 motorway. In the fury that always gripped him when he encountered recalcitrant inanimate objects, he got out and kicked it. When he finally arrived it was not all that much easier. He was bewildered by the men who were running the wholesaling company that he was trying to merge with. "All they seem to want to talk about is something called Aston Villa," he told his colleagues in Cavenham when he got back to London. Some of the Cavenham men were pleased to hear it, they did not share their young chairman's enthusiasm in the first place. "There's nothing to stop you buying companies, Jimmy, but can you run them?", more than one of his executives asked him. But Jimmy Goldsmith plunged ahead. The more he did so the more complex his problems became.

For a start he encountered the first major opposition in his relentless desire to expand. Joe Lyons may have fought him over Carrs of Carlisle, and the Holland family over J. A. & P. Holland, but this time the opposition was much more formidable. Late in April 1966, just as he thought he had reached an agreement for a merger, Singleton and Cole suddenly appointed the merchant bankers S. G. Warburg to advise them and a full-scale takeover battle developed. In a rage he demanded that the chairman and deputy chairman of Cavenham Foods, he and Alexis de Gunzburg, should be appointed to the Singleton and Cole board of directors. Singleton's chairman responded crisply in a letter to his shareholders, saying that the merger talks had not come to anything, "because Cavenham wanted to get control of S & C without any cash payment". He turned down completely the suggestion that Singleton and Cole should have either of the Cavenham men on its board of directors. Jimmy Goldsmith was furious. "It's a fine old company," he explained to the *Observer*, "but its recent profit record leaves much to be desired."

The *Sunday Times* neatly summed up the battle by suggesting: "Singletons argue that if Goldsmith wants the business he must pay for it – in cash or in underwritten paper. Goldsmith in turn says he won't pay cash because the shares are too high, buoyed up by his own market dealings. Moreover he wants Singleton to retain its quote for future takeovers." To the traditional City of London that may have looked an unorthodox manoeuvre, but it was very much Jimmy Goldsmith's style. He liked to do deals that way and he still did not have much money.

By the end of April George Waddington, who was later to become a friend, was circularizing the Singleton and Cole shareholders again, in even more forthright terms. This time he attacked every aspect of Cavenham's performance, particularly its profits. "I think I can sum up your directors' views by saying that agreement to the Cavenham proposal would be equivalent to exchanging the substance of Singleton and Cole for the shadow of Cavenham", and he called on his opponent to "come out into the open and make a realistic offer for the whole of the share capital". After the letter was published few men in the City of London believed that the proposed takeover would ever come about. But, as many were to do in the future, they underestimated the chairman of Cavenham Foods' determination and tenacity when it came to a fight.

Within a week of Waddington's attack on Cavenham's record, and with the help of his merchant bankers Keyser Ullman, Jimmy Goldsmith had offered two Cavenham shares for every one of Singleton and Cole's. The new offer valued the capital of the Birmingham-based company at some £1.4 million, and it was decisive. A fortnight later the Singleton and Cole board of directors capitulated and recommended the revised Cavenham offer to their shareholders. The battle was over, but Jimmy Goldsmith's problems had only just begun. Singleton and Cole was to prove an indigestible acquisition for the new predator in the British food industry.

Nevertheless, by July 1966, with Singletons assimilated into his group and just two and a half years after he had quietly bought his first shareholding in Procea, Jimmy Goldsmith was announcing to the shareholders of Cavenham Foods, in his chairman's statement, that the company had restructured its management and started its drive to "make the most of our household names". It disclosed that he was now responsible for a group whose sales amounted to more than £46 million a year and which made everything from sugar mice to the royal family's favourite table water biscuits. Certainly there were some highlights in his report. The trading profits of the Bakery division had doubled since Procea and Slimcea had been advertised on television; while a similar technique with Carrs Table Water biscuits had also meant that sales had doubled.

But that was almost the only good news. The Confectionery division's reorganization and modernization was not progressing as fast as had been hoped – "it was a disaster" in the words of one executive at the time. The new wholesaling division – which now included Singleton and Cole – "was just about as bad"; even the company's annual report described it as "barely profitable". Cavenham Foods as a whole could only boast a trading profit of £582,000, a little over one per cent of its sales.

For once Jimmy Goldsmith's timing had been wrong. No sooner had he taken over Singleton and Cole than the Labour government announced the introduction of Selective Employment Tax, which would cost Cavenham's newly expanded Wholesaling division £50,000 in its first year, and £90,000 in a full financial year.

Cavenham Foods looked strong enough on paper, with its vast sales and range of products and services, but in reality it was a disparate amalgam of companies lacking any true sense of direction. And from the summer of 1966 it presented its small board of directors with a series of particularly intractable problems. The group still had very little money itself, and it was held together by the energy and expertise of a comparatively small management team, led by Goldsmith as chairman and joint managing director, and Alexis de Gunzburg as deputy chairman, Jack Greenhalgh as the other joint managing director, and the finance director, Lionel Ross.

There was no doubt that Jimmy Goldsmith could buy and sell companies, but now he had to prove that he could actually run them. Certainly Cavenham's Confectionery division was a headache.

TOP: The new member of the Goldsmith dynasty: Jimmy Goldsmith as a baby with his mother and brother Teddy
ABOVE: Jimmy Goldsmith (left) aged three, again with his brother Teddy
LEFT: The gambling schoolboy: Jimmy Goldsmith at Eton before he won £8,000 on a three-horse accumulator

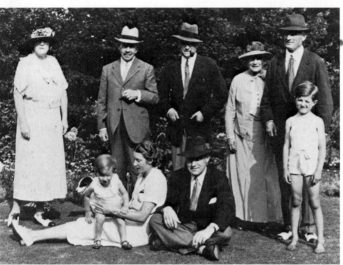

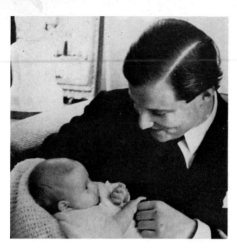

OPPOSITE ABOVE: Isabel Goldsmith at her wedding in France to Baron Arnaud de Rosnay in 1973
OPPOSITE BELOW: The French family Goldsmith: Manes (left), Madame Ginette Goldsmith (second from left), Jimmy Goldsmith and their daughter Alix (right) on holiday in Gstaad

LEFT: The case of the kidnapped heiress: Jimmy Goldsmith with little Isabel after he had won the right to her custody in September 1954
BELOW: The worry of 1957 costs Jimmy Goldsmith his hair: with Ginette Lery, who became his second wife in 1962

ABOVE: Friends who liked to 'make whoopee': John Aspinall and his first wife Jayne with their pet monkey 'Dead Loss' in January 1958, shortly after John Aspinall and a number of others were charged with being found in a Paddington flat alleged to be a 'common gaming house'

LEFT: John Aspinall with his mother, Lady Osborne, who was also charged. All were found not guilty

ABOVE: Other friends in England and France: Selim Zilkha (left) and Jim Slater (right) play backgammon in Scotland as Jimmy Goldsmith looks on
RIGHT: Madame Gilberte Beaux, 'the best banker in France', who joined Jimmy Goldsmith in 1968

LEFT: A career in British politics, or just influence? Jimmy Goldsmith and Lord Ryder, then chairman of the National Enterprise Board, leaving Downing Street after lunch with the Labour Prime Minister Harold Wilson on 25 March 1975

BELOW: Receiving an award as 'Communicator of the Year' from Lord Whitelaw, the Conservative Deputy Prime Minister, in 1980

Nothing anyone could do seemed to help – white sugar mice were not about to become his saviour, and Singleton and Cole had definitely not turned out to be the magnificent addition he had hoped.

In a concerted attempt to sort things out quickly, Jimmy Goldsmith did exactly what he was best at: a series of deals. The first was to go into partnership with the French public company Source Perrier, in which Alexis de Gunzburg was a director and major shareholder, to develop their confectionery interests together. The deal laid the foundation for a merger of the confectionery interests of both groups, by the formation of new companies in both Britain and France in which both Cavenham and Perrier would be equal partners. The publicly declared aim was to "take advantage of the growing confectionery market in the European Common Market", but that was a longish way off. The short-term advantage of the deal was to dissipate some of the Confectionery division's losses, and keep Cavenham Foods' share price up. But that was certainly not enough to sustain the company for very long, because it failed to provide the one commodity that Jimmy Goldsmith still lacked more than any other – money.

Although he reached the same agreement in principle for Carrs Table Water biscuits with the Harrell Corporation of Westport, Connecticut, that he had for confectionery with Perrier, in fact it was never implemented. Once again it was more spectacular window-dressing than the key to Cavenham's financial salvation. Profits would come, but they were still some way off. Something had to be done quickly.

Cavenham had about half the market for slimming breads in Britain, with sales of about £10 million a year, but the competition was hotting up, and it was getting more intense in wholesaling too, where the government's decision to end Retail Price Maintenance had meant a growth in "cash and carry" operations. But the reorganization of Singleton and Cole was accounting for most of Cavenham's borrowing from the bank.

There was no alternative. Something had to be sold. The only question was what, and to whom.

The answer that presented itself came as a surprise to almost everyone, including Jimmy Goldsmith. Though he had hardly noticed it, among Singleton and Cole's interests were two small, but intensely profitable, snuff companies. Even Jim Slater had not noticed them. If he had done so he might not have sold his 20 per cent interest. Certainly he was later to call them "the jewel in the company's crown". One reason was that they offered exceptionally high profits to their owners. Snuff can be made from almost any kind of tobacco waste, and sold at an unexpectedly high profit, particularly if it is flavoured. As soon as he realized it, Jimmy Goldsmith looked around for someone to buy the snuff companies. It did not prove easy. There was hardly anyone in England who was interested, so he tried the United States, and came across the Conwood Corporation of Memphis in Tennessee. And Conwood in turn introduced him to a man who was to become one of his closest business associates, John Burton Tigrett.

Exceptionally shrewd, but with a deceptively relaxed manner, Tigrett had been a successful businessman in his own right in the southern states of America, but at the age of fifty-three had decided to transform his life after the sudden and unexpected death of two of his three sons. He had decided to set himself up as a consultant to the men whom he knew in business in the United States, and had approached the legendary oil men Dr Armand Hammer of Occidental Petroleum and Paul Getty of Getty Oil, as well as Martin Conwood of the Conwood Corporation in his home town of Memphis, to see if he could act for them in Europe. All three took up his offer, and Conwood even asked him to look into the possibilities of Jimmy Goldsmith's snuff companies, "because I had been looking into some other snuff businesses for them".

The slow-talking Tigrett travelled across the Atlantic to see Jimmy Goldsmith, and went to Cavenham's offices at Colnbrook, not far from London's Heathrow airport. Tigrett was not all that impressed by what he saw. "The offices looked a bit run down," he remembers. "I told them they should move." But he was very impressed indeed by the eager young man who came out to meet him. "He seemed to know every figure in the business by heart, and I figured he must have spent the last week rehearsing them. It wasn't till later that I realized he hadn't."

Jimmy Goldsmith was clearly so anxious to sell his snuff companies that Tigrett knew he would have no difficulty in doing a deal when he wanted to. But the more he talked to him, the more fascinated he became.

The following Sunday morning the two men went for a walk in Regent's Park and Tigrett told Jimmy Goldsmith: "I'm going to buy your snuff companies, but I'm only going to buy half."

Jimmy Goldsmith's face fell. "Why?"

"Because you and I are going to Switzerland to raise the money to buy the other half. I know a few people in Switzerland."

Jimmy Goldsmith still looked a little confused.

"That way Cavenham will have all the money it wants from the sale," Tigrett explained. "It will still own half the snuff companies, and, more important still, you and I will be partners."

"But why do you want to go into partnership with me?"

"Well, I'll tell you," Tigrett said slowly, "because you're the best financial mind I've ever come across, and I've met hundreds. I don't ever want to lose you."

By the time the two men had completed their walk across the park, they had become partners, and they have remained so ever since. To this day few other people have as much influence with Jimmy Goldsmith as Tigrett. Tigrett took Jimmy Goldsmith and Alexis de Gunzburg to Switzerland to raise money for the purchase of their own snuff companies, and advised Conwood Corporation in the United States to buy into Cavenham's snuff companies. The sale raised more than £800,000 which Cavenham Foods badly needed, and gave their snuff products outlets in the United States.

As John Tigrett was to remind him for many years to come, "The thing about us, Jimmy, is that we've never had any money." It was an exaggeration. Neither man could honestly be called conventionally poor, but both knew that every other businessman with ambitions they came across was probably richer than they were. That did not matter in the least, it made them try that little harder to grab a firm foothold in the financial world, to keep on fighting. Jimmy Goldsmith was not about to give up now. He was more intent than ever on proving that he could overcome any obstacle to do so.

Indeed, as the affairs of Cavenham Foods began to absorb more and more of his time and energy, Jimmy Goldsmith decided that he could not go on living at the Ritz. He needed a London base again. So as 1965 came to an end, he rented another house in

Regent's Park, and encouraged Ginette to bring the children over to London to stay with him. He was still having an affair with Lady Annabel Birley, but he wanted his family with him nevertheless.

Ginette was still not keen to return to London. Her English was not particularly good, and she preferred the French way of life. Besides, she knew that her young husband was not likely to spend his evenings at home playing with his children. He was a doting father, certainly, and brought them magnificent presents, but he was usually too busy doing something else to spend very much time with them. But Jimmy Goldsmith insisted and she gave in. Manes, Alix and Isabel Goldsmith arrived in England and Annabel Birley helped to find schools for the eldest of Jimmy Goldsmith's children.

But the arrival of his wife and children at their new home in Regent's Park could not conceal the fact that Cavenham was not going according to plan. As Jimmy Goldsmith admits now, "When I went into business again in England, I set down all my ideas in an edition of 'Cavenham News', the house newspaper, and almost every single idea I put down turned out to be wrong. Yet I had managed to assemble around me an outstanding group of executives, and very quickly I started to change. In the hard light of reality we had to." The experience was to convince Jimmy Goldsmith of an adage that he would repeat to his friends for years to come: "How can you get it right the first time? There are too many variables. It's only by changing that you discover what is right."

The hard light of reality was proving exceptionally bright. It was becoming all too clear that Cavenham was not going to meet any of the forecasts it had made to its shareholders. There was even a danger of it going broke. Reluctantly, Roland Franklin, who still worked for the merchant bank Keyser Ullman but had also become a director of Cavenham, came to the conclusion that something drastic was called for. The directors had to inject £500,000 into the company if it was going to survive. In practice that meant that Jimmy Goldsmith and Alexis de Gunzburg, who were by far the biggest shareholders in the company – with more than five million shares between them – would have to find the extra money.

Jimmy Goldsmith did not have £500,000, he did not even have £50,000. Successful French businessman he may have been, but he was not in the class of his cousin Alexis. Gustin-Milical was bringing in a profit of about £120,000 a year (some £600,000 at 1986 prices), but he had an expensive lifestyle to support. There was no family inheritance in trust for him, no shares from the death of his uncle Teddy in England in 1951, or his father's hotel chain. After a great deal of heart-searching, Jimmy Goldsmith and Alexis de Gunzburg agreed to try and find £500,000, and they decided it would be best to make it an outright "gift" to Cavenham. That way the money would boost the assets of the company, and help to keep the share price up. Jimmy Goldsmith arranged for Gustin-Milical to borrow the money in France, as Alexis de Gunzburg was also a director, and his cousin also had to put up certain extra guarantees. It was a desperate measure, and hardly the style of a man who would later be called a "financial genius", but there was no alternative.

Worse, just as the crisis over Cavenham deepened in the first months of 1967, so Major Frank Goldsmith's health finally began to fail. Not that his younger son had relied on his father's advice, any more than he had relied on his money, but he had always been exceptionally close to the elderly man of just under six foot, who never took very much interest in his clothes but always seemed to be enjoying himself.

The shock was all the greater therefore, when on 14 February 1967, Major Frank Goldsmith died in Paris. He was eighty-eight. In its obituary *The Times* commented: "'Monsieur le Major', as he was always known, was probably the leading figure in the French hotel world in the inter-war period, and certainly the most popular." His son Jimmy was distraught. Perhaps more than any other single individual in his life, his father had been his inspiration. Two decades after his father's death, he still says, "I think a lot of what I've done, I have done to satisfy my father, because it would have amused him. I often wish he were alive today to see what I've accomplished."

Finally, with the help of the loan raised by Gustin-Milical he managed to buy a little time for Cavenham. Enough time certainly to do what had become increasingly obvious he had to do: sell off the intractable Singleton and Cole, which he had gone to such trouble to acquire. The gift of £500,000 may have saved his company, but it had not eradicated its difficulties.

When the company issued an interim report to its shareholders in October 1967 he explained: "For the fifty-two weeks ended 1 April 1967, Cavenham made a trading loss, including reorganization expenditure, of £947,000," but added "the results for the first thirty-two weeks of the current year demonstrate that the reorganization has to a large measure been completed and is beginning to produce the desired effects." Cavenham had survived, but it had been an exceptionally narrow squeak.

Indeed, its troubles were not at an end. The company's assets may have been inflated by the "gift" of £500,000, but the auditors were expressing some reservations about the price paid for some of its assortment of companies. When they came to produce the accounts for the year ending March 1968 they noted: "The directors state that, in their opinion, the amount of £949,049 attributed to goodwill in the consolidated balance sheet, by virtue of their valuation of the holding company's investment in subsidiaries, is justified by the future prospects of the group. This is a question on which we do not feel able to express an opinion."

Once again some influential members of the City of London wondered whether their suspicions that Cavenham was a company with an uncertain past, and an even less certain future, were not true. In the years to come the "qualification" of the accounts was to become one of the ghosts that would haunt Jimmy Goldsmith's progress. The memory annoys him still. "Much has been made over the years about the auditors' qualification. But it was not a question of the auditors being happy or unhappy about the board's decision. There are qualifications every year to the accounts of many leading companies in Britain. The qualification to the Cavenham accounts was because there was a figure for goodwill in the balance sheet, because we paid a premium over net assets for Procea. As the group was not making money, it was difficult to assess the value of goodwill. Auditors look to the past and not to the future. We thought the company would become profitable – which it did."

Jimmy Goldsmith knew he had to sell the troublesome Singleton and Cole as quickly as possible. It took a little longer than he might have hoped, but by the summer of 1968 he had managed it. The company's northern division was sold to Robert Sinclair and Company, part of the Imperial Group of companies; the Midlands and what few interests it had in the south of England to Palmer and

Harvey, another wholesaler; and the final section – a small Grimsby sweet warehouse – to P. Panto confectionery. Each time Jimmy Goldsmith adopted the tactic he had refined over the past few years. He never approached the management team, but always went directly to the company's chairman. Some of his colleagues were privately convinced that if he had gone to the managing directors in any of the three companies, he might not have been able to sell.

In his annual report to shareholders he explained the decision to sell Singleton and Cole. "We took this decision because our investment in wholesaling of approximately £2.1 million, or about half our capital and reserves, was not profitable." He went on to blame some of their difficulties on the Labour government's policies, adding "the industry itself was becoming progressively more difficult as a result of increased Selective Employment Tax; the deliberate squeezing of distributive margins as recommended by the Prices and Incomes Board; and the ending of retail price maintenance in both confectionery and tobacco." That was true, but it somewhat overlooked the fact that Cavenham Foods had found its expanded wholesaling division exceptionally difficult to run.

Nevertheless the sale meant that by the end of 1968 Cavenham had £1.5 million more in assets than in liabilities, and had just two manufacturing divisions, Slimming Foods and Grocery, and the three joint ventures – Cavenham Confectionery with Perrier in England, Compagnie Française de Confiserie in confectionery with Perrier in France, and Conwood SA, the snuff company in partnership with Conwood of Memphis. Not all of them were doing badly. Procea, Slimcea and Nutrex, for example, accounted for more than half the £20 million a year market for low-calorie bread in Britain, and 3 per cent of all the bread sold, and profits had more than doubled, from £1.1 million in 1965 to £2.4 million in 1968. But the Grocery division was struggling, and the Confectionery company, even though it was in partnership with Perrier, was a mess. Altogether the company was not in the most inspiring shape. In less than three years Cavenham had shrunk from fifty-one companies to fewer than eight.

Nevertheless there was one tiny bright spot on the otherwise gloomy horizon. Hidden in J. A. & P. Holland were a tiny chain of just twenty-two newsagents, confectioners and tobacconists in

Liverpool and Sheffield, which traded under the name of Hayes Lyon. Just as the snuff companies were to introduce Jimmy Goldsmith to one man who was to become a central part of his business life, John Tigrett, so the shops were to introduce him to another. To run this small chain Cavenham had recruited a former athlete, Jim Wood, who had been manager of a Co-operative store in Liverpool. In a matter of weeks he had turned their substantial losses into trading profits – "Mainly by cutting down the rate of theft at the start. People were walking out with stuff in armfuls", one colleague remembers. Those shops were to form the basis of what would become the largest section of Cavenham's business within three years.

Never keen to overlook an opportunity, Jimmy Goldsmith bought Jim Wood a further sixty shops from the official receiver, which had come on to the market after the suicide of their owner. After selling eleven of them to recoup his small purchase price, he proceeded to hand them over to Wood, thereby creating a chain of seventy-one shops. They were small, unfashionable and unlikely, but they rapidly brought Cavenham a steady, and increasing, supply of its most elusive commodity: hard cash. For while the manufacturing companies had to wait for their customers to pay their bills, the shopkeeper took his money over the counter and kept his suppliers waiting for their money. For a man who had learnt in 1957 how important it was to have a supply of money to ensure the future of a business, that was one of the most significant attractions of Cavenham Foods' newly formed Retail division.

Shops were to be the turning point in Cavenham's fortunes. Procea, Slimcea and the rest continued to do well, and the reorganization of the Confectionery division was finally completed, but it was Jim Wood's chain of retail shops that was to lead Jimmy Goldsmith's disparate group of companies into substantial profit and, by doing so, make Cavenham strong enough to expand in the way Jimmy Goldsmith had always wanted it to. The good fortune of the two snuff companies and the tiny chain of shops was significantly to help Jimmy Goldsmith's management team turn Cavenham round.

By the summer of 1969 he was able to tell his shareholders that "your Company today consists of three profitable and growing trading divisions, a 50 per cent interest in a substantial international and confectionery group, and considerable surplus cash. All the trading divisions did appreciably better than forecast in the last annual report." After scrambling up a slurry of problems, some of which threatened to bury him completely, he could now say confidently: "Your Company is now ready to expand both by internal growth and by acquisition." Finally, the commando force which he had brought ashore in 1964 had sorted out what exactly it was they should be doing; but it had taken some time.

The Cavenham team knew their chairman's strengths, and weaknesses. "Jimmy wasn't terribly good at actually running companies," Greenhalgh explains, "but he was absolutely superb at choosing a team and letting them get on with it. And then he was superb at establishing the strategies for the companies and handling the financial engineering." Every member of Cavenham's senior management believed that their chairman was capable of making the most of whatever they could provide for him in the way of profit.

The effort cost Jimmy Goldsmith dearly. The need to sort out Cavenham's problems had made him more than usually aloof at home in Regent's Park, and Ginette and the children had begun to feel it. It had also become increasingly clear that his old habits of disappearing for the weekend had not changed. He still had interests in France, and he would go to see them whenever time allowed. One person who went with him from time to time was Lady Annabel Birley. For Madame Ginette Goldsmith it was an ironic situation. A woman who would always rather have been in Paris, found herself in London with her children, while her husband was in Paris with someone else. Gradually the strain became too much and she came to the conclusion that she would be far happier in her own city again, rather than struggling to enjoy London – and only seeing her husband from time to time. She knew very well that her husband would never neglect her, he had always been far too loyal for that, but she had decided she would prefer to return to Paris. In the first weeks of 1969 she began to look for a house there again. It was a great relief.

As the summer of 1969 progressed Ginette Goldsmith gratefully took Isabel and Alix back to Paris with her, and left Manes to stay in England to go to his father's old school, Millfield in Somerset. She had found a house on the left bank of the Seine, near the massive monument to Louis XIV and later Napoleon, Les Invalides. With its magnificent courtyard, and moulded ceilings, it had once belonged to the songwriter Cole Porter and had been named in honour of Louis XIV's brother who was known as "Monsieur Frère du Rois". Now it was to become Jimmy Goldsmith's permanent home in Paris, and it was destined to remain so. One of the ports of call in the captain's voyage had been permanently established, and Ginette Goldsmith was far from unhappy. It was still not the most conventional arrangement, but she had come to understand only too well the man she was married to.

For her part Lady Annabel Birley was equally philosophical. She was living in the small house in South Kensington that she had always lived in with her children, and her husband Mark was still there too. Her affair with Jimmy Goldsmith was known to her friends, but it had not appeared in the press. For the time being at least she could appear as she had always done, immensely attractive, organized and a good mother to her family. If she occasionally disappeared to Chester Terrace or Paris with the chairman of Cavenham Foods, it was nobody's business but her own.

Both Madame Ginette Goldsmith and Lady Annabel Birley knew that although the man they loved accepted in his business life, "If you're wrong, you change", in his private life that was one thing he was most unlikely to do.

11

The Turning Point

Jimmy Goldsmith may have spent the past half dozen years of his working life more active in England than in France, but he was still, indelibly, French. He may have gone to Eton, and spent some time in, if not at, Oxford, but he was still more a Parisian than a member of the English upper class. Extravagant and romantic, he saw nothing wrong in maintaining an English mistress while living happily with his family in France. It was the attitude of a man determined to live by his own code. Some men in the City of London might call him eccentric, but that was their mistake. It was to judge him by English standards rather than French ones.

"What does eccentric mean?" he asks now. "It means being outside the culture. In France the life I lead would not be considered all that eccentric, a little perhaps, but not very. In England it is regarded as very eccentric." Many men in England would forget that Jimmy Goldsmith could never share their attitude to life. His heritage, his upbringing, and his attitudes were distinctively European. Somehow he always seemed happiest speaking to his old friends in French.

Certainly, even if Jimmy Goldsmith's principal interest in the past few years had been building up Cavenham, that did not mean he had forgotten France, or Lanord and Gustin-Milical. The drive to remind the English that the Goldsmith family was not to be ignored may have been compelling, but he knew only too well that without his French companies it would not have been possible. Without them his position would have been distinctly perilous. For while Cavenham had struggled, Gustin-Milical had quietly gone from strength to strength – almost without his paying it any attention. England may have been where his most public ambitions lay, but France provided his strength. That was to remain one of the realities of Jimmy Goldsmith's career, and one that many of his competitors would overlook.

But if Jimmy Goldsmith had partly set out to restore his family's, and his father's, reputation in England, he certainly had no intention of neglecting it in France. After his father's death in February 1967 he set his heart on ensuring that the directors of his father's old company, Hôtels Réunis, should not forget the Goldsmiths. Monsieur le Major's son decided that they should have another Goldsmith on the board – him. The decision did not endear him to his father's old colleagues.

In 1967 the Société des Hôtels Réunis had come under the chairmanship of one of his father's old friends, the uncle of the future President of France, Valéry Giscard d'Estaing, and he tried everything he could to prevent the aggressive younger son of his old colleague from joining the board of his company. He and his fellow directors predicted gloomily that "he will only cause difficulties". Monsieur le Major had been a "valued colleague", the directors explained, but they wished to remain as they were for the present. The attitude only served to annoy Jimmy Goldsmith. It made him more determined than ever. There was not a great deal he could do at first, as his father had sold most of the shares he had owned in the company over the years to his fellow directors whenever he needed a little extra money, but when the Hôtels Réunis board decided to go to the Paris Bourse to finance the purchase of the freehold of the Carlton Hotel in Cannes, Jimmy Goldsmith seized his chance. He bought as many shares in the group as he could, until the size of his shareholding made it impossible for the directors to do anything but invite him to join the board. Reluctantly, they did so.

The tactic confirmed the opinion of the directors of Hôtels Réunis about Jimmy Goldsmith, especially as he then proceeded to use every opportunity at board meetings to tell them firmly that they had to adopt a policy of rapid expansion. Unimpressed, the board kept him firmly in his place, as a director but not the decisive force in the company. The more they did so, the angrier he became. No Goldsmith was to be ignored, least of all one in a company his father had helped to create.

Finally, early in 1968, desperate to provoke the board into action, Jimmy Goldsmith suggested a deal to each of his fellow directors. "I told them, 'Look, this is hopeless. Let's set a figure at which you are obliged either to sell me your shares or to buy my shares.' Then I set the price and gave them eight days to decide what they wanted to do." He hoped it would break the stalemate. It didn't.

The directors of Hôtels Réunis agreed to the plan. But after eight days they refused to do anything. In a rage he decided to begin negotiations to sell his shareholding to the Grand Metropolitan group of hotels, run by Max Joseph. And then he proposed to the board that they sell the entire company to Grand Metropolitan. About that, at least, every member of the board was agreed. It was the only way of breaking the stalemate, and they would be rid of the young man who seemed desperate to make them do things they did not want to do, even if it meant they lost control of the company. Towards the end of 1968, after a series of negotiations, Max Joseph took over Hôtels Réunis, and almost the only director to remain on its board was Jimmy Goldsmith, where he was to remain until 1981. But it was still a disappointment to him.

What few of his fellow directors on the Hôtel Réunis had grasped was that Jimmy Goldsmith was now responsible for the financial future of his entire family. Since his father's death his mother and brother had decided that he was to carry their financial hopes. He was to decide which investments should be made. He was to protect them all. He may have been barely thirty-five but the role suited him admirably; as he progressed towards middle age Jimmy Goldsmith saw himself even more firmly than he had done before as the leader of a tribe. He was perfectly prepared to acknowledge that fact formally by accepting responsibility for every member of his family.

In fact he had already proved conspicuously successful at sustaining his father's name, and his family's ambitions, in France. Not only had Gustin-Milical continued to expand in the slimming market, but he had decided to take over a small "shell" company in France and use it as a holding company for all his companies. Alexis de Gunzburg had discovered a company for sale, and although it did not look all that promising – it had formerly been an Algerian tram operator – it served Jimmy Goldsmith's purpose admirably.

At Christmas 1967 Jimmy Goldsmith bought Union de Transport et de Participations as a French holding company for all his interests, including Cavenham and Gustin-Milical; and he shortened its name to Union des Participations. Two months later, again partly at Alexis de Gunzburg's suggestion, he went on to buy the Société Générale Foncière, which also included a small bank in Paris. After finding partners in the Union Bank of Los Angeles, and the Central National Bank of Cleveland with John Tigrett's help, Jimmy Goldsmith and Alexis de Gunzburg then transformed the former Algerian tram company into Société Générale Occidentale, and named their new French bank, the Banque Occidentale. Almost before anyone had noticed, Jimmy Goldsmith had become a banker.

That meant that he would never again have to put up with an elderly banker telling him loftily, when he wanted to finance an acquisition: "Young man, you cannot do that."

"Why not?" Jimmy Goldsmith would ask.

"Because it is impossible."

"How do you know?"

"Because, Monsieur Goldsmith, I have been a banker for fifty years."

"I have been a banker for 500 years," Jimmy Goldsmith was in the habit of replying firmly, even though he neither looked nor acted like a banker.

Ironically, it was the woman who sold him Union des Participations and Société Générale Foncière who was to show him exactly what a good banker was capable of. Once again, almost by accident, Jimmy Goldsmith came across a particularly valuable asset hidden in one of his new companies. This time it was not two snuff companies, or a tiny chain of shops, but a small, demurely dressed Frenchwoman who talked faster and more ferociously than almost any man he had ever met. Madame Gilberte Beaux was to become one of the most important figures in Jimmy Goldsmith's financial life, but when he and John Tigrett first met her, in the basement restaurant of his father's hotel, the Scribe, he did not even know whether to hire her. She, together with Count Thierry de Clermont-Tonnerre, had been senior members of the staff of the Union Financière de Paris, and she had been responsible for selling off the parts. Inevitably the question had arisen: did he wish to take them over as well? Jimmy Goldsmith wanted to.

John Tigrett agreed, "I'd hire them right now. He's going to be a marvellous man to represent the bank, and she could just be the toughest white woman I've ever met." In the first months of 1968 Gilberte Beaux and Thierry de Clermont-Tonnerre both joined Union de Transports et de Participations.

Then just thirty-seven Gilberte Beaux had already been described as "the best banker in France". For the Paris-born daughter of a Corsican father and a French mother, who had started work in the Seligman Bank in Paris at sixteen with no academic qualifications to speak of, it was a remarkable tribute, but richly deserved. By the time she was twenty-three she had become one of Seligman's officers, and the same year had won a diploma in banking. Married to a half-Russian chemist fourteen years her senior, with whom she had a daughter, banking had become her passion. And in the next few years she was to convince her new employer of its charms and its possibilities. Though no one could ever have described Jimmy Goldsmith as a natural banker, Gilberte Beaux provided him with a unique understanding of its value and its strengths; and she was never, ever, to ask for any concessions for being a woman. Quite the opposite. If there were detailed negotiations to be conducted, she would conduct them. If there was an argument to be put forcefully she was never afraid of putting it. If money needed to be raised she raised it. She was to become his business counsellor and friend, even though she was the first to admit, "Jimmy does not like women very much. There is something of the misogynist about him." Even so he was to make her rich beyond the wildest dreams of her childhood.

"Jimmy is really everything *except* a banker," she explains now. "He is a wonderful financial mind, a kind of genius, but financial matters and banking are totally different. Banking is for little margins and little risk. A financial man takes bigger risks for bigger profits. It is exactly the opposite."

Jimmy Goldsmith agrees. "The whole of my belief about business is that if you take a risk there has to be the potential for reward at least as great as the risk, if not greater. But when banks risk £100 all they get is the interest on the money and their profit margin is about one per cent after tax and overheads. They're risking £100 to make £1 net profit and I think that's lousy business. If I take a £100 risk I want at least a £100 gain, not a £1 gain. Banks tell you 'We don't take risks', but they do, that's why almost every bank in the world would be bust if it had to pay all its debts."

Gilberte Beaux recalls that when she first met him in 1968 "Jimmy was applying almost exactly the same philosophy that he has applied ever since. He first tried to concentrate in a group all its activities – to give more leverage and more power. Then he always uses the same technique, which consists of selling off what in his mind is the weak parts and sticking with the other parts of the assets that he can make stronger and better, and which may or may not be saleable in the future."

By the middle of 1968 Jimmy Goldsmith and Alexis de Gunzburg had created the basis of Générale Occidentale with its holdings in Cavenham and Gustin-Milical. Now he wanted to dilute its control of Cavenham slightly, by expanding his English company by acquisition. As Gilberte Beaux explains, "Jimmy considers every morning that he has nothing. Every morning he believes he is only rich up to a point – the point at which his company has the ability to make growth and profits."

Jimmy Goldsmith had come to the conclusion that sensible acquisitions in England were essential for the future of all his companies. With the help of Jack Greenhalgh, he had refined the technique of "taking over a run down company, putting it through the sausage machine of a highly professional management", as Greenhalgh describes it now; before rushing on. He intended to export that same technique to Europe, with acquisitions there, which would have the added benefit of sustaining his share price in the City of London, because they made Cavenham look an exciting prospect. And the higher the English share price of Cavenham Foods, the easier it would be for him to launch a major takeover bid in England. The benefits of being both French and English were a decisive advantage.

By the time he launched Banque Occidentale in Paris in 1968 Jimmy Goldsmith had completed the sale of the few remaining Singleton and Cole wholesale depots, and sold off the troublesome Cavenham Confectionery division to the Swiss company Conwood

SA for a profit, although Cavenham still had a 50 per cent share. With a flourish he announced a profit for the year from March 1968 to March 1969 of £640,000, and told the City of London that the group had "considerable surplus cash". His share price rose immediately. The influential *Investors Chronicle* noted: "It looks as if Cavenham Foods might see better days after a lengthy period of disappointing results."

It did. In 1969 Cavenham bought Melchers, its first company in the Netherlands, a distillery producing a range of Dutch gin, including the famous Oliphant, as well as other spirits and liqueurs. It then added another Dutch company, the liqueur chocolate making firm Ringer's Cacao. And in February 1970 Jimmy Goldsmith bought back the half of Conwood SA that Cavenham did not own, to bring the snuff and confectionery interests back under the Cavenham umbrella. The alarums and confusions of the past had been sorted out – and Cavenham's share price protected.

To sustain the new momentum, Jimmy Goldsmith then announced Générale Occidentale's acquisition of 60 per cent of the French public company, Financière et Industrielle de Pétrole et de Pharmacie, FIPP. Gustin-Milical still had Right Tan and Milical, and had recently acquired the company which produced one of the staples of the French bathroom, the disinfectant Synthol, as well as a chemical company called Agrifurane. Gustin-Milical had then gone on to buy Laboratoires Grémy-Longuet, another of France's leading pharmaceutical companies. As 1969 drew to a close he injected all his French companies into FIPP, of which Générale Occidentale owned 60 per cent. Jimmy Goldsmith then added almost 25 per cent of the shares in the Eiffel Tower to the assets of Générale Occidentale.

The London Stock Exchange was suitably impressed. Even more so when Jimmy Goldsmith asked for his shares to be suspended on 4 February 1970 "until such time as shareholders could give their approval to the completion of the major transactions". The price of Cavenham's ordinary shares, which had been 4s 6d in 1967, rose from 6s to 15s 3d almost overnight. It made Cavenham Foods look an even more exciting proposition than it had before, and one which the City of London could not afford to ignore. To confirm his company's new status, Jimmy Goldsmith also brought Martin

Conwood of the Conwood Corporation, Sir Geoffrey Kitchen, the chairman of Pearl Assurance, and Count Thierry de Clermont-Tonnerre from Banque Occidentale in Paris on to the Cavenham board. By the summer he was announcing a pre-tax profit for Cavenham of £731,316, more than 15 per cent higher than the previous year, and stating confidently: "This result, coupled with our strong cash position, has allowed us to initiate a vigorous policy of expansion and acquisition as a result of which Cavenham will become an international producer of foods, drinks and pharmaceuticals." It also allowed the company's chairman to plan a major takeover in England to take advantage of his strong share price.

Jimmy Goldsmith was about to bring off the deal that would ensure that he would never again be dismissed as simply the playboy chairman of a disparate amalgam of companies in Britain and Europe. To help him secure the financial strength for his first major acquisition he bought a chain of 150 shops from Birrell Ltd in the summer of 1970, and then added a further 272 shops from the group R. S. McColl Limited (which Birrell controlled). The 422 shops cost him a little under £1 million, and he paid for them with £650,000-worth of shares with the balance in cash over three years. Within three months he had sold 105 of the shops to raise the purchase price, and amalgamated the rest with his existing chain of seventy-one called Hayes Lyon and Alex, which were still being run extremely successfully by Jim Wood. From nowhere Cavenham suddenly had a chain of 388 confectionery, tobacconist and newsagents' shops in Britain, all of them operating profitably. Within a short time they were making a profit of more than £250,000 on sales of £8.7 million.

Even some of the more conservative major British investment companies, like the Prudential Assurance, were impressed. As one of their managers, Roy Artus, was to explain several years later, Jimmy Goldsmith convinced them that there was far more to him than some men in the City had been prepared to accept: "The impression which he gave overall, despite perhaps the reputation which he had acquired in his youth, was of being a very serious person, very much in charge of the operation, having provided himself with adequate management to make a start on this programme of his. And in the position of the company and market share at the time it seemed this was a reasonable thing to back."

If everything over the past six years had been created by living hand to mouth, taking over badly managed or loss-making companies, making profits where he could and getting rid of any difficulties as speedily as possible, "the poor man's way of building a big group" that he had described in the summer of 1967, Jimmy Goldsmith was now determined that things should be different. Now he was really going to make an impression on British business. Cavenham Foods might have begun as a ragbag of companies, but it now controlled some of the most familiar names in British shopping. Besides Slimcea and Procea, there were still Carrs Table Water biscuits, and Carson's liqueur chocolates, as well as Elizabeth Shaw mints and Holland's toffees. Cavenham's manufacturing group in the year from March 1970 to March 1971 had sales of £18.8 million, and made profits of £1.16 million.

His expansion into Europe had gone equally well. FIPP, which now embraced Milical, had beaten its profit forecasts, and so had Melchers gin, while the German snuff company, Wittman, was also prospering. Only Ringer's chocolates had turned out to be a disappointment, and after seven months he had sold them. It did not deter him in the least. Jimmy Goldsmith felt ready to launch a major takeover bid. He could use his shares, with their higher price; the cash from his sales of assets; bank borrowings and his support from major investors like the Prudential Assurance company to support the bid. The only tricky question was, what to go for?

Given his interest in brand names there were not many possible targets. He had considered almost all of the potential companies in the past, but he wanted an acquisition that would finally mark his emergence as a financier to be taken seriously. Shortly after his thirty-eighth birthday, in February 1971, Jimmy Goldsmith settled on his objective: a bid to take over the long-established British food company Bovril, which manufactured three of the staples of the English grocery shop, Bovril, Marmite and Ambrosia Creamed Rice. But it was not his intention simply to walk into the office of the new chairman of Bovril, Hugh Lawson Johnston, who had taken over from his elder brother Lord Luke at the beginning of the year, and announce his plans. First he wanted to find out exactly what the company was like, what it was worth and whether it was susceptible to a takeover. In particular he was interested to know exactly how much the Bovril company's diverse assets – which included milk farms and dairies in England and Ireland as well as land and property in Argentina – were worth. The dairies were hardly valued at anything in the Bovril balance sheet, and he wondered if they were worth more than anyone suspected.

With a little research he discovered that they might be. One private estimate valued them at between £7 and £9 million. Yet they were valued at only a fraction of that in the company's balance sheet. Why had nobody noticed that before? Goldsmith had no idea, but he did know that it meant he could afford to launch a takeover bid for Bovril. As soon as he got the company he would sell the dairies and recoup his purchase price. If he had to he would buy the company's shares in the market. He felt he could not lose.

"We were just through the tunnel of reorganizing Cavenham," he remembers now, "with all the problems of confectionery and bringing together a ragbag of tired companies – which had to be totally brought back from the dead – and we had almost died doing it. But I felt the market was just about to turn up. I had missed the 1968 boom because Cavenham was struggling for survival, and in June 1971 I was 100 per cent certain that we were about to get back to a new cyclical boom in the market. Fortunately I was able to cash in because Cavenham was coming right just in time."

On 27 June 1971 Jimmy Goldsmith announced Cavenham Foods' takeover bid for control of Bovril. It valued the company at £9.7 million, and he offered to pay for it with a mixture of shares and cash. But he encountered far more ferocious opposition than even he had expected. "We had battled with Joe Lyons for control of Carrs of Carlisle, but this was the first time that we had gone into a major competitive battle for an established company." The City of London's old suspicions that he was no more than a playboy who had got lucky in recent years were repeatedly thrown in his face. He was made to feel that he had no right even to consider bidding for a household name, but he was not disturbed by that. Privately he might admit to his friends that his bid could be called "cheeky", but the more criticism that was voiced, the more he relished the fight.

To prove that he was to be taken seriously, and that he had the money to buy Bovril, Jimmy Goldsmith announced within a week of launching his bid that he had "signed a letter of intent" with the Southland Corporation, a retailing group with 4,100 shops – many of them the 711 chain – based in Dallas, Texas, for the American company to buy half the newly expanded Cavenham retail shop division. John Tigrett had helped to bring him the deal. He told the astonished City of London that the Americans had agreed to pay Cavenham £3.3 million in cash for the privilege, and that he had even negotiated that the price could rise by up to 20 per cent if the shops showed annual profits of more than £375,000 after tax. The odd assortment of shops that had cost Jimmy Goldsmith hardly anything, once he had sold off some of the sites to finance the purchase of the others, had suddenly made him a very substantial cash profit indeed and given him the money to be taken seriously in a major takeover battle. Backed up by the money from Southland, and the knowledge that he could probably sell part of Bovril at once at a substantial profit, Jimmy Goldsmith plunged into the takeover battle for Bovril in earnest.

Two weeks after he announced the details of his deal with South-land he raised his bid still further, to £10.6 million. Bovril could hardly believe it. In desperation the directors looked round for a "more respectable" company to bid for them, and protect them from this ambitious young man who seemed in rather too much of a hurry. On 21 July 1971, when his bid was three weeks old, the giant Rowntree Macintosh confectionery company stepped into the battle, offering to take over Bovril themselves for £10.9 million. The City heaved a sign of relief.

Jimmy Goldsmith was not deterred. On 30 July he raised his offer for Bovril to £13 million and set out to buy as many shares as he possibly could on the open market. From his house in Chester Terrace, Regent's Park, where he and Madame Beaux were now working side by side – rushing out in the evening to buy the first editions of the newspapers to judge what the opposition were doing – Jimmy Goldsmith forged ahead. The battle grew distinctly bitter. Some City men even insisted that Cavenham Foods' share price was being supported by a "mysterious figure", who was buying Cavenham's shares to keep their price high in the market, thereby sustaining the attractiveness of the offer for Bovril which was to be paid in both shares and cash. "A little creative massaging," they muttered to one another. Jimmy Goldsmith denied it firmly.

"There are always stories of mysterious figures buying shares, but it was absolute nonsense in this case. The explanation was that our profits were going up, we did a spectacularly good deal with the Texans, and the market was on an upswing. We had picked a good time." Even the *Investors Chronicle* was forced to ask "How can Bovril shoot at this target, which is moving so fast?"

"Our share price stayed high for a number of reasons," he says now. "During the battle I sold 49.9 per cent of the retailing division to Southland, and the market was pulling us up too. We bought a great deal of Bovril stock ourselves, often from people who did not actually have it, but who thought they could get it in the period before they had to deliver it to us." While in France Madame Beaux had also been successful in finding supporters for Cavenham's bid. "For me the underwriting of the Cavenham shares in Britain and France was the nucleus of the Bovril operation," she explains now.

"But it was then that I first encountered the destructive power of the press," he remembers. "My only experience of the British media until then was my marriage." Jimmy Goldsmith became convinced that his opponents in the takeover battle for Bovril were spreading rumours about him, and especially suggesting that he was only able to achieve so much because of the "mystery buyer" of his shares.

To this day there are some in the City of London who do not believe him. But, when it happened first, Jimmy Goldsmith became more convinced than ever that there was a conspiracy against him. His view was sharpened when the London *Sunday Times* sent a reporter from its business section round to see him at Chester Terrace on 12 August 1971, just after he had increased his offer for Bovril for the third time to £14.5 million in response to Rowntree's increased offer of £13.4 million. "He seemed to have his mind made up even before he started to talk to me. It was clear he thought that I wasn't going to get Bovril, and that my group did not deserve to." Jimmy Goldsmith was so angry that he rang the paper's proprietor, Roy Thomson, to complain. "I've never encountered anything like it in my life," he told him.

When the article appeared, on 15 August 1971, it concluded that

"Bovril shareholders considering the Cavenham offer must assess the risks and rewards offered by this remarkable man, who combines the talents of a financial Houdini and a commercial Master Builder", and cast some doubt on the precise strengths of Jimmy Goldsmith's Cavenham Foods. But it did not stop him winning Bovril.

Two days before it was published Jimmy Goldsmith announced that Cavenham now had the share content of its increased offer for Bovril underwritten with cash, and he also forecast that the company's profits would show a 30 to 40 per cent increase when they were announced. And he attacked the Bovril board's criticism of his company. To underline his latest move, he sent every single Bovril shareholder a telegram announcing the new cash offer, and followed it up with a letter and a brochure about Cavenham's success. He also announced that Cavenham now owned 24 per cent of Bovril's shares, while the Bovril board owned 8 per cent and Rowntree less than 10 per cent.

On the day after the *Sunday Times* article appeared he went back into the stock market and bought a further 12 per cent of Bovril shares; the following day a further seven per cent, and the day after that a further four per cent. By Wednesday 18 August Jimmy Goldsmith owned 47 per cent of Bovril's shares: and he announced that two institutional shareholders, one of them the Prudential Assurance company, had promised him their holdings – "which will put us over the top". Jimmy Goldsmith had got control of Bovril by the simplest method of all, he paid rather too much for their shares in the stock market. On Thursday 19 August he announced that Cavenham owned more than one and a half million of Bovril's three million shares, which gave it control of the company. Altogether Cavenham had bought more than one million Bovril shares in the market for nearly £5 million – half of the money had come from Cavenham's own reserves, the other half from a subsidiary of Keyser Ullman, which Cavenham had acquired.

"It was perfectly obvious to me," he says now, "that the battle for Bovril would be won in the market place itself, and that we needed cash to buy there. That was the reason for the Southland deal, and for buying so much stock. That together with our high share price tipped the balance. Finally we had so large a proportion of their shares that Bovril could not turn us away. We had won."

Jimmy Goldsmith was jubilant. "It was the most important bid of my life, and the most important deal: important in every way. Bovril was multi-dimensional. It was our first acquisition of an establishment company, with all the strengths of an established company, a company which has been rich for a very very long time; and had strengths which were quite incomparable with anything else we had bought in the past."

Jim Slater had told him, "If you fail to get Bovril, you will never succeed in a bid in the City of London," and he had taken the advice to heart. From the very beginning Jimmy Goldsmith had never intended to be defeated in his bid for Bovril, almost regardless of the price. "Every penny in the world we had, and every penny of credit we could raise was used to buy Bovril," he says.

But now there was to be no hesitating. Barely three weeks after the Bovril company had capitulated and accepted that Cavenham Foods were their new owner, the dairies had been sold off to Max Joseph's Grand Metropolitan group for almost £7 million, after sealed tenders had been invited; and negotiations had begun to sell the company's lands and haciendas in Argentina. The formidable Gilberte Beaux, who spoke Spanish, was despatched to South America to oversee the details of the sales. Within six months Jimmy Goldsmith and Cavenham's management team had not only increased Bovril's profit from £1.2 million a year to the equivalent of £2.2 million, but he had also got almost the entire purchase price of approaching £15 million back, from selling off what he later called "the flotsam and jetsam" in Bovril. "It was a spectacularly good deal because of the Argentine and the dairies," he explains. "No one realized quite how good at the time."

Even if they did not, the whole operation still earned Jimmy Goldsmith a reputation for financial wizardry. Yet because of its size, its apparent impudence, and its disregard for accepted opinion in the City of London, the bid confirmed the view of some City men that he was somehow a man apart, to be treated warily and, perhaps, not to be entirely trusted. Just as he had at St Andrews College in Ontario, Jimmy Goldsmith was still not prepared to take part in any race except on his terms, and just as it had at Eton, that annoyed more of his contemporaries than it amused. Coupled with his determination never to stand still, it served to convince some that his success was transient and achieved by sleight of hand rather than by financial acumen. It was a less than just conclusion. But from that moment Jimmy Goldsmith became a man whose actions were to be monitored carefully, particularly by those who saw the traditions of the City of London as sacrosanct.

The *Sunday Times* had summed up the suspicion when it had concluded, shortly before Bovril had capitulated, "Somehow this mixed bag of everything from Carson's liqueur chocs to Dr Rumsey's snuff, has grown out of all recognition to a point where it can bid with some conviction for a place among the international food giants."

Charles Hambro, a contemporary at Eton who was shortly to become Jimmy Goldsmith's merchant banker and friend, believes, "Jimmy used the moment of an undoubted financial boom fuelled by an enormous amount of money injected into the system without regard for anything by the Conservative government led by Edward Heath, to use paper – his shares – to buy assets which three or four years before he could never have done, and which three or four years later he would not have been able to do either. He caught the wind, and the tide came in at the right moment. There was a little luck as well as extremely good judgement."

What few people in the City of London, or in Paris, realized was quite how rapidly Jimmy Goldsmith intended to capitalize on his success, and repeat the process. As he told an astonished group of his managers at a lunch at the Savoy Hotel in London late in August, almost before the ink was dry on the Bovril takeover, "We must get on with another acquisition. This bull market is not going to last for ever. We must be quick."

As John Burton Tigrett puts it now, "Every man has a turning point in his life. For Jimmy Goldsmith it was Bovril."

12

"More Fun than Gambling"

The first meeting of Bovril's board after the Cavenham takeover did not take long. "The company has got to change," Jimmy Goldsmith told the directors firmly, "and the only place to start is in the boardroom." Before the meeting on that dull morning of 30 September 1971 had come to an end, two of the directors, Lord Tweedsmuir and Sir John Pitman, had announced their resignation; while their elegant but slightly perplexed chairman Hugh Lawson Johnston had also stepped down to be replaced by James Michael Goldsmith. No sooner had the changes been announced than the Cavenham men descended on their new acquisition like a victorious army, "and cut out the old-fashioned systems in no time", in the words of their managing director Jack Greenhalgh. "Bovril was moribund. It had been making just about a million pounds in profit for ten years. We only got there just in time."

The manner of the victory, and the ruthless energy of the subsequent Cavenham reorganization, was to bring Jimmy Goldsmith enemies, some of them permanent. There were some men in the City of London who never forgave him for taking over a famous and well-established firm like Bovril, and this fostered a distrust that was to colour all his dealings in London in the future. The English dislike of sudden change, particularly in the commercial world, made him a man to be feared as much as admired. He seemed to be stalking the stock market jungle like a tiger looking for victims, and that made many less hungry men a little afraid. He seemed not to abide by the rules that they had always believed would protect them: rules that had emerged over decades to comfort the staid and established order.

But Jimmy Goldsmith did not let it worry him. "People have to accept that things change; the established bureaucracies have to adapt, or perish," he explains calmly. In any case he was already planning the next attack.

One sign that Jimmy Goldsmith was still intent on reminding the world that the Goldsmith family were not to be forgotten was his decision to change the name of his company simply to Cavenham, rather than Cavenham Foods. Confident, quick-witted, and steadfastly dedicated to creating a new giant in European business, he stormed every citadel he could find, and left the markets of Europe distinctly dazed.

In the next two years no one in Jimmy Goldsmith's companies, least of all he himself, had time to pause for breath. He sprinted through the stock markets buying and selling companies like a man moving counters on a backgammon board, hardly waiting for the dice to stop rolling before he moved again. The dream that he had nurtured five years before, of creating a major European food company to rival Unilever and Nestlé, came to possess him. And he pursued it with an intensity that terrified some and mystified others.

In the scramble for financial success and power, beautiful women were still his only true hobby. He also gambled regularly, and had been concentrating on making himself the best backgammon player among his friends – but that was a distraction rather than a pleasure. Women were a relaxation. No one understood that more clearly than Lady Annabel Birley. While Jimmy Goldsmith had been assembling Cavenham, their relationship had become increasingly close and she was more and more aware that her marriage was over. Although her husband had known about her affair since 1966 – Jimmy Goldsmith had stayed away from Annabel's since then as a result – Mark Birley remained devoted to her, and anxious to keep their family together, at least while their children were young. For her part, Annabel Birley took holidays with her family, and remained living with them in Pelham Cottage, even if there were one or two excursions to Chester Terrace or Paris with Jimmy Goldsmith at weekends. When, once, Mark Birley had moved out, she had encouraged him to move back again, "because he was plainly so unhappy".

By the beginning of 1971, however, it was clear that Annabel Birley's affair with Jimmy Goldsmith was not going to wane, quite the reverse; while Madame Ginette Goldsmith had also realized that her husband's attachment to the daughter of an English marquis was not about to evaporate, as some of his previous attachments to striking young women had done. If Ginette Goldsmith felt that she had become the victim of her husband's ambitions, she was never ever to mention it; instead she remained studiously and discreetly silent in their home in Paris; a woman who had, unwittingly, found herself handmaiden to a man whose ambitions she may have found difficult to understand, but whose loyalty she had never doubted.

In London Mark Birley reached the same conclusion, and in the summer of 1971 he moved out of Pelham Cottage for the second, and last, time. He bought a house round the corner in Pelham Street, the garden of which adjoined that of Pelham Cottage so that his three children could visit him whenever they wanted to, and he continued to spend his evenings at his club. There were one or two new friends now, but otherwise his life remained much as it had been for the past half dozen years.

For Annabel Birley, however, things were different. Now she could go away with Jimmy Goldsmith during the school terms, perhaps to Marrakesh or the West Indies in the winter, or Italy in the early summer. She knew that he had always believed in working intensively for a time and then disappearing for a few weeks, only keeping in touch on the telephone, and she liked the idea of sharing those times with him. It was their first chance of a comparatively ordinary life together. For the rest of the time, however, her principal concern remained her children.

Children were also on Jimmy Goldsmith's mind. He remained as devoted to little Isabel as he was to Manes and Alix. He would spoil them, always arriving for weekends or holidays with presents, usually bringing them something unexpected. But he was more like an eternally generous uncle, the man who provided the speedboat or the sledge on holiday, than the bringer of daily intimacy which most fathers make their own. Some might have interpreted his generosity as guilt, but that would have been a mistake. It was the approach of a man who sometimes felt uneasy in human relationships, and covered the unease as best he could; with generosity and charm. He could not conceal that, much though he loved his children, he did not wish to spend his every waking moment in their company.

Both Ginette Goldsmith and Annabel Birley knew only too well that he was not likely to change. But they also knew that he was devoted to them both. Indeed so conscious was he of his responsibilities to their respective families that in the summer of 1970 he even arranged for Ginette and his children, and Annabel Birley and her children, to take their summer holidays in Sardinia at the same time, so that he could divide his time between them, driven between one family and the other in a speedboat.

Had they known about his unorthodox private life, most men in the City of London would have simply shaken their heads in disbelief, but they were growing used to that. It was precisely how the London *Financial Times* had described his takeover of Bovril. He had paid more for the company than many thought it was worth, but Jimmy Goldsmith had then demonstrated that they had seriously underestimated its value and its potential. To the astonishment of those conservative members of the City who suggested his takeover was all a matter of sleight of hand, Jimmy Goldsmith proceeded to sell off those parts of the company which he did not believe were central to its operations, and thereby raise considerable amounts of cash to reinvest in it. "It was asset stripping in its most creative form: selling off surplus and sterile assets to increase the value and potential of a company," he remarked.

Barely four weeks after he got control of Bovril Jimmy Goldsmith offered to buy Wright's, a biscuit-making company in the north of England with sales of £24 million a year from their owner Willie Webster, who had recently had a heart attack and wanted to retire. Then, because Wright's owned 40 per cent of Moore's, a chain of about 600 northern grocery shops with sales of almost £1 million a week, he went on to offer to buy them as well. He ended up offering almost £7 million for the two companies, payable mostly in his shares, and got them.

Yet again he had no intention of hanging on to every part of his new investment. He sold half the new chain of shops to Southland Corporation of Dallas, to allow him to bounce straight back into the takeover market. As he did so, his share price went up again.

The *Investors Chronicle* commented admiringly: "There is never a dull moment with Cavenham."

There was not to be one for some time. Jimmy Goldsmith was already planning his next major bid in Britain. As the stock market began to digest just what he had accomplished in snatching control of Bovril from under the noses of some of the City of London's most respected companies, so he was beginning secret talks with Cob Stenham, then financial director of the giant food and grocery company, Unilever, to buy its shareholding in Allied Suppliers, Britain's fourth largest chain of grocery shops.

Jimmy Goldsmith, the owner of a ragamuffin assembly of 360 newsagents, and the newly acquired Moore's chain of grocery shops, which had been losing money, was planning to take over some of the most famous names in Britain's High Streets, including Lipton's, the Home and Colonial, and Maypole Dairies. His target also had the significant attraction of being one of the select group of thirty companies whose share price made up the *Financial Times* share index, which provided the guide to stock market movements.

He was not the first person to have initiated discussions with Unilever about the future of their shares in Allied Suppliers. The giant Spillers food company had held preliminary discussions about a possible merger in 1970 and so had Allied Breweries; while the legendary takeover expert Charles Clore had also done so a few months later, offering shares in his Sears company for them. But that deal had never been concluded. Years later Clore was to tell his friends that Jimmy Goldsmith's good fortune had been created by a "proper Charlie", Clore himself.

The key to Allied Suppliers' future lay in Unilever's shareholding, because although Unilever owned only a little over 12 per cent of Allied's shares, these actually provided more than a third of the decisive voting rights in the company. Jimmy Goldsmith had calculated that with that block of voting shares under his control, and the purchase of more in the market place, it would not take him long to get control of more than 50 per cent of the voting shares: and therefore of Allied itself. But, unlike some of the earlier prospective purchasers of Unilever's holding, Jimmy Goldsmith had in mind an offer that Unilever would find it difficult to refuse. He intended to sell them Allied's tea interests, "just as soon as I get control".

The bait was decisive. As Stenham explained later, "We wanted a very integral and important part of Allied Suppliers for ourselves, and that was the Lipton tea business, a worldwide tea business. We needed that because we had a very successful tea business in the United States and we wanted to increase that." The only difficulty was that Stenham and Goldsmith could not agree on a price for the tea business. For a moment it looked as though the deal would break down, until, finally, Unilever suggested that after he had gained control of Allied Suppliers, he should agree to the binding adjudication of Sir Ronald Leach, President of the Institute of Chartered Accountants, on the price Unilever should pay for the tea interests. With that simple proviso Unilever accepted the £10.5 million that the Cavenham group was offering for their 12.4 per cent of Allied Suppliers' shares. With that agreement behind him, Jimmy Goldsmith prepared to launch his next major takeover bid.

On Friday 14 January 1972 he unveiled Cavenham's bid for Allied Suppliers. Its size shocked the already astonished City of London still further. Jimmy Goldsmith announced his intention of offering £86 million for the giant company which had sales of almost £270 million a year. Only some £22 million was actually to be paid in cash, the rest was made up of Cavenham shares, but with the Unilever holding already in his control, there was very little that the Allied Suppliers' board of directors could do to stop the takeover.

On the cold wet afternoon of Tuesday 18 January 1972, in a private room in the Ritz hotel in Piccadilly, Jimmy Goldsmith met another board of directors of a company he had decided to take over. Once again he was to dominate them from the very beginning. Although they had come to the meeting uncertain precisely what they should recommend to their shareholders, within three hours they had decided to recommend the Cavenham offer. Jimmy Goldsmith had agreed to increase the size of his offer slightly, to £86.3 million, but there had hardly been any real opposition. Even Goldsmith was astonished. "I thought they would put up more of a fight," he told his Cavenham colleagues, "but they didn't." It was another coup. As Cob Stenham put it later: "In one swoop Jimmy roughly doubled the size of his company."

In the space of barely eight months Jimmy Goldsmith had transformed Cavenham from a food company with sales of about £35

million, and profits of less than £2 million, to a massive combine
whose total sales exceeded £400 million a year, and whose profits
could reasonably be expected to exceed £25 million. In the same
period his share price had rocketed from 69 pence to 229 pence. It
was the most spectacular piece of financial empire building that the
City of London had seen for a decade. And it had been accomplished
only ten years after he had been forced to sell his stake in Mothercare,
just eight years after he had bought his 20 per cent in Procea from
the Doughnut Corporation of America, and barely six years since
he had first turned Carrs of Carlisle into Cavenham Foods, with its
mixed bag of sugar mice, biscuits and slimming bread.

The *Daily Mirror* called him "Britain's Number One Grocer",
and the *Observer* added that he was "the financier with the golden
touch". *The Times* commented: "The speed and complexity of the
many deals put together by the Goldsmith interests in the past few
years have baffled the City as well as the competitors who once
dismissed his presence as of no importance."

The influential *Investors Chronicle* concluded: "At the beginning
of last year Mr Goldsmith's company was worth only £15m, and in
the summer had the greatest difficulty in gaining credibility for the
£14.5m bid for Bovril . . . With this deal, arguably the most astute
of a series of clever financial dealings, Cavenham has moved into
the big league – its market value will be not much short of Tesco's
£200m odd. And the acquisition with some £50m of assets will give
Cavenham much of the solidity and respectability which it has
hitherto lacked."

Only the *Financial Times*, reflecting the attitude of the still
sceptical members of the City of London, struck a note of caution:
"Some people are still shaking their heads in disbelief," it commented. "The argument runs thus: if the events of the past few
months have materially increased Jimmy Goldsmith's reputation
for financial wizardry – a reputation which has not always brought
him universal approval – they have so far done little to prove that
he can actually run the empire of his dreams . . . The new group
is on a different scale altogether than the old Cavenham: and so are
the problems he has brought himself. Does Cavenham have either
the top management or the experience to be able to cope?"

The question had never crossed Jimmy Goldsmith's mind. His

management team had coped so far, and he had not interested himself in the specific details of any of his individual companies since the early days of his forays into the staff canteen. He preferred to leave administration to his executives, and pay them handsomely to make their own decisions. In the four months since he had gained control of Bovril, for example, he had hardly set foot inside its factories. He contented himself with looking at the balance sheet and the monthly sales returns. Jimmy Goldsmith had never seen himself as the manager of an empire; he was its creator and he wanted his generals to run it. His interest was in deals – deals were what made business fun.

The fact that Cavenham was controlled by a man who openly seemed to enjoy himself made his competitors and some men in the City of London all the more suspicious. This was reflected clearly in the *Investors' Review*, shortly after the takeover of Allied Suppliers: "He is almost casual in his business approach, and his free and easy manner has upset a good many of the old breed of City men who remain imbued with the Protestant ethic . . . Goldsmith has never made any secret of enjoying himself, but this doesn't mean he's a playboy, a reputation in the City encouraged by his propensity for gambling and long holidays."

As if to prove their point, no sooner had the Allied Suppliers bid been agreed than Jimmy Goldsmith told the *Financial Times* that he intended to treat himself to a six-week holiday. "I've been sprinting rather hard recently. I think I deserve one." To escape the English February he took off for Corsica, where he had rented a house, while his management team, in particular Jack Greenhalgh, the managing director, Lionel Ross, the financial controller, and Jim Wood, who ran the retail division, began to grapple with the new Leviathan he had found for them.

"We were quite used to it. We had developed a technique over the years," Greenhalgh recalls. "Jimmy would buy run down companies, which were then put through the sausage machine of a highly professional team of industrial management who turned them round; and Jimmy would then use them as a springboard for the next move. You just kept on and on."

In fact, wherever he was, Jimmy Goldsmith never liked doing absolutely nothing. He might disappear for what other people described as a "long holiday", but that did not mean he lost touch with his companies, or stopped thinking about them. Far from it. As he disappeared from Britain in the first weeks of February 1972, he was already considering how to get the most for the tea interests in Allied Suppliers, which he had agreed to sell to Unilever at a price to be settled by an adjudication. When he heard a date had been set for the hearing he summoned his financial advisers to the South of France, and told them that he had no intention whatever of allowing anyone else to represent his interests at the hearing. Jimmy Goldsmith intended to appear himself. "What more important issue can there be than money?" he asked them.

"I spent a whole week going through every single argument that could be used," he recalls now. "I was very anxious to get as much as I possibly could from the sale, and I knew that Unilever only expected to pay about £10 million or £12 million for it." By the time he had finished Jimmy Goldsmith felt that he would be a match for anybody.

So it turned out. Unilever had thought the matter would quickly be decided in their favour. The man delegated to appear at the adjudication had studied his papers only on the night before the hearing. He was no match for Jimmy Goldsmith. After three hours of Goldsmith's evidence, it was quite clear that Unilever were going to end up paying a great deal more than they had expected for Allied Suppliers' tea interests. The Unilever representative left the hearing ashen-faced.

A delighted Jimmy Goldsmith went back to his holiday, this time on a yacht he had hired in the Mediterranean. Annabel Birley and John Aspinall joined him. As they sailed into the Aegean his office in London told him on the radio telephone that the adjudication was to be announced the next day.

"Aspinall and I decided to go ashore, so we told Annabel that I was expecting an important phone call, and asked her to take a note of the exact amount of money that the adjudicator had decided Unilever should pay. We should have known better, Annabel has never been very good with figures." When the two men returned to the yacht, Annabel Birley told them that there had been a message. "What was the figure?" Jimmy Goldsmith asked excitedly. "Now, was it six million, or 16 million, or 26 million," Annabel said. "Oh,

I knew I should have written it down." A slightly bemused Jimmy Goldsmith rang London.

Sir Ronald Leach had decided Unilever should pay £18.5 million for the Lipton tea interests. When the cheque arrived at the Cavenham offices, the senior staff all touched it. "We'd never seen so much money," one remembers.

Jimmy Goldsmith stayed on the yacht, wondering whether or not to sell half his newly expanded retail division to Southland and raise another £25 million. In the end he telephoned to ask if they were interested, but discovered they could not afford it at the time. Rather than sell to anyone else he simply kept it. He contented himself with selling three of Allied Suppliers' properties to Cavendish Land to raise another £18 million. That only took a telephone call too.

By the time he returned to Chester Terrace in the spring, he had also begun to negotiate the sale of the company that had got Cavenham on the road in the first place, Carrs of Carlisle. He wanted to sell it, together with the biscuit interests in Wright's to the United Biscuit Company for £4 million. The deal did not take long, and was quickly followed by another. In June Jimmy Goldsmith sold his friend Jim Slater some of Allied Suppliers' property interests, including some of the company's central London offices, for a further £4 million. Without much difficulty he had raised almost the entire purchase price of Allied Suppliers in hard cash by selling parts that he did not consider central to its business, and which he had paid for largely in Cavenham shares. The lessons of 1957 were not forgotten, he wanted as much cash as he could find to give him freedom to do what he liked. Bovril and Allied Suppliers helped him to refine a technique that he was to export to the United States with devastating effect less than a decade later. But for the moment his interests remained in Europe. As John Tigrett explains it, "You look at everything he has ever done. The pattern is the same. Jimmy likes to take over old, long-established companies, with famous brand names, that have gradually expanded into all sorts of strange areas that, perhaps, they do not fully understand, and then simplify the company again by bringing it back to its roots."

While Jimmy Goldsmith had been active in the City of London, he had also kept up his ferocious pace in France. Even before he launched his bid for Allied Suppliers he bought Sanders SA, a French company which produced veterinary products and animal foods in France, Belgium and Spain, and the Sodep company which had similar interests in Europe. Once again the purchase helped to keep his share price up in London, and to make Cavenham stock more valuable in any takeover. But that was not his only reason for buying the companies. It was a business he understood. Just as Procea was based on the sale of ingredients to bakers, so Sanders sold its concentrates to agricultural merchants who "bulked" the product and sold it under a Sanders label. It may not have been the most glamorous industry, but it delighted him. A leader in its own field, involved in France's largest industry – agriculture – its after-tax profits had been expanding at the rate of 40 per cent a year. This was not a purchase to impress the City of London, this was a "delectable coup", he told the *Financial Times*.

Then, as he was tidying up his sales of various interests in England, he launched out again in France, buying 20 per cent of the giant Générale Alimentaire food group with his Cavenham hat on and a further 5 per cent as head of Générale Occidentale, with a view to merging it with his existing FIPP and creating one of France's largest companies. By doing so, Jimmy Goldsmith was going into partnership with his cousins the Rothschilds, who were among the largest shareholders in Générale Alimentaire, with 25 per cent of the stock through their Compagnie du Nord. The combination of GA and FIPP meant that Jimmy Goldsmith was now a substantial shareholder in France's third largest grocery chain with a turnover of more than £100 million a year. It won him the nickname "Mr OPA", for his persistent talent for the "*offre publique d'achat*".

Yet Jimmy Goldsmith had also begun to accept that not everyone sympathized with his objectives. His new awareness that his attitude and ambitions did not appeal to everyone in London and Paris was clear enough by the time that he gave his first public speech, in June 1972, to a small conference in Paris sponsored by *Le Figaro* and the London *Financial Times* and chaired by the then French Minister of Finance, Valéry Giscard d'Estaing. In it, he roundly attacked the French commercial and political establishment for their "hostility to entrepreneurs" and "statism". It was a theme he returned to over and over again in the years to come, and it was not well received.

"Giscard thought it was heresy at the time," he remembers, "because I was attacking the French government for defending large companies against attack from new entrepreneurs who were trying to build up their businesses." In particular Jimmy Goldsmith had been anxious to defend men like himself who were now being described as "predators" in the stock markets of Europe. "Guard against their image," he told the conference, "their role is not only to devour those who go slowly, but it is also to encourage the rest to go quickly. The function for which nature invented them a long time ago." It may not have been the most popular opinion, but it was precisely what Jimmy Goldsmith believed, and exactly the way he intended to conduct his affairs. He saw no reason why what he called "rotting companies" should be left in the hands of "establishment bureaucrats", even if some of his critics saw that as "evil!"

Jimmy Goldsmith defended every entrepreneur's right to do whatever deal he could, and wherever he wanted. He had no massive board of directors to consider, although he would often discuss his plans with Roland Franklin, John Tigrett and Gilberte Beaux, but his colleagues knew only too well that each and every one of his companies depended principally on his energy, his determination and his ability to seize any opportunity that presented itself. Générale Occidentale and Cavenham were fashioned in the image of one man, their chairman, and their future would be determined by the same man. His instincts were responsible for its creation, its growth and its survival. Like the lion at the head of a pride, the safety of all depended on his ferocity.

It was an attitude that few Englishmen understood, which only further convinced his critics that he was either a man "given to attacks of megalomania", or else "simply a gambler with a gambler's luck". Both views showed a fundamental misunderstanding of him. He was a rebel by nature, who would never feel comfortable in a familiar structure, an established hierarchy. Certainly he had a gambler's instincts, "but those are no bad thing, a gambler knows when to stop". Certainly he also had a dream of creating a major

European company, but he saw no reason to be ashamed of that ambition. Was that not the only way to create new jobs, and sustain old ones? If people called him eccentric, suspected his motives or criticized his style, he rather enjoyed it. He certainly did not mind. They did not have to buy his shares, nor he theirs. It was an attitude more American than English or European in 1972.

Indeed it was the American *Time* magazine, in September 1972, which first placed Jimmy Goldsmith on an international stage: he appeared on the magazine's front cover alongside seven other European businessmen, including Jim Slater, as "one of the eight new young Europeans who are making their influence felt from Iberia to Scandinavia . . . Multi-national in their attitudes, multi-lingual and young, they are quietly changing the style and stepping up the pace of European business," *Time* concluded. It was not exactly true (the change would take some years to come about), but that did not prevent the magazine from going on: "Almost to a man the managers who are coming to the forefront in Europe have a dominant objective, they are reaching out for new markets." Jimmy Goldsmith was particularly singled out as "a true multi-national man . . . who claims to have learned the art of management from the mistakes of the US multi-nationals."

In fact Jimmy Goldsmith was now at the head of a multi-national company himself. He controlled some of the most important groceries and brand names in Europe, and many of the shops that sold them. In England alongside Slimcea and Procea he had Carson's liqueur chocolates, Elizabeth Shaw Mint Crisps, Parkinson's boiled sweets, Holland's toffees, Illingworth's snuffs, Bovril, Marmite and Ambrosia Creamed Rice: all of them sold in a chain of nearly 2,500 grocery shops with names like Lipton's and Maypole. In France he still had Milical, and the drug-producing companies, as well as the disinfectant Synthol, and Sanders animal foodstuffs, not to mention a share in Générale Alimentaire's food brands, which included Amora, which boasted half the French mustard market; Dessaux, with half the vinegar market; Vandamme spiced cake and Aussage spices and peppers, which between them took between 25 and 40 per cent of their respective markets. He owned the profitable Wittman snuff company in Germany, Melchers Oliphant Gin in Holland, and a quarter of the Irma chain of food shops in Denmark.

Above these stretched Générale Occidentale's other interests, which included its shareholding in Banque Occidentale and the Van Embden bank in Holland (now renamed the Occidentale bank), and a Swiss bank, Ralli Brothers, as well as its holding of almost 25 per cent of the Eiffel Tower in Paris. But Jimmy Goldsmith had decided to sell that as soon as he realized that its directors were not as interested as he was in trying to expand the company's activities beyond the operation of one of the most famous landmarks in the world. Even the previously sceptical *Sunday Times* explained: "Through Générale Occidentale Jimmy Goldsmith controls the whole of his proliferating Europe-wide empire, now valued by the stock market at over £200m." (At 1986 values it would be worth almost £750 million.)

GO, as it was known to its French shareholders, also oversaw his new banking and investment subsidiary, Anglo-Continental Investments, which had come into existence shortly after the Bovril takeover had succeeded in England. It had expanded steadily while GO was digesting Générale Alimentaire, and Cavenham was sorting out Allied Suppliers. There was one significant difference, however. While the major companies had gone ahead in the hands of his management team, Anglo-Continental represented Jimmy Goldsmith's own, even more personal, interests. The influential City editor of the London *Daily Mail*, Patrick Sergeant, described it as "what you might call his wheeling-dealing arm".

It had started almost by chance, with a series of deals with Jim Slater. The two men had become close friends since their first meeting in London in 1965. Goldsmith would telephone Slater from wherever he was and ask what he thought of the market in England, or the state of the British economy. And the two men were in the habit of having dinner together every two weeks, usually at Wilton's in London's Bury Street, which had been one of Frank Goldsmith's favourite restaurants. Indeed, it was at one of these dinners, in July 1972, that the first of their deals were struck: they joined forces in the ambitious property company Argyle Securities and also agreed that Anglo-Continental should buy two of Slater Walker Securities' satellite companies, Thomas Stevens (Property) and Tanker Investment Trust for £9 million and £8 million respectively. In return Jim Slater got 10 per cent of Anglo-Continental.

The details of the deal were worked out on the back of a waiter's order pad, which they borrowed for the purpose.

As Slater described it later, "Slater Walker ended up with three satellites less, a lot of cash and a few Anglo-Continental shares; whereas Jimmy had very substantially boosted the underlying asset value of Anglo-Continental by issuing its shares for relatively hard assets." Jimmy Goldsmith told the *Daily Telegraph*, who described him as getting "a fully fledged property arm" as a result of the deal: "It is a mixture of substance and hope."

A month later, once again at dinner at Wiltons, with Jimmy Goldsmith eating caviar at his customary electric pace, Slater offered his friend another deal. Once again the details were worked out on the back of a waiter's pad. This time Anglo-Continental was to acquire the insurance brokers Wigham Richardson and two of Slater's investment trusts, Flag and Irish. But the two men could not agree on the price.

"Forty-two million pounds," Jimmy Goldsmith said between mouthfuls.

"Forty-three," Slater told him.

"Let's not argue. I'll play you for the difference," Jimmy Goldsmith said.

"What game?"

"Let's toss a coin for who chooses."

Slater was well aware that if Jimmy Goldsmith won and chose backgammon he did not have much hope of his million. They tossed a coin, and Slater lost. Jimmy Goldsmith chose backgammon. They returned to Chester Terrace to play the game, and before the end of the evening, Jim Slater had lost both the game, and the extra million he had hoped to get for his three companies.

"Ironically, if I had won the choice of games, and opted for chess, Jimmy would almost certainly have lost," Jim Slater recalls now. "Jimmy's passion for speed made chess a game he never enjoyed."

Nevertheless this was still hardly the conventional way to do business. Life, even as the creator of a £200 million European company, was still to be enjoyed rather than endured. Not that Jimmy Goldsmith was unaware of his responsibilities or lacked a clear view of the strategy required for his companies. Shortly after his controversial speech about "predators", he explained in his annual report to the shareholders of Cavenham: "We believe that companies, if they are significant, should form part of the community in which they are based. National pride is a fact of life which can be a powerful asset in developing any major enterprise. We would think it wrong to inhibit the driving force by attempting to run overseas companies from London, or even to seek total ownership."

Jimmy Goldsmith even insisted that the Cavenham-owned companies in Europe should continue to conduct their board meetings in their native language, and should prepare their reports in their own language. The Cavenham men had to learn to cope in French or Spanish, Dutch or German, "though fortunately the Swedes preferred to hold their meetings in English", Jack Greenhalgh remembers.

It was one of the clearest signs that Jimmy Goldsmith had a far clearer perception of his role as an entrepreneur than a great many men in the City of London had given him credit for. They had not looked at the small print of the Cavenham annual report, which read: "Our policy is therefore where possible to participate in Europe as a major shareholder rather than as an outright owner; it is to back national management with our capital, our technology and our methods of management and to make available our strong international commercial organization. This already consists of Europe's largest food retailing group . . . in this way we can work in full sympathy with national authorities; we can attract the most able management talent; we can have as partners local institutions and the public; and we can compete with locally owned companies on equal terms."

These are hardly the conclusions of a wild gambler intent on grabbing any opportunity that presented itself and using other people's money rather than his own. Too many confused Jimmy Goldsmith's style with his principles.

Looking back now, Jimmy Goldsmith does not believe there was anything particularly unusual about his achievement. "You need application, determination, common sense and luck," he says firmly. "There is no other secret to it than that." He does accept that takeovers demand a concentration that few people understand. "You have meetings all day, and are woken up all night. The pressure is on you. You don't know whether you're going to win or lose. You have huge stakes on the table. On each occasion for me it was 'double or quits'. I stood to lose everything. If Bovril had failed I wouldn't have been able to launch another bid in England."

No matter how spectacular the risk he appears to be taking, Jimmy Goldsmith dislikes gambling too far against the odds in his financial affairs. As Gilberte Beaux puts it: "Jimmy may appear impetuous, but, in reality, he is far, far more cautious than anyone would ever expect. He takes a long time, and thinks very hard, before he launches a bid. But when he has decided to do it, he does not give up easily."

Using that determination, coupled with strategy, financial expertise, guile, opportunism, and the force of his own personality, Jimmy Goldsmith had created an empire, even if not everyone understood how or, more important still, why. Even *Le Monde* in France was confused, asking its readers in November 1972, *"Qu'est-ce qui fait courir Jimmy?"* In the past quarter of a century few other financiers had accomplished so much, or so quickly, and few who had would not have then decided to relax. Once again Jimmy Goldsmith was to refuse to do what the world expected of a man in his position. If everyone assumed he was going to sit still, doing nothing, they were wrong. He had only just begun. The thrill of the game had not left him.

Besides, beneath his confident exterior, and sometimes blustering manner, there still lay the uncertain young man that had almost lost everything in 1957. If everything had been achieved so quickly, it could equally well be taken away again. He knew that there had to be more change, still more expansion, so that – eventually – he would no longer be playing "double or quits" each time he decided on a major move. That way lay safety. That way, he told himself, the future could be assured. To do nothing was to descend to oblivion, which is what the old companies like Bovril had been tempted to do. That way led to a takeover from another hungrier predator. To remain safe demanded movement, and change. The alternative was death.

To prove that he was very much alive, and to celebrate his success, Jimmy Goldsmith was planning a party.

13

The Acapulco Strategy

The rich are different. Scott Fitzgerald was right. And it is not just that they have more money. They *feel* rich, and they have a different attitude to life, one that a poor man will never share. Jimmy Goldsmith did not start out rich but he felt rich, and acted as though he were rich. That single fact set him apart. It kept him in a cocoon separated from the world around him, the inhabitant of a world of confidence and luxury, spiced with a touch of arrogance, in which he felt secure. Those whom he welcomed into his world could rely completely on his loyalty and generosity, but beyond the walls of his citadel he was less comfortable, less at ease.

There was no mistaking the insecurity beneath the surface, but that was a private matter never to be disclosed in public. For alongside the rebellious eleven-year-old carrying his bag of toffees in the cross-country race, still existed the romantic young man who eloped because he was in love and the shy, young father who fought for his infant daughter. He was still naïve enough to be surprised at the personal attacks made on him during the Bovril takeover. Alongside the ambition and the volcanic temper, there still existed a small boy's need for affection.

As his success increased so he gratefully retreated into his carefully protected world, occasionally mounting expeditions into public life surrounded by friends whom he liked and trusted, and, more important, whom he knew liked and trusted him. That had always been his preference, and money simply made it easier to organize.

The triumphs of the past two years meant that by the beginning of 1973 Jimmy Goldsmith had passed through the mysterious door that turns a man who has always felt he was rich, even when he was not, into a truly rich man. But if part of him wanted to delight in public demonstrations of his affluence and power, another part wanted to be comfortable in the knowledge that within his private world he was secure, protected against attack. Financial success bought insulation from the grimmer realities of ordinary life. Poverty or unemployment existed in theory, possibilities to be taken into account, and examined carefully; but they were far from a reality. Even cold weather could be avoided, by a judiciously timed migration to the sunshine: or the creation of a world in which the sun seemed to shine perpetually, and whose inhabitants constantly wore the light tan that only the truly rich can afford. So it was hardly a surprise when Jimmy Goldsmith threw a party for his daughter Isabel which re-created that sun-kissed private world, even if it was held in London in the first days of January.

In all the sixty-seven years of its distinguished history the Ritz hotel in London had seldom seen such a fuss, or such extravagance, for a party. The magnificent mirrored rooms in its basement echoed to the shouts of a team of anxious florists busily removing all the hotel's own flowers and replacing them with the orchids and palms that Jimmy Goldsmith had ordered to be brought in specially. He was determined that his 250 guests should leave the chill Piccadilly air behind them and descend into a tropical night in Louisiana. To sustain the illusion he had arranged for five jazz bands to be specially flown in from New Orleans to provide music for the evening. The floor was to be covered in chopped wine corks to give an impression of sand.

The London "season", in which the débutante daughters of the English aristocracy "came out" into society, had ended five years previously when the official presentations at court had stopped. But it was still possible to launch a beautiful young woman into society, provided her father was rich enough to do it. Jimmy Goldsmith was undoubtedly rich enough, and his daughter Isabel was unquestionably beautiful enough to have graced any débutante's ball in the previous half a century. With dark flowing hair, her mother's fierce flashing eyes, and dressed in white Isabel Goldsmith looked like a porcelain doll as she greeted her guests at the Ritz on 10 January 1973. The British school in Paris, where she had taken her two A levels – French, in which she was as bilingual as her father, and art

– had not turned her into a particularly sophisticated young woman. "I wasn't allowed out. I'd never even been to a nightclub, except for a family outing," she had told *Vogue* magazine. In spite of her striking appearance, she was, in fact, a shy, slightly withdrawn girl of eighteen.

Perhaps Jimmy Goldsmith felt a little guilty about his daughter and knew in his heart that he could have spent more time with her during her childhood, offering her a father's advice and encouragement. Instead, after the battle to decide who should control her future, he had all too often left her in the hands of his wife Ginette, a nanny, or a boarding school. He had treated her generously, but it was the generosity of a slightly guilty father, and she remained a slightly neglected figure in his life: the poor little rich girl who could have everything she wanted, except what she wished for most of all – the love of her own mother.

When the first guests arrived on that January night in 1973, Isabel Goldsmith played her part. She smiled and shook hands, thanked the guests for their compliments, and danced with whoever asked her. There were more of her father's friends than her own, but she did not mind. Sir Max Joseph and Lady Melchett, Lord Lambton and Lord Goodman, George Melly and the Duke of Marlborough, Paul Channon and Georgie Fame, as well as Lady Annabel Birley took their places alongside some of her father's other friends whom she knew rather better, like John Aspinall and her uncle Teddy. There was one guest, however, whom she knew quite well. Tall, with a slight bump in his nose caused by a skiing accident, Baron Arnaud de Rosnay was eight years older than she was, but he was someone she felt she could talk to. He made her laugh, and he seemed quite happy among her father's friends. They had first been introduced at her grandfather Patino's party for his three granddaughters the previous August in Paris, and they had become very close. For a beautiful young girl desperate to conceal her shyness, he was a godsend. She had even begun to think that he might be more than simply a childhood friend.

By the time the last guests had stumbled out into the first rays of dawn, Jimmy Goldsmith was feeling particularly elated. The party had been a success and the past eighteen months had been the most exciting and the most successful of his life. Not only had he managed to pull off the takeovers of Bovril, Allied Suppliers and Générale Alimentaire, but he had also won the crucial support of major institutional investors like the Prudential Assurance company in England, and the Union des Assurances de Paris; not only for Cavenham and GA but also for his holding company Générale Occidentale in Paris.

Indeed it was there, in an office in the avenue de Friedland, looking across towards the Arc de Triomphe, that he had begun to reach the decision that would mean he would not go on "risking everything" each time he embarked on a new deal. Yet it was in England that he spent most of his time. Lady Annabel Birley would travel across London to spend time with him in Chester Terrace whenever she could, and he would sometimes stay with her in Pelham Cottage. Their affair was hardly a secret now, too many people in London knew about it, but he still did not intend to flout it openly. In France he would hardly have hesitated, but in England Jimmy Goldsmith knew there were some things best left unsaid.

But in January 1973 Jimmy Goldsmith decided to transplant his private, protected world. He knew he would be forty in a few weeks' time, and he wanted to take a few of his friends away from the miseries of an English February. They could play backgammon, sit in the sun, and relax. In previous winters he had visited Morocco and the West Indies, but now he was intent on Acapulco in Mexico. The break would give him time to plan his next deal, and to consider what he should be doing about the recession that he felt was about to overtake the economies of the Western world. The only question was: whom should he invite. Annabel Birley certainly, and his old Oxford associate Peter West; John Aspinall, of course; and one of Aspinall's friends from the Clermont club, the Earl of Lucan, who was usually good company; Dominic Elwes, who was Annabel's cousin; and, perhaps, one or two others. But first Jimmy Goldsmith intended to take a trip to the United States and Mexico as well as Venezuela and Brazil, to look at the possibilities for investment in both North and South America. John Tigrett had been stressing their potential for some time, and now, for the first time, he thought he might be in a position to exploit them.

By the time he got to Acapulco late in February 1973, Jimmy Goldsmith had made two decisions that were to change his life.

First he had decided that he would like another, English, family, with Annabel Birley. He wanted her to have his children. They had known each other for nearly ten years, her children were growing up, and so were his; and he wanted to acknowledge their relationship. When he told her about it Annabel Birley knew that every member of the Londonderry family would object (they had not been all that happy when her aunt had married Jimmy Goldsmith's cousin, Lord Jessel), but she also knew that she loved him, and that she had always loved young children. The prospect of another family did not dismay her in the least, it would be a new interest – something to keep her young. The fact that the father of her children might be someone else's husband hardly entered her mind. "It just seemed the natural thing to do," she told her friends later. "We both wanted to have children, and so we thought we would."

His second decision was to sell all his property interests in Britain as quickly as possible as he saw that the country was on the verge of the worst recession since the war. Everything he had worked for could be lost.

"You can't just go forward: you've got to have a reverse," he explains now. "From July 1971 until February 1973 had been a sprint. We had built a small company into a worldwide one, but at the end of that sprint I came to the conclusion that we had to sprint back for cover again. I knew that we couldn't go on like that for ever, and I had to assess where we should be."

It was this decision which proved that Jimmy Goldsmith was more than just an enterprising entrepreneur who had ridden the stock market boom of the early 1970s. It enabled him to survive the slump of the mid-1970s while others all around him, who had ridden the same wave of financial success, including his friend Jim Slater, crashed into bankruptcy.

With the sound of the waves breaking on the Acapulco beach in the background, Jimmy Goldsmith started telephoning his office in London, and instructing Lionel Ross, Cavenham's finance director, to sell all his property for cash. Inflation may have been making it "almost impossible not to make money at the time", according to the *Sunday Times*, but he was still convinced he had to sell.

Years later John Tigrett maintained: "It was all because of a dream that Jimmy had one night in New York. I met him one

Sunday morning at the Carlyle, where he was staying, and asked him if he'd slept well. 'Terribly,' he said. When I asked him why he just said, 'I had this nightmare, and I couldn't get back to sleep again after it. I dreamt I was standing on the seashore, and the waves were coming in, but I couldn't stop them. They kept breaking over my head. I felt as though I was drowning.' I told him to have some breakfast and forget about it, but he said he was going to go back upstairs and send a message to London to sell all his property for cash."

Goldsmith firmly denies ever having any such dream, putting it down to his old friend's "liking for Irish blarney". "The major strategic turn for me was seeing early in 1973 that the market was going to collapse in Britain. It convinced me to sell everything in sight, to run for cover before everyone else."

Some men in the City of London thought he had finally lost his mind. It confirmed their suspicion that he had lacked financial sense in the first place. "For three months the press in London treated me as a complete buffoon. Everytime I sold some property, at what looked like a bargain price, the stories would suggest that I'd gone mad. It went on like that for months: every time I sold something, the speculation would start again that I didn't know what on earth I was doing. Until the property companies started to go bankrupt. By that time I was safe."

Even though the Conservative government's incomes policy had just entered what it called phase two in a desperate effort to slow down the rate of inflation, memories of the "swinging sixties" when England seemed the brightest country in the Western world, were still strong in the City. The possibility of a massive increase in oil prices had hardly occurred to most analysts, and few were predicting a new crisis in the Middle East, and the possibility of another war between Egypt and Israel. Even to those City of London investment analysts who acknowledged that the horizon of Britain's economy was darkening quickly, Jimmy Goldsmith's sudden decision to liquidate his valuable assets in property – and particularly those held by Anglo-Continental – looked like another example of his "over-reaction".

Jimmy Goldsmith smiles at the memory now. "The job of a chairman of an investment company is to decide to invest in the right thing in the right place at the right time. But the right thing is the least important. If you picked the very best share in St Petersburg in 1917 you could be the greatest genius in the world and still go bust. The most important thing is the right place at the right time. You have to be able to see the swings in the market. In 1971 I felt the swing up, and that's when we went into our major expansion programme. But in 1973 I felt a major crisis coming, and I got out just in time."

What the City of London had not yet realized was that Jimmy Goldsmith had decided to do more than just sell some property companies; he had also decided what he was going to do with the money – invest in the United States. Prospects in America looked brighter than they did in Europe, and the more he travelled in the United States, the more convinced he became that it was the obvious place for his companies to develop in the last quarter of the twentieth century. A food group to rival Nestlé or Unilever in Europe was a grand enough ambition, but if he was right, and the European economies were about to fall into a terrifying recession, he had to find a new dimension.

"If I have one ability," he said to himself, "it is to see the changes that are going to take place, and to plan for them."[1] It was a talent that was to stand him in exceptional stead: how exceptional he would not know for almost another decade.

"That conclusion meant that my next major move in Europe was going to be backwards rather than forwards," he recalls now. "Because I had the feeling that Europe was about to go through a very patchy time, I began to sell out of Europe and go somewhere else."

He had been examining the possibility of expansion in the United States for some time. There had been preliminary discussions with Squibb over the possible sale of their Beech-Nut baby food division, and exploratory approaches to the food and tobacco group Liggett and Myers, but both had broken down fairly quickly. According to Madame Beaux: "We had been studying the market in the United States for eighteen months, but we lost opportunities to buy companies because we had not fully realized that it was a very different country, and that we had to be in the hands of lawyers."

In fact Jimmy Goldsmith had already thought of another way to launch himself and his companies into the American market. That was to use his strength in Europe to take over a major English company which already had established American assets. Not long after his takeover of Allied Suppliers he had launched "Project Grand Slam" with his colleagues at Cavenham. It was to be another takeover, but this time of the giant British American Tobacco (BAT) company which had recently extended its already established interests in the United States by buying Sak's on Fifth Avenue, one of New York's most famous stores. If Project Grand Slam succeeded it would be the largest takeover in British financial history.

To try to gain control of BAT Jimmy Goldsmith used exactly the same tactic he had employed against Allied Suppliers. He approached their largest existing shareholder, in this case the Imperial Group who owned 28 per cent of the company, to ask if they would be prepared to sell their shareholding. At a series of secret meetings with Sir John Partridge, the chairman of Imperial, which owned no less than 28 per cent of BAT's shares, he asked if the group could be persuaded to part with its holding. The answer was yes.

It was agreed in principle that Cavenham would buy 14.9 per cent of BAT for cash and the remainder of Imperial's holdings for loan stock. As soon as he had that agreement, Jimmy Goldsmith intended to launch a full-scale bid for BAT. "It would have meant that I had created one of the largest international companies, and my plan was that it would have been followed by a twinning arrangement between France and Britain, similar to the twin structure of Unilever between the Netherlands and Britain."

It also meant that it would take Jimmy Goldsmith into the United States, and create a major worldwide company engaged in the manufacture and sale of consumer products. The new company would have been even larger than Unilever, and although it would be anchored in Britain and France, it would make him a force to be reckoned with in the United States.

Just as the deal to take over Imperial's holdings was about to go through, however, "Project Grand Slam" was trumped. Sir John Partridge believed that he should tell the British Conservative Prime Minister, Edward Heath, about the sale. For the first time, but not the last, a political intrigue was to alter Jimmy Goldsmith's plans.

"Ted Heath asked Partridge not to go through with the deal," he remembers, "unless our takeover of BAT could be a friendly bid. He did not want a massive takeover fight on his hands at that stage in his government."

Sir John Partridge accepted Heath's decision. He would agree to sell his company's shareholdings in BAT only if Jimmy Goldsmith could convince the board of British American Tobacco to agree to the takeover. Both men knew that was almost impossible. The entrepreneur whom some men in the City of London had called "an upstart", barely two years before, was hardly likely to be welcomed into the boardroom of one of Britain's largest companies with open arms. Nevertheless he tried. He had a secret meeting with Sir Richard Dobson, the chairman of BAT, at an anonymous private house, but there was no hope. "The outcome was inevitable," he recalls now. "They did not want to be gobbled up." The grand slam bid had failed.

So, by the time he reached Acapulco the following February Jimmy Goldsmith was certain that the only way forward in the United States was for him to strike out on his own. The Americans appreciated initiative. There, no one was going to ask the approval of the President, or the state governor, before they agreed to sell him some shares. There, no one knew the old suspicions of him as a playboy with a gambler's luck. But before he could press on with his plan he wanted to make sure the sale of his property had been completed. Just as he arrived back in England in April the sale of two of Allied Suppliers' largest buildings, in Finsbury Square near Moorgate in London, and in the City Road a little further north, were sold to Cavendish Land company for £11.7 million in cash. Under the terms of the deal the Allied staff were allowed to stay in the City Road block, a former Lipton's tea warehouse for three years. (By a strange coincidence he found himself a tenant of that same building again six years later; it became the site of the offices of his shortlived English news magazine *Now!*)

All the surplus shops in the Cavenham group were sold to Guardian Properties for £17.5 million – with the proviso that £8.75 million was paid before the end of September 1973, and the balance before the end of 1976. At the same time the company finally disposed of what remained of Bovril's interests in Argentina, which

Gilberte Beaux had spent so long negotiating. Gradually everything was pared down. Anglo-Continental Investments shrank in size, although it still had holdings in Jim Slater's Slater Walker Securities; while Argyle Securities, which also controlled some of his property interests, was similarly scaled down.

By the early summer he had also completed the final purchase of Générale Alimentaire in Paris, buying 400,000 shares from the Rothschild family's Compagnie du Nord, and bringing FIPP inside it, along with his Belgian and Spanish companies Sanders, Laboratoires Grémy-Longuet and Agrifurane, to put his European companies in order. In the meantime Cavenham in England effectively took over the management of GA, as the new food manufacturing company came to be known, because it was the English experience that Jimmy Goldsmith wanted to bring to the French group. Once again the Cavenham management team was asked to brush up its French and descend on a new European company.

As ever, both Cavenham and GA were under the control of Générale Occidentale in Paris, which still controlled the fortunes of every one of his companies, and which was still to be found in a suite of small, discreet offices with marble walls and grey carpets in the avenue de Friedland, barely a stone's throw from the Arc de Triomphe. Jimmy Goldsmith was still more of a Parisian than an Englishman, or an American.

Certainly Isabel Goldsmith was French, and a great deal more like her father than either she, or he, cared to admit. Both concealed their shyness by flamboyance, their uncertainty in grandeur and a taste for luxury. Both were romantic and had a habit of falling spectacularly in love. The young photographer who had encouraged her to overcome her shyness at her party at the Ritz in London just a few months before had become a closer and closer friend. By the spring Isabel Goldsmith had decided to marry Baron Arnaud de Rosnay. She was not quite nineteen, and he was twenty-six, but she knew her father would not mind. After all her mother had been younger when they had eloped together. When she told him her plans, he was delighted.

Another party was called for: an engagement party. Goldsmith was determined that his own daughter would not have to elope or hide in the homes of solicitors before her wedding. Everything would be open and above board. Arnaud de Rosnay's parents, who had been sugar planters in Mauritius, would be invited, and so would Don Antenor Patino. The old rift had healed; this was a time to prove it. For a wedding present he told Isabel that he intended to give them an island of 2,400 acres in the Mozambique channel between East Africa and Madagascar. The marriage was arranged for 28 June at the church of St Clothilde, not far from his house in Paris near Les Invalides. The honeymoon was to be spent on their own island.

At the party itself Jimmy Goldsmith was in an expansive mood. His daughter looked radiant, showing everyone the ring Arnaud had given her – a miniature Salvador Dali painting of a swan set in diamonds. Annabel Birley had come over from London specially with her cousin Dominic Elwes, and so had John Aspinall. The party was held at Laurent, a gilt and mirrored restaurant on the Champs Elysées that he had hired specially. By midnight Jimmy Goldsmith had decided that he liked the restaurant so much he was going to buy it. But when he asked the manager if the owner might be prepared to sell, the young man clearly thought the effect of the night's champagne had been too much for the host. He was not to know that Jimmy Goldsmith rarely drank more than a single glass of anything. The young manager hesitated, and finally agreed to talk about the proposition the following day. Secretly he felt sure the idea would be forgotten by then. Why should anyone decide to purchase a restaurant on the strength of a single visit? Once again someone had underestimated Jimmy Goldsmith's passionate concentration on an idea, once it had settled in his mind. The following morning he held a meeting with the owners of Laurent, and he went on to hold more over the next few days. Within a month Jimmy Goldsmith had become the owner, but not the manager, of Laurent.

"Jimmy thought that, as he was always eating out in Paris, why should he not own his own restaurant," one of his colleagues in Laurent was to explain later. What was wrong with having one of the most respected restaurants in Paris, with two stars from the Guide Michelin? But there was another reason. Owning a restaurant guaranteed a comforting privacy, it meant that you could feel at home. Jimmy Goldsmith had always enjoyed the familiar, especially in France. Adventurous entrepreneur he might be, but he disliked places and people he did not know and trust. Risks were for the market place.

The familiar was all the more important now because he was on the brink of his first major deal in the United States. After months of looking for a business that he thought he understood, and sifting through hundreds of different possibilities, Jimmy Goldsmith had settled on a chain of supermarkets called Grand Union. They had been drawn to his attention principally by André Meyer, the legendary head of the investment bankers Lazard Frères in New York, who had gone on to set up the takeover with a telephone call to Grand Union's president, Charles G. Rodman.

Selling food was a business Jimmy Goldsmith knew and understood; and he had a management team that he knew could run it. Jim Wood, the former Co-operative manager who had shepherded Cavenham's supermarkets to enormous profit from the least promising beginnings, was to be put in charge of Grand Union as soon as he had control.

Like Bovril, Grand Union fitted the formula that Jimmy Goldsmith had set himself for new acquisitions. It was a well established company, which had rather lost its way by diversification over the years. Like Bovril, Grand Union was more than a century old. It had started out as a one-man store in Scranton, Pennsylvania, where Cyrus Jones and his brothers, Frank and Charles, sold coffee, tea, spices, baking powder and flavouring extracts. As their business grew they had opened other shops in the eastern United States, operating under the name of the Grand Union Tea Company. By the 1920s there were more than 200 small stores in the group, with more than 5,000 door-to-door salesmen to back them up; the goods were delivered in horse-drawn wagons. In 1929 Grand Union became a public company listed on the New York Stock Exchange.

Throughout the next forty years Grand Union had continued to expand, until by the late 1960s it boasted more than 500 supermarkets in the eastern United States, with sales of more than a billion dollars a year. But the onset of inflation had caught Grand Union's management unprepared, just as the American food industry went into a sharp decline. Though they were hardly enthusiastic about the prospect at the outset – one critic of the deal called him a "goddam foreigner who doesn't know a thing about American supermarkets" – Cavenham and its holding company Générale Occidentale represented a lifeboat in distinctly stormy seas.

Jimmy Goldsmith could certainly afford the acquisition. Stock market analysts estimated that he had £90 million in surplus cash available in Cavenham, which had expanded to a turnover of £763 million, and that his smaller banking and investment arm, Anglo-Continental, was worth some £41 million. Throughout the autumn of 1973 Jimmy Goldsmith patiently waited for the opportunity to buy it. In November he finally made an offer.

This is how he put it in his chairman's report to the Cavenham shareholders, written only weeks before he unveiled his bid for Grand Union: "We started by acquiring and reorganizing a group of small companies largely in confectionery which for the most part were run down to the point where they would have to be put into liquidation – and which in the process would have put some 2,000 people out of employment. We reconstructed this group of companies by strengthening management, closing and selling out-of-date factories, investing the proceeds to modernize other factories, develop new products, and put the companies back on the road to healthy organic growth. It sounds easy but it was not. We almost failed – but we also gained a great deal of experience."

Jimmy Goldsmith was about to put that experience to use in the United States. On 3 December 1973 he announced that Cavenham, through a new American subsidiary called Cavenham Holdings, had bought control of the Grand Union supermarket chain for $62 million, of which almost $61 million had been raised for them by Hambros bank in the City of London as a Eurodollar loan. It was a considerable coup. When Cavenham acquired it, Grand Union was the tenth largest supermarket chain in the United States with sales of almost $1.5 billion a year, employing more than 27,000 people in its 600 shops, which included 531 supermarkets in eleven States. Within four months of Cavenham's takeover Jim Wood was its new president.

The plan that had formed in Jimmy Goldsmith's mind in Mexico ten months earlier had come to fruition. The Acapulco Strategy had been put into effect. It was not a moment too soon. Just as he announced the acquisition in London, the British stock market began to plummet downwards on a slide which was to take it almost a decade to recover from.

It was not the only part of the Acapulco plan that had come to fruition as 1973 drew to a close. Against her family's advice, and ignoring their sternest warnings, Lady Annabel Birley had gone ahead with their plan to start a new family. By August 1973 she knew she was pregnant, and she told her husband Mark. "He offered me the chance to go back to him, but I had decided already that I couldn't," she explains now.

Annabel Birley had decided on her future, and nothing was going to make her change her mind. Some people might be shocked, but she would never let that put her off. No Londonderry ever shirked a difficult decision. It was part of the family heritage—the tradition that had seen her grandmother become the greatest hostess of her day, and her father a member of the British Cabinet for four years.

When Annabel Birley gave birth to a daughter on 30 January 1974 in the private wing of the Westminster Hospital in London, Jimmy Goldsmith was delighted. He had not wanted to be present during the birth, much to her relief, but he had paced up and down the corridors outside her private room with a look of boyish pride on his face. It was as if this was his first child. Some may have looked askance at the thirty-nine-year-old daughter of a British marquis bearing the illegitimate child of a married man but neither of them gave a fig about that. They were both too happy. The gossip columns and the sceptical friends could say what they liked. They both loved children, and wanted to have them together. "Jimmy adored the idea of a new family," she explains, "and so did I. There was nothing I wanted more."

In fact, almost before Annabel Birley and Jimmy Goldsmith had a chance to christen their new daughter, Jemima, she was pregnant again. "We hadn't really planned it, it just happened that way."

The next Goldsmith dynasty had begun, just as the head of the family was beginning to turn in new directions: towards the United States and British politics.

PART 4

Melodrama

14

Political Ambitions

Before his fortieth birthday Jimmy Goldsmith was little more than an ambitious and successful young financier on the rise. He had made few public speeches, "and when I did I was so nervous I was almost ill", and few public statements beyond announcing his takeover bids. He had one or two political friends, and had contributed to Conservative Party funds, but he saw himself primarily as a businessman. Any views he had of events in the world around him were coloured by how these might affect the fortunes of his companies.

After his fortieth birthday, however, Jimmy Goldsmith's interests began to change. His horizons widened, and for the first time he began to wonder whether he might not have more to contribute to the countries that housed his businesses than simply the creation of wealth or jobs. The strategies that he had used to establish Générale Occidentale and Cavenham had clearly worked, and he had foreseen the collapse in the stock market. The confidence these decisions had given him encouraged him to think he might have more to offer than simply the creation of the third largest food group in Europe.

Perhaps it was admiration for his father that first led Jimmy Goldsmith to consider seriously a career in British politics. That, and a fascination for the workings of power. His meteoric rise as a financier convinced him that, at the very least, his views of the future of the European economy deserved to be taken seriously, and he knew he would not be the first financier to have considered using commercial success as a springboard into a political career. Part of him wanted nothing more than to see another member of Frank Goldsmith's family enter the Palace of Westminster, even if he suspected that he was "a bit foreign" and "a bit eccentric" to fit easily into the House of Commons. "Probably the only other difficulty," says his brother Teddy, "was that Jimmy would never have been very happy as a backbencher. He would have wanted to be Chancellor of the Exchequer at least."

As the affairs of Cavenham and Générale Alimentaire settled down, and Générale Occidentale consolidated its hold on them both, Jimmy Goldsmith had more time to devote himself to politics. His financial survival had been assured by his Acapulco Strategy of moving out of property in England. The move had been completed just in time. The City of London was only just beginning to realize how sensible he had been to sell out so many of his assets for cash. He had even sold the small bank he owned in France to David de Rothschild of the Rothschild bank.

By the beginning of 1974 recession was beginning to threaten major companies throughout Britain which had looked impregnable only a few months before. As the oil price had risen in the wake of the Yom Kippur war and Edward Heath had introduced a three-day working week in Britain for the first time in the country's industrial history, so the stock market had started to plummet. By the end of April the value of some leading shares had fallen by two-thirds, and the City of London stock market share index was lower than it had been in the darkest days of World War II, shortly after the evacuation of troops from the beaches of Dunkirk. But, unlike many of his contemporaries who had risen to success on the wave of the rising market in the early 1970s, Jimmy Goldsmith was safe. In the words of his friend Charles Hambro: "Jimmy was pretty well placed. I don't think anybody really foresaw the extent of the débâcle, the collapse in values, but certainly Jimmy came through it well." To the accompaniment of power cuts in factories and offices as well as schools and homes, Britain had begun a spiral of economic decline.

In the crisis that gripped both the City of London and the Conservative government in the first months of 1974, anyone who seemed to have found a means of insulating himself against the collapse was bound to be a figure of considerable interest – particularly to Edward Heath, the Conservative Prime Minister. When he lost the general election in February in the wake of a bruising miners' strike by the narrowest of margins, he began immediately to look around for help to unseat his opponent, Harold Wilson, in the general election that was obviously inevitable within a matter of months.

One of the men Edward Heath turned to was Jimmy Goldsmith, even though they hardly knew each other. Their meeting was not entirely a surprise. Edward Heath's cabinet colleague Peter Walker was the joint founder of Slater Walker Securities with Jimmy Goldsmith's friend and backgammon opponent Jim Slater. Slater had recommended some of Heath's personal investments for him. It was hardly unexpected, therefore, that Jim Slater should suggest to the newly defeated Prime Minister that the one man who might have ideas about the economic future of Britain was the stock market's most conspicuous success in the past three years – Jimmy Goldsmith. Slater also knew the two men shared an interest in European affairs and the European economy, and he guessed they might well have other interests in common.

At that moment, however, Jimmy Goldsmith was not thinking about British politics. He had just finished simplifying the affairs of his European companies, and adding the Spanish branch of the Sanders company to Cavenham to match their existing Sanders holdings in France and Belgium, and in June 1974 he had negotiated an agreement with the Banco Urquijo in Madrid to enable him to extend Cavenham's activities even further in the Iberian peninsula. At the same time he was negotiating to buy more than 400,000 shares in the French grocery company Générale Alimentaire, in which he already had a 25 per cent holding, from the Rothschild family's company, Compagnie du Nord, and thereby put the ownership and control of GA beyond doubt. By the end of June he had managed it.

His companies rather than British politics were still Jimmy Goldsmith's principal interest. Indeed, he had taken no part in the February election campaign in spite of the bitter debate taking place. Far from it. His only public appearance had been at Eton College, where he had told a group of sixth-formers just before the February election, "For a career in the City one needs to be honourable and trustworthy, but for a career in industry one needs a more determined will to win." He still preferred men who liked to win, rather than those who were content to be "good losers".

By the summer of 1974 that was exactly what Edward Heath was looking for, and Peter Walker and Jim Slater knew it. Without telling Jimmy Goldsmith, Walker arranged a dinner at his Westminster home. He invited three principal guests: Jim Slater, Selim Zilkha (whose Mothercare shops had not suffered in the depression) and Jimmy Goldsmith.

"It was rather a surprise," Jimmy Goldsmith recalls, "because I hadn't really met Heath before, and I didn't exactly know what the dinner was going to be about." It did not take him long to find out. The conversation was about the next general election and what the Conservative Party had to do in order to win it.

Edward Heath appeared to like Jimmy Goldsmith, "though it was sometimes difficult to tell who Ted liked", as one of his advisers put it. Heath seemed to admire his directness and his clear vision. Perhaps he recognized some of his own qualities in Jimmy Goldsmith. Both men could be impatient with other people's slowness or indecision; both shared a suspicion of some parts of the English establishment – which they felt had never quite accepted them; while both also shared a conviction that they were often right about events, even if they were not always acknowledged to be so. Whatever their similarities, the dinner for Edward Heath at Peter Walker's house in the early summer of 1974 created a political future for Jimmy Goldsmith.

Though he had not exactly planned it, Goldsmith was not displeased. The ambience of power had always fascinated him. He enjoyed the gossip of politicians, and closeness to decisions that might affect the fate of millions. It was an appetite for influence he was never to lose, though he was to recognize soon enough that political life in England "was full of weakness".

"Ted Heath saw Jimmy as an example of the new capitalism that he admired," explains one of the former Prime Minister's friends. "For a time he became one of his new heroes, like Arnold Weinstock, the chairman of the huge GEC, and Jim Slater; the sort of man he could call on to help with money for particular projects, for research assistance, and who could be relied upon to be as annoyed as he was by the failings of the Tory party's organization." It is doubtful whether Ted Heath actually saw his new friend as a future member of a Conservative Cabinet, but he certainly saw him as someone who could help organize a Conservative election victory. After the Walker dinner Heath suggested they meet again in the near future.

For his part, however, Jimmy Goldsmith was not all that impressed. After another meeting with Heath and the Conservative Party chairman, Willie Whitelaw, at which the two men asked if he would be prepared to help them win the next election, Jimmy Goldsmith left in a state of despair. "It was my first real contact with politics," he was to say, "and I couldn't believe the weakness of it all: the awful indecision, the vacillation, the uncertainty. They didn't seem to know what to do." Another reason for his disappointment was his conviction that Ted Heath could not win another election. The two men may have shared some characteristics, but Jimmy Goldsmith realized that the Tory leader was hardly a man to inspire public affection. "He is a distinctly cold fish," he told one friend sadly after the meeting. "I'm not sure he can do it."

In fact, Heath and Whitelaw were almost as bewildered by Jimmy Goldsmith as he was by them. His restless energy and apparent dislike for the subtler forms of British diplomacy did not exactly endear him to them, whatever their respect for his achievements. As he strode up and down the chairman's office at Tory Central Office in Smith Square, with its view across to Wren's elegant St John's church, they could hardly believe their ears as he regaled them with what sounded like very grand judgements about the future of Europe and the European economy. That had not been what they had been expecting at all. Jimmy Goldsmith did not sound to them like a politically ambitious young man anxious to set his foot on the first ladder of a career in the House of Commons and the Cabinet by helping them win an election. He seemed far too confident of himself for that. There did not seem much room for the delicate intrigue of political compromise in him.

"Your advertising is terrible, and your organization is worse," he told them firmly. In particular he despaired of the party's tradition of "imposing on the local parties from Central Office. If you want to win the election you will have to revolutionize your constituency parties; and you haven't got much time to do it." Dazed, the two Tory politicians thanked him for coming, and said they would be in touch.

"Frankly, I never expected to hear another word from them," Jimmy Goldsmith remembers now. "I was about to go on holiday, in any case, so I put the whole matter out of my mind." And he left for a villa in Amalfi in Italy, which he had hired for the summer from the Italian film producer Carlo Ponti. Ginette was going to be there, rather than Annabel Birley. As he sat on the terrace of Ponti's villa with its view across the azure blue sea, the thought of an election in England slipped out of his mind.

It was Jim Slater who brought it back. He telephoned Jimmy Goldsmith in Amalfi to tell him that Heath wanted to see him in London, urgently. "They want you to help with the campaign. They think there is going to be an election in late September or early October."

For a moment Jimmy Goldsmith hesitated. "He did not have all that much respect for Ted Heath," as one of his friends puts it now, "and he wasn't quite sure what he could do." But the temptation of being near the centre of political power, and the suggestion that, perhaps, he could make some impact on the Conservative Party's chances of winning the general election finally convinced him. He flew back from Italy early, leaving his friends to enjoy the villa.

Back in London he agreed to help Heath in any way he could. For a start he would work from time to time in the chairman's office at the Conservative headquarters in Smith Square advising on organization, on ways of raising money for the campaign, and providing "whatever other assistance is necessary". His first move was to announce a dinner for British industrialists at which they would all be asked for their suggestions to help the Tory cause, and "establish a debate about the country's future". His friend Charles Hambro was drawn into the scheme too. It was not exactly an original idea – the Americans had been using "$1,000 a plate" dinners to support their candidates for generations – but it was a new departure in England.

Jimmy Goldsmith had himself contributed to Conservative Party funds over the past few years. The first time had been in 1970, when Jeffrey Archer, then still an ambitious young Conservative politician, had asked him to donate £100,000 to promote the "European cause" which was close to Edward Heath's heart. That donation, like every other he had made to the Conservative Party, came from his own pocket, not from the Cavenham group. His companies made no political donations whatsoever in 1973, 1974 or 1975. Their chairman could support whom he liked, and donate what he liked of his own money, but he did not intend to confuse his own interests with those of his companies. While he was working in Tory Central Office in the late summer and autumn of 1974 he made it quite clear that he was there in a private capacity, rather than as chairman of Cavenham.

Life near the centre of political power in England confirmed Jimmy Goldsmith's worst fears. "The leadership of the Conservative Party did not seem determined enough to win," he recalls. "When Denis Healey, the Labour Party's Chancellor of the Exchequer, announced during the election campaign that inflation was going down, I produced detailed research to prove that food prices were rising steeply, and contradict him. But it was never properly used. It was as if they were embarrassed by it." It was left to Goldsmith himself to predict, in a speech at his own dinner for industrialists, that food prices would go up if Labour won the coming general election. "It could have had a dramatic effect on the election result," he reflects now, "if it had been properly used."

The longer the election campaign lasted the more depressed Jimmy Goldsmith became. It was all too clear to him that Edward Heath had lost the initiative to Harold Wilson. "Heath looks like a bitter man," he told his friends. "No one really wants a bitter man as Prime Minister." Even the suggestion in the Conservative Party's election manifesto that "it is essential for the Government to draw upon outside talents" failed to cheer him – though some political commentators insisted privately that it was included specifically to allow Heath to bring men like Jimmy Goldsmith into a Conservative government as ministers.

To cheer himself he planned another trip to the sunshine, this time with Annabel Birley and many of his old friends. "We'll leave the day after the election," he told them. "We shall all know what happened by then." When the first results started to come in on the evening of 15 October 1974, Jimmy Goldsmith's private suspicions were proved correct. The Conservative Party had been soundly beaten. Though he did not realize it at the time, at that moment any real hope he might have had for a political career in England evaporated. Edward Heath was never again to be Prime Minister.

But Jimmy Goldsmith was nevertheless optimistic enough to risk a £5,000 bet with one of the industrialists who had come to his fund-raising dinner, Roland "Tiny" Rowland of the Lonrho group of companies, that "Edward Heath will be returned to power as Prime Minister before the end of 1975". In reality Jimmy Goldsmith was by no means confident of winning, unless Edward Heath took up his offer "to reorganize Central Office once and for all".

"If you allow me to do that," he had told Heath, "it would transform the picture once and for all. If Central Office was a co-ordinator rather than an imposer on the grassroots, it would transform the Tory Party into a party close to its electorate." He was aware that the Left had already seen the value of having well disciplined local party organizations.

The offer was never taken up, and a disillusioned Jimmy Goldsmith revealed his conclusions in a rare public speech, the Lubbock lecture at Oxford University on 5 December 1974. He told the assembled undergraduates: "'Muddling through' is a euphemism for failing to plan forward. It means acting tactically and without a strategy; it means confusing the means with the end. It has been a major contributor to the English disease." The reference to the Conservative Party's failed election campaign, and to his part in it, could hardly have been clearer. "We are ill-adjusted to face the great new challenges that confront us. We have been fortunate in that we have been prosperous for a long time, but prolonged prosperity is not good training. People begin to forget why we have this wonderful thing and what produced it. They start believing that it is their God-given right or natural right. They forget fundamental facts . . . As a result we draw farther and farther away from reality.

"It was once said," he went on, "that democracy can survive only for so long as the majority is willing to sacrifice the short-term for the long-term. When this is no longer the case, when the majority is more interested in the short-term, then the whole nation becomes a vast rotten borough. It chooses its leaders by the number of short-term inducements that are promised . . . To pander to this irresponsibility is evil. The government should make clear our changed circumstances and should explain the perils we face. It must preach civil duties not civil rights."

He ended his speech by saying darkly: "The epitaph on the grave of our democracy would be: 'They sacrificed the long-term for the short-term, and the long-term finally arrived.'"

It was the speech of a man who knew he was out of step with the attitudes and opinions of the Conservative Party under Edward Heath, but it was certainly not the speech of a playboy who had indulged his "gambler's luck" on the stock market. It was one of the first public signs that he now had a political dimension. Even so, it was hardly the speech of a man taking the familiar routes to political power. The conclusions were a touch too sweeping, his suggestions too radical to fit comfortably into the traditions of compromise in British politics in the post-war years. There was a flavour of soothsaying about them that had never been a popular part of English politics. And, even when the speech was widely reported, with headlines like "Financial System could collapse warns Goldsmith" and a long extract reprinted in both the London *Daily Mail* and *Observer*, he did not follow it up with television appearances or interviews. In his business career he preferred to walk a lone path; naturally, he had the same approach to politics.

As one of his friends explains, "Jimmy is simply too intemperate a human being to be a politician in England. He will sometimes say wild things, and he pays no attention to how they are received. If he had been rather more temperate then he might have become a more important public figure in England." Goldsmith contents himself with saying, "I have always preferred to look at the strategy of a battle, and to draw my own conclusions. If, sometimes, those are unpalatable to some people, I am afraid I cannot help that."

But Jimmy Goldsmith had realized that there was another obstacle in the way of any hopes of a political future he might have had in England, and one from which he was certain it would never recover: his personal life. Looking back on it now he admits, "Yes, I would like to have gone into politics. I think I might have been useful. But I have never been prepared to be a hypocrite. Hypocrisy is not one of my flaws." He knew only too well that his relationship with Annabel Birley, and the fact that their daughter Jemima was only a few months old in October 1974 when she was six months pregnant with their second child, was bound eventually to have an effect on his political ambitions. Many a Tory MP might have had a liaison with a married woman, but few would have been prepared to admit it publicly, and to sustain two families.

"I had not tailored my life to go into British politics," he accepts now. "My attitude was different. I was not willing to tailor my personal life to my career, and I was not willing to live in any kind of hypocrisy, so I accepted fairly quickly that a career in British politics was not possible."

Nevertheless he was as upset as he always had been by the suspicion, criticism and distrust with which he was treated. He still maintained that there was nothing particularly eccentric about his attitude to life and to his families in France and England. "I find it extraordinary the fascination with people's sex life in England," he says forcefully now. "The mixture of snobbism and frustrated sex in the country I find depressing."

He had a clearer understanding of his weaknesses, and the attitudes of the society in which he found himself, than some other British politicians in the years to come were capable of.

Even in May the following year, when Edward Heath was replaced as leader of the Tory Party by Mrs Margaret Thatcher, Jimmy Goldsmith got no closer to political power. He did not get on terribly well with the new leader when he first met her. "They were very wary of each other," a friend says, and he admits, "We did not get on particularly well at first." The grocer's daughter from Grantham and the flamboyant son of France's most famous hotelier were hardly the most obviously compatible companions. The Victorian values for which she stood were not reflected in his unrepentantly uninhibited lifestyle. Jimmy Goldsmith may not have been prepared to be a hypocrite, but his personal life did not endear him immediately to the new leader of the Conservative Party. The Somerville scientist who had trained for the bar did not mix easily with a man who had visited Oxford to play chemin de fer; the hardworking bourgeois clashed with the natural bohemian.

Nevertheless when they first met in October 1975, in the Leader of the Opposition's discreet wood-panelled office in the House of Commons, she complimented him politely on his Lubbock lecture at Oxford and thanked him for his financial support for the right-wing Centre for Policy Studies which she and Sir Keith Joseph were in the process of launching to focus a new strand of "free market" economics within the Conservative Party. She was far less complimentary about a speech he had given the week before to the annual conference of editors and publishers of United Press International. In it he had made a sweeping attack on the electoral system and on the voting systems for trade union action; he had urged reform of the House of Lords; condemned the infiltration of the Labour Party by the Communist Party; and criticized the Tory Party for being "haunted by its upper-middle-class origins. If you are an industrial nation, overpopulated, competing for world trade to pay for the imports of food to feed your people, then you need a few winners whether you like them or not . . . Britain must become a meritocracy. The best, no matter what their background, must reach the top. Excellence must unreservedly be encouraged. Our present educational system is incompatible with, indeed hostile to this objective. Our private sector, dominated by the public schools, consists with trivial exceptions of students selected on the criteria of wealth and birth." It was too much for the future Prime Minister. For the time being at least, Jimmy Goldsmith and Margaret Thatcher had almost nothing to do with each other.

His unashamedly idiosyncratic approach was not suited to the blurred compromises of English politics, even in the Conservative Party of Margaret Thatcher. His sweeping conclusions about the fate of the western world seemed too grandiose to a politician nurtured in the distinctively English traditions of the Conservative Party, no matter how radical her own approach might be.

In fact, Jimmy Goldsmith's political generalizations were part of the family tradition. His elder brother Teddy had earlier launched himself into public affairs in Britain. Although their paths had diverged over the years, the two brothers remained close, and while Jimmy Goldsmith was rushing through the stock markets of Europe and the United States, Teddy had preferred to draw the attention of the world to its potential fate. Teddy Goldsmith had founded the Ecological Foundation in 1970 with some financial support from his brother, and then had gone on himself to found *The Ecologist* magazine, which in 1972 had produced an apocalyptic vision of the fate of the world unless it took its ecology seriously. Written almost entirely by Teddy Goldsmith, "Blueprint for Survival" painted a deeply pessimistic portrait of Western industrialized society unless "man could be persuaded to return to smaller communities".

John Aspinall shared his views. He helped to launch "Blueprint for Survival" in the unlikely setting of his gambling club, the Clermont, which he was about to sell. "Gambler that I have always been," he told the assembled press conference, "brave man that I am, I tremble before the oncoming storm." So convinced was Aspinall by his old friend's conclusions that in February 1974 he encouraged him to stand as a candidate for the newly formed Ecology Party in the year's first general election. Teddy decided to stand in his father's old constituency which was now called the Eye division of Suffolk. Cavenham Hall had been demolished in the early 1950s after its sale had proved difficult, but the park that surrounded the house was still there and both brothers saw it as an opportunity to keep the family tradition alive.

To attract the attention of the local press during the campaign John Aspinall provided his friend with a camel to ride, although quite what relevance that had to the Ecology Party was not entirely clear to the press. It was really little more than a joke, but it reflected the two men's friendship. Teddy Goldsmith and John Aspinall had travelled the world together in the years since they left Oxford, usually looking for rare and wild animals some of which were to find their way back into Aspinall's private zoo in the fifty-five-acre grounds of his home in Kent, Howlett's near Canterbury.

Teddy Goldsmith lost his deposit in the general election of February 1974, and never stood again as a parliamentary candidate in Britain. Instead he abandoned his London home in Fulham, where he had lived with his wife Gill and their two spectacularly beautiful daughters – Dido and Clio – and settled on three farms near Wadebridge in Cornwall to practise what he preached, and return to a small community of his own.

Jimmy Goldsmith was aware of his brother's views. Both men were profoundly against nuclear power and worried by its potential dangers for mankind. Even if their contacts were usually restricted to long telephone calls, Jimmy still looked after his brother's financial interests, just as he looked after their mother's, and he often saw his brother on holiday, just as he saw John Aspinall. Even before the first meeting with Edward Heath, both his brother and his oldest friend had been urging him to take part "in the public debate". Gradually, Jimmy Goldsmith had accepted that the chairman of a major public company needed to have a vision of the political future, for his companies' security as well as for any political ambition he might have.

It was already clear that some of his interests, particularly his "wheeling and dealing" arm, Anglo-Continental Investments and Finance, could have benefited from just that sort of political awareness. Shortly after the October election Jimmy Goldsmith had been forced to announce that neither Anglo, nor Argyle Securities, the property company in which it had bought a decisive stake in 1973, would be able to pay a dividend to their shareholders. The *Financial Times* expressed the views of the City of London when it commented, "There have been signs of market unease about the financial and property offshoots of Mr James Goldsmith's empire for some time." Looking back now, however, Jimmy Goldsmith defends both Anglo-Continental and Argyle. "They showed the financial strategy I was aiming at, and they were almost the only survivors among the medium-sized financial and investment companies of those days. The shareholders did well out of them in the long term; but they represented a weak point that people liked to attack me on." In fact the companies allowed him to build up cash resources "to increase our holdings in Cavenham. If we hadn't done that then we would have been liable to a takeover ourselves. That's exactly how it worked, and how we protected ourselves in Cavenham."

As 1974 drew to a close, two events were to transform Jimmy Goldsmith's life, and remove any thought of a career in British politics for ever. One was the first tremors of the collapse of Slater Walker Securities, which announced in November 1974 that it "was pulling out of property in Europe" with losses of more than £2 million. The other was a domestic drama: the disappearance of his old gambling acquaintance, the seventh Earl of Lucan, who had been on holiday in Acapulco with him in February 1973. No matter how unlikely it may have seemed at the time, both events were to do more to alter his vision of Britain than either Edward Heath or Margaret Thatcher. In the end both contributed to Jimmy Goldsmith's conviction that he had little future in England, no matter what he might once have hoped.

The Lucan drama had a particularly bizarre beginning. Goldsmith was in Ireland on business that night and knew nothing about it until the following morning, but, shortly before ten o'clock on the evening of Thursday 7 November 1974, Lord Lucan's wife Veronica burst into the saloon bar of The Plumber's Arms in London's Belgravia with blood streaming from her head. "He's in the house . . . The children are in the house . . . He's murdered my nanny," she screamed at the customers. Then she collapsed.

Half an hour earlier Lady Lucan had walked downstairs to the basement of her house in Lower Belgrave Street to speak to her nanny, Sandra Rivett. The basement was dark, and she called the girl's name. There was no reply. Then, suddenly, a man rushed at her out of the darkness and hit her on the head four times with a blunt instrument. Lady Lucan later insisted that the man who hit her was her husband.

Sandra Rivett had been savagely battered by a piece of lead piping which, police scientists said later, was almost certainly the same weapon used to hit Lady Lucan. She was already dead. Miraculously, Veronica Lucan managed to escape from her attacker and run out into the street. She could not explain why she might have been attacked.

"Poor Sandra," she later told a reporter. "Was she killed by mistake for me? She was exactly the same height as me, and the same build."

To compound the extraordinary mystery Lord Lucan, who was called John by his closest friends, and Lucky by his acquaintances, was never seen again after that night.

The disappearance of John Lucan and the collapse of Jim Slater's company Slater Walker Securities were to turn Jimmy Goldsmith into a public figure in England. They also put paid to his political future. Ironically, they helped to make him one of the richest men in the world.

15

An End to Privacy

Jimmy Goldsmith may have created a massive food group in Britain and France by a series of audacious, unexpected takeovers – shifting his companies around like pieces on a backgammon board – but he was hardly a public figure in Europe. He was still the private man he had always been, a shrewd hedonist who liked to make his business an extension of pleasure, but who preferred to conduct his affairs of every kind in secret. He liked to walk the streets of London or Paris without being recognized. He owned the smart English steeplechaser Garnishee, certainly, but he was seldom in the paddock to see it run. He gambled a little, but usually in the seclusion of the Clermont club in London. He took long holidays, but always in private villas away from the more ostentatious resorts. He was a tall, balding man of almost forty-two years of age, who liked to spend his time in the cossetted anonymity of the rich.

By the end of 1975, however, Jimmy Goldsmith's life was transformed; and within eighteen months he was no longer able to go anywhere – in England at least – without being recognized, and more often than not insulted. For a shy man, who often concealed his reserve with bluster, it was a painful turn of events from which he would never truly recover. It was to send him even further into his own private world; a world where strangers were admitted only after careful consideration, which had its own private rules and its own special loyalties.

Indeed, in the first weeks of 1975, Jimmy Goldsmith's primary concern was less his business than his private life. Lady Annabel Birley was about to give birth to their second child. Once again he had no wish to be present at the delivery, "Annabel had never liked the idea either", no matter what the new theories about a father's presence might be, and instead paced up and down his office in Leadenhall Street in the City, telephoning the private wing of the Westminster Hospital every few minutes. He was a great deal more agitated about the birth of his fifth child than he cared to admit. For, though he hardly admitted it to himself, Jimmy Goldsmith wanted another son. Manes, for whom he had a deep affection, was now nearly sixteen, but the boy did not seem to have inherited the concentration or determination of his father. There was just a chance that another son might display more of an interest in ensuring that the Goldsmith family's revival continued. So when the news finally came in the early hours of 30 January 1975 that Annabel Birley had given birth to a healthy baby boy, Jimmy Goldsmith was delighted. The next generation of English Goldsmiths had properly begun. He and Annabel decided he should be called Zacharias, a name famous in both the Catholic and Jewish faiths as marking the child with a future. When the baby was brought home to Pelham Cottage, Jimmy Goldsmith began to wonder if the time had not come to legitimize his second family. Perhaps he should talk to Annabel about marriage. A son was a significant event.

There was another reason why dynasties were on his mind in the first weeks of 1975. Jimmy Goldsmith was just about to be officially welcomed into the greatest Jewish banking dynasty in Europe: the one operated under the sign of the red shield and five arrows by the Rothschilds. Jimmy Goldsmith had helped his French cousins with their difficulties over Générale Alimentaire in the past year – finally taking the company over from them entirely – and now he was selling them his 70 per cent holding in the Paris Discount Bank in return for a 7 per cent holding in the Rothschild's family bank in France and a seat on the board. The directorship would be the final recognition of his achievements over the previous ten years, and a signal to the world that the Goldsmith family fortunes were now properly restored to their rightful place alongside those of their more famous cousins. No one could impugn the traditions or the methods of the Rothschild bank. It symbolized respectability and substance. The fact that the sale would also raise him some £4.5 million, considerably more than the £5,000 that his English godfather Baron James de Rothschild had left him in his will, was irrelevant.

David de Rothschild, then just thirty-three and the son of Baron Guy de Rothschild, recalls the deals with Jimmy Goldsmith clearly. He had negotiated the sale of Générale Alimentaire, and then the purchase of the Paris Discount Bank. "It meant something to Jimmy," he recalls now, "and a great deal to me, because I was just beginning my career." It also saw the foundation of a friendship between the two men which was destined to continue. "Jimmy had the same characteristics then that he has now: charisma, enthusiasm and keenness, as well as great mental agility. He has never changed." When they were negotiating, the eternally restless Jimmy Goldsmith had told his distant cousin, "We've got to come to an agreement in the next two hours or not at all." The memory of it still makes David de Rothschild laugh: "That is always Jimmy. Always a deal at once. There was great tension, but great fun."

His appointment as a director of Rothschilds, however, was not the critical part of Jimmy Goldsmith's business life, welcome though it was. The affairs of Cavenham and Générale Occidentale counted for much more. Gilberte Beaux had joined the Cavenham board the year before, but it was still Jack Greenhalgh and the original management team who were directing the company, just as they had been doing for almost a decade. And they were still ready for their young chairman to bring them new companies. As Jack Greenhalgh explains now, "My job was to have the management ready before Jimmy got the new companies. Every time we took something over we used to put in the same team to get the strategies right, cut out any bleeding sores and suture them off, and then that team would hand over to the new management and seal off behind them so that they could be ready for the next acquisition."

There was one major difference between Jimmy Goldsmith's methods and those of some other British companies expanding in Europe. Goldsmith recognized the commercial benefits of two languages and two nationalities and this style seeped down into his companies. "It gave us an advantage over some other English companies," Jack Greenhalgh explains, "because we often had to grapple with acquisitions in Europe that had been run by other English companies. We found that they had often chosen a managing director for no other reason than that he was the only one who could speak English, rather than his being the one best suited to actually running the company. We stopped that."

While Jack Greenhalgh and the Cavenham men concentrated on making sense of the proliferating European empire that their chairman found for them, Jim Wood was doing the same for the Grand Union supermarket chain in the United States. Since Cavenham had taken over he and his management team had closed forty-seven small markets and opened nineteen new ones. They had also stopped giving trading stamps to their customers and offered them lower prices and higher quality instead.

In the meantime Jimmy Goldsmith devoted himself as enthusiastically as ever to what he enjoyed most: deals. He negotiated the sale of some of Allied Suppliers' shops for £2 million, and completed the purchase of a further 30 per cent of the stock in the Grand Union company. Every negotiation depended on the approach he had refined in the wake of the bank strike in 1957.

Jimmy Goldsmith liked to have hard cash ready for any eventuality. He was prepared to borrow, no entrepreneur was not, but never too much nor too far to risk what he had already achieved. It was no surprise that in the Cavenham annual report published in March 1975 he announced to his shareholders that the company not only had a profit of £17 million after tax had been paid, but it also had a "cash reserve" of nearly £30 million. That meant Jimmy Goldsmith could act when he wanted to without having to wait to arrange the financing.

Not all his contemporaries in British business had been quite as far-sighted or as fortunate. In particular Jimmy Goldsmith's old backgammon opponent Jim Slater was rapidly beginning to realize that his vast financial and investment empire, Slater Walker Securities, which had boasted assets of almost £300 million in 1972, was in imminent danger of collapse: not least because its chairman had lost some of his confidence and enthusiasm in the storm that had seen the British stock market plunge by 80 per cent in the previous two years. Slater Walker had survived, but only just, and although the first three months of 1975 saw the *Financial Times* 30 share index double, trebling the Slater Walker shares in the process, the damage had been done.

"In its fight for survival Slater Walker had to a large extent lost its *raison d'être* and no longer had a worthwhile role to play," Jim Slater wrote in his autobiography, *Return to Go,* five years later. "If we survived we would have to find a new identity, and it would take years to build. The failure of so many secondary banks and finance companies, such as Jessel Securities, First National, Triumph and Vavasseur would make investors and the City community continue to worry about a company such as Slater Walker for years to come. I had lost my early enthusiasm, and felt it would be much better for shareholders and for employees if a different solution could be found." Slater's attempts to sell his many assets for hard cash, copying Jimmy Goldsmith's earlier decisions, had not proved nearly as successful as his old friend's, and he increasingly found himself under pressure from his creditors. Assets were all very well, but if no one was prepared to buy them at the right price they were useless to a company which urgently needed cash.

Jimmy Goldsmith had more than simply a friendly interest in the welfare of Slater Walker. By the beginning of 1975 Anglo-Continental owned nearly 5 per cent of the company, and he was as anxious as anyone to ensure its viable commercial future. As Slater's difficulties had increased so the two friends began to discuss ways of escape, and even the possibility that they might merge their two master companies.

"Jim Slater had not been at all well," Jimmy Goldsmith recalls now. "He'd had a kidney operation, and when he recovered he started to talk about the possibility of merging Slater Walker with another bank. There were conversations with Warburgs, which broke down, and then with Lazards – which even got to the stage of a press release being agreed before the negotiations broke down. Jim talked to Hill Samuel and even to Weinstock at GEC about their taking a stake in the company, but nothing came of any of it. That was when we started buying some shares." The two men even discussed in principle the possibility of a merger between Slater Walker and Générale Occidentale. But the future looked bleak.

To cheer himself up Jim Slater took four of his friends on a fishing trip to the Tulchan estate in the Highlands of Scotland, on the river Spey, which Slater Walker owned. Selim Zilkha, Jacob Rothschild, Angus Ogilvy and Jimmy Goldsmith spent a week trying to catch salmon, without much success – which was not entirely surprising as Slater was a notoriously unlucky fisherman and Jimmy Goldsmith had hardly held a rod in his life. Goldsmith started to offer substantial bets on which of them would be the first to land a fish and how much it would weigh. At least that way he managed to keep himself amused as he watched the cold, crystal water of the Spey creep up towards the top of his specially hired green waders. Jim Slater was exasperated, but amused.

The fate of Slater Walker was not the only thing concerning Jimmy Goldsmith during the summer of 1975. He was still intent on the policy he had outlined in the latest Cavenham annual report – "of concentrating our efforts on our main activities" and "finding the new capital necessary to support them by eliminating all operations that are either marginal or unrelated to the main stream of our business". That meant rationalizing his companies relentlessly, as his definition of "the main stream" changed with his view of the economic climate and the political future of the countries he owned companies in. One group of companies that were no longer in the "main stream", for example, were the staples that had helped to launch his career: slimming aids and dietary food. In June 1975 he sold two of his longest established companies, including Laboratoires Grémy-Longuet which still produced Milical. The whole company went to the American Smithkline corporation. In July he sold Slimcea and Procea from Cavenham. Together with their baking interest and trademarks they were sold to one of their largest customers, Spillers. Dietary foods and slimming aids were no longer part of Jimmy Goldsmith's plans. "I treated my own companies in exactly the same way as I did companies that I took over. I looked at them constantly to see whether there were elements that were no longer central to our objectives. If there were I sold them."

The Acapulco Strategy was steadily being put into effect. The supply of hard cash available for acquisitions, possibly in the United States, was being built up. Slater Walker was to speed that process up still further.

By the beginning of September 1975 a series of bitter accusations and counter-accusations about Slater Walker's relationship with the Haw Par company in Singapore, and the £37 million in loans that Slater Walker had provided for it, began to shake the confidence of the City's stockbrokers in Jim Slater's company still further. By the end of the month rumours of corruption in the company's affairs in the Far East were circulating, and by the middle of October Slater Walker's share price had fallen to below 50 pence. (Three years earlier it had been 275 pence.) For the first time Slater began seriously to consider resigning from the board. He had already discussed ways of shoring up his company with the Governor of the Bank of England, Sir Gordon Richardson, but now there was no time to lose. If Slater Walker was to survive, somebody else had to be found to run it and to negotiate a settlement with the Singapore authorities who now did not trust Slater at all.

Finally, on Wednesday 16 October 1975 at one of their regular dinners at Wilton's, Slater suggested to Goldsmith that he should take over as chairman of Slater Walker. The two men were convinced that if something was not done quickly the whole City of London might suffer appalling consequences. Goldsmith promised to think carefully about the idea, and in the next few days he consulted one or two of his friends in the City including Charles Hambro. "Jimmy came to me and said, 'Charlie, the only way to save the situation is for him to go; and unless something happens very quickly, it could create a really serious situation – almost a political explosion – which could bring a panic' . . . He asked me if I'd go on to the board after he had taken control."

Looking back, Charles Hambro remembers the alarm with which every senior member of the City of London viewed the collapse of Slater Walker. "It would have been disastrous, not so much because of its size, but because of the enormous following and publicity that Slater had attracted." It was with that firmly in mind that Jimmy Goldsmith decided to launch a bid to save the company. The irony that he, the man whom the City of London had hardly deigned to trust for the past decade, was now volunteering to come to their aid was not lost on him, but it rather suited his "idiosyncratic" view of himself.

"Jimmy did not need to do a damn thing about Slater Walker," John Tigrett insists now. "People said he was only getting involved because his own position was at risk, but that just wasn't true. Sure, Jimmy would have been hurt, but not that badly." Whether his decision to get involved in the affairs of Slater Walker was provoked by hubris or altruism would be the subject of debate in Paris and London for years afterwards, but he would say only: "I did it because I felt I had to, and because the situation was very dangerous. There were people who were only interested in casting doubt on the City of London and all it stood for. Their purpose was to discredit free enterprise." To some that conclusion would seem a grotesque exaggeration, another instance of his paranoia, but to Jimmy Goldsmith it was simple common sense. He was, as always, utterly certain of his own mind.

Following their dinner together, Jim Slater spent the weekend considering what he should do for the best. On the following Monday morning, 21 October, he telephoned Jimmy Goldsmith to tell him that there was going to be a run on the bank and that he had decided to resign. He was going to discuss his successor with Sir Gordon Richardson, Governor of the Bank of England, and would explain that he thought Jimmy Goldsmith would be the ideal candidate. In fact, Jim Slater did not manage to see the governor himself that day, but talked instead to George Blunden, his deputy, who in turn explained the rescue scheme to Sir Gordon.

The following day Jimmy Goldsmith was called to the Bank of England to see the governor. "He asked me if I would be prepared to become chairman of Slater Walker, to explain what I had in mind for the company, and how I planned to get it back onto its feet. I told him that first I wanted to assess the facts, to know how much support was going to be needed." That afternoon Gilberte Beaux and a team from Cavenham arrived at Slater Walker's headquarters to find out the worst. By Thursday they knew. "It needed about £160 million to pay depositors."

Jimmy Goldsmith went back to see Sir Gordon Richardson in Threadneedle Street. "I said I would take over Slater Walker, if I had his support and if I could get a board which was sufficiently establishment to prove to the City and to the world that this was not just me helping out Jim." That night at his temporary home in Tregunter Road, Kensington, Jimmy Goldsmith asked one of his three dinner guests, Victor Rothschild, if he would join the board of a reconstituted Slater Walker with him as chairman. Rothschild said he would sleep on it, and the subject was not discussed with the other two guests – the former Tory Prime Minister Edward

Heath and the then editor of *The Economist* magazine Andrew Knight.

As Charles Hambro puts it now: "I think that Jimmy felt that once one major card in the pack of cards in the City holding up an edifice of that type in the secondary area had fallen, then it might have unfortunate repercussions for a number of people, including Jimmy"; although Hambro, like John Tigrett, rejects any suggestion that Slater Walker's demise could have brought Cavenham, Anglo-Continental or Générale Occidentale to their knees, "but it would have been painful".

On Tuesday 22 October Jimmy Goldsmith held the first of a series of meetings with the Governor of the Bank of England, in which he outlined the details of his rescue plan for Slater Walker. The first step was to bring in a new board composed of men whom the institutions in the City of London would respect. In return he asked for an assurance that the Bank of England would make every effort to assist the company with its reconstruction plans and would in turn urge Harold Wilson's Labour government of the day to do the same, in spite of its public scepticism about capitalism. Richardson agreed, "which I think was very important, because it prevented the panic that there might have been otherwise", in Charles Hambro's words.

In another meeting with Sir Gordon Richardson, Jimmy Goldsmith explained that among the men he wanted to bring on to the Slater Walker board were Victor Rothschild and Ivor Kennington of the Rothschild bank in London; Charles Hambro and Peter Hill-Wood of his own merchant bank Hambros; and Monsieur Dominique Leca of the Union des Assurances in Paris, France's largest insurance company, who was also a member of the board of directors of Générale Occidentale. Sir Ronald Leach, who had adjudicated the value of Lipton's tea interests after the Allied Suppliers takeover, had agreed to act as an adviser, and he also intended to ask Gilberte Beaux to help him sort out the confusion.

The last meeting with the Bank of England took place in the afternoon of Thursday 24 October, and just as they were finishing someone rushed in to say that there had been a leak, and that the stock market was in uproar. With Richardson's approval the announcement that Jimmy Goldsmith was to take over as chairman of Slater Walker Securities, at the head of a new board of directors, was rushed out after the stock market closed that afternoon.

The following morning Jim Slater officially announced his resignation to the press. As the *Investors Chronicle* commented a week later: "Only the abdication of the Queen, one supposes, would command more column inches." Slater explained that his "wish to retire from the City and the interests of Slater Walker Securities are now identical" and went on to pay tribute to his successor "as a man of proven ability with a long record of success" who would do "an excellent job for the shareholders". Because there were so many small shareholders who had followed Slater's lead slavishly over the past decade with their savings and tiny investments, and now saw their financial security threatened, public interest in the affair was considerable. The *Daily Telegraph* captured the mood of the British press when it reported: "Last night's change at the top of Slater Walker Securities marked the end of one of the most remarkable stories in the City's long history – the rise of builder's son Mr Jim Slater – and his creation of possibly the most remarkable investment machine ever seen."

Jimmy Goldsmith may not have realized it at the time, but his decision to try to save Slater Walker was to make him one of the most controversial figures in the modern history of British business. In a profile in the *Sunday Times* of 27 October, the paper commented: "He has emerged as the last survivor of the financial phoenixes whose stars shone so brightly in the 1960s and early 1970s. But although in some ways his early business career showed parallels with Jim Slater . . . and the millionaire-a-minute property men, he is a very different kind of animal." The British press was about to look into just how different Jimmy Goldsmith was. The new chairman of Slater Walker, who was forty-two years of age, would never again be able to live a private life in England.

While the studiously suburban Jim Slater had been the epitome of rectitude and the commonplace, his successor – though infinitely more successful commercially – was far less restrained. As the publicity increased so Jimmy Goldsmith rapidly realized that he could no longer live two separate lives in France and England without the world knowing. He was even forced to explain his unusual private life, and his relationship to Annabel Birley, Jemima and Zacharias, to his daughter Alix, then just entering adolescence. But no matter how intense the public scrutiny was to become in the years ahead Jimmy Goldsmith was never to amend his lifestyle in the slightest.

Goldsmith was convinced that however unconventional his private life, his business affairs would stand comparison with anyone's. While Jim Slater had stretched himself too far and had never consolidated his phenomenal success, Jimmy Goldsmith had carefully and consistently taken pains to surround himself – and his holding company in France – with hard cash and the support of some of the most respected names in European business. It was no accident that the directors of Générale Occidentale in Paris included representatives of the French bank Crédit Lyonnais, alongside others from the French Rothschilds, Lazard Frères, Compagnie d'Electricité, and the Union des Assurances; while the Caisse des Dépôts – France's national savings bank – and the French car maker Renault also had substantial holdings in the company. The French bankers Lazard Frères were also shareholders and directors of his Trocadero holding company. If Jimmy Goldsmith seemed a flamboyant young man in private that was more because they had a suspicion of the unconventional than because they had taken the trouble to examine exactly what he had done. Individualist though he undoubtedly was, Jimmy Goldsmith had also been shrewd enough to know that help from established companies in the European financial community might prove useful.

As he and Gilberte Beaux settled into Slater Walker's cramped offices in London in the last week of October, Jimmy Goldsmith saw himself as the outsider who had become a winner and who was now demonstrating that an outsider could help to solve one of the City of London's least tractable problems, Slater Walker Securities. It was a matter of honour for him to do it, the final proof that the rebel could play the establishment at its own game, and win.

Ironically, just as he was embarking on this task, Jimmy Goldsmith found himself pilloried by men educated at the very heart of the English establishment – in the form of the editor and staff of the satirical fortnightly magazine *Private Eye*. In his official history of the magazine, Patrick Marnham describes how the original editors – Christopher Booker, Paul Foot and Richard Ingrams – all met in

1951 as boys at Shrewsbury, one of England's more distinguished public schools. Ingrams edited the school magazine together with a precocious cartoonist called William Rushton. In the autumn of 1961, after a period as undergraduates at Oxford (Foot, Ingrams and Rushton) and Cambridge (Booker) the four, with the help of Andrew Osmond and Andrew Usborne, founded the fortnightly satirical magazine. It was hardly the work of meritocrats, but it was studiously rebellious, ridiculing – in some cases with brutal harshness – sections of the English establishment of which the editors were comfortably members. Ingrams was related to the German banking family the Barings, and Foot's father, Lord Caradon, was a former British Ambassador to the United Nations. As the Eye had expanded over the ensuing fourteen years it had gathered a reputation for gossip and libel actions.

Now they were interested in Jimmy Goldsmith, who had hardly come into contact with it. In the next year that was to change radically; partly because of the disappearance of Lord Lucan, the previous November, and partly because, he believes, the magazine was determined to undermine his attempt to save Slater Walker, and thereby destroy confidence in the City.

As Jimmy Goldsmith puts it, "The reason I became of interest to Ingrams, the editor of *Private Eye*, was because I had been brought in to try and save Slater Walker Securities. It was suggested to Ingrams that the Bank of England's plan to save Slater Walker could be torpedoed if I were discredited."

But it was to be a tortuous train of events that would eventually lead him into conflict with the satirical magazine which was then selling some 120,000 copies of each fortnightly edition.

They began at the Jesuit Church of the Immaculate Conception in Farm Street, Mayfair, on the morning of 25 November 1975. The occasion was a memorial service for the forty-four-year-old portrait painter and playboy Dominic Elwes who had killed himself ten weeks earlier. The requiem was attended by a number of Jimmy Goldsmith's friends, but not by Goldsmith himself. "In the previous ten years I might have seen Elwes twenty times at most," he recalls. "He was a friend and cousin of Annabel's, but only a very distant acquaintance of mine."

One of the speakers at the service was John Aspinall, who referred

in his address to Elwes's "genetic inheritance" which he suggested
had "not equipped him to deal with life". The remark had so angered
Elwes's cousin, Tremayne Rodd, that after the service he had
punched Aspinall in the face outside the Church. Although Aspinall
laughed off the attack – "I'm used to dealing with wild animals" –
a report of the incident caught Richard Ingrams's eye. Later he
explained that he thought there was something going on which
could make an interesting article for *Private Eye*. Precisely what it
was, and who was involved, Ingrams insists, he had no idea at the
time. "I knew, however, it had something to do with an article
about the Lucan case that had appeared in the *Sunday Times*
Magazine in June 1975."

That article had certainly mentioned Jimmy Goldsmith. It had
even contained a photograph of him on holiday in February 1973
with Lord Lucan, and the magazine's cover had featured a photograph of Lady Annabel Birley and Lucan together. It had incensed
Jimmy Goldsmith at the time. "It was the cover which annoyed me
the most," he says now. "It consisted of a photograph taken after
lunch during the Acapulco holiday as a sort of joke, but printed on
its own it seemed to suggest that Annabel was somehow romantically
linked with Lucan which was, of course, perfect nonsense." The
article about Lord Lucan's disappearance, and his gambling friends
at the Clermont club, written by the Old Etonian journalist James
Fox, also included a painting of a group of Lucan's friends having
lunch by Dominic Elwes – who had been on Jimmy Goldsmith's
fortieth birthday trip to Acapulco as a friend of Annabel's. The
painting, and the accompanying article, suggested that Jimmy Goldsmith had been present at a lunch given by John Aspinall on the
day after Lord Lucan's mysterious disappearance. The implication
was that he might know something about Lucan's whereabouts or
have been involved in his disappearance.

Jimmy Goldsmith was furious. The truth was that he had not
been anywhere near John Aspinall's lunch on 8 November 1974; in
fact he had been in Ireland that day telling the Association of
Chartered Accountants about the "morality of business". He loathed
the suggestion that he had somehow been involved in a cover-up
and he was angry that the painting reproduced in the magazine
implied he was present at the lunch. He became even more angry

when he discovered that Dominic Elwes had been responsible for the painting. "A friend of mine had seen him while he was doing it and told him that I would find it objectionable," Jimmy Goldsmith explains now, "but he answered that he didn't care. It was Elwes who organized the article, and introduced Fox to all concerned. My only reaction *vis-à-vis* Elwes was to say that I would never see him again."

In fact, apart from the painting and the Acapulco photograph – which showed the two men sitting beside each other at the lunch table – there was no mention of Jimmy Goldsmith in the article itself. So, although his inclination at the time had been to sue the magazine for libel, instead he had accepted an apology from the editor and let the matter rest.

Another man who had taken exception to the *Sunday Times* Magazine's article was Mark Birley, who was still legally married to Annabel Birley, even if they appeared to be on the brink of divorce now that she had two children with Jimmy Goldsmith. The magazine's cover photograph, apparently linking her with a man who was sought by the police in connection with the murder of Sandra Rivett, had also angered him. In a fury almost as great as Jimmy Goldsmith's, Mark Birley banned Elwes from his nightclub Annabel's and from a new dining club he had recently started in Mayfair called Mark's.

The reaction of both Goldsmith and Birley to the *Sunday Times* Magazine article came as a profound shock to Dominic Elwes. A depressive, who had attempted suicide in the past, he took the enforced isolation from friends whom he had known for many years particularly badly. He was especially upset that he was no longer able to talk to Annabel Birley. Less than a week after the article appeared Elwes decided to leave England and go to the South of France to think things over. On the flight to Nice he happened to meet the London *Daily Mail*'s gossip columnist Nigel Dempster, who at that time was also a contributor to *Private Eye*. "I drove him to his apartment near where I was staying and we saw each other every day for a week. He often spoke of suicide," Dempster said later. Elwes told him that his father was dying, his mother was "terribly ill", a relation had "invested all my money very badly" and "My friends have turned on me because of the Lucan business . . . I can't understand why they are all doing this to me. I have always been a good friend to them, and when Annabel and Jimmy were going through a bad patch it was me who helped her get over it."

Barely ten weeks later, on 5 September 1975, Dominic Elwes killed himself by taking an overdose of barbiturates at his small flat off the King's Road in London. The forty-four-year-old son of royal portrait painter Simon Elwes, who had three children by his wife, the beautiful heiress Tessa Kennedy with whom he had eloped in 1958, left two suicide notes. One was long and rambling, containing a series of religious messages, but the other was shorter. It read: "I curse Mark and Jimmy from beyond the grave. I hope they are happy now."

On the Monday morning following the memorial service for Elwes, Richard Ingrams rang Nigel Dempster at the *Daily Mail* to call on his "encyclopaedic knowledge of high society". After the phone call Dempster sat down and typed out an eight-page memorandum on Elwes and his friends at the Clermont club and elsewhere, which he then posted to Ingrams. "It contained as much as I knew at the time," he says now, "but it did not say Jimmy had been at the lunch at Aspinall's the day after Lucan disappeared."

For his part Ingrams thought it was "rather extraordinary that the friend of Aspinall and Lucan, the hounder of Elwes, should be brought in to restore confidence as the saviour of Slater Walker with the backing and blessing of the Bank of England", and he asked Patrick Marnham, another contributor, to concentrate the article he had already started preparing on Jimmy Goldsmith.

In the Christmas edition of *Private Eye*, which appeared on 12 December 1975, Ingrams published Marnham's story about Goldsmith and Elwes, which had been written with the advice of another of the Eye's regular contributors, City journalist Michael Gillard. Entitled "All's Well That Ends Elwes" it was to make Jimmy Goldsmith a public figure in Britain. Yet it was almost entirely based on the utterly mistaken impression that Jimmy Goldsmith had actually been present at the lunch John Aspinall gave on the day after Lord Lucan's disappearance. It implied that Goldsmith had played a dominant part in obstructing the course of justice and in assisting the fugitive. It was to prove a costly suggestion.

But why was the suggestion made? Richard Ingrams suggests in his book *Goldenballs*, written four years later, that it was principally a mistake: Patrick Marnham and he had thought that James Fox had got it right when he had suggested that Goldsmith had been at the lunch – "and would naturally have taken charge". They did not know, Ingrams says, that Jimmy Goldsmith had complained to the editor of the *Sunday Times* who had "acknowledged privately that there had been an error". But he accepts that "our article hinged on the lunch" and the belief that Goldsmith had been present.

Jimmy Goldsmith himself takes the radically different view that the article had been conceived to discredit him, and, by implication, his attempts to salvage Slater Walker. "It was decided," he says now, "that I was the weak link in the chain, and that they could not attack Victor Rothschild, Charles Hambro or Ronald Leach. If they could crack me, the whole thing went down. If Slater Walker could be converted into a major scandal, in view of its colossal public impact with headlines day after day, it would discredit the City. That is why the moderate socialist ministers in the Labour government of the day wanted to contain the problem, and why the far Left were trying to do everything they could to make the bomb explode. If they could discredit me they would discredit by association those who came into Slater Walker with me, and the Bank of England."

In the months to come Jimmy Goldsmith came to believe that he was the victim of a politically motivated conspiracy. "I was very very naïve," he says now. "I realized I was taking a risk going into Slater Walker, but I didn't realize it was a political risk."

But when he first heard about the *Private Eye* article, Jimmy Goldsmith was in Singapore "negotiating a settlement to the Haw Par affair for Slater Walker". His secretary in London brought a copy of the magazine out to him. "I didn't know what to do about it. For a while I thought I wouldn't do anything at all." But when he got back to England he attended a lunch given by Paul Johnson, the British author and journalist, a former editor of the left-wing political weekly, the *New Statesman*. Among the other guests was Sir Hugh Fraser, a Conservative MP and a former Secretary of State for Air. "At the lunch people urged me to do something," Jimmy Goldsmith remembers. "When I asked them what they would do, they all said they would 'throw the book' at *Private Eye*."

Several people at the lunch, including Hugh Fraser, went on to offer to help in any way they could. But still Jimmy Goldsmith decided to do nothing.

16

Lord Goldsmith or "Goldenballs"

By any standards *Private Eye*'s second article about Jimmy Goldsmith, published on 9 January 1976, was unwise. It was, to say the least, exceptionally long on innuendo and short on fact. In essence it cast doubts on Jimmy Goldsmith's integrity by attempting to link his name with an imprisoned local businessman from the north-east of England, T. Dan Smith. The only connection it could establish was that Eric Levine, one of Jimmy Goldsmith's solicitors, had been on the board of directors of a number of Smith's companies. The rest of the piece was a collection of insulting information, including allegations of bad behaviour at a nightclub in Gstaad at Christmas with his wife Ginette. But like much else in the *Private Eye* edited by Richard Ingrams it owed more to the arrogant self-confidence of the editor than to factual accuracy. Ingrams was determined to find feet of clay among the mighty whatever the cost.

If Jimmy Goldsmith had thought the first piece about him in December "pretty silly", in the words of a friend, he did not take the same view of the second. By then he was well aware that some people had taken the first article seriously, so he responded to both attacks with the full incendiary force of his anger. Three days after the second *Private Eye* article appeared he issued sixty-three separate writs for libel against the magazine and thirty-seven of its distributors in Britain. It was the start of one of the most spectacular libel cases the English courts had seen in modern times; it lasted for eighteen months and involved ten separate hearings. Three days later, on 15 January 1976, he informed the magazine that he intended to apply to the High Court for permission to bring proceedings against its editor for criminal libel.

It was his decision to sue Richard Ingrams for criminal libel – which carried a maximum sentence of two years in prison – which made Jimmy Goldsmith seem even more extraordinary to those who knew no more about him than what they read in the press, and particularly in the columns of *Private Eye*. It had the effect of making Ingrams a hero rather than a villain.

There had been only a trickle of criminal libel cases in the previous hundred years, and since the end of the nineteenth century very few British editors had been sent to gaol for writing anything. In 1879 Adolphus Rosenberg had been sentenced to eighteen months for suggesting in his magazine *Town Talk* that the Prince of Wales was having an affair with the actress Lillie Langtry, while in 1923 Lord Alfred Douglas, friend of Oscar Wilde, had received six months for suggesting that Winston Churchill had used his position as First Lord of the Admiralty to manipulate news from the Battle of Jutland in 1916 to depress the value of English stocks on the American Stock Exchange and enable the financier Sir Ernest Cassel to make a profit of £18 million and provide Churchill with furniture worth several thousand pounds. But those were almost the only examples of the use of this arcane law.

Since the Douglas case English editors had faced little worse than the payment of damages for libel, although one or two had suffered the indignity of imprisonment for contempt of court. In the 1930s there were barely a dozen cases of criminal libel brought each year, and by the 1960s the figure was down to one or two.

Nevertheless, as Digby Neave put it years later: "Jimmy saw himself as a knight in shining armour riding into battle against people who had been attacking his friends and himself. Possibly it was misguided, as there was no possible gain in it for him, in fact there was everything to lose, but that did not concern him."

For his part Jimmy Goldsmith says now: "Obviously I was angry in myself, but there was also the important factor that I was determined not to pass on to my children a "soiled name". For me that would have been impossible. It would have defeated everything that I'd done. One is passing one's achievements along in a chain. If anybody tries to spoil that they will fight me, not just because of me, but also because I am a part of that tradition. Can there be anything more important than what you hand on? I think that's a fundamental biological instinct." Jimmy Goldsmith saw himself in the libel action, as he does in many dealings, as the leader of his tribe, the representative of a tradition.

There were to be some in England who were convinced that Goldsmith was only responding so aggressively because he felt *Private Eye* was being anti-semitic in its attack on him and his solicitor. But Jimmy Goldsmith denies it firmly. Just as firmly, Richard Reid Ingrams denies that his father Leonard, a merchant banker, and his mother Victoria Reid, who were members of the Anglo-German Fellowship in the 1930s, were sympathetic to Hitler or Nazism. Richard Ingrams later insisted that he disliked Goldsmith "not because he is a Jew but because he is a German".

Certainly one of the undiscussed reasons for the animosity and rancour that developed between the two men in the courts lay in Ingrams's dislike of Goldsmith's less than orthodox personal life. The organ-playing Ingrams, who had given up both smoking and drinking, and was married with three children, found his opponent's less than inhibited personal life deeply offensive. Far from it being the satirical, liberal-minded Ingrams attacking the conservative Goldsmith, it was, far more, the Roundhead Ingrams attacking the Cavalier Goldsmith.

This difference between the two men was underlined firmly three weeks after the first libel writs against *Private Eye* were issued. Jimmy Goldsmith suddenly realized that his less than orthodox family life was about to become the focus of a great deal of publicity in England because of the case. The man who warned him about this was his old friend, the Australian journalist Sam White, who had been Paris correspondent of the London *Evening Standard* for many years. When White had first suggested to Goldsmith in the Traveller's Club in Paris, shortly after the writs were issued, that he ought now to explain his unorthodox private life in public "once and for all, so that it doesn't become an issue in the case", Jimmy Goldsmith agreed to think about it. That weekend he invited White to his and Ginette's house in the rue Monsieur for lunch, and after the meal he drafted a letter which explained – for the first time – his two families. White was to show the letter to *Evening Standard* lawyers, who, he pointed out, might otherwise be rather reluctant to use such a controversial story about a man who had just issued sixty-three libel writs.

On Friday 30 January Sam White's weekly column in the *Evening Standard* included a long piece about Jimmy Goldsmith, under the headline "The Two-Family Family Man". White's article explained in detail the two homes and two families, and pointed out that Jimmy Goldsmith did not try to conceal them. "It is a remarkable situation," White reported, "made even more so because there is no attempt at concealment (no 'Tycoon's Secret Love-nest Uncovered' situation here) and again, as far as I know, no question of divorce." Indeed, White pointed out that Ginette's son Manes was godfather to Annabel Birley's son Zacharias, while Isabel was godmother to Jemima, which served only to bewilder further those people in England – including *Private Eye* – who tried to maintain that Goldsmith's way of life could have been possible only if it were carried out in secret. White went on: "Roughly speaking, of the twenty years Goldsmith has been married to Ginette, he has shared ten with Lady Annabel. The normal pattern of his life is that weekends are spent with his family in Paris . . . and weekdays with Lady Annabel." This was hardly the report of a man trying desperately to conceal a clandestine affair. Indeed White ended by suggesting: "I should think that if there is any renunciation to be done, in furtherance of a possible political career, Goldsmith is much more likely to renounce his French passport than to renounce his wife."

By agreeing to this article, Jimmy Goldsmith had accepted that a British political career was no longer possible. "I realized that I could not tailor my lifestyle to suit the English," he says now, "and I put the idea out of my mind." As a businessman, he had also just agreed to buy a further 1.8 million shares in Grand Union, giving him 80 per cent of the supermarket chain in the United States, and had announced the formation of a new American company called Cavenham (USA) Inc. Just before he left for another holiday, this time in Barbados with Jim Slater, Selim Zilkha and John Aspinall, he announced that Générale Occidentale was to take over Cavenham in Britain. Though the British press, and *Private Eye*, had not realized it, Jimmy Goldsmith was already accepting that his future almost certainly lay outside the British Isles.

Nevertheless, bringing an action for criminal libel with its threat of imprisonment made Jimmy Goldsmith seem a vengeful man with an unpleasant, brutal streak. More than any other single act in his career, it was to cost him public sympathy. By that single decision Jimmy Goldsmith chose to cast himself as a monster.

As one old friend puts it: "I think perhaps Jimmy had a rush of blood, and lost his sense of proportion for a while." It is not a charge that Goldsmith himself would accept. He was certainly encouraged to feel that he was acting on behalf of a substantial number of members of the English establishment when he launched his libel actions against *Private Eye*. The fact that none of those members of the English establishment ever chose to support him publicly over the case remains one of his bitterest memories of the affair. "I don't feel animosity against those who attack me, although I do against those who attack my children, but I do feel animosity against those who would not have the guts to stand up and support in public, but would only do it in private."

To take on the battle at all was extraordinary but Goldsmith was unaware of *Private Eye*'s connections with the British press and politics, and unappreciative of the suspicion with which flamboyance is viewed in some sections of British society. His was the action of a man who saw himself as apart from the ordinary, but it ran the risk of setting him apart for ever from the accepted opinions of a large and influential section of the English upper class, who saw nothing whatever wrong in what they called "the public school humour" of *Private Eye*. To take action against the magazine, to some, smacked of self-consciousness – of being "a bit too sensitive" – the act of a man who was "obviously a foreigner, and probably a cad". To others it seemed the action of a violent and belligerent man seeking political advancement, unprepared to hear any views other than his own. Both conclusions were utterly mistaken, but they contrived to ensure that Jimmy Goldsmith was often cast as a vindictive Goliath smiting the helpless David of Richard Ingrams and *Private Eye*. In fact, Jimmy Goldsmith was implicitly questioning the attitudes and morality of sections of the English upper classes.

Entered into in some haste, but with the decisiveness that was one of his principal assets as an entrepreneur, the battle with *Private*

Eye led Jimmy Goldsmith into areas that previously he had hardly understood – many of them at the heart of the English character. Finally he found himself fighting a battle that he may have been able to win legally, but which would for ever place him apart from a significant section of English society. It would make him uncomfortable with some members, and suspicious of others. It would help to convince him that certain sections of the English press were corrupt, and others were "manipulated" by sinister forces in European politics. It would also help to convince him finally that Britain was not the best place to continue to conduct his affairs, and that British society was in a state of serious decay. He would insist in public that none of this mattered to him, but, in reality, the wounds were deep. Like his father before him, Jimmy Goldsmith watched as England appeared to turn against him.

However, one unexpected member of the English establishment did come publicly to his aid – the Labour Prime Minister Harold Wilson. Shortly after he launched his actions against *Private Eye* he and Annabel Birley were guests at a small private dinner given by the television performer David Frost at his London home in February 1976. Also present were Harold Wilson, whom Frost was encouraging to consider a television series on Prime Ministers after his retirement, his wife Mary, and his personal and political secretary at 10 Downing Street, Marcia Falkender. Jimmy Goldsmith had never met Wilson before, but the two men got on "extremely well", according to Marcia Falkender.

Although there was no discussion of *Private Eye* during the dinner, one person who did talk about it afterwards was Mrs Mary Wilson. She happened to tell Jimmy Goldsmith how upset she had been by one of the magazine's regular features, "Mrs Wilson's Diary". Written partly by Richard Ingrams, this purported to tell the readers what the Prime Minister's wife was really thinking to herself in Downing Street. Jimmy Goldsmith left the table convinced that it offended her far more deeply than anyone might have guessed, and aware that her husband also understood how upset she had been by the magazine. As the guests were leaving Frost's house and standing in groups in his hallway – which boasted a jukebox – *Private Eye*'s attack on Goldsmith and his libel actions against it finally came up. But as Marcia Falkender recalls, "No one told Jimmy that he should sue the magazine. There was no question of that, and Harold certainly didn't suggest it, as so many people have said he did since then."

The dinner at David Frost's house had one fundamental effect on Jimmy Goldsmith. It meant that he saw far more of Harold Wilson. As Marcia Falkender recalls: "Harold found Jimmy quite extraordinary, like James Hanson, a big buccaneering tycoon; and he became fascinated by both of them because they symbolized everything that he didn't believe in, but they also symbolized terrific success, and were equally at home with the moneyed people and the rest. They were classless. In no time Harold and Jimmy got on tremendously well." Then forty-three, and created a Life Peer by Harold Wilson eighteen months earlier, the lean, blonde and sharp-eyed Marcia Falkender was in a unique position to judge. Hardly a political secretary since the war had enjoyed the confidence of a prime minister so completely, though others had enjoyed as much influence.

At Slater Walker Securities Jimmy Goldsmith was still struggling to put right the failings of the last Slater years, and Wilson was well aware, in Marcia Falkender's words, that "everything was so fragile that if Jimmy didn't pull that off it would have been very serious, for the government as well. A terrible panic in the City would have affected what the government was doing and we weren't in a very good position at that time either."

As the first weeks of 1976 extended towards spring, Harold Wilson and Jimmy Goldsmith saw each other again a number of times. Jimmy Goldsmith would visit Downing Street in the early evening and eventually a lunch was arranged for him and Lord Ryder, the chairman of the National Enterprise Board, to discuss "What Britain could learn from Europe". Ironically, the businessman who had spent the previous general election campaign trying to organize a Conservative victory was given his first official invitation to eat at Downing Street by the Labour Prime Minister he had been trying to defeat. "But it was always absolutely clear in my conversations with Harold Wilson," Jimmy Goldsmith says now, "that I was an ideological conservative and I never, in any way, wavered about that."

At this time Goldsmith was not aware that Harold Wilson had decided to retire and hand over to one of his colleagues. (In fact by the middle of March 1976 Wilson had already settled on a date in the middle of April.) "Harold simply warned me that I would be the subject of a bitter attack, and that I would need all the help I could get," Jimmy Goldsmith recalls now. But Wilson also knew that after he had left office there was little help he could offer to Jimmy Goldsmith.

Wilson was already quietly planning the personal list of "honours" that a Prime Minister is allowed to award on retirement. "Harold used to write down names from time to time on little slips of paper," Marcia Falkender remembers now, "and put them into his wallet for safekeeping. Then he transferred them to a card . . . What Harold wanted to do was to have a last Honours list which represented the sort of things he'd been interested in, and the sorts of things he'd like to see. He put in a lot of people he intended to put on future lists."

One name that Harold Wilson jotted down on one of his little pieces of paper and stuffed into his wallet was Jimmy Goldsmith's, even though they had only met a few months before. Hardly surprisingly, another was James Hanson, the other "buccaneering tycoon" that he had come to admire. Both men were to be given knighthoods in recognition of their work. Looking back, Goldsmith believes now that there may have been another reason for Harold Wilson's decision to award him a knighthood. "I think he thought it would be useful for me in Slater Walker, because it showed the government's support," he says now. Although when a rumour of the award first appeared in Nigel Dempster's gossip column Jimmy Goldsmith "didn't pay any attention at all".

Like his criminal libel action, the award of any kind of honour to Jimmy Goldsmith infuriated his enemies, and they saw this particular honour as a sign of the Labour Prime Minister's rank foolishness: he had granted formal recognition to a man who was clearly a capitalist, a defender of the financial institutions of the City of London (which many Labour men wanted to see nationalized or swept away), a self-confessed "womanizer" with a French as well as a British passport. To others it looked as though the ambitious Goldsmith was seeking political advancement at all costs, and had sued *Private Eye* to gain favour with the Prime Minister – who had rewarded him with an honour.

Yet, ironically, by the time the honour was announced, *Private Eye* had already admitted that its attempt to link him to a conspiracy to obstruct the course of justice was untrue. By then, however, Jimmy Goldsmith had taken up his dislike of the magazine, and "all it stood for in English society" as a crusade. The affidavit he had sworn just before he had left for Barbados summed up his detestation. It ignored the question of the cause of Dominic Elwes's death, and concentrated instead on Lord Lucan's disappearance. It directly rejected the *Private Eye* suggestion that he was "the richest and most powerful member" of a circle of "gamblers and boneheads with whom Lord Lucan associated" and which had conspired to obstruct the police inquiries into the murder of Sandra Rivett and Lucan's disappearance. He had, after all, not even been at the lunch at which they alleged the conspiracy had been hatched.

On 5 April, three days before the first hearing of Goldsmith's action for criminal libel, solicitors for *Private Eye* admitted that their original article had been untrue. He had not been at the lunch, so he could hardly have been the dominant figure at it. The magazine wanted to settle the action and pay him damages for the insult. Any other man might have relished the prospect of substantial damages paid free of tax, but Jimmy Goldsmith was not interested in the possibility of damages. An apology for the libel would suffice, provided the magazine "ceased to pillory Eric Levine". *Private Eye* refused and Jimmy Goldsmith embarked unhesitatingly on his crusade against the magazine's whole approach to journalism. He chose to leave any civil claim he may have had against the magazine in abeyance, and pursue instead the criminal libel charge.

He was convinced that the magazine was an "evil" publication with a core of "maggots and scavengers", which attracted a lot of trendy hangers-on who did not understand what they were associating with. And he was convinced that the magazine, together with these hangers-on, was orchestrating a campaign of vilification against him in the British media. He also believed that the object of the campaign was to undermine his rescue of Slater Walker, and cast doubt on the City of London, which would lead to its nationalization. The Lucan affair was simply the pretext chosen to attack him.

Just a few days later, on 13 April, Mr Lewis Hawser QC fired the first salvo in Jimmy Goldsmith's battle against *Private Eye* before Mr Justice Wein in the Royal Courts of Justice in the Strand. His application to institute criminal libel proceedings, which he had made on 15 January, made abundantly clear the seriousness with which he viewed the magazine's allegations against him, particularly because he occupied a position of public trust.

But the editor of *Private Eye*, Richard Ingrams, was not particularly concerned. As he sat in the panelled court room, with its leather-bound law books and faint smell of dust, Ingrams felt confident. He still believed the case was "rather absurd", even as Lewis Hawser told the judge of the "campaign of vilification" conducted against Jimmy Goldsmith in his magazine. So confident that he allowed another attack on Goldsmith leaving Slater Walker to be published just as the hearing was drawing to a close. It referred to him as Goldshidt and Goldenballs.

Ingram's confidence evaporated when Mr Justice Wein began his summing-up the following day by saying that, although he was in favour of freedom of the press "that does not mean that the Press, and in particular any magazine, has a licence to publish scandalous or scurrilous matter which is wholly without foundation". He concluded Jimmy Goldsmith's position of "public importance" and his "association with the Bank of England" over the rescue of Slater Walker meant that "the public interest requires the institution of criminal proceedings".

Richard Ingrams left the court in a state of shock. "What no one had thought possible had come to pass," he wrote later. "We had all been treating it almost as a joke, and now I was going to be charged with a criminal offence with the possibility of a prison sentence at the end of it." Despondent, he went back to his home in Berkshire for the Easter weekend, but when he returned to London he returned to the attack, determined to discover all he could about Goldsmith. At the same time he launched a fund to fight the case for his defence, which the magazine named "The Goldenballs Fund" after one of its contributor's nicknames for Goldsmith. The name stuck for many years and perhaps as much as anything else stiffened the existing battle lines between the two men, though Jimmy Goldsmith never responded by calling Ingrams an equally insulting name.

Just for a moment Goldsmith hesitated. Richard Ingrams now knew that he could pursue him for criminal libel, and he wondered whether the case was worth it. He had proved his point, and the threat was there. In the middle of April 1976, as Harold Wilson began to hand over to his successor, James Callaghan, Jimmy Goldsmith began negotiating a settlement of the libel action with *Private Eye*. The magazine's new barrister, Mr James Comyn QC, was strongly recommending that they accept the out-of-court settlement on the terms that had been suggested to them by Goldsmith's solicitors.

Broadly, the suggested settlement between the two sides included the payment of £15,000 to £20,000 in damages, an apology in open court which would also be published in other newspapers, an agreement not to mention Goldsmith or his solicitor Eric Levine for five years and then only to do so after giving them forty-eight hours before publication to see any proposed material about them, and the disclosure of the names of the authors of the offending articles. Negotiations struggled on, with Goldsmith dropping his demand for damages and a five-year ban, until finally Richard Ingrams brought them to a halt.

"Thinking about it," Ingrams wrote later, "the more reluctant I became to do any deal with Goldsmith whatsoever." He concluded, "I suppose, if I am to be honest, another reason was that in spite of all the stress, part of me was enjoying the excitement of the case and did not want it to end at this point." The two men were now firmly locked in combat. The day after Ingrams broke off the negotiations Jimmy Goldsmith launched his criminal libel case at Bow Street Magistrates Court.

One unspoken reason for the breakdown of negotiations, however, was that while they had been taking place rumours had started to circulate a few weeks earlier that Harold Wilson's "resignation honours list" might include an award for none other than Jimmy Goldsmith. To some at *Private Eye* it may suddenly have appeared that their attacker was about to become embroiled in an even greater public scandal. Why should they reach a settlement with a man who was about to find himself at the centre of another furious public row?

On the first Sunday in May, Jimmy Goldsmith's old antagonist from the Bovril takeover, the London *Sunday Times*, reported that the list – drawn up, according to the newspaper, with the help of Marcia Falkender – had met with objections from the official Political Honours Scrutiny Committee. The *Sunday Times* also reported that Wilson himself had deleted one or two names from the list, including that of David Frost, and that difficulties had arisen over a life peerage for a "City financier" whom many quickly identified as Jimmy Goldsmith.

In the next three weeks the public speculation over Harold Wilson's honours list, and the possibility of its including a peerage for Jimmy Goldsmith, overshadowed even the action for criminal libel against Richard Ingrams. The political storm that burst over Jimmy Goldsmith was to damage his image in England every bit as much as his libel action, for the two became inextricably confused in most people's minds. It appeared to those who did not know that Goldsmith was no more than a vindictive tycoon anxious to further his chances of a political career by launching a libel action, with the tacit approval of the Prime Minister, against a small satirical magazine with a circulation of about 120,000 copies a fortnight. Nine days after the negotiations for a settlement with *Private Eye* had broken down, the *Daily Express* ran a front-page headline, "It's Lord Goldsmith", above a story that reported he was to be given a peerage in Wilson's honours list.

But Jimmy Goldsmith had never asked for, or been offered, a peerage. And Harold Wilson had never intended to give him one. As Marcia Falkender recalls now, "In the last day or so before we left Downing Street Harold handed all the little bits of paper and cards that he had been collecting over the months for his list to me, and asked, 'Could you do a fair copy of them?' I said, 'No, because the typewriters have all gone. They went yesterday, can't the civil service do it?' and Harold went into the private office to ask them if they would." The Downing Street civil servants, however, took the view that, as the Prime Minister's resignation honours list was a personal matter, it should be dealt with by his personal staff. "I grabbed the first thing that came to hand, and I sat down with all

Harold's cards to write the names down on a single list. I did them all in my own handwriting – because there weren't any typewriters, and I handed them back to him." Sitting at a small table just outside the Cabinet Room in 10 Downing Street, Marcia Falkender wrote the list on a sheet of pink notepaper she had found.

The "Lavender List" became the focus of one of the fiercest political storms in British politics in the second half of the century. In the height of the controversy that followed it, Marcia Falkender would sometimes wake up in a cold sweat thinking to herself, "Why did I go and copy the list out for him on pink paper?" She was to be cast time and time again as the woman who manipulated a prime minister. "Everyone even got the impression that I'd wanted Jimmy to go to the House of Lords, but that Harold had back-tracked and given him a knighthood instead," Marcia Falkender says now. "But why should I? I didn't know Jimmy very well then, and in any case there had never been any question of a peerage. Harold had only ever intended to give him a knighthood. That was what I wrote on the list."

For his part Jimmy Goldsmith had not known anything about a knighthood, or a peerage, until he had received a telephone call from Harold Wilson towards the end of April.

"You haven't replied to my letter," Wilson said.

"What letter?" a perplexed Goldsmith asked.

"The one offering you a knighthood," he was told.

After Wilson's departure from Downing Street a formal offer had been sent to Goldsmith's former home in Chester Terrace. But by then he was sharing his time between a newly rented house in Tregunter Road in Kensington and Lady Annabel Birley's home, Pelham Cottage not far away.

A slightly perplexed, but nevertheless flattered Jimmy Goldsmith accepted the offer formally. To be given a knighthood by a Labour Prime Minister whom he had spent the last general election trying to defeat came as something of a surprise: but not all that great a one. "Several other men who had created companies smaller than Cavenham had been given knighthoods, so it did not strike me as all that exceptional. I was always a conservative, so were many others who received knighthoods from Wilson," he says now. "It certainly did not strike me as any cause for a public controversy." But that is what it became.

As the political row broke out, sparked by the *Daily Express* and accusations that Wilson had misused his position as Prime Minister (an unfair charge as any resignation honours list is a personal matter for the outgoing Prime Minister), and had been manipulated by Marcia Falkender, Jimmy Goldsmith told his friends, "All I can think is that I am caught up in an internal row between Harold Wilson's friends and advisers." Certainly some of them were privately convinced that it may also have had something to do with his failure to marry Lady Annabel Birley, whose brother-in-law, Sir Max Rayne, was elevated to the peerage on the same honours list. There were undoubtedly some members of the English establishment who deeply resented any recognition whatsoever of a businessman, no matter how successful, who openly flouted conventional morality.

Jimmy Goldsmith found himself confronting, almost simultaneously, the fury of some sections of the English establishment, astonished that a confessed adulterer should be awarded any kind of honour; and the anger of a substantial section of English journalism which felt that any action for criminal libel in the second half of the twentieth century was the behaviour of a belligerent bully with no sense of manners.

In spite of the persistent rumours and speculation, Jimmy Goldsmith had not harboured ambitions for a political career when he set out to rescue Slater Walker. "Certainly he did not seem to have any political ambitions when I first met him," Marcia Falkender says. "What he developed later, from force of circumstance, was the feeling that 'If you're going to be involved like this, you might as well have some sort of public position.'"

Jimmy Goldsmith found himself no longer a simple entrepreneur, with a complex, but private, personal life. Instead he had become a man about whom hardly anyone in Britain did not have an opinion.

17

The Eye of the Storm

An old-fashioned Victorian entrepreneur who wanted to make deals, and make money, was almost as rare a species in the Labour-governed Britain of 1976 as the dodo had been a century earlier.

By the beginning of the last quarter of the twentieth century there was nothing that a substantial minority of well-educated Englishmen and women suspected more than success: particularly commercial success. It was an attitude that would have horrified their Victorian ancestors, but as England had gradually subsided during the intervening century, so some of its best educated men and women, the guardians of its culture and its heritage, increasingly found nothing wrong whatever in decrying achievement in business. The country which had created the industrial revolution was content to see its industrial fruits taken over and exploited by others, whether in Japan or the United States, West Germany or France. A generation of "You've never had it so good" and "I'm all right, Jack", ushered in the "swinging sixties" which contrived to ensure that the British all too often felt flatulent and self-assured on no basis whatever.

Small wonder then that Jimmy Goldsmith felt very much alone, as he battled with *Private Eye* and the English establishment in the early summer of 1976. Small wonder too that the battles convinced him very quickly that England was not a country that he wished to remain in any longer. Like his father before him, Jimmy Goldsmith discovered that the English remained deeply suspicious of foreigners, and flamboyant successful foreigners in particular. He might have an English mistress, and two small English children, but as the weeks of July and then August passed it became ever more apparent to him that England was to be visited rather than lived in. France was still where he felt most comfortable, and the attractions of the United States were increasing daily.

By the time Jimmy Goldsmith's knighthood was finally officially announced, on 27 May 1976, with its citation "for services to exports and ecology", he was well and truly fed up. Even the award's description was now turned against him. "Services to ecology" ran the rumour, meant for cleaning up *Private Eye*; while another joke ran that the Prime Minister had confused the two Goldsmith brothers and thought that Jimmy was the one who had written "Blueprint for Survival". Neither joke appealed to Jimmy Goldsmith. "I had been of service to ecology and I had given money to the cause. I had actually talked about ecology a great deal, I had helped launch the Ecological Foundation, which I supported financially, and I had recently financed the Friends of the Earth in their campaign against the nuclear plant at Windscale," he says now. "I was and still am a supporter of the environmental movement, but not of its political outgrowth. I think ecology was a useful handle, and I think that's all it was."

The gossip which surrounded his "services to ecology" served to tarnish the award, which he then prized, and it served still more to make Jimmy Goldsmith and Marcia Falkender, the two people caught up in the storm, close friends. There were those, particularly among the supporters of *Private Eye*, who believed he had been included in the honours list only because the Prime Minister's secretary had put him there and that she had been the originator of the joke about his "services to ecology", but in reality Marcia Falkender had never included the detailed citations on the handwritten list she had prepared for Harold Wilson on her last day in Downing Street. "They were not on the list that Harold asked me to write out for him." She had no more idea than Jimmy Goldsmith why the citation read as it did. After it was published, "the list locked me into the Goldsmith ambience", she says now. "It was originally fellow suffering, but we got on like a house on fire."

But there was no doubt of the furore that the award had created. In *The Times* one columnist noted: "No honours list, resignation or otherwise, has ever been attended by such farce . . . no individual recipient, however deserving, can feel altogether happy. Who could wish for inclusion in a roll call giving rise to universal astonishment and derision?" And concluded by pointing out that one recipient, James Goldsmith, was a "declared contributor to Tory Party funds".

The damage was done. Although Jimmy Goldsmith later received the Légion d'honneur from President Giscard d'Estaing without attracting any publicity whatever, he was for ever branded in some sections of English society as a man too anxious for his own advancement. In the Labour Party, in some sections of the City of London and in a significant portion of the British press, Jimmy Goldsmith's knighthood and his prosecution of *Private Eye* indicated that he was a man not to be trusted or taken too seriously. Both made him one of the most controversial public figures to emerge in Britain for twenty-five years.

The columnist Michael Davie reported in the *Observer* on the Sunday before the honours list was officially published: "The time has come, it appears, when we must begin to puzzle over the phenomenon of Mr James M. Goldsmith, chairman of the Cavenham Food Group . . . Until recently, Goldsmith was simply a playboy, or ex-playboy, who had built up a food company at high speed. Lately, though, his friends have noted a new seriousness about him, and he has started taking an interest in politics. What is more, politicians have started taking an interest in him. When big business men show signs of going political, it behoves the rest of us to pay attention."

Ironically, Davie's conclusions would have been more appropriate two years earlier. By the time that they appeared the ambivalence that Jimmy Goldsmith had always felt about England had turned to despair for the country and its future. There was no denying that he enjoyed the company of politicians. Like many successful businessmen before him he relished proximity to power, though not for his own political advancement, as so many critics believed. "If that had been my objective, surely I would have organized my entire life quite differently," he says now. "I would have to have done."

"The only political power I wanted was the power to influence events," he told his friends.

Undeniably he saw himself as a friend and confidante of politicians, just as his father had been. To prove the point, shortly after Harold Wilson retired Jimmy Goldsmith organized a dinner for both Wilson and his predecessor as Prime Minister, Edward Heath, at his new house in Tregunter Road. "I think it was the first time that they had actually ever spent any time together alone; and it was certainly the first time that they had ever had dinner together without a lot of other people being present." One person who was not at the dinner, however, was Marcia Falkender although she learnt later that "Harold and Ted Heath got on very well together, and they found that they agreed on a great many things."

More than anything, it was Jimmy Goldsmith's desire to influence events and ideas that also led him to continue his battle with *Private Eye*. The magazine epitomized the worst features of English society, he believed, and he had the financial power to defeat it. What had begun as a battle to protect himself, and one of his solicitors, Eric Levine, from libel, had quickly escalated into a crusade, taking a great deal of his time and energy. It was also a crusade which he could not hope to win. "The magazine was a club of British journalists, and I did not realize the importance of what I was handling! I did not realize that *Private Eye* was part of the whole British press." It was a telling naïvety.

Private Eye had prospered during the first fifteen years of its life by being the only publication in which British journalists could print stories that their own, more respectable, papers or magazines might refuse. To attempt to crush it, therefore, was to strike at the strain of iconoclasm and scepticism that lay at the heart of some parts of British journalism. The comfortable self-righteousness of many journalists – the notion that they alone knew the truth about everything – was called into question. A similar legal action would probably never have been necessary in the United States or in France, where that level of cloistered certainty was less on display; but when Jimmy Goldsmith started out to teach one small fortnightly magazine a lesson, he found himself questioning the standards and the style of British journalism.

Certainly he had not realized that his case against *Private Eye* would fuel the persistent and bitter criticism of his knighthood. Richard Ingrams did, however. "There can be no doubt," he wrote later, "that a major cause of this upsurge of feeling against him was his campaign against *Private Eye*. It was mainly for this that he was well known. Until he sued *Private Eye*, Goldsmith was a relatively obscure figure." But the more the tide of public criticism swelled against him, the more determined Jimmy Goldsmith became to continue with the case and the more convinced he became that he was doing something vital for the health of the British media. "We have to clean out these stables," he told the *Wall Street Journal* a little later – the "stables" he was referring to were those of the British press.

For his part Richard Ingrams liked to cast himself as a victim of events and Jimmy Goldsmith as a megalomaniac tycoon anxious to destroy a harmless magazine. He subsequently maintained that version of events in his own account of the libel case, *Goldenballs*. In fact, shortly after the announcement of Jimmy Goldsmith's knighthood there was a fleeting moment when their public battle might have been settled amicably – and it was refused by Ingrams not Jimmy Goldsmith. Anthony Blond, who had known Jimmy Goldsmith since his time at Oxford with Teddy and John Aspinall, had been an early supporter of *Private Eye* and owned slightly over 9 per cent of the shares in the magazine's holding company, Pressdram Limited. On the day his knighthood was finally announced Blond sent Goldsmith a telegram: "Congratulations. Why not drop your suit against the Eye. *Noblesse* now *oblige*!"

Jimmy Goldsmith rang up and summoned him to tea at Tregunter Road. Blond recalls their meeting vividly. "Jimmy was indignant – with some justification, I thought – that the Eye were attacking him and his family, and using doubtful evidence to do this. He was determined to pursue them to the prison and their confinement, or to the grave. He was prepared to see weeping widows licking his boots and pleading for the release of their husbands and so on." But Blond perceptively pointed out to him that in Richard Ingrams he had "a dangerous adversary – a martyr – somebody who would enjoy flames licking the soles of their feet". And he ended by saying, casually, that Ingrams was "an amusing fellow" and, "Why don't we all three have lunch tomorrow?"

"Jimmy instantly agreed, so I telephoned Ingrams at the Eye. He said, 'Oh dear, oh dear. You don't know what's been happening. Of course I can't have lunch with him. Come and see me.'" The offer of conciliation was turned down flat, and not by Jimmy Goldsmith. The memory angers Blond to this day because he knows that Ingrams's refusal to meet his adversary – at a time when the case could still have been called off – was never recorded by Ingrams. "Because it shows Jimmy's profound transigence, and Richard could not stand that."

It is now abundantly clear that the reason the libel case between Jimmy Goldsmith and *Private Eye* continued for so long and so acrimoniously owes more to the character of Richard Ingrams than it does to the case itself. As Anthony Blond puts it, "Richard doesn't like anything flash. He doesn't like naked power, and he likes to bring the mighty down – that could explain it." Indeed, Blond also suggests that "Jimmy's existence and success offends Richard's possibly slightly Puritan precepts. Behind the Eye is a very East Anglian, Cromwellian distaste for power, luxury and high level fun and games."

More than anything else it was that British suspicion of the rich and powerful – one *Private Eye* director describes Jimmy Goldsmith as a "megalomaniac tycoon who resembles Napoleon in everything except the Emperor's tiny testicles" – that lay behind *Private Eye*'s continued battle against Jimmy Goldsmith. They saw themselves on a moral crusade against the high and mighty, just as their adversary saw himself conducting a crusade for the honesty of the British press. But he was more prepared to settle the differences than they were. In any event, the opportunity to call off one of the century's most controversial libel cases was lost.

For just as Blond was mediating with Goldsmith, so Ingrams had found that his foe was employing a team of private detectives to search through the *Private Eye* dustbins, to find out "exactly who their sources were". Jimmy Goldsmith wanted to find out whether the attacks on him were "coincidence or conspiracy" because "at that time every journalist wrote anonymously for *Private Eye*". The revelation convinced Ingrams even more forcibly that he could "never deal with a man like Goldsmith".

On the day the *Daily Express* reported "It's Lord Goldsmith", the paper also recorded that he had returned to the High Court to ask for a writ prohibiting "Words, pictures or visual images tending to disparage or cast doubt on the private or personal integrity of Mr Eric Levine". In a bizarre footnote to what was becoming a brutal encounter, Goldsmith had discovered that the magazine was planning another attack on Levine, this time based on his conduct while a member of a firm of City of London solicitors, Leslie Paisner and Company.

When Jimmy Goldsmith heard that the magazine were considering printing a string of new allegations which included the suggestion that his solicitor Eric Levine had been involved in improper currency conversion for an American client, he decided to confront the men making the allegations – Leslie Paisner, the head of the firm of solicitors, and a public relations consultant called John Addey. On Friday 13 May Jimmy Goldsmith saw both men in his office at Leadenhall Street, and both repeated their allegations. He then saw Eric Levine who denied the allegations forcefully.

By Monday 17 May, however, both Leslie Paisner and John Addey had withdrawn their allegations, and had sworn affidavits to that effect. That morning Jimmy Goldsmith telephoned the editors of *The Times*, the *Daily Telegraph*, *The Economist* and the *Sunday Express* to warn them that the allegations might still be made, and to explain that one of *Private Eye*'s regular contributors, Michael Gillard, who was largely responsible for its "Slicker" column on the dealings of the City of London, had been blackmailing John Addey.

As Jimmy Goldsmith was to explain in court three years later, "I felt it was necessary to explain to the editors of leading newspapers what was happening, and the gravity of their case, so that they looked more carefully at articles based on lies, appearing apparently independently in their paper, but effectively part of the campaign of *Private Eye* to put pressure on me." Jimmy Goldsmith had decided to fight back in any way he could. No matter how exaggerated his actions might appear, he was intent on counter-attacking whenever he was attacked, even to the extent of having to fight a slander case in court.

"I had every reason to believe," he would eventually tell the jury in the case brought against him three years later, "that *Private Eye*, as part of their campaign, would try and publish these false allegations, or part of them, for an article about Eric Levine; and the trouble about these articles is that today it is possible to prove that they were all lies, but when they are made they do harm; and you have to be fairly strong to be able to live through such lies." That was why Jimmy Goldsmith had returned to the High Court on the morning of 17 May 1976 to ask for an injunction to prevent *Private Eye* mentioning Eric Levine at all.

As the charge and counter-charge grew more intense, however, so the list of victims of the battle between Jimmy Goldsmith and *Private Eye* grew longer. By the time the injunction was heard formally by Mr Justice Donaldson on a steamy July day, John Addey had disappeared to Italy on an extended business trip, and Leslie Paisner was found by his doctor to be "extremely confused and withdrawn and threatening suicide". Unfit to appear as a witness, shortly after the hearing Paisner retired from his law practice, but his health did not recover. He died less than three years later at the age of seventy.

In fact, on 16 July Mr Justice Donaldson refused to grant Jimmy Goldsmith the injunction he sought to prevent *Private Eye* mentioning Eric Levine. But that did not bring matters to a close. In May the magazine had given a temporary undertaking not to publish anything about Goldsmith or Levine until the hearing of the injunction, which had been breached five times. No sooner had *Private Eye* won a small victory than it found itself arraigned for contempt of court and fined £250. But these were only minor skirmishes as a prelude to the main battle.

On the morning of 30 July 1976 Jimmy Goldsmith's criminal libel case against Richard Ingrams was finally heard at Bow Street court, by the Chief Metropolitan Magistrate, Mr Kenneth Barraclough. He chose that moment to make his first public appearance with Lady Annabel Birley. They walked into court together arm in arm: he looking a shade intimidated by the vast crowd of photographers, she looking determined and supportive, showing a trace of Londonderry fire by having chosen to wear a revealing print dress with a split skirt that flapped open in the summer breeze. It was Goldsmith's only appearance in the witness box during his eighteen-month legal battle with *Private Eye* itself.

For those who knew Jimmy Goldsmith only by his reputation in the press, his appearance came as a surprise. Tall, a little diffident, with an almost boyish voice, he did not look much like the bullying, belligerent tycoon that he was so persistently painted. Richard Ingrams found him a "tall, restless, nail-biting man" who "looked at least ten years older than forty-three. His face was tanned, his eyes a steely blue. In repose, his expression was particularly dead. But his face would frequently crinkle into a smile and – which was disconcerting – from time to time he looked across at me, nodding and grinning, as if to try and convey a message of some kind."

"Until this case," Jimmy Goldsmith told a slightly bewildered Kenneth Barraclough, "I think I had only issued one writ for libel in my life." That provoked James Comyn QC, appearing for *Private Eye* to remark dryly, "You are making up for it now." Goldsmith seemed remarkably agitated as he gave evidence. He paced restlessly, bringing his fist down on the rail of the witness box from time to time, gesticulating as he usually did. To anyone who knew him well it was entirely in character – he always walked up and down when he talked, just as he tended to wave his arms to support his argument, and to bite the corner of his handkerchief in moments of tension – but to those who only believed *Private Eye*'s description of him it came as a shock. An astonished Kenneth Barraclough finally asked him if he would mind behaving "a little less theatrically". Rather taken aback, Jimmy Goldsmith said apologetically, "I am sorry, I find it difficult to keep still."

As he left the courtroom at lunchtime, once again with Annabel Birley by his side, the London *Evening Standard* was already running his name as its front page leadline: "Goldsmith tells criminal libel hearing, 'I'm not trying to smash the Eye.'" He had told James Comyn QC that he had already tried to reach a "generous settlement" with the magazine which would allow it to survive "although perhaps a little more truthfully" and he had also told him that his criminal libel case was the result of "a campaign against me fortnight after fortnight".

Jimmy Goldsmith's evidence helped to convince the Chief Metropolitan Magistrate to allow the criminal libel case to proceed, in spite of the serious reservations about it expressed in some legal quarters. He had won the first round in the battle of what *Private Eye* had called the "antique blunderbuss" put into his hands by Mr Justice Wein. But the price had been terrifyingly high. Jimmy Goldsmith would never again be anything other than a controversial figure in England, beset by enemies he had never met – for reasons he could barely understand. He was cast in stone for many as the belligerent pursuer of a harmless satirical magazine.

What other man, so the argument ran, would have instructed his solicitors to recruit a team of private detectives to search through *Private Eye*'s dustbins in pursuit of evidence against the magazine. What other man would encourage his detectives to follow and then photograph leading members of the magazine's staff, including Richard Ingrams and his contributor Nigel Dempster, if he was not actually slightly mad. It seemed, unquestionably, to many English people, the behaviour of a "megalomaniac financier" who was "determined to win whatever the means".

In fact though Jimmy Goldsmith certainly could, and did, on occasion, present an aggressive face to the world, there was also a strain of boyish insecurity within him which he struggled to conceal. That meant he tended to react violently, even quixotically, to many things – and especially to attack. "I felt *Private Eye* were attacking me with everything they could," he said later, "and I decided to fight back with everything I could. Besides I also had to find out whether the campaign against me was really being co-ordinated, or whether it was my imagination. That is why I took on private detectives to find out who really worked for *Private Eye*, and they produced a substantial list, which confirmed what I had suspected."

Nevertheless his behaviour fundamentally offended the English sense of fair play. Once again he had revealed himself something of an outsider, a man prepared to play by different "rules". When his use of the detectives was finally publicly revealed – as it was at the next hearing of the criminal libel action at Bow Street court on 6 August – it served only further to convince many that he had a mean and vengeful streak alongside his obvious "foreignness". Perhaps more than any other fact during the *Private Eye* case it contrived to turn the vast weight of public opinion in England against him.

But whatever Jimmy Goldsmith's determination to defeat *Private Eye*, there were still the affairs of Cavenham, and Générale Occidentale – not to mention Slater Walker – to be considered. He had already announced that he intended to invest "in excess of £200 million in the next five years" on behalf of Cavenham's "main stream activities". Now he needed to devote himself to the task, especially as shortly after the Bow Street hearing of his criminal libel case late

in July, he learnt that his cousin Alexis de Gunzburg, who had
helped him create his businesses in both Britain and France over
the past dozen years, wanted to resign. For "personal reasons of his
own", as he explained to the London *Daily Telegraph*, Alexis de
Gunzburg had decided to leave the board of an empire which he
had seen expand until it now employed some 66,000 people around
the world, and boasted pre-tax profits of almost £35 million in 1976
(some £100 million at today's prices).

After the Bow Street hearings were over, and Alexis's resignation
accepted, Jimmy Goldsmith decided to take a brief holiday in
Corsica before returning to reveal to the City of London for the first
time the full extent of Slater Walker's difficulties – and what he had
done to try to minimize them for the future. It had not been easy.

On Wednesday 15 September 1976, with the *Private Eye* case
temporarily out of the headlines, the first complete report of the
events at Slater Walker Securities was published, two weeks before
the company's scheduled annual general meeting. Within a matter
of hours the company's share price had fallen by 50 per cent – from
16 pence to eight pence, even though it had once traded at forty
times that amount. Slater Walker was alive, but only just. A few
days later it looked as though it might never survive. Fifteen
summonses alleging breaches of the British Companies Act were
issued against Jim Slater by the Department of Trade and Industry
for his conduct of the company before Jimmy Goldsmith took over,
and on the following day the Singapore government asked for the
extradition of Jim Slater and four other Slater Walker men on
charges of fraud and conspiracy. Exactly how bad a state the
company was in had finally come out into the open.

It was hardly surprising, therefore, that Jimmy Goldsmith was
not looking forward to the Slater Walker annual general meeting at
all. On the telephone he started asking his friends to come along,
and even offered to buy one or two shares for them so that they
could be there officially. "He seemed to want a bit of moral support,"
one remembers, "it wasn't exactly the behaviour of a belligerent
tycoon."

As he feared, the meeting was a stormy affair, not least because
a group of what he later called "Trotskyists" had managed to get in
to disrupt it by shouting slogans. In the uproar Goldsmith had to

shout across the carpeted function room of the Connaught Rooms in London to make himself heard. He explained that without "the support of the Bank of England Slater Walker would not have been able to keep trading" and that altogether the Bank had made available no less than £110 million to keep the company operating while he and his fellow directors had put into effect a "complete reorganization".

As the demonstrators' shouts grew louder so he shouted more and more to make himself heard, and tempers began to fray. Finally John Aspinall's mother, Lady Osborne, and Jimmy Goldsmith's mother, Marcelle, who were both sitting near the front, started attacking the protestors with their umbrellas. A pitched battle raged for some minutes until eventually, with the help of the meeting's stewards, the protestors were ejected. "Afterwards everything was totally friendly," Jimmy Goldsmith recalls, "because the share-holders felt a common cause against the Trotskyists." But when the reports of the meeting appeared in the British press the next day it was not Jimmy Goldsmith's achievement in keeping Slater Walker afloat – if badly leaking – that attracted the attention, it was the demonstration. It seemed to confirm that he was now a figure who could never escape controversy in Britain.

But it was not Slater Walker or the case against *Private Eye* that brought him back into the headlines again, just a few days later. An opportunity had presented itself to put his theories about "cleaning up" the British press into effect. There was a chance that he could take over Britain's oldest Sunday newspaper, the *Observer*, which was in severe financial difficulties. The paper, which was owned by a Trust, was reported to be considering whether it might be sold.

"One morning I was reading an article about Rupert Murdoch's interest in the *Observer*," he recalls now. He was in fact sitting in bed in Tregunter Road eating his breakfast. "In the article I read that Lord Goodman, who was chairman of the *Observer* trust, stated that I would definitely not get the *Observer* and that I would be repelled. I was amazed by this, because I had made no advances. So I wondered how I could be repelled."

Jimmy Goldsmith decided to find out. He rang Goodman, who still acted as his adviser at Slater Walker Securities, and was assured that he had been misquoted. The portly but distinctly shrewd Goodman, a close friend of Harold Wilson's, then invited Goldsmith to join him that morning to meet the owner of the *Observer*, David Astor, and the paper's managing director.

When the four men met, Goodman asked if he would be interested in buying the paper. "I said yes. They then asked me whether I would guarantee editorial independence. I said no. I made it clear I would not buy the paper unless I was invited to do so by all the parties – including the journalists." The following evening he invited a group of the paper's senior editorial staff to dinner. As one of the men invited, Michael Davie, the paper's outstanding columnist, reported later: "Even if Goldsmith were interested in routes to political power, of which he has never shown any sign, they are not open to him. Yet he wants power. Ergo, the obvious step is into publishing . . . But he claimed most persuasively – since he is nothing if not persuasive – that he would always attempt to get his views across by reasoned argument, not by diktat. He would never be another Beaverbrook or Northcliffe. He would never give orders about editorial content."

But his case against *Private Eye* would eventually ensure that Jimmy Goldsmith never owned the *Observer*, or any other existing British national newspaper. The intensity of the legend that gathered around him, fuelled by the magazine and rarely contradicted by him except in a court of law, convinced a generation of British journalists that he would be the reincarnation of Charles Foster Kane. Certainly his decision to return to court again in October to ask for Richard Ingrams to be charged with contempt – for the second time in three months – because of an article in the magazine about Leslie Paisner late in August, absolutely convinced many *Observer* journalists that this was a man they could never accept as their proprietor.

It rapidly appeared that the English courts agreed with them. When Lewis Hawser QC appeared for him again, in front of the Lord Chief Justice, to claim that "the editor and contributors of *Private Eye* have combined to create and maintain a climate in which it will be difficult for there to be a fair trial", he was given very short shrift. The Lord Chief Justice, Lord Widgery, found firmly against Goldsmith.

The two contempt of court hearings during the blisteringly hot summer of 1976, coming as they did in the midst of his criminal libel action against Richard Ingrams, ensured him a reputation for vengefulness, which he was never to lose. All those whom he had felt would explain his position publicly studiously declined to do so. There were no articles by his supporters suggesting he might just be right, no public defence was launched, and Jimmy Goldsmith found himself fighting alone. It was the greatest disappointment of his life.

Even his hopes of owning a British newspaper came to nothing. By November, after a trip to see Grand Union in the United States, Jimmy Goldsmith discovered that the giant American oil company, Atlantic Richfield, had suddenly bought the *Observer*. Though it would be reported that they had foiled his attempt to own it, in fact he had never even made a bid. Shortly afterwards he was offered the chance to buy shares in another British national newspaper group, the *Daily Express* and *Sunday Express*, when Rupert Murdoch, the Australian-born newspaper tycoon, who had just bought the *New York Post*, offered him 4.4 million shares in Beaverbrook Newspapers, which owned the two papers. Jimmy Goldsmith bought them. This interest in becoming a publisher of newspapers or magazines was beginning to grow.

Though few people knew about it, he was so contemplating buying magazines in both France and the United States. Clay Felker, the owner and publisher of the adventurous and successful *New York* magazine, had already discussed the possibility of his buying his magazine, together with two others in his stable, *New West* and the *Village Voice* shortly after Rupert Murdoch had all but gained control of them; but the deal had never come off. It was too late. Meanwhile, in France, Jimmy Goldsmith had also been quietly conducting negotiations to purchase the French weekly news magazine *L'Express* from its politician owner, Jean Jacques Servan-Schrieber. Those negotiations were to prove a great deal more successful.

For the moment, however, there was Britain, and the Express group of newspapers, owned by the Beaverbrook family, to be pursued. In fact there was another, less obvious, reason for Jimmy Goldsmith's purchase of the Beaverbrook shares. He wanted to keep them out of the hands of the proprietor of Associated Newspapers, Vere Harmsworth, the owner of Beaverbrook's principal daily rival in Britain, the *Daily Mail*. And he wanted to do that, he explained later, "as a financial penalty" for the paper's gossip columnist Nigel Dempster, whom he saw as a regular contributor to *Private Eye*.

By the beginning of January 1977 he had built his holding to almost five million of Beaverbrook's A shares, about 35 per cent of the total, but because of the company's structure, that gave him no power whatever in its affairs. That still lay with the voting shares, which were primarily in the hands of the family of the late Lord Beaverbrook, under the leadership of his son Sir Max Aitken. As it turned out, Aitken was "not in the least amused" by Jimmy Goldsmith's intervention in his company, and he made it quite clear that he had no wish to see his newspapers fall into his hands. By the end of January Jimmy Goldsmith was accepting defeat, and telling everyone concerned that he would "push no further into the company" without Aitken's blessing. He was unlikely to get that.

Though few people in England recognized it at that moment, that was to be the last time Jimmy Goldsmith ever seriously considered taking over a major British publishing company. The events of the previous year or so had convinced him beyond doubt that he would never be able to spend much time in Britain again: the dislike he had encountered was too intense. He had no intention of allowing it to continue any longer.

On Friday 18 January 1977, days before he made it abundantly clear he would not push into Beaverbrook any further, he began the process that would see him retire as chairman of Cavenham, the company he had created from almost nothing in just thirteen years. As he put it, "I can't say I've enjoyed it. I've disliked it. Not much is done to make things enjoyable for the chairmen of public companies. They tend to be targets and I see no reason why I should put up with it." But he was not only announcing his intention to step down as chairman, he was also revealing his plan to buy out the 44 per cent of the company that was still in public hands. "Now we are very much following a policy that we should paddle our own canoe in private."

To those who accused him of being a megalomaniac, seeking nothing but public power and influence, it was an eccentric decision, even if it was yet further evidence of his secretiveness. *The Economist* reported, with some surprise: "He has suffered, he says, twelve years of virtually unmitigated press vilification, despite being responsible for one of Britain's post-war industrial success stories: and nobody, least of all the stock market, understands him." Jimmy Goldsmith had actually acknowledged that not only was he an outsider in British business, but that he intended to remain one.

After a brief suspension of dealings in its shares on the London Stock Exchange, Générale Occidentale offered 120 pence for each of the remaining Cavenham shares not in their own hands. The bid was not greeted with universal enthusiasm in the City of London. As some critics quickly pointed out, in 1973 the shares had stood at 230 pence. For a few weeks the bid remained on the table, but without much interest, until in March Jimmy Goldsmith rang up Peter Hill-Wood of Hambros in London from Barbados, where he was on holiday with Annabel and her children, and told him to withdraw it. The bid was off. Some in the City of London nodded at each other sagely, suspecting that he had never had any intention of going through with it. What they did not know was that Jimmy Goldsmith had only postponed his decision, not changed his mind about it. His depression about the state of England had not eased.

While his bid was temporarily stuck he won a small victory over *Private Eye* when the magazine's appeal against his series of libel writs against it and its distributors was rejected by the Court of Appeal, even though two of the three Law Lords thought fit to warn that "no private individual should be allowed to stifle a publication by suing its distributors for libel" and "neither wealth nor power entitles a man to censor the press". Neither opinion affected their decision; and even better to Jimmy Goldsmith's mind was the fact that *Private Eye* had been forced to admit in court that his libel action meant that they had been losing 12,000 in sales every fortnight, and that their legal costs already amounted to more than £30,000.

There was another victory for him to celebrate that month, however. On 16 March 1977 Jimmy Goldsmith finally succeeded in becoming a publisher – in France. Through his subsidiary company, Agrifurane, part of Générale Alimentaire and thereby Générale Occidentale, he paid £3.5 million for 45 per cent of Groupe Express, publishers of *L'Express*, the largest news magazine in France with sales of 550,000 a week. Founded in 1953, it had been a daily newspaper for eleven years of its history (1955 to 1966), and had a strong left-wing and radical tradition.

News of Jimmy Goldsmith's reputation in England had crossed the Channel, and not every French journalist was pleased at the prospect of his takeover. One national paper, *Le Matin*, commented: "A paper which ceases to belong to its founder, journalists sold like part of the furniture – it is more than sad – it is serious."

To the astonishment of his critics, Jimmy Goldsmith did not proceed to interfere with his new magazine's editorial freedom. Instead he appointed France's leading neo-conservative philosopher Raymond Aron as head of the editorial board and a columnist to "create an equilibrium" and insisted that it be run as a business, standing on its own feet. Within a matter of months even some of his critics were admitting that *L'Express* had not lost its radical voice. To the amazement of some of his own journalists on *L'Express* he told *Newsweek*: "Editorially, my own feeling is that there should be access to a broad spectrum of political thought – not the most extreme ones perhaps – and that's what will happen . . . Not only do I believe in a vigorous and free press but I would fight for it as an absolute necessity, as an element in protecting the way of life we wish to see preserved."

To those who knew him only as the scourge of a small satirical magazine in England that seemed an astonishing statement, but once again it underlined the contradiction at the heart of Jimmy Goldsmith's character. He did not believe for one moment that all journalists were bad, or that every one had to be controlled, or that only his own opinions should be accepted by any magazine he happened to own; but he did believe that it should "reflect the highest possible standards of journalism". But he also believed, as he believes still, that there was nothing that would tempt him "to be associated with a newspaper or magazine whose editorial line was one that I considered evil or destructive". Jimmy Goldsmith was certain that "Some people use our respect for the freedom of the press as a screen behind which they can work to transform our society into one which would no longer tolerate this basic and vital freedom. Many of these people are backed by slush funds whose purpose is to encourage subversion in our community." It was a view which he would return to time and again in the years to come, and one which would – inevitably – separate him from some liberal journalists in Britain and France who were convinced it was simply further evidence of his extraordinary paranoia about the press.

The suspicions that many British journalists had of Jimmy Goldsmith were little different from the suspicions held by many members of the City of London. As his libel action against *Private Eye* had gathered pace, so reservations felt by investment and pension fund managers had grown. They did not like to be seen financially supporting the shares of a man who was a bully and a charlatan, and many were asking themselves if they should continue to maintain their holdings in Cavenham shares.

When Jimmy Goldsmith first offered to buy all his firm's shares in public hands some had even contemplated accepting his offer of 120 pence a share, simply to disassociate themselves from a man who had become a pariah in certain quarters. But they had waited to see what would happen. When he withdrew the offer, they assumed, correctly, that it would be made again. Ironically, the attack by *Private Eye* and the suspicions that it aroused and confirmed in the City contrived to make Jimmy Goldsmith a far richer man than he would otherwise have been, for not only did they have the effect of, temporarily, depressing his share price, they also encouraged him to buy all the shares in his companies himself.

"The attacks meant that I decided to reduce the size of the target being shot at," he explains. That allowed him to ensure that he alone owned and controlled his own companies, and allowed him to invest more and more in the United States at a time when the English pound was worth two dollars and forty cents.

18

Retreat to Paris

In the early spring of 1977 Ormeley Lodge, a magnificent Georgian house on the edge of Richmond Park to the south-west of London, was showing unusual signs of activity. The grounds echoed to the sounds of builders and labourers; the tennis court and swimming pool were being cleaned; the cottage on the west side was being refurbished; and the main house itself was bustling with carpet-layers and curtain fixers, plumbers, painters and carpenters.

Lady Annabel Birley was transforming the house from the rather plain country style of its previous owner, Lord Howard de Walden, a senior steward of the British Jockey Club, into something a little prettier and distinctly more patterned. The paintings of horses were being replaced by paintings of the Londonderry family. Upstairs a nursery was being created for Jemima and Zacharias, and downstairs in the basement a room big enough to entertain a hundred guests for dinner was being wallpapered in red and gold. There was a faint hint of chinoiserie, but the predominant style was Queen Anne by way of Chelsea. The sofas were usually pink, the walls a softer shade of brown. And there were photographs of children everywhere.

Behind the tall iron gates that separated it from the quiet road outside, a family house was being created which Jemima and Zacharias Goldsmith would always call home. Though he was already planning to move his business affairs back to France and from there towards the United States, Jimmy Goldsmith was nevertheless setting up one of his homes in England, with Annabel Birley. He moved some of his increasing art collection into Ormeley Lodge, as well as his photographs – decorating the first-floor bathroom beside his bedroom with them – but he had no intention of making it a permanent home. He had never really had such a thing, and he had never missed it. But he was enjoying the pleasure that Annabel Birley was clearly drawing from decorating their first home together. As the battle with *Private Eye* had grown more brutal, so they had grown closer. Though he still spent weekends in Paris with Ginette in the rue Monsieur, it seemed as though he was on the brink of doing something decisive.

"It's an old Jewish trait," one friend remarked to her, "to want to be with your family when you can, and Jimmy hasn't escaped it." Isabel was already twenty-three, and married – if not altogether happily – to Arnaud de Rosnay. Manes was almost eighteen, and Alix thirteen. Indeed, Jimmy Goldsmith had not given up hope of having more children. Annabel Birley had had a miscarriage in the fifteen months since the birth of Zacharias, and she was already telling her friends that she would "not mind in the slightest" if there was another member to add to the family. "I love children, I always have," she told her friends. "They are the most important thing in life to me."

No matter where his young children might be, however, Jimmy Goldsmith was still officially resident in France. He paid French taxes and had a French wife and family. He owned and ran one of France's most successful post-war companies. In France he made the important decisions that affected his life and his companies, wherever they might be, and in France he discussed the future with Gilberte Beaux. In England there was Roland Franklin, who had joined Cavenham from Keyser Ullman, and the affairs of Slater Walker Securities, but it was still to France that he looked first.

Ormeley Lodge was the home that Annabel wanted – she had found it, and she loved it. But Goldsmith felt he was under siege in England, with no respite from the attentions of the press, no hiding from the abuse of the small group of people who appeared to believe he was a tyrant or a demagogue ("although the overwhelming majority of the mail I received was favourable"). He had been forced to take extra security precautions for his new home, his chauffeur was specially trained to be wary of potential kidnappers or assassins, his house and office were screened against bomb attack. In the past year or so, even his closest friends had noticed a subtle, but marked change in him. He had grown harder, more agitated, less relaxed than he had been in the past. And that had added to his secretiveness. The only times that he appeared to feel truly comfortable was with his oldest friends, and on holiday away from England. As his friend Charles Hambro remembers now: "For a time Jimmy did not seem his old self at all."

Yet still he wanted some say in the affairs of Britain. He had dismissed the idea of a political career, and told the local Richmond Conservative Association so firmly when they had sounded him out to see if he might be interested in replacing their retiring Member of Parliament at the next general election. He was to turn down the offer to stand as a Member of the European Parliament with equal speed. But a British newspaper or magazine was a different matter. That offered influence, if not actual power, and proved that he was prepared to play some small part in the life of a country for which he had once nurtured such high hopes. So when he received a telephone call soon after lunch on Wednesday 27 April 1977 at his Leadenhall Street office, from Charles Wintour, the managing director of the London *Daily Express* and a director of the Express Newspapers, he did not hesitate. He invited him round to see him.

By midnight Jimmy Goldsmith had made clear to everyone in the newspaper group that he was seriously interested in injecting money not only to save the London *Evening Standard* from a planned merger with its traditional rival, London's only other evening newspaper, the *Evening News*, but also to save Beaverbrook as a whole. Everything had to be done at breakneck pace, because Associated Newspapers, owners of the *Evening News*, had already planned to announce their agreement to take over the *Evening Standard* on the following day, Thursday 28 April. His intervention made the evening news on television.

But Jimmy Goldsmith could not simply write a cheque and buy Beaverbrook's old newspapers. It was Cavenham, not he, that already owned more than 35 per cent of Beaverbrook's non-voting shares, which they had acquired from Rupert Murdoch, and to take over Beaverbrook might fundamentally change the nature of Cavenham's operations in England – it might also have had a drastic effect on the company's publicly quoted share price. Jimmy Goldsmith still wanted to buy all the Cavenham shares in public hands, and he did not want to be accused of using a takeover bid for Beaverbrook to lower his share price to do it. So after the initial discussions with Charles Wintour, and his expression of "serious interest" in putting in money, Jimmy Goldsmith hovered on the edge for a time, while other potential bidders were approached.

Finally, almost two months after the first discussions with Charles Wintour, he entered the bidding for the ailing Beaverbrook group in partnership with a man whom he had first met with Roland Franklin and Jim Slater, Roland "Tiny" Rowland, the head of the giant Lonhro company with interests in Africa as well as Europe, whose company the Tory Prime Minister Edward Heath had once memorably described as "the unacceptable face of capitalism" and whom Jimmy Goldsmith had not come to like. It was to turn out to be an uncomfortable partnership, and one doomed to failure. But for a time it appeared one way of gaining control of Express Newspapers without transforming the character of Cavenham. "I went on with the partnership partly because I wanted to stop Tiny getting complete control of the papers. I thought that might not turn out to be a very good thing."

The more his interest in the Beaverbrook papers deepened, however, the clearer it became to Jimmy Goldsmith that his libel case against *Private Eye* was an insurmountable obstacle to his ever owning an established newspaper group in England. The intense suspicion and mistrust with which most British journalists viewed him had been clear enough during his negotiations with the *Observer*, and they were unlikely to disappear while the case continued. The Beaverbrook directors were already urging him to settle and so, more significantly, was Madame Beaux. "It is taking too much time, and diverting your attention from more important matters," she would explain.

In the first week of May 1977 Jimmy Goldsmith accepted her advice, and decided to call off his criminal libel action against Richard Ingrams. After a rapid series of negotiations, partly initiated by the young editor of the *Evening Standard*, Simon Jenkins, it was agreed that a full-page apology from *Private Eye* to Jimmy Goldsmith would be printed in the paper; and that the magazine would contribute £30,000 towards his legal costs – to be paid in instalments over the next ten years. There was a profound sense of relief in the *Private Eye* camp. When Richard Ingrams left the dock of the Central Criminal Court at the Old Bailey a few days later, when the charges were formally dropped, he said "I left with the strong conviction that we would have lost the case."

The battle with *Private Eye* had lasted almost eighteen months and cost Jimmy Goldsmith approaching £100,000 in legal fees, but to the millions who understood no more about it than the newspaper headlines it almost seemed as though he had lost. Having gone so far it was difficult to see why he should have given up at the last minute. Few realized that he had all but given up on two previous occasions, and that there was less reason for him to do so now than at any time during the case.

In retrospect Jimmy Goldsmith thinks settling his libel action against *Private Eye* was a mistake. "I regret it now," he says firmly, although he accepts that bringing a case of criminal libel was "a tactical mistake". Bowing out before the case finally came to trial meant that his version of events was never presented properly, and the printing of a single apology – no matter how large – could never completely erase the impression that months and months of media reporting throughout had created. The settlement made him seem capricious, as if he had entered into the libel case lightly and had dropped it with equally little thought. Regardless that the apology insisted that "there was not a shred" of truth in the charges that "Sir James would have been entitled to very substantial damages for what *Private Eye* said about him" and that he had "made it clear that our unreserved apology will satisfy him and he has waived his right to damages", his name was somehow still besmirched. There was no victory: only the sour taste of compromise which haunted him for years. Nothing had really changed, he was for ever "Goldenballs" to readers of *Private Eye*, and to millions more who did not even understand what the case was about.

In the welter of libel writs and court hearings, most people had all but forgotten what the original libel case was about: whether or not Jimmy Goldsmith had been at a lunch on the day after Lord Lucan's disappearance in the wake of the murder of his family's nanny Sandra Rivett. The issue of whether Jimmy Goldsmith actually knew what had happened to Lucan, or whether he had ever helped him, was overlooked by almost everyone, except the police.

Unlike *Private Eye* they asked Jimmy Goldsmith himself.

"A couple of weeks after Lucan disappeared they telephoned and asked if I could go round and see them," he remembers. "All they asked me was what I knew about Lucan's disappearance, and I told them all I knew, about his problems with his wife and his affection for his children." Among other things, Jimmy Goldsmith told Detective Chief Superintendent Roy Ranson, the senior CID officer for Belgravia who was in charge of the investigation into the Lucan case, was that Lucan had gone to Paris to visit him not long before his disappearance to ask for his help. "He asked me to loan him £10,000 to help 'buy' his children away from his wife. Lucan believed she was using them to torture him, and he was absolutely devoted to them. He thought he could get them away from her if he paid enough, and wanted me to lend him the money."

Goldsmith refused. "I hate loans. I said, 'I'll give you the money', but he didn't want that, so in the end I got the Midland Bank to supply an overdraft for him and I guaranteed it." There was not a great deal else to tell the police. "I knew that he was short of money. I knew that he was in terrible trouble with his wife, and I knew that he was under terrible pressure because he absolutely loved his children. But I didn't know anything else."

Jimmy Goldsmith denied firmly that he knew anything about Lord Lucan's whereabouts, or that he had anything to do with the lunch held on the day after his disappearance at John Aspinall's home in Belgravia, where six men who knew Lucan, one of them Dominic Elwes, had met to discuss the events of the previous night; some of them were convinced that Lucan would "turn up in the next day or two". He also denied the suggestion that he might have provided financial help for Lucan's disappearance, or that he was providing him with money and a new identity in another country.

Then, as now, Jimmy Goldsmith was convinced that Richard John Bingham, the seventh Earl of Lucan, had killed himself. "The reason that I'm convinced he's dead is that he was so English the idea of him living anywhere else except England is absurd. The idea that he is still alive is just as absurd. He was a murderer because he went mad under the pressure, and because he loved his children so much. But I don't think his code would have allowed him to do anything except fall on his sword once he had realized what he'd done. That was absolutely his culture – the culture of eighteenth-century, aristocratic, military England."

Nevertheless, rumours that Jimmy Goldsmith was secretly in touch with Lucan, that he was sending him money, that he had organized plastic surgery for him, that he had settled him on a farm in Paraguay like a Nazi war criminal, and that he was protecting him from the police, continued to circulate in London for the next decade. But Jimmy Goldsmith firmly denies there is a single grain of truth in any of them. "Lucan has never contacted me," he says now, "and no one has ever contacted me on his behalf." That was something of a relief, because Jimmy Goldsmith is not altogether certain what he would have done if the missing Earl of Lucan had ever contacted him. It made *Private Eye*'s suggestion that he had somehow engineered or orchestrated Lucan's disappearance all the more ridiculous.

"If there had been a single word of truth in their story," Jimmy Goldsmith says now, "what would have been my reaction? I would have said nothing. I certainly wouldn't have sued them, and submitted myself to all the investigation and everything else, and then highlighted it all with a criminal libel action. How could I have been that stupid? If it had been true the last thing I would have done would be to have talked about it."

But no one in England seemed to have appreciated that fact. The original reason for his libel case had long since been forgotten in the clamour of publicity. The fury and determination with which Richard Ingrams conducted his campaign against Jimmy Goldsmith was hardly mentioned. It was to be several years before Patrick Marnham, the author of the original *Private Eye* story on Dominic Elwes in December 1975 would admit, in his book on the magazine, that Ingrams had been changed by the experience of defending the libel action – "The drastic side of his character became more evident" – while John Wells, one of Ingrams's friends would write, "He is not really open to discussion. He can't argue and he can't admit error." At the time those were qualities that the ordinary *Private Eye* reader attributed to Sir James Goldsmith not the magazine's editor. He was the "megalomaniac tycoon" who was trying to close down a small satirical fortnightly magazine which only ever attacked the high and mighty. It was a travesty of the truth, but that

ABOVE: Lady Annabel Birley in her
house at Pelham Cottage, South
Kensington, shortly after she first met
Jimmy Goldsmith
LEFT: Lady Annabel Birley, who was to
become his third wife in 1978

The Master Builder, or Houdini? Jimmy Goldsmith after the Bovril and Allied Suppliers takeovers in his house in Regent's Park

Plunge into melodrama: Jimmy Goldsmith arriving at the offices of Slater Walker Securities opposite St Paul's Cathedral on his first day as chairman in October 1975

LEFT: The Lucan Case: John Aspinall, after being punched by Tremayne Rodd, another of Dominic Elwes's cousins, at the end of the memorial service for Elwes in November 1975. It was this incident that provoked *Private Eye's* coverage of the events surrounding Elwes's death and led to Jimmy Goldsmith's criminal libel case

BELOW: Dominic Elwes, Lady Annabel Birley's cousin, who committed suicide in 1975

FOOT: The seventh Earl of Lucan with his wife Veronica at their wedding in 1963 – a year before he succeeded to the title.

The first public appearance together of Sir James Goldsmith and Lady Annabel Birley, arriving at Bow Street Magistrates Court in July 1976 for the hearing of his criminal libel prosecution against the editor of *Private Eye*. They were to marry two years later

ABOVE: Richard Ingrams, then the editor of *Private Eye*, after the committal proceedings at Bow Street in July 1976, in which he was committed for trial in Sir James Goldsmith's private prosecution for criminal libel
LEFT: Magazine publisher in his own right: Sir James Goldsmith with the first dummy edition of his shortlived British news magazine *Now!*

OPPOSITE: The British family Goldsmith: Sir James and Lady Annabel with their daughter Jemima (left) and their son Zacharias (second from left) together with Lady Annabel's nephew James Powell at the wedding of Lady Cosima Vane-Tempest-Stewart in October 1982

ABOVE: Raider on Wall Street: Jimmy Goldsmith at work aboard the yacht *Galu* near the Island of Ponza, off the coast of Italy, during the final stages of his successful takeover of Crown Zellerbach
BELOW: In his New York office shortly before his aborted bid for Goodyear in the autumn of 1986

hardly mattered. That was how Jimmy Goldsmith was perceived in England, and there was nothing that he could do to alter that.

Three days after the *Private Eye* apology was published in the *Evening Standard*, Jimmy Goldsmith announced that Générale Occidentale was now offering £80 million for the 25 per cent of Cavenham's shares that it did not own. By the middle of June 1977 he had managed it, just as the merger of Cavenham and Grand Union in the United States had been completed. Though *Private Eye* did not realize it, his libel action against them had brought one critical, and unexpected, benefit.

"The case against the Eye made me richer than I ever dreamed of," he explains now, "because by going private at the bottom of the market, and buying my shares when they were cheap, meant that instead of having a huge empire, in which I had only a percentage, I ended up owning the whole thing."

By forcing Jimmy Goldsmith so mercilessly into the public eye, the magazine had also contrived to make sure that instead of simply being a financier who had built an empire but ended up owning only a tiny portion of it himself, he had become its principal owner. "If the case hadn't happened I'd have built a huge empire, been a notable, but I wouldn't have been a capitalist. I was forced to be a capitalist. The decision to go into Slater Walker, which led to the Eye, turned me from being the head of a company into being rich. It's odd."

Whatever his worth, however, Jimmy Goldsmith's ambitions to be a publisher in England were no nearer fruition. His partnership with "Tiny" Rowland to buy Beaverbrook newspapers was going nowhere. Sir Max Aitken, Lord Beaverbrook's son, was still as uncertain about Jimmy Goldsmith's ownership of any part of his family's publishing company as he had been at the beginning of the year. And two new bidders for the newspapers had emerged, Rupert Murdoch himself and the Trafalgar House group of companies, which owned construction firms as well as the Ritz hotel in London and the Cunard shipping line. To gain control of the papers now Jimmy Goldsmith would have had to enter a full-scale takeover battle, and match the Trafalgar House offer of £13.69 million. He declined; he thought the price was too high.

Without too much regret Jimmy Goldsmith turned his back on

Express Newspapers and began to consider his future. If he really wanted a voice in Britain, he could always start a newspaper or a magazine of his own. That way there would be no need to consult anyone. Within a matter of weeks he had told *The Times* in London, "I am definitely going to be in the newspaper industry in Britain within a reasonably short-term future", although he went on to explain: "First I want to complete my task of reorganizing *L'Express*, which is a thoroughly profitable paper, to learn a little more about what I am doing." It was another year before he announced his entry into the British publishing world. In the meantime he was still determined to remove himself from any public position in England, even to the extent of retiring from chairmanship of Cavenham. As he put it: "The chairman of a public company in Britain must be either a masochist or a fool. I am neither."

None the less, Jimmy Goldsmith was more than prepared to defend himself publicly when the need arose. After BBC television's "The Money Programme" embarked on a critical programme about him in October 1977, he took considerable time and effort, after discussions with David Frost, to prepare himself for a lengthy interview to rebut their criticisms. Instead of being intimidated by the two BBC interviewers, Jimmy Goldsmith decided to dominate the half-hour programme entirely – and he did so, to the delight of those City of London men who had long believed that some journalists, whether in newspapers or on television, neither knew anything about, nor trusted anyone who was involved in, making money. His performance became a training video for executives.

He told the interviewers in the bluntest terms that he was tired of being sneered at for his achievements, particularly when Cavenham had accomplished so much in its thirteen years of existence. The suppressed fury that he had been nurturing for almost two years – since *Private Eye* had first written about him in the wake of his arrival at Slater Walker – was clear for all to see. To many journalists, he was a man "whose icy stare bordered on the lunatic"; but to a vast majority of the hundreds of viewers who wrote to the BBC after the programme, he had acquitted himself admirably.

In fact, the bluster of Jimmy Goldsmith's manner concealed a natural shyness as well as a sadness that his achievements were never acknowledged. The truculence that he sometimes demonstrated in public was his defence against the campaign to demean him. As his friend and business partner Charles Hambro puts it now, "Jimmy was very uptight at one time, and I think over-sensitive, particularly in this country. But his being uptight may have led him down the wrong paths from time to time in his reactions to criticism, because he played into the hands of those who were trying to goad him."

No matter how impressive he looked on "The Money Programme", however, he was still being sneered at in England. At least in Paris he could go where he liked when he liked and do what he chose, certain in the knowledge that it would not be repeated to the newspapers. He felt more comfortable and familiar with French politics and culture. So after the settlement with *Private Eye* and the collapse of his attempt to gain control of Express Newspapers in Britain, Jimmy Goldsmith retreated to Paris.

His office in the avenue de Friedland looked ordinary enough from the outside: six storeys of conventional respectability restrained behind glass and iron doors but decorated with the touch of marble in the halls that marked its affluence and its origins in the 1920s. In the corridor of Générale Occidentale's suite on the fifth floor there was one discreet door among the pale wood and soft grey carpets. It led to a single stairway, and to an office which was very far from ordinary. Beyond an ante-room for a secretary there was a small boardroom, two sofas, a coffee table and a small antique desk, but one end of the room was panelled not in wood, but in glass. Beyond it was a magnificent, low-walled terrace as long as an English cricket pitch and as wide as the Royal Lawn at Ascot, complete with its own grass lawn, shrubs and flowerbeds. The terrace looked straight across to the Arc de Triomphe, with nothing whatever to obstruct the view. Napoleon himself could not have devised a better grandstand from which to view the monument that he ordered to be constructed in 1806 to commemorate his greatest victories. This was the heart of Goldsmith's empire, the place where he could retreat from the world, secure in the knowledge that now he had wrapped his companies around him like battalions, all of them now directly under his control.

Without anyone in England noticing it, Jimmy Goldsmith proceeded to transfer the headquarters of all his businesses back to Paris. By the end of 1977, he had decided, everything in his control, whether in the United States or in England, should be run from the avenue de Friedland. By the summer of 1978 he was telling the 26th International Congress of Chambers of Commerce, in the unlikely surroundings of Disneyworld in Florida: "British industry has become a cripple and the British nation has been impoverished . . . Great Britain is an example of a society which has purposely reduced the scope for entrepreneurship." Emotionally Jimmy Goldsmith had decided to leave British industry and commerce to their fate.

Though some would accuse him of "trying to freeze out the little investor", he relished the fact that he now owned 50 per cent of GO himself, while the other major shareholders, each of whom owned less than 10 per cent, were to be large institutions in France. The Union des Assurances and the car maker Renault had been investors for some time, and his merchant bankers in England, Hambros, had recently joined them. Now he was looking for others. In the past four years he had completed his plan to consolidate his companies and eliminate anything that was marginal to their main business of manufacturing and retailing food. Now he was anxious to expand again, and he felt sure that he now had a firm base to work from.

One man whom Gilberte Beaux contacted as the plan to move back to France gathered pace was her old friend Ambroise Roux who had heard of Jimmy Goldsmith but did not know him well. After a string of meetings, Roux, the head of the giant French Compagnie Générale d'Electricité, became another partner in Générale Occidentale. At the same time Jimmy Goldsmith launched a new holding company in Hong Kong, called General Oriental, which would own his holdings of slightly more than 50 per cent in Générale Occidentale, and in turn that Hong Kong company was to be controlled by another that he intended to found in Panama, Lido SA. He wanted to ensure that no shares in Lido could be sold to a non-resident of France without express permission; he wanted to be secure against every intruder, whether from another commercial company or *Private Eye*.

Even in New York, where he was spending more and more time on the lookout for new opportunities, the offices were run in the name of Générale Occidentale. His other interests, like John

Aspinall's new gaming club in London, which he had helped with loans and guarantees of almost £2 million – in exchange for the right to be an equal partner with Aspinall himself with 50 per cent of the equity if he exercised the right before 1988 – were little more than a hobby. He liked to allow himself one or two hobbies, providing of course they turned out to be profitable and they were run by friends. "Aspers" might say that ten of his twenty closest friends were animals – he had always had a thing about tigers, insisting they were wiser than men – but Jimmy Goldsmith knew he was one of the ten, and one who could be counted on.

But it was America that was preoccupying him. By the time that John Aspinall's new club opened in June 1978, Jimmy Goldsmith had already launched a bid for the supermarket chain Colonial Stores, based in Augusta, Georgia, which boasted sales of more than a billion dollars a year in 369 stores throughout the south-eastern United States. By August 1978 Colonial had accepted the offer, which had cost $133 million, and he controlled the group. Together with Grand Union, his was now the eighth biggest super-market chain in the United States, with 840 supermarkets from the Canadian border to Florida and the Gulf of Mexico. The Acapulco plan was still in operation, and he was intent on expanding still further.

In New York he stayed in a corner suite kept specially for him on the twenty-second floor of the Carlyle Hotel on Madison Avenue, which Annabel had decorated in a rather modern style – with strong stark patterns and brighter colours than a man who has a taste for Louis XVI would usually find attractive. She visited him there from time to time and he would be as he always was with her: immensely friendly, a little combative but ceaselessly charming. She knew Jimmy Goldsmith had not changed and that there were still one or two pretty young companions when he was away. But in the winter of 1977 he met a young reporter on *Paris Match* who was to become very much more than an occasional companion. Laure Boulay de la Meurthe was then just twenty-six, a niece of the Comte de Paris, the pretender to the French throne. Bright, with blonde hair and a sharp sense of humour, she had established a career as a journalist working in Paris, where she lived quietly with her sister in an apartment on the left bank. Though even some of his oldest friends could hardly have suspected it at that moment, she was to come to play an essential part in Jimmy Goldsmith's life.

Yet at the same time, early in 1978, he had finally decided to marry Annabel Birley. He had already quietly divorced Ginette, as quietly as he had married her seventeen years before. The shy young girl who had worked alongside him in Laboratoire Cassene had watched him create one of Europe's greatest post-war companies, but had found his success difficult to keep up with. She had brought up Manes, who was now nineteen, and Alix, who was fourteen, certainly as well as Isabel, but Ginette Goldsmith realized that she could no longer hold on to the tall young man she had met in a tiny office opposite the Hôtel Scribe. The children could now cope with the change, and she knew that her husband had always believed that "marriage is more than a piece of paper, it means supporting your family". He would always support her, and their children together, but now he had decided that the time had come to change.

Jimmy Goldsmith's attachment to Lady Annabel Birley may no longer have had quite the flush of the passion that it had seen more than fourteen years before. But it had lost none of its strength for that. She knew he had never lost his eye for other companions, wherever he might be, but she also knew that he liked to come back to their new house on the edge of Richmond Park to see her and her children. When he did they argued occasionally, but never permanently, and they still got on well. If he went back to stay with Ginette in the house in the rue Monsieur every week that was all right: "Jimmy has always lived his life that way", she told a friend. "He always says that he's not a humbug." It may not have been a conventional life, but it had always been his custom, and he made no secret of it. If now he wanted to get married that was fine.

Late in October 1978 Jimmy Goldsmith began arranging his third marriage. It was to take place in Paris – he was after all still a French citizen, though he had both a British and a French passport – away from the prying eyes of Fleet Street. Annabel was to fly from London the night before the ceremony under an assumed name, and to stay in the Ritz. They were to meet the following morning, and go off to get married. But he would not tell her where the ceremony would take place, for he was determined that his private life would not, once again, be the subject of speculation and gossip in the British press.

Once again the London *Daily Express*, even though it was no longer in the hands of Sir Max Aitken, was to prove his tormentor. The paper's gossip column, William Hickey, revealed his intentions even before he had finished the plan. Worse, the paper then despatched a reporter and a photographer to Paris to describe the event. The *Express* reporter, Christopher Wilson, even managed to travel on the same plane from London to Paris with Annabel Birley – who was calling herself Mrs Vane – and introduced himself. He followed that up by sending two dozen red roses to her at the Ritz. Events were certainly not going according to Jimmy Goldsmith's plan. Worse was to come.

On the morning of his marriage, when Annabel Birley arrived at the Générale Occidentale offices, an *Express* photographer, Bill Lovelace, appeared to take their photograph. Jimmy Goldsmith was incensed. The rage that he had felt against the British press since the case against *Private Eye* burst out again. He grabbed Lovelace, pulled him into the doorway of his office building with the help of one of his staff, and wrenched the film out of his camera. In the scuffle the photographer had his camera and his glasses broken, his knuckles skinned and his ribs bruised. As Jimmy Goldsmith whisked her away, Annabel Birley could not help thinking that it was the most bizarre wedding morning that she could have imagined.

The marriage was hardly over before her new husband started dictating a letter to *The Times* in protest. "When a middle-aged couple who have shared their lives for fourteen years are able to marry it is appropriate that they should choose to do so with the dignity of silence," he wrote. "That is still possible in Paris . . . However I would be ungrateful if I were to finish this letter without thanking the *Daily Express* for a wonderful wedding present – the legal opportunity to 'manhandle' a representative of its gossip column." Jimmy Goldsmith maintained steadfastly that he had submitted the *Express* photographer to a "citizen's arrest" under the French laws of privacy.

The explanation convinced neither the *Daily Express* nor the rest of Fleet Street. Once again he had given the impression of being a man given to absurd rages and outrageous behaviour, who was obsessed with secrecy. As Christopher Wilson of the *Daily Express* wrote in reply to the letter in *The Times*: "It seems extraordinary that a man of Sir James's position should then admit to being pleased to engage himself in a public brawl on his wedding day."

But Jimmy Goldsmith had a surprise for Fleet Street. He had decided to launch an English equivalent of *L'Express* in Britain, a weekly news magazine, which would reflect what he believed to be the proper standards of journalism. He had already asked a small management team in Cavenham to look into the project while he searched for an editor. This was his personal project. The company's money might be used, but he alone was keen to see it off the ground. The rest of the Cavenham team in England, including the company's managing director, Jack Greenhalgh, were extremely sceptical: they did not believe it would ever work.

As he and Annabel Birley left for their brief honeymoon, Jimmy Goldsmith was unrepentant. He was going to show Fleet Street what could be done, and he had no intention of changing his opinions about Britain or the British press to suit the views of British journalists, any more than he had any intention of altering the unconventional way he was accustomed to leading his private life.

After the honeymoon, he spent Christmas with Annabel and the children in London. Then, as he had done for years, he went to Gstaad to spend the New Year with Ginette and his other family. When the *Daily Express* reported this somewhat unusual behaviour for a newly married man, Jimmy Goldsmith ignored them.

19

Operation New New World

Everything about Britain depressed Jimmy Goldsmith. It was not just *Private Eye*, or the inquisitiveness of Fleet Street, or the lack of acknowledgement that he had created one of the country's most successful companies in Cavenham, or the whispered sneering that seemed to greet him everywhere he went; it was also an atmosphere of snobbish disregard for any kind of success that seemed to him to permeate everything, dragging the country down. Nothing and no one seemed capable of stopping the rot.

In March 1979 he told the annual convention of the Institute of Directors: "Britain's share of World Trade has declined from 25 per cent to 8 per cent. Twenty-five years ago the income of the average Englishman was among the highest in the world. It is now lower than that of Iceland and Finland and is being caught up by Spain and Greece . . . Output per man in the British Steel Industry is less than one-quarter of its American counterpart and about one-sixth of its Japanese counterpart. In the car industry with the same equipment, output per man in Britain is about half that of any other European country . . . So, economically, in one generation we have been transformed from a rich country into a poor one." His message was all too clear: Britain was in rapid decline, the only question was whether the decline was terminal.

His criticisms did not end there. It was not just the economy which was in a state of collapse; individual freedom, the subject closest to his heart, was also under threat: "Today in Britain the average man is in fact no longer able to choose the school to which he will send his child. He is no longer free to choose the doctor who will care for his family. He is no longer free to choose the hospital which will look after his children when they are ill. He is no longer free to work for a company without first paying obeisance to the trade union that, by law, he is forced to join."

Five thousand businessmen sat in silence in the Royal Albert Hall as he continued: "That is where we are now. But most people consistently refuse to face these facts. Perhaps it is because our national decline has taken place at a rate which allows people to get used to it step by step." There was not even a murmur of approval, but Goldsmith was used to being out of step with opinion, or being a rebel. If other people chose to ignore his advice and warnings, that was their concern. However, he did feel compelled to suggest what might be done: "Those who create prosperity must be encouraged and rewarded. They must not be encouraged to emigrate to create prosperity for others. Enterprise is the creature of individuals, not of councils, nor of committees, nor of pension fund managers, nor of governments. It is the product of individual initiative. My proposal is that we now cast away false ideology and accept unequivocally that we wish to be a meritocracy based not on equality but on equal opportunity." He wanted the great state bureaucracies to be radically scaled down, and those who had emigrated to be encouraged to come home to work for Britain. "Thereby we would unleash a great wave of enterprise and prosperity in which we would all share."

He sat down to sustained, respectful but not exactly enthusiastic applause. The leaders of some of Britain's most important companies felt that he was still making wild judgements; he was a maverick to be watched from a distance rather than emulated. Besides, they told themselves, he was exaggerating; things in Britain were already looking up. A general election was only a matter of weeks away, and the new leader of the Conservative Party, Margaret Thatcher had already promised to revive Britain's fortunes. Her party's election posters, showing a long line of unemployed men and women queueing for a job over the slogan "Labour Isn't Working", seemed to show a new determination to get the economy moving again, and there was even the suggestion that individual initiative would be prized. Goldsmith wanted far too radical changes, far too quickly. This was moderate, sedate Britain, after all.

As Margaret Thatcher settled into Downing Street just six weeks later, in the first days of May 1979, there were not many British businessmen who were prepared to agree with Jimmy Goldsmith that all Britain ever seemed capable of was "muddling through without a strategy". Life was going to work out quite well enough without any need for his "meritocracy" or an end to the class system. The old school tie still seemed quite efficient. Privately some might agree with one or two of his conclusions, but he was still the man whom the pension fund managers were not entirely happy to support, who had taken his company back from public hands, and appeared to disregard every accepted standard of the City of London.

Not everyone in a country which had just experienced a winter of strikes by hospital porters and dustmen, which had left piles of stinking rubbish on the streets of Britain, was quite so complacent. In some his sentiments struck a chord. The biggest-selling daily newspaper, the tabloid *Sun*, put his speech proudly on its front page, encouraging him not to give up the battle but to push on with his plan for his own British news magazine.

By this time he had hired an editor-in-chief, Tony Shrimsley, formerly a political columnist on the *Sun*, even though he had never had experience of editing a national newspaper or magazine; the managing director was to be Tony Fathers, who had been responsible for the dietary food division of Cavenham, before Slimcea and Procea had been sold off in 1975. Fathers, too, had no experience of running a magazine. When his friends, including Marcia Falkender, were told about the men he wanted to run the magazine, they stayed a little more silent than usual. Privately some of them wondered whether he might not be entering a field that he did not entirely understand. Their fears were borne out when Goldsmith began to encounter difficulties in recruiting the journalists he needed. Some British journalists simply refused to work for a man who had been "the scourge of *Private Eye*" for so long. The unofficial network that lay at the heart of Britain's national newspapers and magazines was too clannish to allow anyone to try to destroy one of their members without some reprisal. But not every journalist who refused to work for him did so because they supported *Private Eye*, there was another group who were far from convinced that a news magazine could ever work in Britain. They knew only too well that the firmly established national daily newspapers, complemented by a strong collection of Sunday newspapers, often with free colour magazines, were certain to make the task of launching a news magazine both lengthy and exceptionally costly. It took Jimmy Goldsmith and his editor almost six months to assemble their staff.

Ironically, just as the final touches were being put to *Now!*, as he had decided to call it, Jimmy Goldsmith's attention shifted decisively to the United States. The Acapulco plan had never been forgotten. In the latter part of 1978 he had come across the old Diamond Match Corporation of New York which had introduced the safety match to America in 1882. Now renamed Diamond International, it was a conglomerate which packaged and retailed timber in various shapes and forms. It produced half America's playing cards, as well as paper plates for fast-food chains like McDonald's. With more than $1.2 billion sales a year, it was one of the 250 largest companies in the United States.

The potential of Diamond had first been drawn to his attention by the legendary Ira Harris of the Chicago-based investment banking firm Salomon Brothers Inc. The elegant, shrewd and intensely competitive Harris had been one of the first men in the United States to recognize Jimmy Goldsmith's interest in investing in America, and had introduced him to the owners of Columbia Pictures early in 1978 when, for an instant at least, it looked as though the studio might be for sale. There had been talks but no deal had ever materialized. Not long afterwards Harris mentioned Diamond's possibilities to Jimmy Goldsmith.

In the previous eight years or so the forty-two-year-old Harris had become one of America's leading investment bankers and dealmakers, conceiving and fostering mergers and acquisitions like Norton Simon Incorporated's purchase of the Avis car rental company. Harris and Goldsmith got on well together and during the summer of 1978 Jimmy Goldsmith's fascination with Diamond gradually increased, just as his disillusionment with Britain was increasing. Even as *Now!* magazine was on the brink of being launched in September, Jimmy Goldsmith was beginning to sense that Diamond was the deal that would finally shift the focus of his business life to the United States.

Diamond International held a special advantage for Jimmy Goldsmith. It fitted his favourite criteria for a takeover. "It was a perfect situation as far as I was concerned. A conglomerate, rather tired, with lots of pieces which were worth more sold off." Just as he had done with Bovril almost a decade before, he began to examine quietly what the potential values of those assets might be. In particular he commissioned a survey of Diamond's holdings in forest lands. Hidden among its chain of do-it-yourself shops and lumber mills were 1.6 million acres of forests in the north-east and north-west of the United States. His brother's old idea of an ecologically sound asset still appealed to Jimmy Goldsmith, but not as much as the chance of becoming the owner of a vast area of American forest for very little cost. The forests throughout the United States appeared in the Diamond balance sheets as little more than a passing reference.

At a meeting in Ira Harris's office in Chicago the analysts told Jimmy Goldsmith that it was entirely possible that Diamond's forest holdings could be valued at some $800 million. If Jimmy Goldsmith could get control of the company he could not lose. As John Tigrett used to put it, this was another of those deals without "a down side". Once Jimmy Goldsmith got control of the company all he had to do was to sell the assets he did not need, use the money to pay for the purchase price, and he would be left with the forests for almost nothing. It was too good to miss.

Unbeknown to almost anyone, except Madame Beaux and Roland Franklin, Jimmy Goldsmith had begun to take a closer and closer interest in Diamond International throughout 1978, codenaming the company for the purposes of internal memoranda at Générale Occidentale's new offices on the 24th floor of an office building on the corner of Fifth Avenue New York, as "Operation New New World". On his behalf Bovril (Canada) Limited, the Cavenham Pension Trustees, and Banque Occidentale began quietly buying small amounts of Diamond stock in the open market. In January 1979 he showed part of his hand by declaring publicly that his new American subsidiary, Cavenham Holdings Inc., had bought 4 per cent of the company's stock for some $15 million. Diamond did not take much interest. No one had really heard of Sir James Goldsmith, and the best-informed Wall Street men assumed that he was too committed in Europe to make much of an impact in America, although the *New York Times* admitted rather grudgingly in February 1979 that his takeover of Grand Union "appeared to have matured successfully", even if it had suffered from "severe growing pains on the way".

What the Americans did not know was that the new Conservative government's dedication to "seeing Britain back on its feet again", had not been sufficient to cure Jimmy Goldsmith's pessimism about Britain. He had no wish to see the country's decline threaten his own success. Besides he also believed that its political future was in grave danger from left wing infiltration. As early as October 1975 he had warned a conference of editors and publishers in London about the infiltration of the British Labour Party by the extreme Left. "Unlike many other countries," he had told them, "the communists in this country have not fielded a major political party at general elections. They know that in Britain only a very few would knowingly vote communist. So their strategy has been to capture the trade unions and the Labour Party machinery." At the time he was accused of paranoia, and scare-mongering.

Reasons for moving to the United States seemed to be multiplying day by day. Not only was Grand Union clearly showing improvement, but the Diamond deal looked more and more attractive. And Jimmy Goldsmith relished the idea of taking on Wall Street, and trying to play in the far bigger financial market of the United States. It offered a new challenge. In addition, Charles Hambro and others were pointing out with increasing force the attractive possibilities of the United States. "I rather advised him," Hambro recalls, "that from his point of view there was a strong case for liquidating his situation in Britain, and to a certain extent in France, and perhaps moving to the United States. Because at that time sterling was extremely strong against the dollar – about $2.40 to the pound – and that, therefore, there were certain advantages in the purchasing power of his money which were not likely to last all that long."

There was also a purely personal reason for his interest in Diamond. He was seeing more and more of Laure Boulay de la Meurthe, the young *Paris Match* reporter whom he had met the year before. She seemed to represent his new life, the opportunity to put the unpleasant memories of Britain and Fleet Street behind him with a new beginning. He would discuss his life with her in French rather than in English, take her with him on trips – except those to see his families in England or in France – and he spent any spare time he had talking to her about the future.

Now! did nothing to alter his reputation in Britain. His attempts to ensure that it maintained the tradition of *L'Express* and publish the views of two left-wing columnists alongside those of two right-wing ones, were ignored. In Britain he was seen as a wild, right-wing figure, and the fact that he had managed to attract the respected philosopher Raymond Aron to join *L'Express* from *Le Figaro* in an influential position on the magazine seemed to have no effect in England whatsoever. No matter what he did Jimmy Goldsmith was portrayed in Britain as an apostle of arch-conservatism, intent on sustaining his philosophies in his magazine. If he maintained consistently to anyone who came to work for him that he did not take every decision on his magazines himself, there were many in Britain who believed him.

"I believe the proprietor of a newspaper or a magazine is responsible for what goes into it, and I could never overlook that responsibility," he would explain to those coming to work at *Now!*, which was due to be launched in September. "But that does not mean that I am not prepared to have conflicting opinions in any magazine or newspaper that I may own, of course I am."

As if to confirm that he was indeed the scourge of journalists, in June 1979 Jimmy Goldsmith returned to the High Court to criticize a British journalist. His bitter relationship with the British press was destined to take yet another extraordinary turn. The air of distrust and suspicion on both sides had become so dank that every action of either only served to fuel the other's prophecies. That was now to be demonstrated for all the world to see once again.

On the morning of Monday 11 June 1979 he and Lady Annabel Birley once again walked into an English courtroom, just as they had done almost exactly three years earlier to launch his criminal libel action against Richard Ingrams of *Private Eye*. But this time there was a significant difference, this time it was Jimmy Goldsmith who was being sued for libel and slander.

Michael Gillard, who wrote the "Slicker" column in *Private Eye*, was suing him for suggesting that he had blackmailed the public relations consultant John Addey into helping the magazine with its

defence against his libel action against them in 1976. It was a serious
charge, which Jimmy Goldsmith had not only repeated on the
telephone to the then editors of *The Times* and *Daily Telegraph*,
among others, but which he had followed up in writing.

Michael Gillard told the jury that Jimmy Goldsmith's "terrible,
wicked and very damaging" allegations of blackmail had meant
that he had lived under a "black cloud" for three years, and, worse,
they could gravely affect his employment as a journalist. Yet again
Jimmy Goldsmith became the rich, bullying monster seeking to
destroy the career of anyone who got in his way, while journalists
were poor, victimized figures anxious only to find out the truth
about the rich and powerful. But as the hearing progressed it became
increasingly clear that the jury were not convinced by this familiar
scenario.

Goldsmith not only steadfastly refused to retract a single word of
his accusations, but also defended them stoutly on the grounds that
they were true. In the words of one reporter who sat through
the five-day hearing, Jimmy Goldsmith gave "one of the most
remarkable performances in a courtroom I have ever seen", and
even *Private Eye* later described it as a "tour de force". For a day
and a half he stood in the small witness box alongside the judge,
Mr Justice Neill, and answered questions from his lawyer, Lord
Rawlinson QC, a former Attorney General. Time and again he
referred to "an orchestrated campaign of ridicule and vilification
against me" as an attempt to cast doubt on the City of London, the
future of Slater Walker and the foundations of his own company,
Cavenham. Time and again he made the point to the jury that he
was only defending himself against attack.

At 12.20 in the afternoon of Friday 15 June, the fifth day of the
trial, the jury retired to discuss their verdict. After returning briefly
to ask for a legal definition of blackmail in a civil case, they returned
shortly before four o'clock. When the foreman announced that they
had found for Sir James Michael Goldsmith there was a cry from
Annabel Birley. The jury had accepted that the accusations of
blackmail Jimmy Goldsmith had made against Michael Gillard in
1976 were true. And although Gillard was to launch an appeal
against the verdict in the British Court of Appeal and the House of
Lords, that decision was never reversed. For the first time in his

battles with *Private Eye* and its supporters in British journalism, Jimmy Goldsmith had been vindicated, and by a jury.

Jubilant, he immediately launched an attack on the British Press Council, the body responsible for upholding the standards of British journalism, for its unwillingness "to address itself to the fundamental problems concerning the good health of the nation's press". The enmity that existed between Jimmy Goldsmith and a substantial group of British journalists showed no sign of abating.

It was not the most auspicious background for him to launch any venture in British publishing which required the talents of journalists, let alone one as uncertain as a weekly news magazine. When *Now!* finally went on sale on Thursday 13 September 1979 its chances of success were hardly helped by a persistent campaign of criticism in *Private Eye*, which helped to convince some advertising agencies and readers that to support the magazine was to support a man of extreme right-wing opinions and unconventional habits.

But by then Jimmy Goldsmith hardly cared. He had proved his point. "Publishing in Britain is only going to be a hobby in any case," he told his friends, and he began to devote himself with ever increasing energy to the United States. Now there was nothing to keep him in England except Annabel and the children, and they could always move to a new house near New York. He would keep a small base in London, but that was all that would eventually be necessary. His fascination with British journalism would not obscure his other interests.

There was Grand Union to be attended to, and the possibilities of Diamond International to be pursued. And a third intriguing possibility had also presented itself. In the course of a series of negotiations in Paris, Madame Beaux had been asked whether Générale Occidentale might be interested in investing in the oil business in Guatemala, by putting some $2 million into a small oil company called Basic Resources International, run by former American air force major and oil man John D. Park. "It was basically just a high-risk investment banking transaction we decided to get involved in," Jimmy Goldsmith recalls.

Park had worked for Standard Oil, and in 1970 invested more than $6 million of his own money in a reconnaissance exploration of 4.5 million acres of Guatemalan jungle, not far from the border with Mexico. Like Jimmy Goldsmith, Park was a maverick. The major oil companies had paid little or no attention as he built a small airstrip deep in the jungle, and proceeded to start a geological survey of what was known as the Tortugas Salt Dome. Even when Park became convinced that he had discovered "a sizeable oil play" and asked the Guatemalan government to grant him a petroleum concession for the most attractive one million acres of the area he had surveyed, most American oil men had dismissed him as a crank who was wasting his money. He had even built a barge and floated an oil-drilling rig down the Rio Negro to start drilling two wells on his concession. Undeterred, Park put his tiny oil field into production. The first well produced 1,200 barrels of oil a day, and the second 1,800 barrels.

Suddenly Basic Resources was taken very seriously indeed. In no time Basic had gone into partnership with Shenandoah Oil from Texas and Saga Petroleum from Norway to extend their exploration and drilling; and once again the exploration proved a success. More oil was discovered on what were known as the Rubelsanto and West Chinaja fields, and Basic began constructing camps for its workers, a network of simple roads and a crude oil processing plant. There was only one difficulty – the oil was being produced 125 miles from the nearest sea port, Santo Tomas on the Gulf of Honduras, in the middle of some of the most difficult jungle terrain in the world. If it was going to succeed, Basic needed a pipeline and partners with financial muscle. As John Park was to admit later, "Basic was a small company, and, in retrospect, grossly underfinanced to undertake such a massive project."

Then, to make matters worse, Park's original partners had encountered financial difficulties themselves, until late in 1978 he had been forced to look for new investors in his company. One of the people he talked to was Gilberte Beaux, who introduced him to Jimmy Goldsmith. "Jimmy told me that GO was always looking for new investments," Park recalls, "but that he wanted to see the country for himself. So we flew to Guatemala."

No sooner had they landed in Guatemala City, where Basic had its head office, than Park's new potential investor had rented a helicopter and taken off to look at the country. "He went to the beaches in the east, and to the mountains and the mountain villages, and he became fascinated." The man who had relished Mexico for a decade or more, discovered he liked the country across the border just as much, and the possibility of becoming an oil man – even on a small scale – intrigued him. Central America offered a new horizon. In the first months of 1979, even with the Diamond deal in the offing, the launch of *Now!* magazine growing ever more controversial in Britain, and the future of Grand Union giving rise to some concern, Jimmy Goldsmith still felt he had time for another project. By May GO had invested a little over $5 million in Basic Resources, most of it to go towards the construction of a pipeline to the coast, and Jimmy Goldsmith had become the company's chairman.

Basic had needed a major oil company as an operating partner, however, and earlier in 1979, Park had formed a new company with the French nationalized oil company Société Nationale Elf Aquitaine, known as Basic Elf Aquitaine (BEA) Petroleum. Basic had 75 per cent of the joint company and Elf Aquitaine just 25 per cent.

Jimmy Goldsmith was now an oil man in addition to being a grocer, a food retailer, a publisher and a financier. And he still controlled the strategies of all his interests himself, preferring to be consulted about them at almost every stage, even if that meant tracking him down on the telephone half way across the world in the middle of the night. He trusted his managers, certainly, but he liked to feel that he was the single person round whom every part rotated.

Goldsmith still could not resist a good deal when he saw one. Even as he had begun to take an increasing interest in Diamond International, he had also started to look into the prospect of expanding his supermarkets by adding further chains to their existing outlets. By November 1979, two months after the launch of *Now!*, he had bought the Texas supermarket chain of 100 stores, J. Weingarten, to add to Grand Union, as well as the Cater's chain from Debenham's in England to add to Cavenham's supermarkets.

Not for the first time Jimmy Goldsmith looked like a man who was in too many places at once, a moving target that it was impossible for his observers or his enemies ever to pin down. At any one moment he might be in Paris, London, New York or Guatemala City, if he was not on holiday in Corsica or Sardinia or the Côte d'Azur. He might be in his house near Les Invalides, or on Ham Common on the edge of the Royal Park at Richmond, or his suite on Madison Avenue. Only one thing was certain: he would not be in any one of them for very long. He preferred it that way. The nomadic habits of his childhood in his father's hotel suites had never left him; neither had his old appetite for secrecy.

But as the 1970s came to an end, Jimmy Goldsmith was preparing to make one of his activities extremely public. He was on the brink of breaking up Cavenham. The massive food manufacturing and retailing group he had created over the past decade was no longer the focus of his interest. The new horizons of the United States and Central America were so much more interesting, so much more of a challenge. Besides, the constant questioning he subjected all his own companies to had revealed that the original basis of his business in Europe, created only a few years before, had changed almost beyond recognition. The man who had broken through by buying three of the staples of the English pantry, including Bovril, was no longer really a food manufacturer. Selling groceries now accounted for the major part of Cavenham's business and the larger part of the profits, while manufacturing food accounted for a far smaller part of the business, and far less of the profits. "We are the third largest food retailer in the world after Safeway and Kroger with sales of £3,000 million a year," he told the *Daily Mail*.

With Diamond and Basic Resources demanding more and more of his attention, there seemed little point in sustaining the pretence that he was simply Britain's "Number One Grocer" any longer. In his chairman's statement he told the shareholders of his British company: "Cavenham had reached the moment when it had to decide whether to concentrate its resources on manufacturing or retailing. In view of the results achieved, the decision to concentrate on retailing was obvious."

Early in 1980 Jimmy Goldsmith sold Bovril to the Beecham Group, who had expressed their interest in it when he had beaten Rowntree Macintosh in the takeover battle nine years before. They paid him £42 million in cash. Within a few weeks Générale Occidentale had sold its food manufacturing interests in France to BSN Gervais-Danone, while Felix had been sold in Sweden and in Austria. No sooner had that deal been completed than Générale

Alimentaire was sold, as were other interests in Spain, Belgium, Holland and Austria. Within six months almost every remnant of what had been a massive European food manufacturing group, the largest in Europe after Unilever and Nestlé, had been dismantled. It was the quickest dismemberment of a major company witnessed in Europe since the war. But it was absolutely typical. When it came to the future Jimmy Goldsmith was not sentimental. He had never believed in standing still.

Like a conjuror he wanted every member of his audience, be they in Paris, London or New York, only to watch the hand they commonly looked at, the hand which they recognized as their own. The fact that his other hand, in another country, or another continent, was doing something entirely different, which may well fundamentally affect the first hand was his own particular secret: that was Jimmy Goldsmith's cleverest trick. It was one he was about to demonstrate to a 114-year-old American company.

PART 5

Raider on Wall Street

20

The Sparkle of Diamond

No one could have been less like Sir James Michael Goldsmith than William J. Koslo, the president and chief executive of Diamond International. Koslo was every inch a Corporation Man. He had spent virtually his entire career with Diamond, joining in 1955 and rising to become an executive vice-president and then chief executive in 1977. Solid, upright and respectable, he epitomized the familiar virtues of American companies: loyalty, industry and determination, to which he had added his own particular brand of competitiveness and pugnacity. Happily married with four children and three years older than Jimmy Goldsmith, no one would honestly have described him as a buccaneer or a raider. Koslo was certainly not a freewheeling entrepreneur intent on racing round the world in search of excitement and a fresh deal. But for the first six months of 1980 Bill Koslo, a former High School maths teacher from Mount Carmel, Pennsylvania, who had joined a New York printing business that merged into Diamond, found himself in a prolonged bout of arm-wrestling with Sir James Michael Goldsmith, over what one of Générale Occidentale's directors was later to describe as "Jimmy's last real game of 'double or quits'". At the end of the bout Koslo was to admit: "They were the most exhausting, the most traumatic and I guess I'd have to say exciting times in my life."

On Monday 28 April 1980 Jimmy Goldsmith announced that Générale Occidentale might offer to purchase "a substantial proportion" of the common outstanding stock of Diamond International Corporation "at a significant premium" over the current market price through its subsidiary Cavenham Holdings Inc. In a letter to Koslo, Bowman Gray III, a vice-president of Cavenham, explained that his company was considering the offer because Diamond had "chosen to ignore" Cavenham's opposition to the proposed acquisition of Brooks-Scanlon.

In fact, Jimmy Goldsmith was considerably angrier than Gray's letter suggested. "I objected to the Brooks-Scanlon deal because they were buying the business in undervalued shares – their own paper – and they were paying an overvalued price, which made it twice as bad. And I thought it was, at least to some extent, designed to dilute our holding. I had to interpret it as an aggressive act." Had Diamond but realized, they would probably have been better advised simply to allow Jimmy Goldsmith's comparatively small holding in their corporation to remain as it was, at about six per cent, because as he has explained consistently, "I need a stimulant before I can get going. When they came up with this load of nonsense about Brooks-Scanlon, that really triggered the fight."

But Bill Koslo did not know that. His response was exactly that of any loyal American manager in similar circumstances. On Wednesday 1 May he wrote to the Diamond shareholders angrily suggesting that Cavenham were attempting to "gain control of Diamond International for the lowest possible price". As the letter left Diamond's New York headquarters on Third Avenue, barely four blocks from its adversary's office on Fifth Avenue, Diamond's shares stood at $32.65 on the New York Stock Exchange – and they were on the way up. Diamond was not going to allow itself to be bullied by Jimmy Goldsmith.

Neither was he to be deterred. No sooner had Diamond's response reached him than Cavenham launched a law suit in Delaware to stop Diamond from holding its annual general meeting on Wednesday 14 May, at which it was scheduled to discuss the Brooks-Scanlon merger. It was to be only one of a string of law suits that would punctuate the battle between Bill Koslo and Jimmy Goldsmith.

In a further attempt to stop the Brooks-Scanlon deal Cavenham announced on Friday 9 May that it was offering what *Fortune* magazine in the United States later called "an unusual dual package". Jimmy Goldsmith was offering $45 for each Diamond share – providing the shareholders defeated the Brooks-Scanlon proposal or postponed the decision long enough to allow Cavenham to use any shares it acquired by the offer to vote against it. But if the

shareholders accepted the Brooks-Scanlon deal he would only offer
$40 a share. His objective was to bring the Cavenham holding in
Diamond up from 5.9 per cent to 35 per cent or so, and in the
process he was offering to buy some 4.5 million shares in the
company.

Sensing a profit whatever happened, the Wall Street arbitrageurs
(investors with a special interest in takeovers) started buying Diamond shares. By Tuesday 13 May the stock stood at $38.25, even
though the Cavenham law suit in Delaware to prevent the Diamond
meeting had been thrown out by a federal judge. After the Diamond
meeting in Bangor, Maine – which Jimmy Goldsmith attended
himself – Bill Koslo announced that he was considering launching
his own law suit to prevent Cavenham's "grossly inadequate" offer,
which was "not in the best interests of the company". The two men
eyed each other cautiously across the ballroom of one of Bangor's
motels. The *Wall Street Journal* described their exchanges as "civil,
if less than cordial".

What the *Journal* did not know was that Diamond had employed
private investigators to gather information that might be damaging
to Jimmy Goldsmith; and that, in particular, the detectives had
come up with the familiar allegations from *Private Eye* in England.
The innuendo and rumour that had stalked him for the past five
years had not been forgotten. "I was investigated and they came up
with all the old *Private Eye* stories," Jimmy Goldsmith remembers
now. "They said I was a front for Giscard, that I should be exposed.
But they were wasting their time. I had nothing to hide whatever.
They were all dead issues."

After the annual general meeting was over and Jimmy Goldsmith
had flown back to New York, Bill Koslo went on the attack. In a
letter to shareholders he insisted that the Cavenham offer was not
"consistent with the long-range goals of Diamond", and twisted the
knife by adding, "according to Cavenham's own offer to purchase,
most of the funds to be used in the purchase of 4.5 million shares
aren't yet in place and the rest of the funds are presently in Europe".
Koslo and his fellow directors clearly thought, as one Wall Street
analyst was to put it shortly afterwards: "Goldsmith just hasn't got
the money." Were the directors and the sceptics right?

It was exactly that question which the *Wall Street Journal* set out to answer the following day. It succeeded. Although *Fortune* magazine was later to estimate that Générale Occidentale's sales amounted to some $7 billion a year, New York's most respected financial newspaper concluded: "Générale Occidentale – which owns the Cavenham group bidding for Diamond – is a privately held company in France that had revenue in the year ended March 30 estimated at the current equivalent of $6bn". It went on to pay tribute to Jimmy Goldsmith's talent as "a stock market operator", adding: "Beginning with a small company, Sir James merged it into a large group through a number of takeovers, installed energetic management that ran the companies profitably and concentrated on strategy aimed at increasing the stock price and thereby financing even more acquisitions."

But to the dismay of many men on Wall Street, and the Diamond directors, the *Journal* found it difficult to unravel the precise means by which Sir James Goldsmith controlled Générale Occidentale, beyond admitting it was "through an astonishing complex tangle of companies based in Paris, where he lives, Hong Kong and Panama."

In fact, Jimmy Goldsmith's empire was not all that elaborate. "GO's controlling ownership is anchored in France through a company called Trocadero Participations, of which Sir James is president and in which he holds a 30 per cent stake", the *Wall Street Journal* acknowledged. In fact, major French institutions held another 40 per cent of Trocadero, while the remaining 30 per cent was held by General Oriental Limited (GOR), his Hong Kong company. But Jimmy Goldsmith and his family owned over 80 per cent of General Oriental, so that with General Oriental he and his family owned at least 50 per cent of Générale Occidentale. In turn the majority of GOR was owned by a Panamanian company, Lido SA "which is 40 per cent owned by Sir James", and the remaining 60 per cent was owned by a foundation "whose income, by statute, has to be devoted to charitable causes".

The suggestion that this ownership structure was designed to avoid paying taxes was hotly denied by Jimmy Goldsmith. The reason for its existence, he told the *Journal*, was "freedom of action . . . I want to be able to act without asking people". It was not exactly the style of Bill Koslo, or his fellow Diamond directors, but at least it appeared to make sense.

"When Diamond found out that they had nothing that they could prove against me," Jimmy Goldsmith explains now, "we came to a deal." Neither Diamond's private detectives nor Wall Street had been able to unearth anything that threatened to undermine his companies, and neither had the Securities and Exchange Commission. By the time the *Wall Street Journal* published its own analysis it was clear enough that there was no basis for the rumour and innuendo. Shortly after the piece appeared Koslo telephoned Jimmy Goldsmith in Paris to suggest that they meet. Before the results of the shareholders' ballot on the directors' proposed Brooks-Scanlon merger had even been announced, the two men had done a deal. Koslo and Jimmy Goldsmith had reached a "standstill agreement" after two hours of conversation in his suite in the Carlyle Hotel in New York. In addition to the "standstill" they had agreed that Cavenham would get 25 per cent of Diamond. "We were both kind of conciliatory," Koslo said afterwards. On Friday 6 June 1980 they called a truce.

Even though the Cavenham bid, which was due to expire on Thursday 12 June, was still in place, the two men had also agreed that Cavenham would be represented by three directors on Diamond's board and that, in exchange, the company would not press ahead to gain more than 40 per cent of the company for five years. Jimmy Goldsmith also agreed to increase his offer to $42 for Diamond shares if the company's existing shareholders voted to go along with the Brooks-Scanlon proposal. The New York Stock Exchange took the news hard. Diamond shares dropped from $50 each to $38.825 in the day. It looked to most Wall Street observers as though Diamond had won and Jimmy Goldsmith had been repelled. They were even more convinced when, on Monday 9 June, Diamond announced that the shareholders had voted to allow them to go ahead with the Brooks-Scanlon deal if they wanted to.

Wall Street could think what it liked. Jimmy Goldsmith was a long way from defeat. Cavenham extended its offer for 4.5 million Diamond shares to $42 and Diamond countered by announcing it was going to go ahead with the Brooks-Scanlon deal which would dilute the Cavenham holdings to only 34 per cent of the company if it managed to add 4.5 million shares to its existing 756,560 shares: without the dilution Cavenham would have 41 per cent of the company. Certainly the two companies had agreed that Cavenham should limit its holding to "approximately 40 per cent" for five years and both companies had agreed to drop all the litigation that had been set in train, but now Jimmy Goldsmith, together with Roland Franklin from GO and Cavenham, as well as Bowman Gray III, were to be directors of Diamond. Though some Wall Street men predicted Jimmy Goldsmith had "given up all hope of ever getting Diamond", one or two others wondered if he was building a Trojan horse. The next twelve months were to tell.

By the end of June 1980 Cavenham had got an additional 2.5 million Diamond shares in response to its tender offer, and had raised the $105 million to pay for them with the help of Crédit Lyonnais, Crédit Suisse, and the London branch of New York's Citibank. It meant that Jimmy Goldsmith had got control of some 24 per cent of Diamond. As Bill Koslo told the *New York Times*: "It's not exactly a business as usual situation, but we're going to do the best we can." What he did not know was that Jimmy Goldsmith had never been a man to leave decisions half made, or deals half done – whatever the standstill agreement might have said.

Bill Koslo would have known that he would hear more of his adversary, however, if he had kept an eye on the affairs of Cavenham in the United Kingdom. At the beginning of July 1980, just a few days after the final details of his fresh shareholding in Diamond had been revealed, Jimmy Goldsmith quietly announced that he was resigning as chairman of Cavenham in Britain. As he put it formally in his last annual report: "As I am domiciled in France, it is wisest that I should concentrate my efforts on my job as chairman of Générale Occidentale." The same thing had been true for the past dozen years of the company's existence, but Jimmy Goldsmith needed a public explanation, preferably one which would not reveal his true intentions.

Had anyone in Diamond, or in the British press, cared to think about it, the announcement was the first clear sign that Jimmy Goldsmith was about to sever most of his ties with England. The man whom *Punch* magazine had only recently called "as recognizable as Robert Redford" wanted privacy again away from the prying eyes of the British media. In Paris he could still walk the streets un-noticed, and in the United States the only people who might recognize him were the readers of the *Wall Street Journal* or the business pages of the *New York Times*. He could walk into the B. Dalton bookshop on Fifth Avenue, just beneath his office, and no one would come up and bother him. It was something he could never do in London. There he would take refuge in his office in Leadenhall Street, or in John Aspinall's new casino, and in Ormeley Lodge in Ham, where Annabel and the children lived. But he would rarely venture out into a shop on his own.

Annabel and the children were the one immutable tie that bound him to England. Jemima and Zacharias were still occupying the nursery on the top floor of Ormeley Lodge, although Jemima was just starting infant school, and Zacharias was going to nursery school. Manes had been spending time there as well. Now twenty-one the boy had not turned out to be quite the success his father had hoped; he seemed charming and excellent company, but lacked ambition. There had been one or two attempts at a job, including a rather unsettled period running a newsagent's shop not far from Ormeley, but for the most part Manes seemed happiest doing comparatively little. It was not exactly his father's style, and this occasionally led to strained relations between the two of them. Alix was in Paris with her mother, and Isabel, now divorced from Arnaud de Rosnay, lived in London. Jimmy Goldsmith enveloped his new dynasty in his own protection. That had always been his ambition.

And he saw no reason why his dynasty should not increase in size. Although the demands of America and Guatemala had forced him to spend more and more time away from his new wife, he knew she still enjoyed bringing up children. In the past four years Annabel had had three miscarriages. And in the spring of 1980, just as the battle with Diamond was getting under way in America, she discovered she was pregnant again. It was to be her sixth child and her third with Jimmy Goldsmith. Even though she was forty-five years old, Lady Annabel Goldsmith was delighted. "I hadn't really intended to have any more children," she told her friends, "but Benjamin just popped out."

As ever his father did not attend his birth. While Annabel was in labour at St Thomas's hospital opposite the Houses of Parliament, Jimmy Goldsmith was pacing up and down his office in Leadenhall Street, phoning every five minutes. Eventually his secretary packed him off to Aspinall's, promising to phone his chauffeur on the car's telephone "the moment there is any news". Jimmy Goldsmith was in his own casino as his third son, and sixth child, was born on 28 October 1980. He went straight to the hospital to see him. But he was not destined to become a familiar figure in the boy's daily life. There was too much to be done, and too many projects to be attended to in the United States and Central America for that to happen. He loved his son certainly, just as he loved all his children, they were all to be kept and maintained properly, but they were only a tiny part of his life; one of the many compartments that he liked to keep separate from one another.

Just as he liked to keep his businesses in distinct groups, whether in Paris, London or New York, so he liked to keep his private life in equally distinct compartments. "Not one iota of my relationship with Ginette has changed since our divorce," he would explain; nor had any part of his relationship with Annabel since their marriage and his affair with Laure Boulay de la Meurthe in New York. "If you marry your mistress, you create a job vacancy," he had once remarked; it was only partly a joke. No one was being deceived, everyone knew where they stood, everyone would be protected; he would see to that. Loyalty was a quality he prized above almost any other.

Whatever his attachment to Annabel and their children, nothing could conceal his despair with England. His hopes for the country had evaporated, even though Mrs Thatcher had agreed to address a dinner at the Savoy Hotel to honour the first anniversary of the launch of his English news magazine *Now!* He had wanted to regenerate some interest in the magazine, which he thought privately had rather failed to sparkle, and the Prime Minister's after-dinner speech, which was televised live in the middle of September 1980, had given the impression that *Now!* was of some significance, even if its circulation had fallen steadily from the launch figure of 400,000 copies a week to barely 125,000 copies.

Jimmy Goldsmith's conviction that England was no longer the place for him remained unaltered, both by the Prime Minister and the British press. Even though he had won the Gillard libel case, and the Court of Appeal had rejected Gillard's appeal against the jury's verdict, Jimmy Goldsmith felt he was being cast eternally as the villain. Worse, *Private Eye*'s campaign against *Now!* had the effect of making it difficult for almost anyone in any section of the English media, whether television, radio or advertising, to be seen to support Sir James Michael Goldsmith. Once again his achievements seemed to be ignored, neglected in favour of the all too familiar English sneer, and the thought depressed him still further. So it made sense to devote more and more of his energies to the United States. The rewards were so much greater there; and he had already made a start. There was Grand Union, with its new Weingarten arm, which had become, according to the *New York Times*, "one of the fastest growing supermarket chains in America"; there was his 24 per cent holding in Diamond International, and his investment in Basic Resources.

In fact, Basic's oil explorations in Guatemala were turning out to be far more of a problem than he had ever imagined. Major General Fernando Lucas Garcia's military government was demanding greater and greater control of the oil companies that had suddenly spotted the possibility of a vast new oil field in his country's jungles. In August 1980 Basic had been forced to relinquish its petroleum rights under Guatemalan law. When the company had asked to convert its exploration rights into exploitation rights in order to drill wells and begin full commercial production, their routine request had been categorically refused, in spite of advice from six leading Guatemalan law firms that it could not be.

The Guatemalan Ministry of Hydrocarbons, which was responsible for the new oil industry, had received a report from one of its own experts that Basic's petroleum rights could have a value of $3.3 billion, in return for an investment of just $200 million. The Ministry's report suggested that this was an "immoral profit" and concluded that Guatemala was quite within its rights to renegotiate any agreement it might have had with Basic Resources with that in mind.

At the same time Basic's partner in BEA Petroleum, Elf-Aquitaine Guatemala, was holding private discussions with the Guatemalan government to discover if there was any way in which they might obtain a direct interest in the exploitation of Basic's oil field. It did not take long for the government to decide that Basic had to relinquish its existing rights, and enter into a new contract which gave them 80 per cent of a new joint company with Elf-Aquitaine (who would have 20 per cent) to explore and develop the field at their own expense, in return for just 45 per cent of the production they achieved. The other 55 per cent was to go straight to the Guatemalan government.

John Park, still president of Basic to Jimmy Goldsmith's chairman, fought the proposal inch by inch from his office in Guatemala City. "There was such a fight in Guatemala that my name was becoming mud," he says now. "And that was the first time that I really saw a lot of Sir James Goldsmith." The new chairman of Basic Resources International calculated that it might be in the best interests of protecting his investment if he took over some of the principal negotiations with the Guatemalan Ministry of Hydrocarbons. Générale Occidentale had gradually increased its stake in Basic until now almost $30 million was at risk. "Jimmy came down and stayed in Guatemala for a month," Park recalls, "and Madame Beaux came for two months." As 1980 wore on the chairman and chief financial officer of Générale Occidentale also recruited the help of retired American General, Vernon Walters, a Vietnam veteran (who was later appointed US Ambassador to the United Nations by President Reagan), in the hope that one general might be able to help talk sense to another in Guatemala. But the ploy was not an unqualified success. After weeks of heated negotiation Basic managed to hang on to its concession areas, but found itself forced to allow Elf-Aquitaine to become the operating company to drill for oil. Goldsmith was not particularly dismayed. "I was delighted when Elf agreed to come in, because I thought at the time they would be a good operating company, and I knew I wasn't in the oil business, I was in the financial business. We were really just passive investors."

John Park explains: "Jimmy thought that they should know how to operate an oil field because of their experience, and because we had bloodied the nose of everyone in the government it might be better to give them a new face." It did not turn out to be a good decision. On 15 August 1980 Basic handed over the running of its Guatemalan operation to its former junior partner, Elf-Aquitaine, who had agreed to drill six new exploration wells at a cost of $42 million over the next three years. The change turned out to be little short of a disaster, and one which threatened every single penny of Jimmy Goldsmith's investment in oil. But it was to be some time before that became clear.

At this point Jimmy Goldsmith was also considering exactly what he should do with Cavenham in Britain and Générale Occidentale in France. He had already sold off their food manufacturing companies – the original foundations of Cavenham which he had laid seventeen years before had been quietly dismantled. Certainly some of his British supermarkets, like the Presto chain, remained as a counterpart to Grand Union in the United States; but there was little else of significance left. There was still *L'Express* and the Laurent Restaurant in Paris, as well as *Now!* in England, but otherwise Jimmy Goldsmith had manoeuvred himself into a position which would allow him to disappear from Britain and Europe at a moment's notice.

Before his new son Benjamin was three months old, he was beginning to consider whether the time had come to liquidate everything else in Europe, and follow the Acapulco plan to its logical conclusion. "I had originally decided to invest in the United States, but it had become clearer and clearer that it would make sense to move all our interests there," he explains. One factor very much in his mind was the possibility that France would elect François Mitterrand as its socialist president in the elections in April 1981. If that happened, Jimmy Goldsmith believed, none of his company's interests in France would be safe for a moment. Ronald Reagan's America looked a far more solid proposition. As Olivier Todd, one of his journalists on *L'Express* at the time, put it later: "Jimmy became convinced that if Mitterrand won, it would only be a matter of time before the Russian tanks started rolling up the Champs Elysees." If that happened, no one was safe, least of all an entrepreneur with a reputation for defending capitalism against all attackers.

The obvious thing for Jimmy Goldsmith to do was to refine his escape route; there was already one in existence in the shape of Grand Union, Diamond and Basic Resources. Throughout the second half of 1980 he and Gilberte Beaux spent increasing periods of time in Central America and New York, laying the foundations of a future outside Europe. They even offered a conciliatory hand to Diamond. In September Bill Koslo was invited to join the GO board, and accepted; the earlier antagonism had softened, and Jimmy Goldsmith – through Cavenham Development Inc. – acquired a little over 300,000 extra Diamond shares as 1980 came to an end, to prove that he was "going to stay with the company". By the beginning of 1981 he owned almost three million of the company's 12 million shares, about 25.9 per cent of the outstanding Diamond stock. The escape route had been precisely mapped out.

In Guatemala similar plans were also being laid, although with rather less success. Elf-Aquitaine's performance as the operating company of the Basic Resources oil concessions was not living up to everyone's expectations, least of all Jimmy Goldsmith's. Elf-Aquitaine's original agreement in August to drill six new wells at a cost of $42 million over three years was already under threat. "By the end of 1980 they'd spent $14 million, but they hadn't accomplished all the work they had to do," Park remembers now. Things were to get worse. "For 1981 they made a budget for $50 million, which we weren't too pleased with because $50 million plus $14 million made $64 million, to be spent in eighteen months – much more than the $42 million we'd agreed should be spent over three years. But we were partners so we approved it."

A few months later Elf-Aquitaine returned with another budget for 1981, this time for $72 million which, together with the $14 million already spent, would bring the cost of the operation to $86 million by the end of the year – twice the original estimate for three years. From being a straightforward investment, Basic was turning out to be an extremely expensive interest. According to the terms of their August 1980 agreement Basic had to provide 80 per cent of the funds for the project, against Elf-Aquitaine's 20 per cent. John Park remembers telling Jimmy Goldsmith, "Oh my God! We're going to be in a problem financially."

Générale Occidentale could raise funds in Paris and New York, but Jimmy Goldsmith had other plans for those; not least Diamond International. Strapped for immediate hard cash to provide the extra finance Elf-Aquitaine was demanding, Basic had to allow the French national oil company to increase its percentage interest in their agreement from 20 to 43 per cent. "It was the only way we could keep going," John Park explains, "but we still didn't get any accounting from them." Park was told firmly that his responsibility in the operation was to provide the money when it was needed.

Back in Paris, Jimmy Goldsmith was beginning to wonder whether Elf-Aquitaine's plan was not rather more elaborate – to grab the oil concession for themselves. He knew only too well that the French national oil company was unlikely to run out of money, and the more it demanded the more likely he would be forced to dilute his interest in Basic Resources, because he would need to find partners to supply extra hard cash.

"When we started getting reports of a string of disasters, drilling after drilling going wrong, well after well being lost, production going down, John Park would come and say 'They're sabotaging it' and I'd say 'Nonsense, I don't believe it for a second'", Jimmy Goldsmith recalls now. "Then they started overspending, and I just thought it was inherent in the high-risk element of the oil business; until I heard a rumour that they had decided to put pressure on Basic, so that they could pick up the concession. That's when I started to say, maybe John's got a point."

Jimmy Goldsmith's old dislike of state capitalism came bubbling to the surface again. He might be privately planning the removal of his companies from Europe, but he was not about to be forced out with his tail between his legs, especially when John Park was claiming on the telephone from Guatemala City that Elf were guilty of deliberate negligence.

Suddenly there were problems everywhere. In the first weeks of April 1981 it became increasingly clear to him, and to the staff of *L'Express*, that France was about to elect François Mitterrand as its president for a seven-year term. His worst fears had come to fruition. Now he was determined to get out of Europe as quickly as possible. There would have to be one or two sacrifices – *Now!* magazine would have to go, it required too much money and time, he had already spent almost £10 million in less than two years on it – and so would Gilberte Beaux's beloved Banque Occidentale, which could well be nationalized in any case. There was no alternative, he had made up his mind.

On Monday 27 April he announced that *Now!* magazine was to be closed, with the loss of more than 120 jobs, including eighty journalists. What one English newspaper had called "the boldest publishing launch since the war" had come to an unceremonious end just nineteen months, and eighty-four weekly issues, after it had begun. He had been a dabbler in the British press not a magnate, which depressed him slightly, but the magazine no longer fitted into his plans.

On the same morning he announced to an astonished City of London that Cavenham would be changing its name back to Allied Suppliers, the company it had taken over so spectacularly nine years before. Few people realized at the time that the Cavenham name had not disappeared altogether – it was very much alive in the company holding Jimmy Goldsmith's stocks in Diamond International. He might be prepared to sell a company called Allied Suppliers, but he would never willingly sell one called Cavenham; he was too superstitious and too proud for that. Wherever Cavenham was so he would be.

No sooner had he announced the sale of *Now!* in England, and the end of Cavenham, than Jimmy Goldsmith found himself plunged into an argument with his journalists on *L'Express*. The French magazine had published a cover showing photographs of the two candidates for the forthcoming presidential elections. The pictures chosen showed François Mitterrand looking a great deal younger than his opponent, Valéry Giscard d'Estaing, even though he was in fact nearly ten years older. In the words of one Paris newspaper: "Jimmy Goldsmith saw red."

The opinion polls were already predicting that the presidential election would be close, and the obvious inference was that his magazine was encouraging its 2.5 million readers to dismiss the ageing Giscard in favour of the more youthful and energetic Mitterrand. That was the opposite of what Jimmy Goldsmith wanted. He may have insisted that the magazine have columnists from both ends of the political spectrum, but that did not mean he approved of its apparent decision to throw its weight behind a socialist president.

Determined to sack whoever was responsible, but intent on waiting until the election itself was over before taking any action, Jimmy Goldsmith remained in London. The obvious candidates were the magazine's respected editor, Jean François Revel, and its managing editor, the Cambridge University educated former BBC television presenter Olivier Todd. Then immediately after Mitter-and's victory, and only a matter of hours after he landed at the private airport at Le Bourget, Jimmy Goldsmith summoned Todd to the publisher's office in *L'Express* and fired him. Within a day Revel had offered his resignation as well.

Once again Jimmy Goldsmith and a group of journalists found themselves at loggerheads, only this time they actually worked for him. When the rest of the editorial staff voiced their anger at a mass meeting two days later, he was unmoved. The editorial staff had just one choice, he told them bitterly: "Submit to my new role as editor-in-chief or resign." In case they were in any doubt that he was serious, he also told them forcefully that he would shut the magazine at once if there was any trouble. Though more than twenty staff eventually resigned, *L'Express* continued successfully under a new editor, Yves Cuau.

After the firing, Goldsmith was given a hard time in the French press. Olivier Todd explains now: "A lot of people thought there was a terrible political logic to it, but I personally don't. He was perfectly entitled to fire me, and he did it as a gentleman, I got every penny I was owed." Nevertheless the crisis at *L'Express*, only a matter of days after a crucial presidential election in France, confirmed the opinions of many critics that Jimmy Goldsmith was nothing but a fanatical supporter of the right wing. Yet, once again, it was a misunderstanding of his attitude.

"When Jimmy arrived at *L'Express*," Olivier Todd says now, "he made it quite clear that he was not going to be a 'sleeping owner', but at the same time he wanted to show his 'liberal self'. He wanted to give an ideological direction to the ship, but also wanted to recruit men like me to talk about the left wing – but you can't have your cake and eat it too."

In fact, Todd is convinced that no matter what Jimmy Gold-smith's good intentions, the idea of a single magazine which tries to include differing political views is doomed to failure in France, "because we are not a consensus society, not a tolerant society – you are either Left or Right, anyone who is liberal gets crushed". But Todd is also convinced that Jimmy Goldsmith was probably happy to see liberal opinions reflected in his magazine only when there was a right-wing government in France. "As soon as the government became socialist that was different – that's where his liberalism stops."

The same could have been said of Lord Beaverbrook or Lord Northcliffe in England, or of Henry Luce at *Time* magazine in the United States, but given Jimmy Goldsmith's reputation as a manipulator of the press, those were parallels that were seldom drawn. To many people he had established himself once and for all as the enemy of journalists whether in Britain or France. This is not a view supported by Olivier Todd in spite of their arguments. "I see Jimmy as someone who probably should not have got into the newspaper business, because he didn't see that if you do go into it you either do what some proprietors do and let your publications say exactly what they want regardless, or you become the editor yourself, especially if you buy an old liberal institution like *L'Express* with socialists everywhere."

But Jimmy Goldsmith's fury at the events of *L'Express* in the last days of April 1981 were only a momentary diversion from the more significant decision of where he should be conducting his businesses. A single news magazine, no matter how influential, was irrelevant to the principal thrust of his commercial life, and that was not to be left to the caprice of journalists.

"If I have any talent at all," he says now, "it is for seeing major developments and acting on them before anyone else." The development that he had most feared, a socialist president in his native France, was just about to come to pass. Jimmy Goldsmith had no intention of sitting still and allowing it to threaten his commercial future. If the attractions of the United States had always been strong, they were all the greater now that his future in Europe was threatened.

21

No More "Double or Quits"

By the time that François Mitterrand had settled into the Elysée Palace, almost everything Jimmy Goldsmith owned in Britain and France had been sold. Even Madame Beaux's beloved Banque Occidentale had been sold to Crédit Lyonnais, who were already shareholders in Générale Occidentale. With it had gone his old London office in Leadenhall Street. Now all that remained in Europe were the 970 food stores of Cavenham – for which he had committed a budget of £145 million for capital investment over the coming five years – and one or two hobbies, like Laurent and Aspinall's club. Even Cavenham had become Allied Suppliers again in 1980, which should have given the City of London a clue about what was actually going on in Jimmy Goldsmith's mind.

As he was to write in his book *Pour La Révolution Permanente* five years later, Jimmy Goldsmith had become "successively worried, frustrated, angry, disenchanted and alienated" in England and in France. "It seemed to me that both nations were set on paths which, unless radically changed, would lead to decline, poverty and unhappiness. And perhaps to subjugation." That was something he was not prepared to tolerate for himself. "In 1973 I made my first major investment in the USA. I expanded it sharply after the socialist and communist alliance gained power in France in 1981."

He was convinced nothing in Europe was safe any longer. There were family ties still, certainly, but Jimmy Goldsmith was more convinced than he had ever been than his future lay in the United States. Surely his family could move too. It was to be his only disappointment in the completion of the Acapulco Strategy. When he had discussed the idea with Annabel she had not been at all enthusiastic about the prospect. He might be a financier on three continents but that did not mean his children had to share his peripatetic habits. "I'm English, the children are English, and I would like them to be brought up in their own country," she had explained firmly. "Besides, all my friends are here. You can go where you choose, but I don't want to live in New York." Whether his attachment to Laure Boulay de la Meurthe, who was spending more and more of her time in the United States, had influenced his wife's decision was not clear, but nevertheless her resolve to stay in England depressed him for a time. Jimmy Goldsmith knew very well that he intended to spend between three and six months of the year in the United States in future, and he wanted his family to be with him. But there was nothing he could do, Annabel's mind was made up.

The problems with Elf-Aquitaine now reached crisis point. At the outset his interest may have been simply that of an investment banker with $2 million at risk "which we could have walked away from and taken our loss", but as the French national oil company had increased their expenditure further and further so Basic had been forced to provide 80 per cent of the money. As 1981 wore on his investment had grown towards $30 million and then $45 million, "a great deal more than an investment banking transaction".

Jimmy Goldsmith, as chairman of Basic Resources, knew that he had little choice but to continue to provide the extra money that Elf-Aquitaine were demanding – "If Basic had been in default Elf would automatically have received the whole concession free." By the autumn of 1981 the extent of the overspending and under-production in Basic's concession area in Guatemala became so apparent that it could no longer be ignored or attributed to the high risks of the oil business. "Finally at the end of 1981, Elf came back and asked for another revised budget," John Park remembers, "and I said 'No, absolutely no'." Undeterred, the French oil company told him that he had no right to refuse, because his function under the terms of their agreement was to provide money when it was called for. Park told them he was going to stop paying until he received proper accounting. Elf responded by placing their partners in default with the Guatemalan government, and insisting that their legal responsibility was to ensure that their financial demands were met within ninety days.

For the first time in Guatemala Jimmy Goldsmith lost his temper, and he decided to find out everything he could about Elf. While John Park was accusing the French national oil company of "deliberate negligence" and Elf was responding by claiming he was "in default", Jimmy Goldsmith hired a firm of private detectives to examine his adversary's affairs. What they discovered made less than appetising reading. "It appeared there had been corrupt practices of one kind or another," he explains now. But for a time he was too busy elsewhere to do anything about it.

Just at the moment when Basic Resources was demanding more of his time and attention, an opportunity to increase his stake in Diamond International in the United States presented itself. The Brooks-Scanlon company, which had provoked him to tender for "a substantial portion" of the Diamond shares when Diamond had proposed to merge with Brooks-Scanlon in April 1980, suddenly seemed to have become his ally rather than his adversary. Towards the end of September 1981 Jimmy Goldsmith was offered 1.6 million extra shares in Diamond by some of the former stock holders of Brooks-Scanlon, including Mr Conley Brooks, who had become a director of Diamond after the two companies merged in June 1980. The asking price for the new shares was exactly the same as the one he had offered for Diamond's shares the year before, $42 each, and the reason for the offer was all too clear. Diamond's shares were now trading on the New York Stock Exchange at $29, and the timber industry was in the middle of an exceptional recession. The possibility that Jimmy Goldsmith might still be prepared to pay the original price was too great a temptation to be missed.

In fact, Jimmy Goldsmith was still prepared to pay his original price, because he was convinced that Diamond was still fundamentally undervalued on the stock market. On 2 October 1981 Cavenham Holdings Incorporated announced in New York that it had purchased a further 1,645,828 Diamond shares for $69.1 million. They were not paying for these shares entirely in cash, however, as they had for the 2,858,332 they had bought in June 1980. This time Cavenham was offering 62.5 per cent in cash and the rest in two-year promissory notes bearing interest, payable half yearly, of 9 per cent per annum. The purchase was to be financed by three banks, including Citibank. The announcement did not exactly please every director of Diamond International – some felt Brooks-Scanlon had effectively rendered their company into Jimmy Goldsmith's hands – so it was not exactly a surprise when, at the next Diamond board meeting, Mr Conley Brooks resigned his directorship because he felt it was "no longer appropriate".

After the deal Jimmy Goldsmith owned 5,577,640 of the 13.7 million Diamond shares in circulation, slightly more than 40 per cent, although that did not breach the "standstill" agreement he had reached with Diamond in June 1980, because the number of shares in the company had been diluted by the Brooks-Scanlon merger. But it was becoming abundantly clear to the directors of Diamond that they would not be able to repel the interest of its largest shareholder for very much longer. The takeover that Jimmy Goldsmith had launched in the spring of 1980 had suddenly become inevitable, especially as there was no sign that the stock market was going to stop falling and the timber industry suddenly start booming again to save the company.

In the middle of October Générale Occidentale announced in a document lodged with the Securities and Exchange Commission in New York that it was considering "on a more active basis than theretofore various courses of action with respect to Diamond", including buying more Diamond stock or proposing a merger with one of its own subsidiaries. By the end of the month Diamond had accepted the inevitable, and on 5 November 1981 the company announced that it had begun discussions with Goldsmith to explore the possibility of his acquiring all Diamond's outstanding stock. Diamond's shares were suspended on the New York Stock Exchange. Hardly a Wall Street analyst was surprised.

In early December Jimmy Goldsmith offered $42 a share for the remaining seven million or so Diamond shares – to be payable $21 in cash and $21 in debentures with a marketable value of $21. At first Diamond refused the offer, because the investment bankers it had retained to examine any offer made, Bear Stearns, did not regard $42 as a fair price to the public stockholders of Diamond. On 14 December 1981, however, Jimmy Goldsmith increased his offer to $44.50 in cash for each Diamond share, and he gave the shareholders until 23 December to accept the deal. They did so. Jimmy Goldsmith had got what he had wanted for almost two years – control of Diamond – but it was a considerable gamble.

After all, Diamond did not look all that wonderful a catch. Regarded by many industry experts as "a heap of junk", the company's net income in 1980 had been only $40.6 million, down from $61.7 million the year before, while its sales had stayed almost steady, at $1.28 billion. But Jimmy Goldsmith had not created Cavenham in England, or Générale Occidentale in France by buying glamorous successful companies; he had done it by carefully assembling the less glamorous, and certainly the less successful, and making a success of them. The only difficulty with doing the same thing with Diamond was that he did not really have the money to pay for it. Stretching to find extra funds for Basic, with Grand Union clearly needing more investment in the near future, and his few remaining assets in Europe still locked away in his holdings, he did not have the cash resources available. To buy it Jimmy Goldsmith realized that he would have to borrow against its assets and then sell some of the assets again as quickly as possible to release his debts. As *Fortune* magazine was to point out two years later: "When he proposed to buy out the last 60 per cent of Diamond in December 1981, Goldsmith was a lonely leveraged bull pawing the ground for a stock market rally. He needed a sharp run up in stock values if he was to sell off Diamond's divisions at a profit."

In essence Jimmy Goldsmith knew that he had no alternative other than to raise the $378 million he would need to get the remaining 60 per cent of Diamond shares entirely from borrowings – about one-third of it from Générale Occidentale itself and the rest from a bank consortium, probably led once again by Citibank. It also meant that the total cost of the company to him would be in excess of $660 million. "I was going to be borrowing $660 million at 16 or 17 or 18 per cent," he recalls now. "The interest payments alone were $120 to $130 million a year, and Diamond was losing money." To more than one Wall Street analyst it looked like financial suicide. "It wasn't just double or quits, it was worse," Jimmy Goldsmith admits looking back. "It could well have been costing me more than $180 million in a year to hold on to the whole company when it was losing money."

Jimmy Goldsmith was banking on his absolute conviction that 1982 would see a fundamental recovery on Wall Street, and a major rally in the New York stock market. "If my view was wrong – even by a year – I was blown away, bye-bye."

As *Fortune* was to acknowledge later, "Success hung on timing."

As 1982 began, however, it was by no means certain that the American economy, and the New York stock market, was on the brink of a turnaround. A less determined and less self-confident entrepreneur might have hesitated, or at least hedged his bets by looking round for partners to share the burden of the debt, but Jimmy Goldsmith did neither. He went out and raised the money he needed with the help of New York investment house Drexel Burnham Lambert. It was a precise expression of the entrepreneurial style that he had refined for himself over the previous two decades. And not for one moment did he regard it as dangerous.

"My criterion has to be, what do I think is going to succeed, not what do I think is the least risky," he says now. "That is not the same criterion that an investment manager might have, because he is assessed not on how well he does, but how well he does in comparison with other investment managers. So if every other investment manager loses a vast amount and he loses just a little less then that's OK. To protect his job, and his image as a sound, respectable, stable man, he is bound to do precisely what his peers are doing, only just a little bit better. But if he suddenly goes counter-cyclical, and starts selling when everyone else is buying, or vice versa, then he's wrong. People start saying he's unstable. But I don't mind that. I'm not looking to be just like the others. If I lose three-quarters of everything I've got, it's no comfort to me that everybody else did as well.

"You don't need courage to do what I do," he insists, "you need it to do the same as everybody else, because that is certain death. If everybody agrees that you should increase capacity in ball bearings, for example, you can be absolutely sure that there's going to be a glut of ball bearings, and you'll end up losing your money. But an investor on his own account cannot care about what everybody else thinks, he can only care about what he can do, and what he can achieve."

Not that Jimmy Goldsmith came to those conclusions entirely alone. He still discussed his plans in detail with both Madame Beaux in Paris and Roland Franklin in New York. If they could persuade him he was wrong, he would usually abandon the plan, or at least shelve it. As Gilberte Beaux puts it: "Every time we have a medium-term strategy it comes from Jimmy, but it is a strategy which is like the block of stone for a statue, it needs to be chiselled and polished, and that he certainly does not do by himself; he would not want to." With the help of his two closest and longest-standing advisers he refined the plan to finance the purchase of the remaining 60 per cent of Diamond, and began to convince them that he was right to believe that the American stock market was about to turn. And he convinced them with one of his favourite arguments about stock markets anywhere in the world.

"I don't often invest in the market," Jimmy Goldsmith explains, "but I sometimes do, and when I do I will never invest if I don't first telephone half a dozen supposed experts and find them unanimous. Because when 90 per cent of people are thinking the same thing, you can be certain that if you do exactly the opposite you'll make a fortune; and there's a very good structural reason for that.

"If everybody thinks that the market is going up then one thing is certain – they've already invested all their funds because they think they're going to increase them. So there's no more money left to go into the market. Therefore the market can only go down. If everybody thinks that the market is going to go down then they will have already sold, so they're full of cash, and at the slightest turn they're going to plunge in again and buy. The market can only go up. Structurally if you can find unanimity and do the opposite you can be certain to be successful."

It was the conclusion of a man who had always felt at his most comfortable doing the unusual, or the unexpected; standing outside the crowd, never allowing himself to be pigeonholed, never caring to be described as a conformist. And in March 1982, while the first stages of the money-raising for the Diamond purchase were being arranged in New York, he explained his conclusions to an institutional conference organized by the New York investment house Drexel Burnham Lambert, who had first had dealings with him in the purchase of the Brooks-Scanlon shares in Diamond in October 1980.

"They had invited me to speak, and I agreed to go because I thought I might need to borrow money." The man who really had little reputation in the United States at that point told the assembled fund managers and investment analysts that he was convinced that the Dow Jones index would go past 1,500 before long, even though it had been just 700 not long ago. "Everybody looked at each other as though I was a complete lunatic," he remembers.

But that did not stop him working flat out to finance his purchase of Diamond. The only difficult question was – how was he going to raise the money? It was Drexel Burnham Lambert who came up with one of the solutions. Chris Anderson, the sharp and pugnacious managing director of the firm's business solicitation division, a man given to wide braces and short sentences, quickly grasped that the key to the Diamond deal for Jimmy Goldsmith lay in the company's 1.6 million acres of forests. "In that transaction what you are really concerned with – at one level – is how does one view an asset, in this case forest land. Clearly it was an asset which people were intrigued by, but on the other hand puzzled by."

Together, Goldsmith and Drexel tried to discover how they could finance the purchase of a company with its forests valued in its accounts at virtually nothing. "The question was – how do you convince other people of their value?" Anderson explains. "At the time it took an extraordinary amount of courage to step up to the forest products and paper industry. It was in a long slide which had gone on since 1979." But if they could find a way of proving that the forests were a valuable asset then they could raise money against them to finance the purchase of the company.

Drexel were no strangers to risks, or takeovers. Gradually during the 1970s they had gathered together a number of investors who had become famous for their raids on sleepy American corporations – including T. Boone Pickens of Mesa Petroleum and Saul P. Steinberg of Reliance Holdings – many of whom had first been attracted to the company by the activities of its young bond dealer Michael Milken, who was by then running Drexel's bond-trading operation in Beverly Hills. And the firm had expanded rapidly and successfully in the process.

In spite of Drexel's reputation and Jimmy Goldsmith's determination, it took longer than either expected to put together the finance to complete the purchase of Diamond. The original agreement to the merger had specified that the deal should be completed by the end of July 1982, but that was extended, with the Diamond directors' agreement, first to 30 September, and then to 31 October 1982.

By that time Drexel Burnham Lambert had come up with a scheme which would value the company's forests, and therefore allow Jimmy Goldsmith to borrow against them to buy the company. They created a "put" on the forests by finding a guaranteed buyer for them if Jimmy Goldsmith decided to sell them. For a fee of $12.5 million Travellers Insurance agreed to pay him $250 million for the timberlands at any time before the end of 1984, if Jimmy Goldsmith decided to sell. With a guaranteed buyer, the syndicate of banks that had been approached by Jimmy Goldsmith to provide $440 million of the $660 million necessary to finance the entire purchase price of Diamond were much more willing to lend.

Diamond itself had eased the difficulties of the transaction at the last moment by selling its principal packaging operation to the Irish company Jefferson Smurfitt for $80 million and one of its group of playing card companies for a further $45 million. As *Fortune* later commented: "The proceeds reduced Diamond's corporate debt by $44 million, making it easier for Goldsmith to borrow against the assets that remained."

But even while he was struggling with the finance for Diamond, Jimmy Goldsmith did not forget his other American interests, and their demands for money.

On 11 May 1982 the London Stock Exchange suddenly, and unexpectedly, suspended dealings in the shares of Argyll Foods, a food manufacturing and retailing group run by a single-minded Scottish entrepreneur called James Gulliver. On the following day it was announced that Allied Suppliers had been sold by its parent company Générale Occidentale to Argyll for £101 million. Of the chain of 1,650 grocery shops and supermarkets, with names like Home and Colonial, Maypole and Lipton's, which Jimmy Goldsmith had bought ten years before for £86.3 million, there were now just 918 shops left, 128 of them called Presto supermarkets. When the sale of Allied was announced Jimmy Goldsmith told the *Wall Street Journal* that the sale was not intended to raise money for the

Diamond offer but to help Grand Union finance "a transformation of its stores, which will cost £119 million a year over the next three years". Not every Wall Street broker believed him.

Whatever the use the proceeds from the Allied Suppliers' sale were to be used for, one thing was certain: the final commercial link between Jimmy Goldsmith and Britain was broken. One English newspaperman compared him to "a storm that had been blown out to sea". As he told the influential City editor of the London *Daily Mail*, Patrick Sergeant: "I now come to Britain only for my hobbies." Before his son Benjamin was eighteen months old, Jimmy Goldsmith had severed all that remained of his principal financial connections to England, apart from his home on the edge of Richmond Park and his share in Aspinall's club in Mayfair. He was, as he put it himself to anyone who asked, "no longer a factor in Britain". The man who just six years before had all but dominated the British press for months at a time was now as remote as an offshore Scottish island, and as little understood by most Englishmen.

To most men in the City of London he was now an enigmatic figure who had chosen to occupy his own remote stratosphere, away from the world that most of them knew and understood. He seemed to many of them more interested in the complexity of his shareholdings, and their tax position in different continents than in what exactly he was buying. It was less than a fair judgement, but he made no compromises to alter it, just as he had made no effort to contradict the caricatures put forward of him by his opponents during the first stages of the tender for Diamond in the United States – "I never bother to say anything because it really doesn't matter." People could say whatever they liked. He intended to act in whichever way he chose, regardless of public opinion, which concerned him less and less.

Indeed, he had decided the deal for Diamond should be conducted by a new company, DUSA, which was directly a subsidiary of his Hong Kong based holding company General Oriental (GOR). DUSA's role was to act as the holding company for his interests in Diamond. Having an off-shore company as the ultimate holding company for one of his acquisitions was nothing new for Goldsmith. Générale Occidentale had been the holding company for Cavenham, in England, just as GOR was the holding company for his interest in Aspinall's in London, and Basic Resources International (Bahamas) Limited his holding company for his interests in Basic Resources in Guatemala. He was already examining ways of moving his GOR's base from Hong Kong to the Cayman Islands in case the change in the colony's allegiance from Britain to China were to affect it.

The attacks he suffered in the City of London, or in the New York money markets, however, were trivial in comparison to those he suddenly started to face in Guatemala. The row with Elf-Aquitaine, far from cooling towards a settlement, had grown more acrimonious as the first months of 1982 had passed. So in the middle of discussions with Drexel Burnham Lambert about Diamond in New York, with the Argyll group in London about their purchase of Allied Suppliers, and with Madame Beaux in Paris over the final winding up of Banque Occidentale and the structure of the shareholdings between Générale Occidentale and General Oriental, Jimmy Goldsmith was also forced to visit Guatemala City regularly to decide what should be done about his less than satisfactory partners in the jungle oil field there. Basic Resources and its president John Park were still not receiving the accounting records they wanted, even though on 23 April 1982 Park had provided specific details of what he claimed was overspending to the tune of some $16 million. Elf had remained silent.

Finally, almost two years after they had welcomed Elf-Aquitaine into their concession area as the operating company, with a 20 per cent share, Jimmy Goldsmith reluctantly decided that they should put their disagreement with the company into official arbitration before the International Chamber of Commerce in Paris and Geneva. In Paris Basic would claim that Elf-Aquitaine had not honoured their contractual obligation to pay royalties to them, while in Geneva they would argue that Elf had shown gross negligence in their operation of the oil field. Basic would then present a claim for damages for $294 million.

In the Basic head office in Guatemala City Jimmy Goldsmith asked John Park, "John, we're taking Elf to arbitration – do you know what they'll do?"

"I assume they'll act decently," Park replied, a little confused.

"Remember it's a state company, and as a state company they believe that they're above the law."

Park looked even more confused.

"You'll be surprised," Jimmy Goldsmith told him. "They'll cut you off, they will do everything possible to cut you out, and they will try to drag this thing out for ever – and it's going to cost a fortune."

"But they must be reasonably responsible."

Jimmy Goldsmith snorted. "They won't play by any rules that you recognize. But, John, I don't mind that, I just want to ask one question. Are we right?"

"Yes, we're right," Park told him firmly.

"OK, so don't worry about the finances, I'll take care of them."

As John Park recalls now: "Everything Jimmy said Elf would do they did. They blocked our supplies of oil, they tried to claim our assets, it was a bloody battle."

It was also not a cheap one. Already committed to an investment in excess of $50 million at the beginning of 1982, Jimmy Goldsmith saw that figure rise to $90 million before the dispute with Elf-Aquitaine came to an end. At almost any point before Basic Resources launched its arbitration claims against Elf-Aquitaine Jimmy Goldsmith could have, as he puts it now, "walked away and taken our loss". There was even the possibility that he could have sold his section of the company to Elf-Aquitaine itself, whose bankers Crédit Lyonnais were old friends and shareholders in Générale Occidentale. But he chose not to. "It was an emotional decision," he accepts now, "and because of that a stupid mistake I suppose; but I was angry at everything that had happened.

"At one time in Guatemala I was told that my losses were not just going to be financial." To a man who had always preferred a fight to almost anything else, there could have been no greater encouragement to continue the dispute with Elf-Aquitaine to its bitter end. "How could I have walked away? I was absolutely repelled by the whole sickness of it."

Nothing improved for Jimmy Goldsmith in Guatemala after he launched the arbitration action against Elf. An attempt to bring in a further partner, the Spanish national oil company Hispanoil, to share the expenses and take over as operator was blocked by Elf, who proceeded to ask for an embargo on Basic's assets in Guatemala. Throughout 1982 and into 1983 the bitter charge and counter-charge over the Basic concession area in the Guatemalan jungle continued. It could hardly have come at a worse time. If he was wrong about the American stock market, and it failed to rise, Jimmy Goldsmith could have found himself "comprehensively blown away".

To his intense relief, as the humid summer air began to seep into his apartment in the Carlyle Hotel on Madison Avenue, it became abundantly clear that his predictions were correct. The Dow Jones index started to rise steadily. The dark days of the 700 level rapidly faded into the memory, and 1,100 came back on to the horizon followed by 1,200, on the way to 1,500.

"It all happened exactly as I'd predicted at Drexel's conference," he remembers. But there was a snag. "It was after I'd agreed the deal with the Diamond board but before it had actually gone through." Jimmy Goldsmith started to worry that somebody might get suddenly optimistic again, and that his deal would collapse as a result. In the weeks after Labour Day in September 1982 his drive to complete the Diamond deal became a rush. Jimmy Goldsmith could sense the profits that he could get from selling off sections of the company. He had no wish to lose them now, he was too far stretched.

His luck held. On 1 November 1982 Bill Koslo circulated the Diamond International stockholders with details of the proposed merger into DUSA, and invited them to the annual general meeting at the Waldorf-Astoria Hotel on Park Avenue in New York on Wednesday 1 December 1982. "The Board of Directors of the Company unanimously recommends that the stockholders vote in favour of the proposals to approve the plan of sale and the proposed merger," Koslo wrote, although reminding everyone that "the affirmative vote of the holders of 85 per cent of the outstanding shares of Common Stock of the Company is required to approve the proposed merger." On 1 December 89.6 per cent of the shares in Diamond International were voted in favour of the merger, and Jimmy Goldsmith gained control of the company he had first taken an interest in almost five years before.

Clearly delighted, he told the crowded annual general meeting that he would be relying on $435 million in bank loans to pay for the entire company, which he would be repaying by selling off some of its constituent parts. He went on to explain that the merger particularly pleased him because he believed that the United States offered greater opportunity for growth than the economies of "various foreign countries" where he had holdings.

Not for the first time, Jimmy Goldsmith was to celebrate the foundation of a new commercial life with a new child. Barely had the details of the Diamond merger been agreed than Laure Boulaye de la Meurthe discovered that she was pregnant with her first, and his seventh, child. It was like a confirmation that the latest branch of a new Goldsmith dynasty was beginning to take shape: this one with its roots firmly in the New World. He was already planning to acknowledge his success in Diamond by creating a home for his latest family in New York. A hotel suite, no matter how well appointed, was certainly not sufficient for a financier who had become the first European to join America's small and exclusive group of "corporate raiders". He wanted a firm base from which to expand his operations, and to complete the necessary sales of Diamond's constituent parts that he had in mind. There was still some way to go before he would finally see the benefits of the Diamond deal, although with Wall Street now climbing steadily, he knew it was not going to be long.

There were still some on Wall Street who condemned him, and others like him, as no more than a "hostile predator preying on unsuspecting companies and their shareholders"; but it was clear to those who worked with him that he was unlike those who made a reputation by taking over soggy American corporations and splitting them up for a quick profit. Chris Anderson of Drexel Burnham Lambert explains: "For a start, the manner in which the Diamond deal was conducted placed Jimmy in a very singular position in the United States marketplace. It proved he was a gentleman acquisitor. And I think one reason for that is that he accepted a standstill agreement, and stood by it, and he only proceeded with the merger after he had agreed it with the Diamond board."

Even more important to the common stockholders who came to the company's annual general meeting on that first Wednesday afternoon in December 1982, Jimmy Goldsmith also demonstrated that he would give them their money quickly and efficiently, and more money than they were expecting. As Anderson puts it: "If someone makes an offer which is friendly to 65,000 shareholders and places $2 billion of extra value in their pockets, by finding a way of revaluing their company's assets, and is opposed by a handful of people at the top of an organization – you have to ask 'hostile' to whom and 'predatory' to what?"

But, as ever, Jimmy Goldsmith was not in the least concerned with what anyone else thought. He was delighted with the Diamond deal, and he celebrated his fiftieth birthday in February 1983 by planning his new house in New York. After considerable trouble he had discovered two adjoining brownstones off Park Avenue, and now he wanted them brought into one.

In the space of the next six months Jimmy Goldsmith was to demonstrate not only that he could convert the assets of Diamond International into hard cash for the shareholders, but also that he could, by so doing, finally ensure that he would never again find himself playing "double or quits" in a takeover battle, risking almost everything to gain his objective. As Gwen Kinkead put it in *Fortune* magazine almost a year afterwards: "In complexity and risk the Diamond deal ranks as one of the financial events of the 1980s."

Within a year of Diamond's merger with DUSA, and his taking control of the company, Jimmy Goldsmith had demonstrated to the world that the risk had been well worth it. In the first seven months after the merger he sold six of Diamond's divisions, five to other corporations and one to its managers, to raise more than $334 million. In the three months after that, he arranged for the sale of another three divisions for a further $253 million. The sales drew comparatively little attention because they happened one by one. The James River Corporation of Virginia bought the pulp and paper business for $149 million in July; the Michigan General Corporation of Dallas bought the retail lumber chain for $120 million in September 1983; while Wesray Corporation, led by the former United States Treasury Secretary William Simon, had snapped up the Heekin Can Division for $98 million almost before the ink was dry on the merger in December 1982.

In the space of a single year Jimmy Goldsmith and the tiny Générale Occidentale staff in his offices on Fifth Avenue brought off one of the largest liquidations of a United States company in modern times. The proceeds of the sales enabled him to pay off the total of $435 million in bank loans that he had raised to purchase Diamond, as well as to liquidate almost all the company's remaining corporate debt, which *Fortune* magazine later estimated stood at some $162 million. Jimmy Goldsmith left himself with his debts to Générale Occidentale itself for the Diamond acquisition, but, more important still, he also left himself with 1.6 million acres of timberland in Northern California and New England. And that he divided between GO and GOR. In the summer of 1983, one timber industry analyst estimated that the forests were worth at least $723 million. If he were to sell them and pay off his final debt to Générale Occidentale, Jimmy Goldsmith would be left with a profit of more than $500 million.

"Whatever the ultimate profit," *Fortune* explained admiringly, "most of it will flow to Goldsmith himself and a Liechtenstein foundation he controls."

For the purchase of the new Diamond, DUSA, Jimmy Goldsmith had arranged for Générale Occidentale to put up $225 million in return for 37 per cent of the profits. But the principal owner of the new company, through a holding company in the Dutch Antilles, was General Oriental, who were to get 67 per cent of the profits. Jimmy Goldsmith himself, together with the Bruneria Foundation in Leichtenstein, which he controlled, owned almost 90 per cent of GOR, while GOR and he owned almost 50 per cent of Générale Occidentale.

By the summer of 1983, six months after the completion of the Diamond merger, his own holdings in GO and GOR were estimated to be worth $940 million – four times what they were worth before the merger. There would never be any reason to risk everything again. In future Jimmy Goldsmith would always have $100 million or more to hold back.

As Ambroise Roux, still a director of Générale Occidentale, puts it: "Before Diamond, Jimmy was taking risks that were practically the dimension of his empire. After it the risks were never quite so big." As if to acknowledge his change in fortunes, just as the success of the Diamond deal was becoming clear to Wall Street so the High Court in London awarded him £85,000 in damages from *Private Eye* for an assertion in August 1981 that he had in some way been an associate of the murdered Italian banker Roberto Calvi. It was then the largest sum ever paid out by the magazine in a libel action, and the success delighted Jimmy Goldsmith. It seemed to mark the fact that in both Britain and the United States the tide had turned in his favour.

Or as Jimmy Goldsmith prefers to explain it himself: "If Bovril was the first turning point for me then Diamond was the second, and the decisive one. I've never made any secret of the fact that everything was 'double or quits' until Diamond. But I think risk is a good thing for a business, and I think people are now beginning to realize that."

He was about to demonstrate that he had not lost his own appetite for it.

22

The Jewels in the Crown

Wall Street now began to take Jimmy Goldsmith "very seriously indeed" as Chris Anderson of Drexel Burnham Lambert puts it. On 8 March 1985 no less an American institution than the *New York Times* began its principal editorial by suggesting, "T. Boone Pickens . . . Carl Icahn . . . Saul Steinberg . . . Irwin Jacobs . . . Sir James Goldsmith. Their names are spoken with a shudder in board rooms from Pittsburgh to Bartlesville. They are the new buccaneers of capitalism, making millions by taking over, or just threatening to take over, America's largest corporations." Jimmy Goldsmith had become one of the most famous of America's new band of "corporate raiders".

The idea delighted him. He was more convinced than ever that the United States offered him a unique opportunity to make a considerable fortune for himself – and to improve the basis of the American economy. For, just as he had condemned the suffocation of England and the bureaucracy of France in the past, now he was attacking the stuffy "corporatism" of the United States. That was the new windmill he chose to tilt at on the road to Wall Street.

"Although corporations belong to their shareholders," he wrote not long afterwards in the *Wall Street Journal*, "corporate managements sometimes believe that the business that employs them has become an institution and that they are the trustees of that institution. Some believe that they have developed some sort of proprietorial rights. Shareholders then become no more than an inconvenience." That was not Jimmy Goldsmith's view, particularly if and when he intended to become one of an American corporation's major shareholders. He had every intention of making himself extremely inconvenient to any corporate management that failed to take him seriously when he launched a takeover bid. "The principal difference between a friendly merger and a hostile takeover is that management agrees to a merger. A hostile takeover is carried out without their approval. A hostile takeover is only hostile to established management."

The established managements of large corporations who failed to move with the times were still Jimmy Goldsmith's enemies, whether they were in Paris, London, Guatemala City, New York or San Francisco. "The management of large, tired companies, fearful of the free market, plead with the government bureaucracy for special protection to protect the status quo and avoid change." In the America of the mid-1980s, with the mania for massive takeovers running at the highest level for almost two decades, Jimmy Goldsmith suddenly found himself perfectly placed to do what he had always done best – topple the established order.

America seemed to prize a piratical predatory individualist stalking established companies. Even the *New York Times* had concluded its March 1985 editorial by arguing that "Corporate raiders don't perform their useful function altruistically. But their self-interest usually leads to a collective good." He had been preparing himself for precisely this opportunity all his life. "In a free economy the inefficient are eliminated and the efficient – as long as they remain so – grow for the benefit of all," he wrote in *The Financier* magazine. There were no rules that Jimmy Goldsmith liked better than the rules of the jungle and the free market.

Indeed, nowhere was that more clearly demonstrated than in the jungles of Guatemala. For while the Diamond merger had finally been completed in New York in the winter of 1982, so the battle between Basic Resources and Elf-Aquitaine had grown ever fiercer. By the winter of 1984 the two sides were facing each other frostily across the conference tables of the International Chamber of Commerce in Paris and Geneva at arbitration hearings. As chairman of Basic Resources International (Bahamas) Limited, Jimmy Goldsmith was claiming $294 million in damages from Société Nationale Elf-Aquitaine for "gross negligence and wilful misconduct", as well as a little extra by way of unpaid royalties. It was another fight against a major corporation, and he loved it.

In Guatemala City Basic's founder John Park was growing increasingly concerned that even if they won their case in Geneva for "substantial damages" there would be no company for them to claim against. He feared that Elf-Aquitaine Guatemala, their actual partner in the drilling operations in the Rubelsanto and West Chinaja fields, would simply be declared bankrupt if Basic won the arbitrations in Paris and Geneva. Basic would then be left with nothing at all. To prevent this and to forestall a lengthy and expensive law suit, Park and Goldsmith decided to sue the French parent company, Société Nationale Elf-Aquitaine, in Houston, Texas, for around $290 million in damages. Basic Resources wanted its money.

France's largest company responded by remarking that there was no possibility that they could be sued in Texas as they did not operate there. Undismayed, Basic went ahead and, in one of the most unlikely moves in any corporate battle, proceeded to ask a firm of Texas private detectives to stake out the largest hotels in Houston – in particular the French-owned Meridien – in case any executive of Elf-Aquitaine ever appeared there. For almost six months the detectives made a regular sweep of Houston's leading hotels, asking the staff if there was any sign of a booking by any Elf-Aquitaine executive. Finally they discovered that Elf had made seventy-six reservations at the Meridien in Houston, including rooms for the chairman, the managing director and the chief financial officer.

In a scene worthy of a television soap opera, the three principal officials of Elf-Aquitaine were approached in the marble lobby of the Meridien hotel in Houston shortly after nine o'clock on a hot summer evening by two soberly dressed Texas lawyers and handed subpoenas on behalf of Basic Resources. Before the French company's own American attorneys, who had been at dinner with them, could knock the documents out of their hands in an effort to prove that they had never received them, Basic's private detectives had taken photographs of the Elf-Aquitaine men actually holding the subpoenas. "We caught them doing business in Houston," Park remembers gleefully.

The Houston Federal Court Judge who was asked to hear the case was not impressed by a battle between two corporations; one run by a company two-thirds owned by the French government, the other apparently controlled by an Anglo-French financier with a colourful reputation. But the court was exceptionally distressed that the French company simply returned the subpoenas it had issued, claiming "sovereign immunity". In the firmest terms Elf-Aquitaine was instructed to return to Houston at once to answer the claim for damages. That decision brought the battle between Basic and Elf-Aquitaine to a head. In Paris the French company decided to do a deal with Jimmy Goldsmith and pull out of the partnership with Basic in Guatemala.

Basic went on to win both its arbitration hearings in Paris and to discover that the Geneva hearing would also come down in its favour. Seven days before the official judgement was promised, Elf-Aquitaine offered Basic a deal – the astonishing sum of $130 million in cash in damages. It was reported in France that Elf was found guilty of "gross negligence" in the operation of their joint company in Guatemala but the final judgement was not made public. As John Park put it now: "It came out very well, we even got a guarantee from Elf of 80 cents a barrel in royalties for every barrel of oil produced in our field for the next twenty years." Basic used its cash to pay off $65 million in debts, distributed $43 million to its shareholders, but kept $20 million as working capital to expand its operations. Then it took a new partner in Guatemala, the Spanish national oil company Hispanoil, who took a half share in a new partnership, and Basic went back to what it wanted to do all along, watch oil being produced by an operating company from the three fields it had already discovered, as well as exploring new ones. Park was still convinced that the experts he had consulted were right, and that his existing three fields contained 200 million barrels of oil, which could be produced at the rate of 65,000 barrels a day. Even with the oil price at $15 a barrel, it still promised to be a profitable investment.

But Jimmy Goldsmith never liked merely to sit and watch. Once the heat had gone out of the Elf-Aquitaine battle and the Texas court had effectively forced the company into a compromise, he was more interested in new opportunities. Although John Park sat in one corner of Générale Occidentale's offices on Fifth Avenue, Basic could now be left to look after itself. Besides, he had no wish to spend long periods of time in the fierce tropical humidity of

Guatemala City, let alone in an oil-drilling camp in the jungle. By the end of 1984 Gilberte Beaux had replaced him as chairman.

Firmly established in a new house provided for him by General Oriental, just off Park Avenue, with a magnificent glass atrium spanning two brownstones and stretching back almost a block, Jimmy Goldsmith now spent at least part of his time living quietly in New York with Laure Boulay de la Meurthe and their daughter Charlotte who had been born in the summer of 1983. As blonde as his other young children in England, Charlotte was being brought up to speak primarily in French, just as he had been by his own mother. The birth had caused his wife Annabel some heartache, not least because she knew only too well her husband's fondness for legitimizing his children by marriage. However, nothing seemed to have changed on his visits to England to see her and their children. They still spent the school holidays together as they had done for years. "He seems as fond of them as he has always done," Annabel Goldsmith told her friends, "there's no difference whatever." Some of the friends still shook their heads in disbelief, but they should have known better. Jimmy Goldsmith was still content to live his life in compartments just as he had done twenty years before. The only difference now was that rather than commuting between London and Paris, he was commuting between London, Paris and New York.

When he arrived in any of the three cities he could not have been more cheerful. "Jimmy is happier than ever," Annabel would explain. The reason was clear enough. Now there was nothing for any of his families to fear: there was now financial security. After the success of Diamond Jimmy Goldsmith knew that his families would always be protected. The spectre of 1957 had finally been erased from his mind.

Besides, new opportunities seemed continually to be coming through the small street door of his new house, with its door mat bearing the legend "I Love New York". Hardly was the ink dry on the final sales of Diamond's assets than he was offered five per cent of the stock of the New York based forest products, energy and insurance conglomerate St Regis Corporation, which had profits of $55 million on sales of $2.8 billion in 1983. "I wasn't really ready for it," Jimmy Goldsmith explains now. "I wasn't ready financially, but when a block of shares was offered to me I bought them, because I thought St Regis was grossly undervalued, and by then I knew a bit about the industry." Significantly, St Regis owned some 3.2 million acres of timberland which were valued at only $223 million in the company's accounts. It made the shares, which cost General Oriental $59.8 million, seem exceptionally good value. It looked like Diamond all over again.

With the help of his friend Jacob Rothschild in London and a group of other investors, Jimmy Goldsmith then built up his St Regis shareholding, spending an extra $50 million. And in February 1984 he filed documents with the American Securities and Exchange Commission, revealing that he and his associates held 3,069,600 of the company's shares, some 8.6 per cent of the total, and had acquired them "for investment purposes". Wall Street analysts put the value of the company at more than $1.4 billion. On the day before St Valentine's Day 1984 the New York Stock Exchange saw a flurry of activity in St Regis shares.

The success of the Diamond takeover meant that no sharp-eyed investor on Wall Street wanted to miss out on what promised to be another spectacular takeover battle with the possibility of exceptional profits. "I went to see St Regis that week," Jimmy Goldsmith recalls now, "and they were panicking all over the place. I couldn't understand it. I remember saying to myself, 'Why are these fellows so scared? They've got a big big company.'" He could hardly believe it. "Anyhow, they wanted to do a deal. So I told them 'OK, I'll do a deal with you, I'll buy 25 per cent of the company. I'll come on the board and I'll stay with you. We'll build this company into a major business.'" Goldsmith made a single condition for his investment of more than $300 million in the company. "If you want to make a significant acquisition or investment, or a divestment of some kind, and the board is not unanimous in its agreement, then I want it to be submitted to the shareholders. If they agree then I'll go along with it."

The chairman of St Regis Corporation, William R. Hasleton, agreed to Jimmy Goldsmith's condition, and the two men began to discuss what would constitute a "significant" acquisition or divestment. "I think I suggested $100 million," Jimmy Goldsmith recalls now, "but they wanted $300 million. I told them 'There's no way that I'm going to be strapped into a vehicle going at very high speed spending hundreds of millions of dollars of my money in it without my having a right to put the brakes on.'"

After a string of meetings in the St Regis offices and at Jimmy Goldsmith's house over the next three weeks, the negotiations gradually ground to a halt. Some of the St Regis directors wanted to turn their company into a diverse amalgam of insurance and other services, while he was insisting that it should concentrate on its core business: forest products.

Finally the St Regis directors told him: "We'd like to buy you out." Without a moment's hesitation Jimmy Goldsmith replied: "Well, I'd like to buy you out," and he contacted Drexel Burnham Lambert to help him do it. Within a few days he had agreed to offer St Regis Corporation $52 for each of its shares, which valued the company at more than $1.8 billion. But St Regis countered by offering him exactly the same price for his shares.

"I told them that getting rid of me would serve them no purpose whatsoever," he remembers, "but they would not listen, so finally I accepted the deal. But I warned them that if they went around looking for a white knight to save them, and finally settled on one, the next morning when they woke up he would be black." Besides, he told them: "If you're looking for a white knight, I'm white and I'm a knight." It did no good at all.

Exactly a month after Jimmy Goldsmith had announced his 8.6 per cent stake in St Regis, the *Wall Street Journal* reported that the corporation had paid him and a group of his associates $52 a share for their 3,069,600 shares, a total of some $159.6 million – "thus averting a possible takeover bid". Jimmy Goldsmith, in association with Jacob Rothschild, the Australian television tycoon Kerry Packer, and the head of the Italian motor company Fiat, Gianni Agnelli, had paid between $33.50 and $38 each for their shares. In the parlance of Wall Street, St Regis Corporation had paid Jimmy Goldsmith "greenmail" (a higher price in dollar bills for their shares than they had paid) for not pursuing them in a hostile takeover. As the *Wall Street Journal* reported: "The Goldsmith group acquired the St Regis shares at an average price of $35.50 a share, or a total of about $109 million. Its profit on yesterday's transaction was thus about $51 million."

Jimmy Goldsmith insists he would rather not have had the profit. "Technically, in today's terminology, they paid us greenmail in the sense that I was getting a premium over the market price of the shares, and they were buying a block of hostile shares at a premium. But my intention was not to do that, I wanted to stay in the company with 25 per cent. I had geared myself up to do that, and I was much more excited by that than the profit." In his mind the bid had been a failure, not a success.

Jimmy Goldsmith's prophecy that getting rid of him "would do St Regis no good at all" turned out to be painfully true. A matter of days after the forest products corporation had paid the Goldsmith group their profit, and seen their share price fall to $37.50 in New York as a result, the Loews Corporation (the hotels, cigarettes and insurance group led by Laurence and Preston Tisch) paid out $100 million for an 8.5 per cent stake in the company. By the end of April St Regis had arranged for the Loews stake to be bought out by Georgia-Pacific, another forest products company. But in June the Australian publishing and television magnate Rupert Murdoch, through his News Corporation and News International companies, bought 5.6 per cent of the company for $65.1 million, and in the middle of July he launched a full-scale offer for the company at $52 a share. St Regis was still not free of corporate raiders. The wheel had come full circle in only four months.

In despair St Regis turned to a white knight to save it from the unwanted attentions of Rupert Murdoch. On 1 August 1984 it announced that it had agreed to being acquired by Champion International for about $1.8 billion. Champion, a Connecticut-based paper, building products and packaging company, had agreed to pay $55.50 for each of the St Regis common shares. Ironically, within three months many of the St Regis directors, including the chairman and deputy chairman, were to find themselves no longer working for the company. "I think they rather regretted afterwards that they hadn't accepted my offer to stay at 25 per cent," Jimmy Goldsmith says now. "I was sorry they didn't, because I didn't want the money, I wanted to build up the company."

But Jimmy Goldsmith never looked back. By the time St Regis had fallen into the hands of Champion, he was already pursuing another forest products conglomerate, the Continental Group. The idea of mounting a takeover for the Connecticut-based Continental, which had sales of almost $5 billion a year, had been brought to him by Robert S. Pirie, the president and chief executive of Rothschilds Inc. in New York. With interests in insurance, oil and gas, as well as in packaging and canning, Continental exactly fitted the pattern Jimmy Goldsmith had set for himself for any company he was planning to take over in the United States. It had the benefit of 1.4 million acres of timberland, as well as an oil reserve estimated at nine million barrels.

On the afternoon of Tuesday 5 June 1984 Jimmy Goldsmith telephoned S. Bruce Smart Jr., Continental's chairman and chief executive officer, to tell him that he wanted to take the company over "on a friendly basis", and that he intended to offer the Continental shareholders $50 in cash for each of their shares. That valued the company at $2.12 billion, but the conversion of all Continental's convertible shares would add a further $300 million to the price. Bruce Smart did not say much on the telephone. He was too stunned. As the *Wall Street Journal* commented the following morning: "The proposed $2.42 billion takeover would be among the largest non-energy acquisitions ever."

There was more than one analyst on Wall Street who was convinced that Jimmy Goldsmith simply did not have that kind of money. As the *Wall Street Journal* put it: "Some professionals were wondering yesterday how Sir James would pay such a tab." Certainly some of Continental Group's advisers doubted he could raise the money, and they told the company's directors so. That was, once again, to underestimate Jimmy Goldsmith.

"We had not built up a very big stake in Continental when we decided to launch the bid," he remembers now, "only about one per cent; but we thought it was another undervalued stock in the market. I explained to the Continental people that I wanted to sell off the extraneous parts, perhaps organize a management buyout on the canning side, and concentrate on the core of the business again." These suggestions were not exactly welcomed by a company which had spent the previous seven years reshaping itself, had specifically expanded into new businesses, and had even bought back some of its own stock in an attempt to stave off any potential takeover bid. So when the rumour started to come back from

Wall Street that its pursuer "just didn't have that sort of money", Continental did not take the bid too seriously. It did not take long for them to change their minds. Jimmy Goldsmith was very serious indeed, and he certainly did have the money.

When negotiations got under way in earnest in the third week of June, he produced a certified cheque for $1 billion to prove it, to go along with guarantees of at least a further $1.4 billion. Continental were still not convinced, so Jimmy Goldsmith raised his "informal offer" to $55 a share, bringing the total size of the bid to $2.66 billion, the biggest foreign takeover bid ever launched in the United States. Still Continental did not accept; instead they decided to put themselves up for sale, and asked for sealed bids. Jimmy Goldsmith's last offer was $58 a share.

On Friday 29 June 1984, barely three weeks after he had first telephoned Continental to express an interest in it, Jimmy Goldsmith learnt that he had been beaten for the company by the private mining and construction company Peter Kiewit, in association with the California-based financier David Murdock. Kiewit at one stage had been one of his informal partners in the takeover – with a 20 per cent interest. The Kiewit/Murdock sealed bid was $58.50 a share. It was the largest acquisition of a publicly-held company by private investors in the history of American business, and the biggest takeover outside the oil industry in Wall Street history; and Jimmy Goldsmith had lost out by just 50 cents a share. The fact that his shareholding was to bring him a profit of about $10 million, and that he was to receive a further $25 million in private compensation payments, was no consolation. Like St Regis, Jimmy Goldsmith thought Continental had been a failure.

"Although Continental was unsuccessful," Robert Pirie of Rothschilds explains, "I think Jimmy came out of it feeling that he could achieve almost anything. And in particular one of their advisers told him that he was mad to go for them, he should be pursuing another forest products company, Crown Zellerbach."

It was not long before he did precisely that although, even while he was considering it, he bought a stake of just under 5 per cent in the famous New York based soap and toothpaste conglomerate Colgate-Palmolive for almost $100 million. It was by no means the only company that he was to take an interest in during the summer of 1984. Jimmy Goldsmith still liked to create the impression that he was doing several things at once to confuse anyone who might want to guess precisely what was in his mind.

When he returned to Europe for a holiday with Annabel and the children in August he made up his mind what to do next. He knew that the problems of Basic were all but resolved. He also knew that the problems of Grand Union seemed finally to be sorting themselves out: a new chief executive, Floyd Hall, had taken over the company. The "dull stores" and the "dull profits" that Jimmy Goldsmith had complained about so fiercely just three years before were being replaced by brighter stores and substantial profits. The affairs of Diamond International were completely sorted out; he had even sold a little timberland for $170 million, but his holdings through General Oriental and Générale Occidentale still amounted to almost 1.4 million acres.

"I knew we were ready to move again," he recalls now. "St Regis had really been too soon, but everything was settled by the autumn of 1984."

When he got back to New York in September he had his first meeting with the new president and chief executive officer of Colgate-Palmolive, Reuben Mark, who asked him directly why he was buying their shares.

"Because I want to buy a major stake in your company, and because I think it's wrongly thought out," Jimmy Goldsmith told him firmly. "You're a conglomerate. You should get rid of the extraneous pieces and use the money to buy in your shares and shrink the capital while the market is cheap; and then you should develop the basic core of the business. As long as you're *not* doing that the business is unsound."

A slightly bemused Reuben Mark said he would think about it. But for almost the first time in an American takeover Jimmy Goldsmith found himself rather liking his potential opponent in a battle. It was eventually to make it impossible for him to proceed against Colgate-Palmolive. Usually there had to be an enemy to be fought for him to pursue a company in a takeover – even if he ended up liking the men he was pursuing enormously (as turned out to be the case with Bill Koslo of Diamond). "Normally I can't go after somebody I like," he would tell his friends privately. But he would pursue to the death any company chairman or chief executive who patronized him, or made the mistake of insulting him or underestimating his achievements.

William T. Creson, the fifty-five-year-old chairman of Crown Zellerbach, made exactly that mistake. When Jimmy Goldsmith sent a tersely-worded telex to the forest product corporation's head-quarters on Bush Street, San Francisco, on the morning of Wednes-day 12 December 1984 announcing that he intended to buy between 15 and 25 per cent of the common stock in Crown Zellerbach Corporation, the company's spokesman immediately described his plan as "unsolicited" and "not in the best interests of the company". Nothing was guaranteed to make Goldsmith angrier, or more deter-mined. He had already begun quietly to buy shares in the company, which were then trading at $28 each in New York, through one of his subsidiaries. By 12 March 1985 he owned 2,375,000 of Crown's 27.2 million ordinary shares, about 8.6 per cent of the company, and he had paid an average price of $33.25 for them, an investment of almost $80 million.

On 19 March, during a trip to Los Angeles to address another Drexel Burnham Lambert conference for institutional investors, Jimmy Goldsmith flew up to San Francisco to have lunch with the blunt and energetic Creson, whose company had $2.4 billion in assets and owned more than two million acres of forest in the United States. The meeting did not go well. While Reuben Mark had kept studiously calm when Jimmy Goldsmith approached him, Creson was rather less so.

"I told him that we were now the largest shareholders," Jimmy Goldsmith recalls now, "that we thought the value of the shares did not reflect the value of the underlying assets, and that we thought there was a possibility of restructuring the company for the benefit of everybody."

Creson did not take kindly to this. But Goldsmith was undeterred. "I also told him that we were not going to go away, and that he had four choices. He could sell the company by tender, as Continental had done; he could work with us and let us build up our stake to 25 per cent as we had wanted to do with St Regis; he could search around for a white knight to save him; or he could bluff himself into thinking we would go away – which we wouldn't. And I told him that we would not accept any kind of greenmail to disappear."

The meeting ended with Jimmy Goldsmith suggesting to Creson that he should telephone him in Los Angeles in the next week; if he didn't telephone it would be assumed that he was taking one of the last two options – a white knight or a bluff. Creson did not telephone.

In the first week of April 1985 Jimmy Goldsmith decided to move quickly and make a takeover bid for Crown Zellerbach. There was only one problem: to defend itself against a potential takeover the company had adopted what Wall Street called a "poison pill" the previous July. Anyone acquiring 100 per cent of the company's stock immediately found themselves facing the prospect of having to compensate the surviving shareholders by effectively paying them double the price of their shares for doing so. It made buying the company outright an exceptionally expensive proposition. Devised by the American attorney Marty Lipton, of the New York firm of Watchtell, Lipton, Rosen & Katz, who also advised Colgate-Palmolive, its objective was to make Crown Zellerbach too expensive for any outside investor to take over.

Undeterred, on Monday 1 April 1985 Jimmy Goldsmith wrote to Creson explaining that if the board of directors withdrew their poison pill he was prepared to buy the company for more than $1.14 billion in cash, offering the shareholders in excess of $41.625 a share, the price that Crown Zellerbach's stock was trading at on the previous Friday afternoon in New York. He gave the directors one week to make up their mind. If they refused to pull the pill he announced that he would immediately launch a legal battle to seek representation on the board of directors at the company's annual general meeting on 9 May.

Creson's response was swift. He announced firmly that the Crown Zellerbach board would not "be hurried, bullied or intimidated", and that they would reply to his letter "at an appropriate time, which may or may not be on or before the April 8 ultimatum". Creson told the *New York Times* that the "poison pill" was in place because of the board's obligation to protect the rights of all shareholders.

A week later Creson had not replied, neither had he withdrawn the poison pill. The *Los Angeles Times* noted that morning: "Crown

Zellerbach, a 115-year-old fixture of the West Coast business community, is engaged in a fight for its corporate life." On 10 April Jimmy Goldsmith, advised by Drexel Burnham Lambert and Rothschild Inc., offered to purchase for cash up to 19 million shares in the common stock of Crown Zellerbach at $42.50 a share. It was an offer that could cost more than $800 million.

Not that Crown Zellerbach looked all that much a prize to some. Like Diamond it had been called "a load of junk" and "sluggish" before Creson himself became chief executive in 1981. Then it was still "saddled with some of the most antiquated paper mills in the country" in the words of one Wall Street analyst. Creson had cut 9,000 of the corporation's 28,000 employees and sold off some of its loss-making Canadian operations, as well as pursuing the lucrative markets for tissues more actively. The company's Marina and Chiffon toilet paper, Nice 'n' Soft tissues and Spill Mate paper towels had the largest share of the towel and tissue market in California. Creson had even branched out into computers, launching Eczel Corporation to distribute ribbons, discs, print wheels and cables for the computer industry. But although the company had climbed back into profit, and its sales had exceeded $3 billion a year again in 1984 for the first time for two years, its recovery had not convinced every observer.

The Crown Zellerbach directors were convinced, however, and they eventually responded to Jimmy Goldsmith's tender offer of $42.50 a share by putting themselves up for sale – at $60 a share. The company's spokesman announced: "We're telling shareholders that if we can't find a white knight we'll liquidate the company." The battle was on. Four days later Jimmy Goldsmith and Crown Zellerbach traded law suits: one demanding the withdrawal of the poison pill, the other claiming that Goldsmith was in violation of securities laws in offering $42.50 a share.

William T. Creson even found time to address a hearing of the Senate Finance Committee in Washington on Monday 22 April 1985. He compared Jimmy Goldsmith to "the men who pillaged England and Ireland in the ninth and tenth centuries", condemned him for creating no real wealth "but rather taking over assets painfully built up by others" and destroying companies "that built our nation's long-term wealth". He even suggested that it was not clear whether Jimmy Goldsmith paid any United States income tax on his "pirating".

By then Crown Zellerbach thought that they had found a white knight, in the shape of Burnell R. Roberts, the chairman of the Mead Corporation, to save them from the attentions of the pillaging Jimmy Goldsmith. Over the weekend private negotiations had led to a Mead offer of $50 a share. Creson could afford to insult Jimmy Goldsmith, or so he thought. The only difficulty turned out to be that Mead did not proceed with their offer. After protracted arguments over the precise price per share, the negotiations broke down.

Without its white knight Crown Zellerbach decided to counter-attack by revealing its own plans for the future. "We believe our board of directors is better positioned to maximize values for all our shareholders than Sir James Goldsmith," the company stated firmly; although they did try in some small way to appease him. In the last week of April they privately offered him two seats on the board of directors and to withdraw their poison pill, providing he would enter into a "standstill" agreement which would prevent him from buying any more than 19.5 per cent of the company for three years. Jimmy Goldsmith turned the offer down flat. After the insults of the previous few days he refused to accept less than 33 per cent of the company, and demanded that his two directorships should be reinforced by a new rule that less than unanimous decisions by the Crown Zellerbach board should be referred to a vote of the shareholders "to eliminate any further unilateral actions – any future poison pills". When, predictably, Crown Zellerbach's board turned down his demands Jimmy Goldsmith withdrew his tender offer.

Then Crown Zellerbach announced it was going to split itself into three separate companies: one would be composed of 1.6 million acres of their timberlands (with an estimated value of at least $800 million); another of their speciality plastics and packaging business (which might have annual sales of $500 million); and the third consisting of the rest of the original company – which might have annual sales of $2.25 billion. Jimmy Goldsmith became more determined than ever to take over the company. The only question was exactly how? The poison pill was still in place, and the share price had risen to more than $44 in the wake of his bid, in the belief, as

Business Week magazine put it at the end of April: "Goldsmith or another suitor will eventually topple the company." While he decided what to do he left America for England, to spend part of the Easter holidays with Annabel and the children.

By the time he got back to New York at the end of the first week of May he had made up his mind. "It was the Bovril plan all over again." He went back into the market place and bought more of Crown Zellerbach's stock. By 8 May 1985 he owned 5,356,700 of Crown Zellerbach's 27.2 million shares, 19.6 per cent of the total. In the previous two days he had bought 2.8 million more shares in the company, at a cost of nearly $120 million, more than two million had come from the New York arbitrageur Ivan Boesky – a professional dealer on Wall Street with a reputation for buying stock in companies that were the subject of takeover battles. He also demanded that Crown Zellerbach postpone their annual general meeting the following day because "shareholders have been presented with a most confusing picture". On behalf of Crown Zellerbach William T. Creson called the move "without merit and it will be vigorously resisted". There was still no sign of a compromise or a white knight other than Sir James Michael Goldsmith.

In his New York house Jimmy Goldsmith came home after dinner on the evening of 9 May, the day of the Crown Zellerbach annual general meeting, turned on the giant television in his first-floor sitting room, and discovered William T. Creson telling his shareholders fiercely that "there's no way we're going to pay Goldsmith greenmail". As he had already told Creson specifically in March that he would not accept it, and put that decision in writing "to make it legally binding", the announcement contrived to make Jimmy Goldsmith even angrier. "They had been trying to push greenmail down my throat and I'd been refusing it," he says now, "and three days after that meeting the Crown directors offered me $100 million in greenmail to leave them alone. But I turned them down. By this time I was boiling."

But there was still the poison pill to protect Crown Zellerbach: or so the company believed.

"When we got to 19 per cent," Jimmy Goldsmith remembers now, "I told them I was going to explode the pill and buy more shares. They didn't believe me. All along they thought I was bluffing."

Crown Zellerbach found that he wasn't. He filed papers with the Securities and Exchange Commission warning that he intended to buy more than the limit of 20 per cent, and accepted the risk. What Crown Zellerbach and the lawyers of Watchtell, Lipton, Rosen & Katz had not taken into account was that Jimmy Goldsmith, or anyone else, might not actually want 100 per cent of the company their poison pill was designed to protect. What they had failed to realize was that Jimmy Goldsmith might stop short of 100 per cent of the company – in which case the poison pill would have no effect whatsoever.

Even worse than that, however, once Jimmy Goldsmith had "exploded the pill" by buying more than 20 per cent of Crown Zellerbach's shares, the company could not retrieve the rights it had given its shareholders by the poison pill provision in July 1984. That meant it could not turn to anyone else to buy 100 per cent of the company, because to do so would have the effect of triggering their own pill – and doubling the price of the purchase. Once Jimmy Goldsmith had bought more than 20 per cent of the company their own poison pill effectively isolated them from any white knight that might suddenly appear. As Robert S. Pirie of Rothschilds put it later: "Eventually the poison pill was an enormous help to us because once it was exploded Crown could do no deals and we were able to buy the stock for less than our tender offer price of $42.50."

By the end of the third week of May Jimmy Goldsmith owned 26 per cent of Crown Zellerbach's shares, and it was all too clear to the company that he could be kept at bay no longer. Finally, on Saturday 25 May, Creson came to his house off Park Avenue and called a truce. As Jimmy Goldsmith paced up and down his sitting room, chewing the end of his Davidoff Number One cigar and waving it in the air, the fifty-five-year-old forest products executive, who had not long before had open heart surgery, sat stiffly on one of his cream sofas and agreed on a restructuring plan for Crown Zellerbach. In return for Jimmy Goldsmith's agreement that General Oriental Securities Limited, which had been buying Crown Zellerbach's shares, would buy no more unless it gave ten days' notice of intent to do so, Jimmy Goldsmith was to join the Crown

Zellerbach board of directors, and all litigation between the two sides was to be suspended.

The battle looked over. As the *Wall Street Journal* reported on the morning of 28 May: "Crown Zellerbach and Sir James Goldsmith moved toward ending their six-month struggle for control of the forest product company." Once again it did not turn out to be the case.

Throughout June the two sides discussed a restructuring plan, but as the month dragged on it became increasingly clear that they could not agree. In particular Jimmy Goldsmith did not want Crown Zellerbach to sell 1.6 million acres of its timberlands to a partnership, "because I believed it would saddle the shareholders with a tax bill of almost $180 million". But at "one of the harshest board meetings I've ever attended", on Monday 1 July at the company's head-quarters, Jimmy Goldsmith thought he had finally got a deal. The timberlands would be sold to a corporation not a partnership, and a string of other less significant issues were settled. "It was everything that I'd asked before, but which had been turned down," he recalls now.

A delighted Jimmy Goldsmith left San Francisco, first for New York and then for a holiday. He had hired a yacht and intended cruising in the Eastern Mediterranean, off the coast of Turkey, for about a month. But he had taken the precaution of installing a satellite telephone on the yacht to keep in touch with what was happening in San Francisco. Roland Franklin was to stay there in case there was anything to be sorted out while the lawyers were drawing up the agreement made at the board meeting. The deal was to be ratified at the next Crown Zellerbach board meeting on Tuesday 9 July.

By the time Jimmy Goldsmith reached his yacht off the coast of Turkey on Thursday 4 July 1985, however, it was clear that not everything was going according to plan in San Francisco. "Roland could not reach anybody, and things were rather strange." He was not unduly concerned, because he had agreed to participate in the board meeting the following Tuesday by telephone. It may not have been quite what the Crown Zellerbach directors were accustomed to, but their company's largest single shareholder had never particularly cared for convention.

His satellite call from the Eastern Mediterranean to San Francisco did not go well. "Over the telephone I heard that we had pulled out of the deal, which is why it was not now going forward, and the board was now going to vote against it."

A shocked Jimmy Goldsmith shouted into his telephone, "We pulled out of the deal? I don't understand. Why?"

"Because the lawyers couldn't agree on it."

"Of course lawyers can't agree on things, lawyers always bring up problems, that's why Roland Franklin has been in San Francisco, to sort things out. Why didn't you call him and tell him there was a problem?"

"Your people lacked faith in the deal," Creson told him over the telephone.

An incensed Jimmy Goldsmith shouted: "Look, it's very straightforward. There are two minor technical points to be settled, but I am willing to sign the agreement. You say we pulled out, I say you pulled out. The proof of the pudding is who is willing to sign and who is not willing to sign. I am, are you?"

The Crown Zellerbach board was asked by its chairman William Creson if it was willing to sign their agreement with Jimmy Goldsmith. The answer was no. Creson told him they had lost faith.

"This is an incredible situation," Jimmy Goldsmith fumed from 8,000 miles away. "Here is an agreement you say I'm reneging on but which you're not willing to sign, and you say I'm the one who's reneging on it. I can't understand it."

The Crown Zellerbach board of directors did not budge. It voted to reject the deal done with Jimmy Goldsmith only eight days before, and put the timberlands into a partnership.

"As far as I was concerned that was war, total, absolute, final and irreversible war," Jimmy Goldsmith remembers now. "The next morning we went into the market and we started buying. We bought and bought and bought until we got 51 per cent of the company." That took barely a week. While Crown Zellerbach's senior executives went on a rapid tour of their principal shareholders trying to persuade them not to sell their stock in the company, Jimmy Goldsmith's representatives acquired a further 9.6 per cent of the company, giving him about 35.6 per cent. And between 15 and 19

July they bought a further 13.7 per cent, giving him 49.3 per cent. At the same time they assured him of a further 1.4 per cent.

Just ten days after the Crown Zellerbach board had refused to sign their agreement with Jimmy Goldsmith he effectively owned 51 per cent of the company – even if he was sailing in the Mediterranean. And he had bought the extra shares at less than the $42.50 he had tendered for them in April. On the evening of Sunday 21 July there was another conversation between Creson and Jimmy Goldsmith on the satellite telephone. This time the tone was rather different. The battle was over.

On the morning of Thursday 25 July Jimmy Goldsmith flew into New York from Paris on Concorde for just one day to become chairman of Crown Zellerbach. "I was no longer angry. I'd won, so I tried to do a deal which people could live with rather than destroy them." He now controlled a majority of the directors on a new eleven-man board of directors. William T. Creson became the company's president, and stayed its chief executive officer. The poison pill had been overcome, as the *Wall Street Journal* explained formally the following morning, "by withdrawing a formal tender offer and simply acquiring majority control of the company through stock purchases on the open market". Wall Street put it a little more bluntly: "Jimmy swallowed Crown and spat out the pill." The investment had cost him a little over $550 million.

But the final capitulation of Crown Zellerbach was not the only deal Jimmy Goldsmith did in New York that day. While the lawyers were drafting the final details of the Crown agreement he slipped next door to the Waldorf-Astoria where Reuben Mark of Colgate-Palmolive kept an apartment. Mark told him that Colgate-Palmolive was adopting some of the plans that he had suggested almost nine months before, and asked for his support "because we will be fragile while we're doing it and we could be liable to a takeover". Jimmy Goldsmith told Mark that he would do nothing at all, and wished him good luck. Indeed, within six months he was to sell his stake in the famous toothpaste and soap company "at a reasonable profit". The shrewd and diplomatic Mark had avoided the fate that had befallen Creson and Crown Zellerbach by not making Jimmy Goldsmith angry, and by listening to what he was saying.

As he caught Concorde back to Paris on the morning of Friday 26 July 1985 Jimmy Goldsmith was in no doubt who he would rather be doing business with, but in no doubt also that the battle to win control of Crown Zellerbach had been worth it. When *Business Week* magazine suggested two weeks later that he might find the company "a thorny problem", particularly as it had announced declining profits for the second quarter of 1985 on the very day he had become its chairman, Jimmy Goldsmith was not about to abandon his holiday in Europe. What the magazine did not know was that he had already decided on his first deal to recoup some of his investment: he intended to sell the principal paper and tissue-producing parts of the company to the James River Corporation of Virginia, who had bought paper mills from him in the Diamond deal in 1983.

By mid-December 1985 James River's chairman Brenton S. Halsey had agreed to exchange up to 22.6 million new James River shares for Crown's, giving the Crown Zellerbach shareholders stock worth betwen $41 and $44 for each of their shares, which had been trading at $28 just a year earlier. As *Business Week* admitted: "Christmas came early this year to James River Corp., Sir James Goldsmith, and, most of all, the shareholders of Crown Zellerbach Corp." That was not quite the full extent of Jimmy Goldsmith's presents. James River also agreed to pay $225 million for a Crown container business if he could not find a higher bidder for it before 1987.

In exchange for his $550 million investment in 13.6 million Crown Zellerbach shares, Jimmy Goldsmith had won control of 1.9 million acres of timberlands; $90 million in cash, and assets he could sell worth more than $330 million, plus Eczel. Most important of all he had gained control of the timberlands at a price of less than $100 an acre, at a time when most industry analysts argued they were worth at least $500 an acre if they were not sold quickly. When anyone asked him what he intended to do with them, Jimmy Goldsmith just smiled. "We'll just have to wait and see if I'm right that the value of timber will go up."

If Diamond had been the breakthrough deal for Jimmy Goldsmith, Crown Zellerbach was to confirm his place as one of America's most adventurous, but least predictable, corporate raiders. And everyone in the United States seemed to know it. After spending Christmas in Europe, with Annabel and the children in London, and paying a visit to Ginette in Paris, he flew back to New York to see Laure and Charlotte. As he flew into Kennedy Airport on 26 December 1985 the customs officer stopped him.

"Say, are you the Goldsmith that made the $500 million on that Diamond deal?" he asked.

Slightly taken aback, Jimmy Goldsmith admitted he was.

"Say, fellas, this is the guy that made the $500 million," the customs man shouted in the all but deserted baggage hall. "Listen, I wanna shake your hand. Any guy that can do that has to be something."

Slightly sheepish, but utterly delighted, Jimmy Goldsmith suddenly found himself surrounded by a group of enthusiastic, back-slapping Americans, all of them anxious to shake his hand and congratulate him for doing what he had always liked: deals. "I'm not used to people being so nice to me," he said afterwards. Suddenly he felt very much at home in the United States.

In celebration he and Laure took off on a six-week trip to Bali and South America in the private Boeing 727 he had hired to travel across America during the height of the Crown Zellerbach negotiations. But even while he was on the plane he was still planning. There was a property company in France that looked interesting, and a new magazine to be launched by *L'Express*, not to mention the new oil exploration rights in Guatemala that Basic had just been offered. Even on holiday Jimmy Goldsmith still did what he liked doing best – thinking about a deal. By the time he got back to Europe again in March 1986 Gilberte Beaux had all but got the property company, and Roland Franklin had devised a way of restructuring Crown Zellerbach for the best profit. *Forbes* magazine estimated later that it would bring him between $65 and $70 for each of his Crown shares; a paper profit of between $340 and $400 million.

In just five years in the United States Jimmy Goldsmith had made profits from his deals estimated at more than $1 billion, and seen the annual turnover of Générale Occidentale and General Oriental rise towards $4 billion. In the process he had made himself a dollar billionaire – "at a conservative estimate" – and he was well on the way to becoming one of the richest men in the world. If his companies were to sell their holdings of timberlands alone at a price of $500 an acre that would raise $1.75 billion; and that was before the holdings in Guatemalan oil, Grand Union supermarkets, or even Aspinall's casino in London were considered. Not that he was content to stop there. As he had explained to *Fortune* magazine in the middle of the Crown Zellerbach deal, takeovers may be interpreted by some corporate raiders as "for the public good – but that's not why I do it. I do it to make money."

As he had once said: "The secret is to create new ambitions the whole time."

In the late summer of 1986 he found two. Sitting in his new house in Spain, surrounded by Annabel and the children, he settled on a new American target – Goodyear Tire and Rubber, the 35th largest company in the United States with sales worth more than $10 billion a year. In late August he began quietly buying Goodyear shares and on 29 October he announced that he had acquired 11.5 per cent of the company's 109 million shares, at a cost of some $530 million. By 5 November he was telling Goodyear's executives that he was prepared to offer $49 for every share he did not own to gain control of the company – a move that would cost him $4.7 billion. It was the beginning of one of the most acrimonious takeover battles Wall Street had witnessed in the 1980s, but one which was destined to last barely two weeks.

In the face of his bid Goodyear rapidly came up with a restructuring plan almost identical to the one he had in mind for the company, "and the rationale for the bid evaporated," he explains now. "On top of that, the political situation in Ohio [where Goodyear had its headquarters] was at such a nuclear level that I'm not sure we could have managed to do what we wanted to do as well as the present management." Finally, on the night of 19 November, Jimmy Goldsmith reluctantly called off his takeover bid for Goodyear and sold his shareholding back to the company for more than $620 million, a profit of $93 million. But there was some consolation in Europe. Just as he announced the end of his Goodyear bid he gained control of France's second largest publisher, Presses de la Cité, after outwitting the Italian industrialist Carlo De Benedetti. The company cost him just $450 million.

23

The Power to Influence

So not everything in the United States had gone as well as Diamond and Crown Zellerbach. The boyish, almost naïve, enthusiasm which had taken Jimmy Goldsmith into America in the first place had not always ensured success. While the peaks of his major corporate take-overs were being scaled, and the jungle battle against Elf-Aquitaine was being fought, so the difficulties of Grand Union, his American supermarket chain, had multiplied. If Guatemala had been an expensive headache, Grand Union had quickly developed into a nightmare, and one destined to cost him $150 million in just one year.

On the surface Grand Union had looked all right. The chain had traded successfully enough since its purchase in 1973. A few of the older stores had been closed, and some others modernized. In August 1978 the Colonial group, 359 additional supermarkets, had been added – after Jimmy Goldsmith had initiated a deal on the telephone from Bombay – bringing the chain to almost 700. And in November 1979 he bought a further 100 J. Weingarten stores based in Texas to go with them.

A new-style Grand Union "Food Market", bringing the flavour of a European delicatessen into the traditional American supermarket, was launched successfully in Wyckoff, New Jersey, in 1979, and for a time everything seemed to be going smoothly. In fact, the merger of three separate supermarket chains, each with a different tradition and different systems, turned out to be unwieldy and expensive. As Floyd Hall, now chairman of the Grand Union company, puts it: "I guess the Colonial people didn't really want to hear anything the Grand Union people had to say and vice versa – so instead of a merger and a blending together of the two companies they got exactly the opposite result." When Weingarten was added the problems grew still faster.

Then, in 1981, Jim Wood, Jimmy Goldsmith's old ally from Cavenham, the Co-operative manager who had transformed the British supermarkets, was tempted away from running Grand Union by the A&P chain. Shortly after his departure the underlying difficulties in Grand Union finally surfaced. In October 1981 the company reported rapidly declining profits, and it became abundantly clear that a crisis was looming. Not quite sure what else to do, for a time Jimmy Goldsmith took control of Grand Union himself.

One thing became abundantly clear to him as he looked more and more closely at his supermarket chain in the last gloomy months of 1981, Grand Union may have been the eighth largest chain in the United States, but what he saw was "a dull company with no vision, no new thinking, bureaucratically managed and producing dull profits which were set to decline". Jim Wood had turned the company round brilliantly, but Jimmy Goldsmith was less certain that he had set it on a path that guaranteed financial success. He decided to treat Grand Union as if it was a newly acquired company. He might not be a natural manager but he was confident he knew the strategy to ensure its future.

Seizing on his European experience, Jimmy Goldsmith encouraged Grand Union to invest even more heavily in the "Food Market" concept it had already tested in New Jersey. He wanted to establish supermarkets with specialist and gourmet food departments – fresh fish shops and working bakeries within the stores – with higher levels of customer service than was usual. And he also wanted a new design concept to differentiate his Grand Union (and Big Star) supermarkets from all the others in the United States. Together with the New York designer Milton Glaser he decided that the graphics were going to be bolder, the entrances more exciting, and the displays more like those of a local grocery store than a modern supermarket. It was a considerable risk. If Diamond was to see some of its assets sold off, so Grand Union was to demand that its assets be expensively improved. "It's the exact opposite of asset stripping," Jimmy Goldsmith was to say wearily during the process. "But Grand Union has always been a long-term investment."

As the transformation of the Grand Union chain began, so the financial difficulties increased. Sales fell by almost 15 per cent, from more than $4 billion a year to about $3.5 billion – although the gross profits as a percentage of those sales crept up marginally. Jimmy Goldsmith decided his chain was too large; the Colonial supermarkets did not fit in with his new idea. Throughout 1982 and 1983 Grand Union closed supermarkets, gradually shrinking the chain from more than 700 stores to less than 400. From sales of $3.5 billion in 1982 – which brought in profits of just $226,000 – sales fell to $3.4 billion in 1983 and the group made an operating loss of $115 million ($48 million of it set aside to pay for the closures).

"At the time I was considered mad," Jimmy Goldsmith recalls now. "The trade press said we were gambling with the business like a chip on the table. But I had to do something. If I'd let Grand Union go along as before the whole thing would have died."

His mind was made up, and – significantly – he had also accepted that he could not run the chain himself. After a lengthy search, in March 1984 he managed to persuade the talented chairman and chief executive of Target Stores in the United States, Floyd Hall, to take over as chairman and chief executive of Grand Union. Tall, relaxed and able, Hall had started in the B. Dalton bookstore chain and seen his career blossom spectacularly. One American retailing magazine called him "the leading shopkeeper in the USA".

By the time Hall arrived Jimmy Goldsmith had already made the emotional decision to pull out of Texas, where his Weingarten chain had its base, as well as Florida and Washington DC, and to concentrate instead on the north-eastern United States. Hall implemented the strategy and pulled the company out of the red in six months. But he also put in new management systems to get rid of what he still calls "the old seat-of-the-pants style".

Nevertheless, when Hall took over Grand Union he inherited a supermarket chain which had been through a traumatic two years. In his first annual report, almost eighteen months later, he wrote: "If there can be a Year One for a 113-year-old company, it would be 1984/85. Some things were ended but much was begun." One thing that was begun again was profit. In 1984 Hall managed to shepherd Grand Union to a $5 million profit to set against its $115 million loss the previous year.

In retrospect Hall pays tribute to Jimmy Goldsmith's style of leadership. "I'd say probably the overriding thing is that Jimmy is a gentleman. He would never humiliate, ridicule or embarrass anyone. That's probably just the opposite of most of the dynamic individuals in America, who almost always ride roughshod over most of the individuals they come into contact with, certainly their employees. How many people do you know who would spend $115 million of their money doing what they think is right for a chain they could have sold?"

Looking back Jimmy Goldsmith admits: "It was a very hard period for me. I spent a great deal of time on Grand Union." He also spent a great deal of money which at the time was sorely needed elsewhere, notably for the Diamond and Crown Zellerbach takeovers. It may take a decade or more for his investment in new stores, new designs and packaging, new advertising and management styles, to pay dividends.

By the end of 1985 Grand Union had just 379 stores and 23,000 employees, an annual turnover of just $2.6 billion, and it had become the tenth rather than the eighth largest supermarket chain in the United States. But it was making an annual profit before tax of about $60 million. Floyd Hall is convinced that the financial corner has been turned. "I see us closing five or six stores a year, but I'm hopeful we'll open five or six a year, and when we shake out about twenty we're currently operating, then I think we'll be opening faster than we're closing." For his part Jimmy Goldsmith believes: "Grand Union is now booming, and the best US companies are now copying us. The current year's pre-tax profit should exceed $50 million." He has no intention of abandoning the business which first helped Cavenham in England to expand significantly – supermarkets. "I have been a grocer for almost thirty-five years; I intend to remain one."

But the problems of Grand Union highlighted one of Jimmy Goldsmith's weaknesses. They demonstrated clearly that he is not, and never has been, a natural manager. He is a strategist and a risk-taker, but not a man content – or equipped – to run a single business for a prolonged period of time. Goldsmith is not the legendary Texas oil man H. L. Hunt, a man fascinated by the complexities of a single industry, whose fortune grows as the industry that is its focus prospers. Jimmy Goldsmith is too restless for that, and too concerned with far horizons. The concentrated vision necessary to run a single concern inhibits him and makes him uncomfortable. In recent years he has preferred to devote his attention to wider and wider issues: judging the swings of the markets in the United States or Europe, trying to sense the shifts in political climate for his commercial benefit. Indeed, it is this more than anything else that now principally occupies his energies. And it brings him – elliptically – into the political arena. For though he may have long since abandoned the thought of a political career in England, the possibility that he may have political influence as a result of his commercial power and success, coupled with his strategic vision, is now firmly part of his ambitions. Jimmy Goldsmith sees himself as part of the political debate in Europe and the United States: with the financial strength to exert influence, often substantial influence.

As his old friend Arnaud de Borchgrave, now editor of the *Washington Times* puts it: "Jimmy is not interested in power. He is a man who is interested in influence, which is quite different."

One particular subject, above any other, concerned him: the susceptibility of Western governments and the Western media to infiltration and covert manipulation by the Soviet Union. One of the first indications of his interest in the subject was a speech to the Media Committee of the British Conservative Party in the House of Commons in January 1981. In it he described the way in which he believed European newspapers and magazines were being used, often without their appreciating it, by communist propagandists. In particular he cited Major-General Jan Sejna, a defector from Czechoslovak intelligence, who insisted that the campaign by the German news magazine *Der Spiegel* to discredit Franz Josef Strauss was orchestrated by the KGB.

The flamboyant, portly Strauss, a butcher's son from Munich who had been West Germany's Minister of Defence from 1956 until 1962, and is still Prime Minister of Bavaria, had been subjected to prolonged and bitter criticism by *Der Spiegel*, West Germany's most influential news magazine, throughout his period in charge of the defence ministry. This came at a time when many West Germans were predicting that Strauss would eventually become the successor to the German Chancellor Konrad Adenauer. The possibility was effectively brought to a halt by the magazine.

Jimmy Goldsmith's swingeing criticism of *Der Spiegel* and its campaign against Strauss during the early 1960s projected him back into European politics again. Shortly after his speech was reprinted in *Now!* in February 1981, during the last few weeks of its existence, the publishers of *Der Spiegel* issued a writ for libel. And the West German magazine demanded damages and costs. They claimed that Jimmy Goldsmith had inferred that *Der Spiegel* and its management "either were owned or had been subsidized by, or on behalf of, a foreign power; had been penetrated by journalists sympathetic to communist propaganda or, alternatively, had been bought by Soviet agencies in the most direct sense of the word".

"I never suggested that *Spiegel* was *knowingly* used," Jimmy Goldsmith says now. "I said it had been used. So have most newspapers, including, on occasion, my own." But this was one political issue on which he was determined to fight. Some might accuse him of using it as a springboard to gain political influence, others as yet further evidence of an obsessive anti-communism, but he was unconcerned. As soon as *Der Spiegel* announced the libel action, he responded by saying that he would defend against it. And he set about collecting as much information as he could on the techniques applied by the Soviet Union to manipulate the Western media organizations. He also had a more personal reason for the fight.

"Obviously my interest in the case was aroused by the fact that the methods used by *Der Spiegel* to discredit Strauss were almost identical to those used by *Private Eye* and their friends against me. The false association with bad people, etc."

Jimmy Goldsmith applied himself to the cause with the same intensity that he had brought to his case against *Private Eye* six years before. He spent the next three years personally interviewing defectors of every kind in his houses in New York, Paris and London, gradually assembling information on the techniques the Soviet Union used in the Western media. In September 1981 he even announced a £50,000 prize in England for "the best investigative journalism into subversion in the media" and he grew increasingly convinced, as Chapman Pincher of the London *Daily Express* also concluded, that "the threat to our freedoms from the active-measures campaigns is far more serious than even the British and European secret services, with all their knowledge, are prepared to accept". Yet once again, to many people in Britain it seemed to underline his tendency to exaggerate. Not for the first time he was portrayed as a wild-eyed right-wing demagogue. Few people noticed when late in 1985 he finally announced that he had awarded his prize jointly to the Greek journalist Paul Anastasi – for his investigation of Soviet agents in Greece which had seen him imprisoned – and John Barron of *Reader's Digest* for investigating other infiltration. (The London Press Association news agency thought it so insignificant they declined to put the announcement on their wire.)

His attack on Soviet manipulation of the Western media was not ignored or decried in the United States, however. Quite the opposite. It turned Jimmy Goldsmith into one of the country's experts on Soviet disinformation. In recognition of the fact, in May 1984 he was invited to address the Defense Strategy Forum of the National Strategy Information Center. As Dr Roy Godson, professor in International Relations at Georgetown University and an expert in Soviet propaganda techniques, explains: "Jimmy is beginning to have an intellectual impact on the United States because he is a supporter of study in Soviet disinformation. But he does not fit into the conventional Left–Right moulds; those labels do not fit him at all."

His Washington speech was, in effect, an enlarged version of the one he had given three years before in the House of Commons, except that he now had the results of his own research and conversations with Soviet bloc defectors to inject into it. He began by reminding his audience that "Freedom of the press is fundamental to the protection of the citizen against the power of the State. It is a prerequisite to liberty . . . But how should we react when allies of a totalitarian system try to use the freedom of our press as a protective screen behind which they can conspire to destroy freedom itself?"

Then Jimmy Goldsmith told the large Washington audience, which included representatives from the American Central Intelligence Agency: "There are lessons to be learned from the conflict between Carthage and Rome. The Carthaginians were a great semitic people. When they needed to, they knew how to fight. Their greatest general, Hannibal, led his troops to victory in battles against Rome. But the Carthaginians were a mercantile civilization. They were traders and merchants and they interpreted the motives of the Romans according to mercantile logic. Rome was different. Rome's purpose was military conquest and imperial expansion. This the Carthaginians were never able to understand, and so ultimately Carthage was destroyed . . . Today in the West we are like Carthage, and Moscow like Rome. We seem incapable of understanding Moscow's way of thinking."

He went on to list at length the evidence he had compiled from Russian defectors and dissidents; to explain that many of the most influential agents recruited by the KGB were in fact journalists; and to outline the difficulties that some journalists who had attempted to establish that connection had faced. But in particular he devoted himself to the details of the case of Franz Josef Strauss and *Der Spiegel* whose campaign the American columnist William F. Buckley later described as "Strauss's Chappaquiddick".

He encouraged the American press to take up the fight. "The media face a major challenge. How can they defend themselves from these campaigns without restricting freedom of expression?" And he specifically pointed out that all too often a campaign was carried along by journalists only following what had become "fashionable opinion" among their profession. "It takes no courage to be fashionable, to express conventional wisdom and comfortably to join the pack in attacking some wounded stag. Courage resides in saying the truth that does not please and which can make you a pariah in the eyes of your peers. That precisely is the duty of the press and one of the great justifications for the freedom of the press."

Jimmy Goldsmith was identifying himself with Franz Josef Strauss, and every other man who had been pilloried unfairly in a Western newspaper or magazine, whether the orchestrators of their fate had been the KGB or journalists themselves. His speech was received enthusiastically in a Washington that was about to see the return of Ronald Reagan for a second term as President. As Roy Godson puts it, reflecting a substantial strain of opinion in the

American capital: "I know few men who have such a firm grasp of strategic reality in politics as he does nor many who can be as constructive." While Arnaud de Borchgrave is convinced that ultimately, "Jimmy will be an important media influence in the United States, because he is interested in restoring balance to journalism in this country."

Yet, by a strange irony – just as in his case against *Private Eye* – when it finally came to the crucial hearing Jimmy Goldsmith did not get a chance to present his evidence on the manipulation of *Der Spiegel* in court. On this occasion it was not he who chose to settle without going through with the hearing – quite the opposite; *Der Spiegel* itself backed away from going through with the libel case against him at the very last minute. "I was the defendant in the action," he says now, "and the defendant cannot force the plaintiff to pursue the case." When the publishers of *Der Spiegel* let it be known through their lawyers in September 1984 that they wished to settle their libel action against him out of court, Jimmy Goldsmith had to accept. "As far as I was concerned we had won, and without the need to spend three valuable months in court."

In the High Courts of Justice in London on the sunny morning of 8 October 1984 Lord Rawlinson, a former British Attorney General, acting for Jimmy Goldsmith, explained gravely that his client was convinced, and could prove, that "the Soviets conduct massive and continuous propaganda campaigns both overt and covert . . . the ultimate object of the campaigns is the undermining of free Western societies and political systems".

Rawlinson told the court that, "It is Sir James's position that in pursuance of these policies, the Soviets made a conscious decision to seek to discredit the West German politician Franz Josef Strauss and mounted a campaign of defamation, disinformation, and provocation against him," adding "the Soviets decided to make use in that campaign of the fact that *Der Spiegel* was well known as opposing Dr Strauss's political views and regularly published articles expressing that position".

The tall, grey-haired barrister concluded by stating that "had the case continued Sir James would have called high-level Soviet and Soviet bloc defectors, who in their former capacity as officers of the KGB or satellite intelligence services, had themselves been involved in disinformation or the penetration of Western media including the recruitment of Western agents of influence, among them journalists".

What had promised to be both a spectacular and politically significant case for the European and American media, however, was never heard. No sooner had Lord Rawlinson finished his statement than Mr John Wilmers QC, appearing for *Der Spiegel*, announced that his clients "fully accept that broadly speaking Soviet Intelligence seeks to operate in the way stated . . . although they themselves were not conscious of having been used in the manner mentioned by Sir James Goldsmith. My clients are conscious of the dangers to press freedom posed by Soviet covert propaganda".

The court statements were repeated in advertisements in the *New York Times* and the *Wall Street Journal*, as well as in *The Times* in London. To Jimmy Goldsmith that was conclusive proof of his victory. "Once *Spiegel* had decided to withdraw our only course was to repeat the words complained of. This we did in our advertisements and this was publicly accepted in the High Court by *Spiegel*."

Though his laborious collection of evidence from Soviet defectors on the influence of Soviet intelligence agencies on journalists in the West was not revealed in open court, "the evidence was disseminated in the appropriate places", he says now. And a year later one of the British journalists who took his case seriously from the start, Chapman Pincher, formerly of the *Daily Express* and an expert on intelligence, published much of his research in the book *The Secret Offensive* in Britain and the United States.

Standing outside the London court Jimmy Goldsmith told the waiting reporters enthusiastically: "It was never my intention to imply that *Der Spiegel* was at any time aware that it was being used by the KGB." He went on to say firmly: "I made no concessions whatever on the substance of my 1981 speech . . . The agreed Statement of 8 October 1984 is a famous victory for the defence of the West against its main enemy, Soviet imperialism."

As he puts it now: "The acid test of which side has won is very simple – can the words complained of be repeated without fear of being sued or can they not? In the Lucan case anyone who repeats the allegations made by *Private Eye* against me is going to be whacked for six. In the *Spiegel* case anyone is freely entitled to repeat my words which were complained of by *Der Spiegel*."

But his "famous victory" turned sour in the hands of parts of the British press; so sour that it might well seem to anyone who did not look closely that Goldsmith himself had backed down at the last minute and lost the case. The impression given in some British newspapers was that he was an obsessive anti-communist anxious to seize every chance for personal publicity, but who could not prove his case. That was a gross distortion of the truth, but it still gained currency.

"The *Spiegel* propaganda machine suggested that this was a settlement initiated by me," he says now. "That is not true. But my 'admirers' in the British press preferred the *Spiegel* version. That was just par for the course. In fact I sued *Spiegel* in the German courts so that they did not repeat the lie."

Jimmy Goldsmith wrote a letter to *The Times* ten days after the settlement of the *Der Spiegel* case explaining that the request for an out-of-court settlement came from *Der Spiegel* (which Lord Rawlinson confirms). But, as so often before in England, that did nothing to dampen down the suggestion whispered in some quarters that he had not been able to prove his case. That was a grotesque distortion of the facts, but no matter how many letters he wrote to *The Times* he could not entirely dispel it, just as he had been unable to eradicate other distortions in the past.

In West Germany and the United States, however, his victory was acknowledged and complete. *Time* magazine commented shortly afterwards: "The issues in the *Spiegel* case probably are, as its editors asserted last week, beyond conventional proof. But the broader problem Goldsmith raised is one that knowing journalists cannot easily dismiss."

The settlement in the *Spiegel* case did not mean Jimmy Goldsmith was uncertain about his conclusions or his convictions. In the following years his fears for liberty in the West became his single passionate interest outside his financial affairs. By the beginning of 1986 he had codified his thoughts into a book, published in France, explaining the importance of a "permanent revolution" in the West's attitudes to freedom. "It is something that has to be fought for persistently," he insists still. It is not a conclusion that many English people, or many English politicians, find easy to accept.

In 1985 that conclusion, more than anything else, led him finally to announce formally his decision to abandon any political connections in England. Not only were his financial interests now predominantly in the United States, but there too his political opinions were listened to with greater seriousness and purpose. Jimmy Goldsmith had become convinced that the same would probably never happen in England. He believed that the English would very seldom fight for what they believed in, particularly if it meant contradicting "fashionable opinion" or questioning the common sense of their class system.

To test his theory, and provide his last public statement of a political philosophy in an English political context, he agreed to give the autumn address in 1985 of the Conservative Centre for Policy Studies, founded by Sir Keith Joseph and Mrs Thatcher in 1975, which he had helped to finance. The speech was given during the Conservative Party's annual conference at Blackpool in October. Before it he explained: "I expect this to be the last public statement that I will make in Britain." The despair and gloom that he felt about the English, and the English class system in particular, once again rose to the surface. He had decided that all he could do now in British politics was to act as a soothsayer.

Once again he began by drawing a parallel between Roman civilization and Soviet Russia, and asserting that British intellectual thought was hostile to business: "At the very moment of its triumph, the entrepreneurial class turned its energies to disguising itself in the image of the class it was supplanting. To be accepted successful businessmen went through an accelerated process of gentrification. They became ashamed of the very virtues that created their and their nation's success."

Looking a trifle nervously over the lectern provided for him in the balcony foyer of the Winter Garden in Blackpool at an audience of more than a hundred, he continued: "The hunger for gentrification led to a consolidation of the class system. Progressively there was a mingling of the old landed aristocracy with the new industrial class and the emergence of a gentrified middle class . . . And so emerged the extraordinary upstairs/downstairs society. Upstairs admiration was reserved for amateurs, dilettantes and a somewhat effete set of values which were supposed to represent a cultured way of life. Adventurers, risk-takers, tough and ambitious professionals were considered rather uncouth and vulgar. To be a good loser was more important than being a winner."

No one was left in the slightest doubt on which side Jimmy Goldsmith felt himself to be. After suggesting that the House of Lords should be fundamentally reformed, that there should be primary elections for the selection of parliamentary candidates, further curbs on the power of the trade unions, and a reform of British education, he sat down to what he later called "surprisingly enthusiastic" applause. Far from throwing things at him the audience appeared to rather like this tall nervous man with a slight stoop who was palpably not nearly as terrifying as his reputation. It was as if, for a moment at least, Jimmy Goldsmith had ceased to be the shadowy indistinct monster portrayed by *Private Eye*.

When he replied in answer to a question, "A mercantile system is based on freedom to do what each man wants", there was no question that it was all that he had ever asked for himself. This view was confirmed when, with his wife Annabel and his daughter Isabel sitting in the front row of the audience, a man asked him why he was not Chancellor of the Exchequer. For an instant Jimmy Goldsmith, who at one point in his life had wanted nothing more, paused. Then he replied: "If I had been Chancellor I'd have lasted a lot less time than Mr Parkinson." A prolonged burst of applause and laughter greeted him as he sat down. There was no doubt that he would have been every bit as controversial as the former chairman of the Conservative Party, who had been forced to resign from the British Cabinet after the revelation of an affair with his secretary – but it was the remark of a man who accepted rather than tried to conceal his way of life.

Jimmy Goldsmith ended his speech by saying: "In a great civilization people are individually free; they have equality of opportunity; they are united in a common objective. None of these circumstances exist in Britain today. If the nation is to be saved, this must be recognized and put right. And let it not be forgotten that those who are not willing to fight for their freedom deserve to be enslaved." It was a more human and a more personal conclusion than his audience had been expecting. He was expressing his sadness that his hopes for England had faded.

The same was certainly not true of the United States or France. In spite of his predictions of what would follow the election of a socialist President, by the autumn of 1985, four years after Mitterrand came to power, Jimmy Goldsmith had become convinced that France was swinging rapidly back towards the Right, and he was already planning to re-invest some of his resources in the country in recognition of that fact – principally in buying 64 per cent of the $260m real estate investment company Cogifi which owned 3,000 residential apartments and approximately 38,700 square metres of commercial property and offices, mostly in the Paris area.

Jimmy Goldsmith had long loved France more than any other country he worked in. It was where he felt most at home, and where he had come to prize his political influence. It was also the only country in which he had so far achieved his ambition of becoming a successful publisher. *L'Express* had become the country's most successful news magazine, selling more than 515,000 copies a week and spawning a Belgian edition, and he had taken over the influential weekly literary magazine *Lire* in 1983. With the help of Milton Glaser's designs, Jimmy Goldsmith and Tom Sebestyen, the managing director of *L'Express*, had helped *Lire* increase its sales from just over 80,000 to more than 125,000 copies a week – far more than any other literary magazine.

In France he had also just underlined his commercial strength by extracting $130 million from France's largest company, Elf-Aquitaine – the biggest sum in damages ever paid in French commercial history. "It was government-controlled and the government was hostile to us," he later said delightedly. "This sort of thing does not happen in France. It confirmed us as dangerous warriors."

That alone confirmed that Jimmy Goldsmith was someone no one in French politics could afford to ignore. His influence became increasingly clear as his friendship grew with a group of influential and rising French politicians on the Right, including the new French Prime Minister Jacques Chirac (whose candidature he had supported in a signed editorial in *L'Express*), and the clean-cut François Leotard, who became France's new Minister of Culture after Chirac's victory in the 1986 elections. For the first time in his career he had become a figure of considerable political significance in France, and though he had not set out to seek it, he enjoyed it none the less. At lunch or dinner in Paris he would discuss the country's future with politicians of every kind, refining his own philosophy as he did so.

In September 1984 he published his own philosophy in a lengthy article in *L'Express* called "Un Programme Libéral". It concentrated on the rights of the citizens in a free country to decide their own fate and their own economic priorities. The article had started out as an internal memorandum to the staff of the magazine, designed to give them guidance about his own political views. "Jimmy hadn't intended to publish it," Tom Sebestyen says, "but after some persuasion he agreed we could print it in the magazine."

The article provoked a storm. Jimmy Goldsmith was attacked from the Left for being determined to bring down the socialist President. But Tom Sebestyen believes that it gave "the young turks of the liberal opposition someone to look up to". It was not the manifesto of a man anxious to see himself elected a deputy in the French Assembly, quite the reverse. It was the statement of a man who had always acknowledged his own individuality, and wanted the same freedom for everyone else. It was the philosophy of a rebel, or "a prophet of absolute liberalism", as the French magazine *L'Evénement* was to conclude not long afterwards.

Tom Sebestyen specifically denies that Jimmy Goldsmith is interested in political power in France. "A man motivated by power is a man who tends to interfere in everything, and Jimmy is not like that. That is totally absent in all the businesses I've known Jimmy in for twenty-five years. Jimmy is not, and never was, a politician. He does not adapt his opinion to what he thinks people want to hear."

In particular Sebestyen argues: "He wants the editorial people on his magazines to produce the sort of paper that they want to, and which they believe will interest people, convince people and amuse people. He is not on the telephone every day saying, I want you to cover this and I want to make sure of that. He's never done that. He does not even want the Générale Occidentale group to advertise in *L'Express*, in case there was the suggestion of his influence."

Olivier Todd, who was managing editor of *L'Express* until he was fired in the wake of the French presidential election of 1981, believes that "Jimmy is in favour of multi-opinions and the liberal left-wing being represented on his magazines only as long as the French government was right-wing. As soon as it became socialist, that was different. That was where his liberalism stopped." It is a view shared by a substantial number of French journalists. "Even if people in France are very anti-communist and anti-socialist they don't know quite what to make of him. I think the left-wing suspect him of being a populist, but they find it easier to dismiss him as a die-hard, or a total nut. That is a mistake. I think in some ways he is really an English eccentric."

In the past three years Jimmy Goldsmith has demonstrated an appetite for explaining his political philosophy. The views he expressed in *L'Express* in the autumn of 1984 were expanded in a privately published collection of his speeches and articles, *Counter Culture*, which appeared in Britain a year later. That was followed by another book in France in the spring of 1986, *Pour La Révolution Permanente*. Written during his trip round South America in the wake of victory over Crown Zellerbach, the book reiterated many of his already clearly stated convictions, including his belief in the need to defend freedom at all costs, the significance of Soviet attempts to manipulate the Western media, and his conviction that a liberal programme was vital for France. He maintains now that he wrote it not necessarily to influence events but "because I did not want to make it easy for my detractors to deform my views, or for my staff on *L'Express* to be in any doubt what I thought." As Olivier Todd admits: "Unlike many entrepreneurs Jimmy is interested in ideas."

It is too early to predict exactly what influence Jimmy Goldsmith may have on French politics in the 1990s. Some believe it will be considerable, particularly if François Mitterrand loses the Presidential election in 1988, for several of the potential Presidential candidates who may run against him, including Chirac, Leotard and Alain Madelin, the Minister of Industry, have paid considerable attention to his ideas. His influence in France, even if only as an adviser, could well be decisive. The court of Jimmy Goldsmith, whether it is in Paris or New York, is seldom without a French politician. The future of his native country has become another of his abiding interests.

Yet one area where Jimmy Goldsmith's influence has already proved considerable is the United States, and particularly on Wall Street. Though he numbers American politicians among his friends – including former Treasury Secretary William Simon and former President Richard Nixon – it is his success as a corporate raider, and his eloquent defence of takeovers that have won him the most acclaim in the United States. Some of the other raiders, including the Texan T. Boone Pickens Jr, head of Mesa Petroleum which attempted to take over the giant Gulf Oil in 1984 and made a profit of $760 million when Gulf was finally taken over by Chevron, have angered American corporations by their apparent ruthlessness, and their relentless pursuit of profit. As *Time* magazine commented in 1985: "The Gulf episode proved to speculators that virtually any company, no matter the size, was vulnerable to a takeover. All a raider needed to get rich in a hurry was a gambler's nerves and access to enough borrowed cash to make an offer."

But Jimmy Goldsmith has convinced a significant and influential section of American corporate opinion that some takeovers, including his own of Diamond International and Crown Zellerbach, can be beneficial both to the companies involved and to the economy in general. Nowhere was that more vividly demonstrated than at a hearing of the United States Senate subcommittee on corporate takeovers in Washington in the summer of 1985. On 12 June Jimmy Goldsmith appeared in the committee rooms most famous on television for the activities of Senator Joe Macarthy in the 1950s and Senator Sam Ervin's Watergate committee during the 1970s. On that stuffy June morning Jimmy Goldsmith found himself appearing as a witness alongside T. Boone Pickens. By comparison with the eternally sad-faced Pickens, Jimmy Goldsmith looked exceptionally cheerful, perfectly relaxed, and as though he had very little to hide – or to be ashamed of.

In his opening speech to the committee he made no apologies whatever for what some called his "hostile takeovers" of major American corporations. Even though he was in the final stages of the battle with William T. Creson and the board of Crown Zellerbach, beneath the light suntan and well-cut suit, he looked as though he had hardly made a commercial effort for a year. But the takeover battle had sharpened and hardened his opinions.

"Who would have believed a few years ago," he told the committee, chaired by Senator Alfonse D'Amato of New York, "that conglomerates, created at the time by freewheeling entrepreneurs, today are described by some as sacrosanct institutions which should be protected from the marketplace by special legislation . . . All that has changed in many of these companies is that the flame of the founder has been replaced by the complacency of the bureaucrat. And because the members of such bureaucracies control the disposition of vast amounts of other people's money and the power and patronage that accompany it, they feel they are part of the establishment and therefore deserve special privileges."

The committee were left in no doubt that Sir James Michael Goldsmith did not approve of that modern American habit. "I would only like to make one obvious point," he explained, taking his half-rimmed glasses from his nose for a moment. "Corporations are owned by their shareholders. Management is employed by shareholders to look after shareholder interests. Devices like poison pills, paying greenmail, defensive acquisitions, super majority voting, staggered boards, etcetera, should all be subject to a prior and free vote by shareholders and should not be imposed unilaterally by management . . . When management acts unilaterally, without consulting shareholders, it is seeking protection not for their shareholders but from their shareholders."

And he concluded by arguing vehemently that the American industrial revolution was based on freedom. "My most fervent hope is that one day my fellow Europeans will learn that freedom works, and I also hope that Americans will never forget it."

The tone of the questions that followed his introductory speech was distinctly welcoming. When Senator Chic Hecht of Nevada asked him, "How come you stayed in Europe and did not come to America many many years ago?" Goldsmith said without a pause: "Stupidity actually. The main answer is that people are not aware of lack of freedom until they taste freedom, and I was never aware of the inhibitions and constrictions in Europe until I fully tasted those on the other side in America."

It was something he had been seeking his entire life: the freedom to be judged by his actions and their effect on the marketplace. Bending down towards the microphone on the dark mahogany table in front of the committee, Jimmy Goldsmith said quietly, "There's nothing hostile about a hostile bid. There's no difference between a raid and a merger except that the established bureaucrat loses his job, not the owners and not the business . . . The word hostile is merely a bureaucratic term to try and create a nobility to entrenchment." With a wry smile he went on to admit to the Senate subcommittee: "Raiders shouldn't put on a halo. They are doing it for personal gain. The important thing is whether their action is generally beneficial or generally detrimental, not why they are doing it . . . The dead hand of the bureaucrat does not produce growth. It does not produce innovation. It produces complacency, ossification and decline."

A delighted Hecht told T. Boone Pickens, "Hey, Boone, this guy does a better job of talking than you do," adding: "Sir James, personally I would like to invite you to be an American citizen and join the Republican Party. You could be one of our top spokesmen." Jimmy Goldsmith looked across the committee room in surprise.

"It was one of the most remarkable days of my life," he admitted afterwards. "On the whole they thought like me, and I've never had people so nice to me in my life. I'm not used to it." It seemed, finally, as though the years of suspicion and derision which had greeted his achievements had come to an end.

He had told the Senate how the "mass of heterogeneous medium-sized businesses had weakened Diamond", and that, "We liberated and sold the pieces that would be better off independent, kept the piece we wanted, which was the forest products side . . . We did it for one purpose – profit. The question is whether or not it was profitable generally. In my view, our action was entirely beneficial." The man who created Générale Occidentale and General Oriental, and nurtured their growth into major international companies, was convinced that "liberating companies from tired old conglomerates is good for everyone – shareholders, employees, the economy and, of course, the raider".

Not every American banker and corporate executive shared his view. Bruce Smart, the chairman of the Continental Group, which had just escaped him in 1984, told *Time* magazine in 1985: "There are other stakeholders in a company beside the shareholders, and they all lose." (Smart himself had retired as chairman of his group shortly after its takeover by David Murdock and Peter Kiewit.) Felix Rohatyn of Lazard Frères, one of New York's most respected and influential investment bankers, also told *Time* that "The takeover game as it is practised today is really a little like the arms race. You have to stop it before it gets out of control." While Senator William Proxmire, one of the members of the Senate subcommittee, also argued: "The rising tide of hostile takeovers threatens the very foundations of our American business system. They undermine productivity, wreak havoc on entire communities, and saddle wellmanaged companies with billions of dollars in excessive debt."

Jimmy Goldsmith fundamentally disagrees. He defends his takeover and "liberation" of Crown Zellerbach in exactly the same way as he defended his takeover of Diamond. "In December 1985 the readers of *Fortune* magazine voted it the second worst managed major company in America. We transferred the paper-making activities to James River, which was voted one of the best-managed companies, and we have reorganized our pieces, with new management dramatically improving results and cutting out approximately $42 million a year of waste and losses."

Jimmy Goldsmith is convinced that the only people "damaged" in the Crown Zellerbach deal were those in the head office in San Francisco. "The companies themselves succeeded brilliantly. But when you dismantle an eighteen-floor head office to some extent you're wounding some. We paid sufficient compensation to the rest to see them through their change without too much pain. If you look at the record I don't think there is anybody who feels they have been treated badly. What I did was to minister to their wounds and I've had letters from Zellerbach people who were wounded saying they agreed with our decision that the head office was totally unnecessary."

Joe Flom, the Manhattan attorney who advised him on the Diamond and Crown Zellerbach deals, defends him by saying: "More people are working in Diamond today than there were before, and the management has prospered." Flom calls his client "a genius in his own way, with an infinite capacity for taking pains, flair, imagination and a great deal of charm" and he pays tribute to the fact that "one of the pleasures of working with Jimmy is that he looks beyond just making money – in terms of people and politics". But Flom does not deny that Jimmy Goldsmith pursues a deal with relentless, unflinching energy: "He gets very tense, he doesn't leave it alone. He works at it constantly. But he understands what he is doing and he has a philosophy."

Robert Clark, law professor at Harvard, for example, believes that the control of major United States corporations which began as capitalist enterprises is bound to move from entrepreneur founders to professional managers and finally to institutional investors and savers. The corporate raiders, he told *Fortune* magazine in 1985, are the catalysts of that change. "They are really breaking the vice of the managing class."

Jimmy Goldsmith has been preparing for exactly that opportunity throughout his working life. It is an approach and style which may not endear him to every executive in corporate America, but it is one which has won him greater influence on Wall Street than many of the other, perhaps less articulate and persuasive, American corporate raiders. And it could well turn out to be his decisive influence on the commercial world.

24

Rich as Croesus

No one could honestly describe Sir James Michael Goldsmith as the epitome of England's "verray, parfit gentil knyght". Though this tall, perpetually tanned man in his fifties, with a slightly embarrassed stoop and soft almost reticent manner, eternally displays the elegant courtesy of a Medici prince, beneath that veneer there lies a tumultuous, volcanic energy: too consuming ever to allow him aristocratic languor. Alongside that there lies a rage for perfection.

Comparatively few people have sought to try and unravel that skein of tradition and emotion that inhabits Jimmy Goldsmith. For many within the business communities of Paris, London or New York he remains a curiously remote, elusive figure, existing in the golden twilight of immense luxury and power. Although a character of weird and forceful originality, he is dismissed as neurotic by some, yet recognized as genuinely imaginative by others. The contradiction has stalked his life.

This eloquent, unquiet son of a German-born Jew and a French Catholic from the Auvergne, who speaks French as frequently as he does English, has been known to throw his breakfast tray out of the window if his fresh orange juice has not had the fragments of pith removed from it, and his wine on to the floor if the vintage does not live up to his expectations. Jimmy Goldsmith behaves more like a mongol chieftain than a twentieth-century businessman, pitching his tent wherever he intends to conquer. An old friend once described him as "Attila the Hun with financial genius", and it was not meant as an insult. In some ways he is a man born out of his time. He can roar like a lion when he is angry, beat the table in frustration and hurl papers that displease him across the room. But just as quickly he can be consumed by remorse, the outbursts are forgotten in a matter of minutes, and his mercurial spirit suddenly directed to apology rather than intimidation.

His is the character of a giant beast of the jungle, an animal whose prodigious strength can frighten all but the brave, but who is also, ironically, always a little afraid himself.

There is an incandescent, untamed energy about him that can terrify those who do not know him well. But there is also an unquenchable, boyish charm. Like a schoolboy his tie is always just a little askew, and it is no surprise that he can seldom wait to take it off. There are those who suspect that, like an adolescent, his every public action is somehow a little exaggerated, every habit carried deliberately to extremes; every decision in some way a rebellion against the established order.

That idiosyncrasy has done him no harm, however. He has made himself one of the richest men in the world by never allowing himself to be predictable, by questioning and flouting conventional wisdom, and by unashamedly casting himself in the role of maverick. A volcano may be rumbling ceaselessly within him, but it provides his power.

Undeniably Jimmy Goldsmith is one of the most eccentric tycoons of the second half of this century. And he is also one of the most successful. In the past decade alone he has made himself an estimated billion dollars. If he were to sell his assets they might provide him with a personal fortune in excess of $2 billion.

In addition to the 3.5 million acres of American timberlands of Diamond and Crown Zellerbach, which at the most conservative estimate are worth $1.75 billion, he controls the Grand Union chain of supermarkets in the United States, worth more than $1 billion; the Basic Resources oil fields in Guatemala, which may be worth $500 million; a publishing empire in France, led by Presses de la Cité as well as *L'Express*; and the successful gambling casino Aspinalls Curzon in Britain, in which his stake could be worth more than $75 million. These are augmented by occasional speculations in the market, and currency manoeuvres to take advantage of fluctuations in the exchange rate. And his appetite for new investments shows no sign of abating. There is already Cogifi, the real estate investment company in France, while speculation about his move on Wall Street after Goodyear never ceases.

Fortune magazine called his takeover of Diamond "one of the financial events of the 1980s", bringing him a profit that it estimated would exceed $500 million. When the dust finally settles after his takeover of Crown Zellerbach, the world will see that "it turned out to be much better even than Diamond", in Jimmy Goldsmith's own words. After all his debts are paid he is left with the 1.9 million acres of forest lands, the eighteen-storey headquarters building in San Francisco, $90 million in cash, and the computer company Eczel – "which after deep surgery we have turned round to making a profit". If he were to liquidate all those assets at the right price it might bring him a profit approaching a billion dollars on this deal alone. "But that is only on paper and if you believe in wood." The deal confirmed his place among the richest men in the world.

"I really haven't the slightest idea how much I'm worth today," he says firmly, pacing the ground floor sitting room of his Queen Anne house on the outskirts of London like a caged tiger, waving and chewing his Davidoff Number One cigar so excitedly that he is finally forced to tear off the crumpled end to keep on smoking. "I don't know what my assets would sell for, I really haven't any idea. For me something you don't want to sell you can't put a value on."

At the annual general meeting of Générale Occidentale in Paris in September 1986 a shareholder asked him how much GO was worth. Jimmy Goldsmith smiled. "I've no idea. You want me to sell it and we'll find out?" The shareholder sat down smartly.

Though he controls both GO, through Lido SA, his Panamanian company, and General Oriental Investments Limited, the Cayman Islands based company that succeeded General Oriental in 1985, he has no intention of relinquishing control of either. Just as he has no intention of selling Grand Union, *L'Express* or Basic Resources, "which makes it impossible to say what I am worth". Even trying to estimate the value of his holdings in General Oriental Investments, by taking their share price on the London Stock Exchange, is fraught with difficulties. For after his own 90 per cent holdings are taken into account, along with those shares held by old friends like John Aspinall and John Tigrett, or those in the hands of his senior executives, only about 3 per cent of the shares are in other, private, hands. The market price of General Oriental shares is based on a tiny proportion of the capital. Their value depends, as he puts it, "on the skill one would have in selling it". He has no intention of doing anything of the kind.

Even Jimmy Goldsmith would admit that he is now rich beyond the wildest dreams of most ordinary men. Capable of walking into an American bank and leaving with a certified banker's draft for a billion dollars a few minutes later – as he did during the Continental takeover in 1984 – he is worth more than most men can dream of. There may be more than 800,000 millionaires in the United States, but the club of billionaires is significantly smaller. *Forbes* magazine, in its annual list of the 400 richest Americans, lists barely fifteen.

Yet he has always known that he would do it. "If anybody asked me at the age of eight what I was going to do I never had any doubt whatsoever – I was going to make a fortune. I had some doubts along the way, but it never entered my head when I was very young that I was going to do anything else."

His brother Teddy likes to tell the story that when Jimmy was six their father was worried that he hadn't yet learnt to read. When he asked what he intended to do about it his youngest son told him firmly, "When I'm old enough I shall be a millionaire and have someone to read to me, so I won't need to." As one old friend says: "Jimmy has not always had money, but he's always believed he would have." Digby Neave, who flew to Casablanca with him in 1953 in search of Isabel Patino, agrees: "Jimmy does not have the same attitude to money as other people. He's never understood what it means not to have money, he has always been a millionaire. Even when he didn't have millions he was a capitalist without capital."

Teddy Goldsmith is convinced "Jimmy was always driven. Even when he was young he was always buying and selling things. He was always competitive and ambitious." The urge to make a fortune consumed his younger brother from childhood.

And Jimmy Goldsmith still finds it difficult to understand why the same passion does not inhabit everyone. "I find it hard to explain why more people don't do it," he says. "But I cannot envisage going into business for any other purpose than to make money. There is no vocation about business. The purpose is to make money." There is a pause, then he adds enigmatically, "I don't particularly like business."

Though he may not, it has provided the focus of his life. He may read incessantly, devouring newspapers wherever he is, filling his shelves in London with biography and memoirs, in New York with corporate history and modern novels, and in Paris with politics and philosophy; but his fascination with the opportunities of a deal has never left him. The instincts of an entrepreneur lie at the very heart of his nature. Together with his idiosyncrasy they drive him on.

As Jimmy Goldsmith puts it himself, "I think motivation comes from a certain disequilibrium in the personality. I'm sure that applies to me. Someone who is perfectly balanced is not likely to be very determined. A cow in a field may be perfectly balanced, and perfectly contented, but it doesn't do much." He pauses as he says it, aware that the acknowledgement itself sets him apart from more conventional businessmen. "Perhaps my disequilibrium comes from the very fact that I'm a foreigner . . . I'm a Jew to Catholics and a Catholic to Jews, an Englishman to the French and a Frenchman to the English. I've always been neither one thing nor the other – which can be a very unsettling thing to be." But that is not the only explanation. There is also the reputation of his family.

Jimmy Goldsmith has never forgotten that he is a member of a mercantile dynasty. The restless child brought up in the grandest hotel suites of Europe grew into an adult with the appetites and style of a Turkish emperor or a Florentine prince. It is no accident that the first-floor drawing room of his New York town house is decorated with the bust of a Medici, and his marbled hall with those of the Florentines Cardinal Soderini and his brother, at one time the employers of Machiavelli. His too is a great dynasty which he intends to sustain.

When taxed with excessive regard for the Goldsmith name he replies: "I don't think of my family as anything particularly unusual, just one that had a minor role in the mercantile development of Europe. But one is passing one's achievements on in a chain. And if anyone tries to spoil that they will fight me, not just because of me, but because I am part of that tradition. Can there be anything more important than what you hand on?"

This awareness of the Goldschmidt family and its tradition

provides another of the fires that burn within him. As a young man his father told him, "My father handed on a respectable name to me, I hope you will be able to do the same for your children." The determination to do so, more than anything else, lay behind the intensity of his battle with *Private Eye* in England. But beneath even that desire lies another, even deeper, and almost unacknowledged: to prove to the world that it underestimated his father. "I think a lot of what I've done I have done to satisfy my father," he will admit privately, "because it would have amused him. I often wish he was alive to see what I've accomplished."

In Europe he has been described both as "an inspired entrepreneur" and "a Machiavelli"; a combination of Houdini and *The Master Builder*. One old French colleague pays tribute to his "prodigious intuition and intelligence" while another dismisses him as "in the grand tradition of gamblers who will bet whether someone coming through the door is wearing red or black". Jimmy Goldsmith is both "gentleman and adventurer, self-made man and cousin of the Rothschilds, a liberal and a man of the extreme Right, a man of pleasure and a man of principle" to the left-wing Paris newspaper *Liberation*.

Undeniably he is a man who likes to be liked, and yet is capable of exciting intense enmity; a man who can appear without sentiment yet who carries pictures of his children around with him in a tiny silver case; a man whose financial timing is legendary yet who seldom wears a watch; a man who relishes extravagance but who will never pay too much for a company; a man who likes acknowledgement and yet craves privacy; a man who loves his children and yet may not see them for weeks at a time; a man who is married but has the attitudes of a bachelor; a man who is immensely rich but rarely carries money.

To those who do not know him those contradictions reinforce his own exaggerations, so that more conventional and moderate men become convinced that he is possessed by a dangerous arrogance and self-delusion. To them his success is based on bluster and the trickery of a mountebank. For them Jimmy Goldsmith remains a financial juggler whose hands move too swiftly for them entirely to trust him, especially as he seems intent on refusing to tread any of the conventional paths of the modern commercial world.

It is not true, but the myth remains.

One person who understands the myth is his closest confidante, Gilberte Beaux. She knows that almost every fixed view of Jimmy Goldsmith is mistaken. "People cannot understand his success so they say that he must be a gambler, because they think it has to be based on something that they do not understand, and therefore something bad. No one is prepared to say that we may have worked a little harder and thought a little more. I would not say we have taken no risks, that would not be true, but before Jimmy takes a risk he looks at it more carefully than anyone can imagine."

As she speaks she taps the light wood desk of her office in Paris with a pencil, like a baton. "He has never been something in the middle, he is not a bourgeois. He does not put a little money here and a little money there. He prefers to believe he can continue to create for the group, and that is because he is both a peasant and a member of a great Jewish family.

"Jimmy wakes up every morning convinced that he has nothing at all. Every morning we are rich only up to a point, the point at which the company has the ability to make growth and profits. All the money is tied up in the group and he is therefore only as good as the group's performance. If he is in the group he has to work, if he does not want to work he has to sell his participation, there can be no middle way."

Gilberte Beaux is in a better position than anyone to judge. One of their closest friends describes them as "like Richard Burton and Elizabeth Taylor, always arguing, but for ever close". The legendary investment banker, André Meyer of Lazard Frères, once called her "the best banker in France". She insists that Goldsmith "has the ability to change, to move, to adapt very quickly; and to abandon what he thought would be a strong point. Jimmy is far less of a gambler than we hear when it comes to business".

It is a conclusion which helps to dispel a myth that even Jimmy Goldsmith sometimes likes to perpetuate about himself – that he is prepared to sacrifice everything for one more throw on the red, regardless of the risks; that he is the slightly thoughtless playboy who got lucky. That is a fantasy, but one which he has – on occasion – been happy to sustain, because it allows him to appear less thoughtful and more foolish than he is. From the chrysalis of a six-year-old who "didn't need to read" emerged the entrepreneur who likes his opponents to underestimate him.

His apparent appetite for mystery is not restricted to his deals. It also appears to affect his companies. To the outsider the intricate structure of Générale Occidentale and Trocadero Participations in France, General Oriental Investments Limited in the Cayman Islands, and Diamond International Holdings in the Dutch Antilles, all coming as they do under the control of his privately controlled Bruneria Foundation in Liechtenstein and Lido SA in Panama, serves to make him appear a conjuror with a great many hats, from any one of which he may produce a rabbit, or a profit. In fact all the companies simply lead back to Jimmy Goldsmith.

He explains the structure by saying simply, "My family and I own the overwhelming majority (over 80 per cent) of General Oriental, and together with General Oriental own 60 per cent of Trocadero; so that we also own more than 50 per cent of Générale Occidentale." And Gilberte Beaux adds: "All our holdings are vertical and logical, so that in terms of operating companies and teams of people we are probably the cleanest and smallest that can exist for a group of our size."

Whatever the myths of the gambler that may have gathered around him, one essential element in Jimmy Goldsmith's success since the bank strike in France saved him in 1957 has always been "to have sufficient finance so as not to have to depend on a bank in the short term", as Gilberte Beaux puts it. "He always wants sufficient liquidity not to be obliged, because speed can be very important."

Charles Hambro, a contemporary at Eton and now a director of General Oriental, agrees. "His great instinct is always to have enough cash to pay the bills on a week-to-week basis. He may be long-term borrowed, but never too much short. He's got that quality today, he always has – and he has always liked to buy real assets."

So Jimmy Goldsmith was not entirely joking in 1984 when he told the *Sunday Telegraph*: "A man should always keep $600 million in cash available, in case a good deal comes along." It reflected his style and his boyish pleasure in seizing deals when they presented themselves. Charles Hambro believes that a key to his friend's success lies in exactly that timing, and luck. "Luck in the sense that he had this little Cavenham in England at a moment of undoubted financial boom fuelled by an enormous amount of money injected into the system without regard for anything by Edward Heath's government, and timing in the sense that Jimmy used that moment to use paper to buy assets which three or four years before he couldn't have done and which three or four years later he couldn't have done. He caught the wind."

Jimmy Goldsmith's delight in making himself richer by the speed of his reaction and his skill in anticipating the movements of the marketplace, whether it is in Europe or the United States, has never palled, especially if it has involved a fight against the established order of any country he found himself in.

His former partner in Mothercare, Selim Zilkha, who is still a close friend, explains: "People do not understand that business is both his hobby and his passion. He probably enjoys it more than anything else he does." While Jim Slater, another old friend, also believes: "Jimmy likes to feel the world is against him, it makes his adrenalin flow. He likes the fight to overcome them."

This combative quality leads Sir Gordon White, the British industrialist who built up the vast Hanson Trust alongside Lord Hanson, to call him the Don Quixote of the financial world: "Jimmy's always cocked a snook at authority. He's prepared to tilt at windmills providing he can see the pot of gold at the end. He can be mercurial, but he is also highly intellectual, and he's got the one other thing that is missing in modern-day business – common sense, which means he has the ability to buy something at the right price, and sell it for a profit."

Ambroise Roux, a director of Générale Occidentale, says: "He has exceptional qualities that you meet rarely in your career. He is completely out of the ordinary because he can see things that nobody else sees – he has a sort of 'vision' in business, which when you ask him to explain he can't." But the phlegmatic and shrewd Roux adds: "When he has a design for a financial deal it is Gilberte Beaux who transforms the scheme into a practical reality. I am not sure that he is a perfect administrator, but he has very good people working for him, like Roland Franklin in America, and he has a very good commercial sense."

It is precisely that quality which Jack Greenhalgh, managing director of Cavenham in England for more than ten years, identifies as a reason for Jimmy Goldsmith's success. "He wasn't terribly good at running companies, but he was absolutely superb at choosing a team and letting them get on with it. He had tremendous creativity and imagination, but he also had this famous expression – 'If you can see a bandwagon, it's too late to get on it.'"

David de Rothschild, president of the French arm of the Rothschild Bank, believes that "Jimmy's success lies in integrating his financial skill and his imagination. He has a talent to make money, and that is based on his abilities as a risk-taker – he is psychologically able to take larger risks than I could. He is much too ambitious, in terms of making money, ever to like a 'fee business' like banking. He has never liked acting as an agent, he likes to be the principal."

Robert S. Pirie, the ambitious president of Rothschilds Inc. in New York, who acted for Jimmy Goldsmith in the Continental and Crown Zellerbach deals, entirely agrees: "We can all sit around and cook up great schemes. How many people have the balls to go out and risk their money? There are a lot of great stock pickers who are poor because they will never commit and will not take a risk. Jimmy, in contrast, is totally comfortable with his own judgement, and he has a gambler's ability to analyse the loss potential and know how to avoid it. That's a critical ability." Pirie also insists that "Jimmy Goldsmith is very much a loner in his thinking. In every deal we've been involved with he disappears at all the crucial periods. I think the reason for that is that he doesn't want to be cluttered with a lot of people talking to him. He wants to think it out himself."

The London investment banker Jacob Rothschild, a partner in the consortium that attempted to take over the St Regis Corporation in 1984, also agrees that another of Jimmy Goldsmith's crucial advantages as a businessman is this very isolation – coupled with cosmopolitanism. "Jimmy is completely international. He's equally at home doing business in the London market, the Paris market or the New York market, and there are few people who have the intellect or the capacity to transcend national boundaries. People just aren't used to dealing with someone who is as independent and outspoken as he is. He doesn't compromise, he doesn't suck up, he isn't accommodating to the second rate, and he doesn't like people who are hidebound, or do nothing of interest."

Jacob Rothschild believes that his friend's ability "not to have a domestic centre of gravity – being able to wander between these three centres – is very difficult and takes great courage". While Charles Hambro also accepts that "Jimmy has no fixed roots. He likes to pop in and out all the time, and he doesn't care too much about things like which picture is on the wall". Teddy Goldsmith, who shares his younger brother's lack of interest in convention – is convinced that "Jimmy could never live in any other way. He's always lived a nomad's life. He enjoys it." While Digby Neave, who has known both men for forty years, adds, "Teddy and Jimmy are still living out of suitcases mentally."

It is one reason why Jimmy Goldsmith does not care for commercial empires. Although some may find it difficult to believe, he is not interested in establishing a giant corporation which will remain long after his death: a monument to his achievements. On the contrary. "When I started I think I had a vague romantic notion of re-creating the great nineteenth-century companies, like Shell, Unilever or ICI. But I realized very quickly that empires like those were bad things, because most of these major companies are just private bureaucracies. I came to the conclusion very quickly that they were pure ego trips, pure searches for power."

A despiser of vast institutions supported by bureaucracy, he does not even have a desk in his offices in New York or Paris. "I haven't had one for twenty years. I don't like the idea of sitting behind one, in the same way that I don't like files. I tear almost everything up when I've finished with it. I don't like bureaucracy of any kind.

"Some people want to build companies as memorials to themselves, but I don't. I strongly believe that companies that are put together by one person or a team should be broken down when those people get old and die, and that they should go through a massive change. The idea of leaving a nineteenth-century industrial empire as a mausoleum to myself sickens me."

That conclusion colours his view of other entrepreneurs and of inheritance. "On the whole people who inherit are weak and soft because they've never had to fight in their lives, and I somewhat despise those who inherit as opposed to those who've made it." Although he admits, "passing things down to one's children is a natural human ambition". One area where his dislike of inheritance is clear, however, is in his reaction to the J. Paul Getty Foundation's art collection, housed in its museum in California. "Setting up a massive trust fund to scavenge history and art to glorify the memory of this rather arid, dull old man I thoroughly disapprove of. If he had established a trust to encourage the best new art and crafts that at least would have been alive, but he did not even do that."

Certainly he disapproves of the appetite of some entrepreneurs to create empires. "If James Hanson had kept SCM in the United States and Imperial Tobacco in Britain after he had taken them over he would have been creating a Ministry, and I profoundly disagree with that. But by taking them and breaking them up he's done an immense service."

It is the reason that he also disagrees with the $6 billion merger of General Electric and RCA in the United States in 1985, and disapproved of the proposed merger between Sir Arnold Weinstock's GEC and Plessey in Britain. "The merger would have been a disaster. What would it have produced? A bit of short-term profit because they'd have cut out some overheads. It would not have helped the British electronics industry; a bust-up would have been infinitely better."

Nevertheless his conviction of the importance of those entrepreneurs who take over decaying conglomerates and sell off their assembled parts to those who can run them more profitably and effectively is one reason for Jimmy Goldsmith's respect for the British-based businessman and newspaper publisher Robert Maxwell. "He's a good predator, a shark." Early in 1981 he described Maxwell's activities, though he did not name him at the time, in a speech in Paris. Part of it took the form of a parable – which could just as well describe Jimmy Goldsmith's view of entrepreneurship.

"Not long ago a friend of mine visited the Galapagos Islands. He witnessed an incredible sight. In the sea were hundreds of thousands of anchovies being attacked by diving birds. Over and over again the birds dived and killed. The sea was a gory mess. The anchovies could not escape because they were also being attacked from below. Large mullet were rising from deeper seas and forcing the anchovies to the surface. It looked as though they would be wiped out. But all of a sudden the mullet dispersed, the anchovies swam to deeper waters and the birds flew away. The reason soon became obvious.

Sharks had been attracted to the scene and attacked the mullet who fled to safety. The anchovies were liberated and thus the sharks saved the anchovies."

Jimmy Goldsmith does not believe the shark – the predator on Wall Street or in the City of London – "does it for any motivation other than being a shark. The shark is acting according to his nature. But you cannot have a community which protects everybody. Life is not like that. Struggle is what we're built for. You can kill everyone, every animal, by totally protecting them." It is an argument that infuriates many on the Left in Britain and France, particularly when he goes on to add, "It is absurd to ask, Are entrepreneurs nice? The question is irrelevant. Nice or not, they are necessary to an industrial society. Risk-taking, adventure and pioneering are not characteristic of committees."

In defence of his raids on Diamond and Crown Zellerbach he explains: "People cannot abide change. But in breaking up an old conglomerate you're not killing companies, you're not buying them to shut them down and sell their assets. You are simply killing off the bureaucracy and letting the companies inside the conglomerate free. But people find that very hard to understand. They can't quite make out the difference between Unilever headquarters, for example, and the Vatican. They think it's immovable." Nothing would convince him that is true. "The secret of a successful community is to be able to align the results achieved by those making money to the interests of the community as a whole."

It is not a conclusion that will ever make him popular with those strands of political opinion who see the modern state's responsibility as ensuring the comfort and sustenance of its poorest and weakest members. His is the philosophy of economic Darwinism. In the end he believes that the State has to supply a safety net for those who need it but not "a suffocating blanket of assistance for all". To those with less certainty than Jimmy Goldsmith that can be an intimidating, even terrifying, conviction.

Yet nothing can extinguish the charm with which he proposes it, or the eloquence of his explanation. Even in England, where he is probably regarded with the greatest suspicion, Lord Rothschild, former head of the British government's "think tank", calls him "dynamic, highly intelligent and extremely quick-witted – and I rarely use such adjectives. He has much charm, vitality and intellect. He is somewhat of a gambler in that, unlike me, he believes in "runs of luck", but he is one of the few people apart, of course, from my wife and family, that I greatly enjoy meeting whenever the opportunity arises." Lady Falkender, who has become a close friend since her departure from Downing Street in 1976, maintains firmly: "It was unreasonable that Jimmy should have become the focus for so much criticism in England."

When anyone describes him as "eccentric" in England, he tends to reply: "What does eccentric mean? It means outside the culture. In France the life I lead would not be considered all that eccentric, a little perhaps but not very. But in England it is regarded as very eccentric." The thought depresses him, just as English puritanism throws a blanket of gloom over him. "I find it extraordinary the fascination with people's sex life in England; and the mixture of snobbism and frustrated sex in England I find depressing." The attitudes of a young man brought up in France, and whose mother always spoke to him in French, remain an indelible part of his character. It is no surprise that, although he is officially a resident of Britain for tax purposes, he increasingly spends more and more of his time in France. The French appreciate that. As Humbert Frérejean, of *L'Express* puts it: "He could well have left France and moved everything to America, but he did not do that, and there is great sympathy for him here. We French are not quite sure of ourselves and we like to be liked, and people here think he likes us."

Jimmy Goldsmith is far more French than most Anglo-Saxons realize. His reactions and his attitudes owe every bit as much to his mother Marcelle as to his father Frank. There is something of Marcelle's sense of drama in him – as a young woman she would burst into tears or scream with excitement or impatience. Like her son she could never be described as a stoic. And like him she loved hotels. She spent the last years of her life, until her death in 1985, living in a suite in the Grand Hotel in Paris, only a few yards from the Scribe where she and her husband had spent so many years. There, surrounded by family paintings and mementoes, she would receive telephone calls from her sons and grandchildren: a bright-eyed woman with a formidable determination. Both her sons adored her, "although she irritated Jimmy sometimes too", as one old friend puts it – perhaps because in some ways they were so alike. Yet she bequeathed her younger son a passionate intensity that he has never lost.

Like his father, and the other Goldschmidts of Frankfurt, there is also a tribal quality about him. Like a chieftain he ushers his tribe of family and friends around after him – providing them all with food, shelter and protection. Even some of his superstitions are medieval. He will never describe a transaction he is involved in to an outsider while it is taking place for fear that doing so may bring him bad luck, and he is convinced that certain people and places bring him either good luck or bad. He will touch wood when describing a deal, and he is especially superstitious about the bad luck that rubber bands – indeed almost anything made of rubber – can bring. He once walked off a commercial airliner shortly before takeoff because he saw a rubber band in the aisle. He was followed from the aircraft by a group of local shepherds who thought he knew more than they did.

His political opinions, too, are unashamedly archaic. Just as he despises the far Left in Britain or France so too he sees the British Conservative Party as "sickened by its own weakness, dominated by an old ruling class whose day is gone". It is not a conclusion that he restricts to Britain. He has condemned the liberal opposition in France for not being "sufficiently courageous", and attacked American foreign policy for not understanding the Soviet Union's "imperial ambitions". He insists "the United States cannot develop a long term and harmonious relationship with Russia". His is the philosophy of a Tartar chieftain who prefers to rely on his own strength to protect himself from what he sees as a dangerous world. He is intensely suspicious of those whom he regards as his enemies, but equally loyal to those he regards as friends. And like many ancient princes he is wary of the potential influence of spies.

Like a chieftain Jimmy Goldsmith also relishes the sensual. His suits are tailored in London, and he consumes his food at speed. "I've seen him steal food from somebody else's plate if he likes the look of it," one old friend says, "though he doesn't do that now as much as he used to. He's mellowed in the last few years." In his New York town house off Park Avenue the first-floor sitting room sofas are white silk, the walls golden, the coffee tables cream, the rugs Persian, the effect palatial. It is the home of a modern emperor. And it is there that he usually works rather than in his office on Fifth Avenue, and there too that he does business and entertains.

That does not mean he has lost his capacity for enjoying himself, or taking holidays. There is a summer house on Long Island for Laure and their young daughter Charlotte, where he will often spend the weekend when he is in the United States; just as there can be a rented Boeing 727 sitting on MacArthur Field nearby, to take him wherever he needs, or would like, to go. In the first months of 1986 that included Bali, Rio de Janeiro and Argentina. His business interests in the United States do not mean that he has forsaken his nomadic habits. Yet he has long since ceased to be a playboy. He avoids most parties, and prefers small dinners with friends. He does not spend his evenings in nightclubs; he simply divides his time between New York, London and Paris, and the families in each.

In England there is still Ormeley Lodge on the edge of Richmond Park, where his wife Annabel looks after Jemima, Zacharias and Benjamin (always known as Ben-Ben). All three children are now at school, his daughter Jemima an exceptionally keen horsewoman, his eldest son on the verge of going to Eton as his father did. Both older children are aware of his separate lives. "They found it difficult at first," explains one old friend, "but he seems so happy when he sees them, everything seems to have settled down." His eldest daughter Isabel, who has become a keen collector of paintings, also lives in London.

His relationship with Annabel is certainly more settled and happier than it has been for years. "I have the nicest times, without any of the aggravation," she says, "and he gets on better with the children now than ever." To some she may appear like a bird in an exceptionally gilded cage, but his devotion to her and his family has not faltered in spite of the increasing amounts of time he spends in Paris and New York. They now have a house in Spain, where he tries to spend at least part of the school holidays.

In France there is still the house in the rue Monsieur, where Ginette lives. Their daughter Alix has moved to the United States to spend more time with her father, and their son Manes is in Mexico City assisting the Mexican national football team. Jimmy

Goldsmith stays in the rue Monsieur, where he keeps some of his collection of Louis Napoleon furniture, whenever he goes to Paris, and he insists "not one iota of my relationship with Ginette has changed since our divorce, not one".

For her part Ginette prefers to retain a discreet silence about her former husband, although she has said when pressed, "Jimmy is loyal and warm hearted, the most generous man I know, and I don't mean in the financial sense. It is his whole character that is generous." The girl who shared his tiny office in the rue de la Paix has lost none of her devotion, though she has certainly suffered as his interests have spread across the world. "Perhaps more than anyone else Ginette has been the victim of Jimmy's unconventional lifestyle," says one old friend, "but neither he nor she would accept that." Certainly he still protects and looks after her interests, just as he does those of the other members of his families in other countries. At Christmas he visits them all one by one, as he has always done.

"Jimmy has always lived his life in compartments," is how more than one friend explains it. "And I could not exist in any other way," Jimmy Goldsmith admits. He believes the modern attitude to divorce is mistaken. "The vertical polygamy practised in the West is ridiculous. The custom is that if you divorce you abandon your wife. That is pure moral turpitude. I do not agree with it and I never have."

An unpleasant streak of envy is almost always visible in some of the harshest criticism of his personal life, particularly in England. "A middle-class figure would always resent me," he says fiercely, "but the Governor of the Bank of England or the ordinary working man might like me." Lady Falkender is convinced he is right: "I think the ordinary man in the street warms to him." Charles Hambro adds: "Jimmy is not ashamed of his personal life. It may be unconventional, but he is extremely loyal." He attracts an equal loyalty in return. His friends defend him intensely, just as his wife and his former wife have never criticized or threatened his relationship with Laure Boulay de la Meurthe. It may be difficult for the more conventional to accept, but he lives, as the Manhattan lawyer Joe Flom puts it, "as other people might like to live".

Yet in spite of his wives and mistresses there is a strain of misogyny in Jimmy Goldsmith. Though he has been hypnotized by beautiful women in the past he also views them with suspicion. "I do not consider men and women either superior or inferior to each other but different," he says. Certainly he can sometimes treat them as though they were ornamental additions to his life rather than equal partners, though he insists that men and women are "complementary by nature". Like a lion he enjoys a pride of wives, but there is also the lingering suspicion that he might prefer to spend periods of time apart from them. Not long ago he admitted wistfully, "I've only been a bachelor for about two years of my life."

In the past handful of years Jimmy Goldsmith's passion for living every day as though it were his last has mellowed, settling into an equanimity that he never enjoyed as a younger man. The principal reason for that lies in the fact that in the past there was always a chance that he might lose everything – "which would only have meant he would start again tomorrow", according to one old friend – but now that possibility has gone. In 1981 he could say with conviction, "If the next takeover comes off I could be as rich as Croesus, or I might be as poor as Job." After the Diamond and Crown Zellerbach takeovers, he could never again be as poor as Job.

The success has brought calm. The rages are still there, but less pronounced and less frequent; the ambitions remain, but only those which he feels he can accomplish. There is now no need to tilt at every windmill. "I'm not willing to compromise in any way with anybody to achieve something," he says now. "I couldn't have said that all my life, but I've reached that stage now."

His refusal to compromise or to tailor his behaviour to the conventions of some of the countries he has lived in has brought him one major regret, however: a career in politics has escaped him. Jimmy Goldsmith was never able to take up his father's mantle in the British House of Commons. "If you'd asked me at the age of twelve, What are you going to do? I would have said: 'First make a fortune, then go into politics.' The second hasn't happened. The first, for the moment, looks as though it has." His wife Annabel still believes it is one of the "greatest sadnesses of his life". But it is one that he has come to accept, contenting himself with influence and the company of politicians.

Indeed, he now insists: "I wouldn't accept another political honour, for the simple reason that my ideas have mutated to the fact that you've got to remain totally independent of the state. If my ideas then had matured to what they are now I would never have accepted an honour in either Britain or France, but to turn them back would cause an unnecessary scandal." Instead in every new public document in the United States, Britain or France – whether they are the annual reports of his companies, tender offers or share certificates – he refers to himself simply as James Goldsmith. There is no mention of his knighthood or his Légion d'honneur.

Standing in front of the great windows in his New York drawing-room, he says, "I am totally uninterested in trying to obtain acceptance. I don't mind at all what other people's reactions to me are, though I would hope they were positive. I have none of those constraints."

There is a pause, then, the chieftain concludes: "I am a free man – with all the advantages and disadvantages of that."

It is a freedom that comparatively few men or women will ever share, and it has yet to be seen whether it can be exercised for the benefit of all. To be as rich as Croesus is magnificent, but it alone is not enough. Even a modern emperor has a responsibility beyond wealth, to the quality of life itself. That will prove to be Jimmy Goldsmith's last and greatest test.

Index